The Visible Words of God is an exposition of the sacramental theology of Peter Martyr Vermigli (1500-1562), together with a biographical introduction.

Martyr, who was the central figure in many of the sixteenth-century debates on the Eucharist, is of the greatest importance in our understanding of Calvin and the Reformed theology. The author demonstrates that the three figures of Bucer, Calvin, and Martyr hold the key to that theology which is basic to the Reformation in all its aspects.

No book in English has ever appeared on Martyr and no bibliography of him has appeared in any language within the last hundred years. The biographical section on this work, which is based on original materials, traces Martyr's life in its stages in Italy, Strasbourg, Oxford and Zurich.

The bulk of the book consists in a detailed exposition of Martyr's doctrine reign of Edward VI. The question of his relationship to Thomas Cranmer is studied, and a much greater influence on the Prayer Book and English Reformation on the part of Martyr is suggested.

DR. JOSEPH C. MCLELLAND was educated in Canada and earned his Ph.D. at Edinburgh. He was, for a time, a Minister of the Presbyterian Church in Canada. He has served as Tutor in New Testament Greek at Knox College, Toronto. In 1955-56 he was Lecturer in Christian Ethics at the Presbyterian College, Montreal, and during 1956-57 Lecturer in Church History at Knox College, Toronto.

THE VISIBLE WORDS OF GOD

THE VISIBLE WORDS OF GOD

*An Exposition of the Sacramental Theology
of Peter Martyr Vermigli
A.D. 1500-1562*

BY

JOSEPH C. McLELLAND
M.A., B.D., Ph.D.

Wm. B. Eerdmans Publishing Company
Grand Rapids, Michigan

FIRST PUBLISHED . . . 1957

Published in Britain by Oliver & Boyd

PHOTOLITHOPRINTED BY CUSHING - MALLOY, INC.
ANN ARBOR, MICHIGAN, UNITED STATES OF AMERICA

FOREWORD

IT is one of the tragedies of Reformation history that the theological works of Martin Butzer and Peter Vermiglio Martyr should have been so sadly neglected. That defect in the case of Martin Butzer is being remedied with the appearance of a number of valuable monographs in recent years and now at last of an excellent edition of his *Opera Omnia*. But nothing has yet been done for Peter Martyr, apart from a brief introductory work by C. Schmidt a hundred years ago. Peter Martyr was undoubtedly one of the finest scholars and ablest theologians of his generation and must be ranked close to Calvin himself with whom he stood in the highest estimation and with whom he was in the fullest agreement. But the theology of Peter Martyr has distinct characteristics of its own and rich qualities not shared in the same measure by the other leaders of the Reformation—characteristics and qualities, however, which are much more congenial to the Anglo-Saxon outlook. Brief though his sojourn in England was, his work has had a permanent influence particularly on the Church of England. It is indeed his type of Reformed theology, particularly in the doctrine of the Church and Sacraments, that appealed strongly both to the Church of England and the Church of Scotland, and still reveals the basic theological unity between the two.

It gives me great pleasure to commend this very able and lucid exposition of Peter Martyr's teaching by Dr J. C. Mc-Lelland, not only because in it Dr McLelland has given a faithful account of Reformation theology at its best but because his own discussion of it is a signal and brilliant contribution to theological literature today.

THOMAS F. TORRANCE

INTRODUCTION

A BOOK ABOUT PETER MARTYR is really about the Reformed doctrine of sacrament. The pattern of historical circumstance combined with his person to produce a remarkable unity of life and teaching. The construction and defence of this doctrine, especially in terms of the Lord's Supper, became his life's work. Unfortunately, Martyr is little known today, except incidentally through the historical theology of Heppe or Schweizer, or the problems of the Anglican Reformation. In his own day, however, he was acclaimed a theologian of first rank. His name was joined with Calvin's in the defensive polemic of the Reformation, and together they gave positive shape to the Reformed theology. For these reasons, it seemed necessary to introduce his teaching by way of a biographical 'Portrait', which gives the historical context of our study. It also provides some excuse for beginning the theological portion with an examination of the doctrine of analogy. For the more one reads Peter Martyr the more one sees that his use of this concept is the key to his theology. It is the sacrament of the Lord's Supper which is not only the central office of the service of God but also the action in which the problem of analogy becomes most clear and most crucial. It is therefore no coincidence that Martyr wrote more about the Sacrament than about anything else. This work offers itself, therefore, as a contribution to our knowledge of Reformed theology in its original form, and by this token as a help towards the solution of our contemporary problem of intercommunion.

The opportunity to pursue the research of which this book is a result was afforded by a scholarship from Knox College, Toronto. From that institution, whose late Principal Walter Bryden had posed for me a problem in epistemology of the deepest moment, to New College, Edinburgh seemed a natural step. Here it was Professor T. F. Torrance who guided me to the Library's depth where the old Latin tomes of Peter Martyr lie. Thus began the fascinating task of search and research, culminating in a doctoral thesis presented at Edinburgh and now revised in book form. Because Martyr has been given voice only in cursory historical treatments, he has been allowed to speak for himself as much as possible on every page. Latin phrases or quotations have been relegated to the footnotes, along with matters of secondary interest.

Thanks are due to many patient librarians, particularly Dr Lamb of New College, Edinburgh, and those at St. Andrews, at Corpus Christi and the University Library, Cambridge, and at the Bodleian, Oxford. Those in the Church of England whom I approached were most cordial: Professor Norman Sykes, Dr G. W. Bromiley, and by correspondence from Lambeth Palace and Canterbury Cathedral. The solution of problems of genuine texts and manuscripts was due largely to the work of Professors F. Wendel of Strasbourg and J. Courvoisier of Geneva, and the Librarian of the University of Zürich. The original typescript and its revision were most capably accomplished for me by Miss Grace Normand of Cupar-Fife, Scotland and Mrs A. M. Deans of my Bolton congregation.

A special word of thanks is gratefully offered to Professor Torrance for introducing me to Peter Martyr, for his constant help and advice as I sought to steer a somewhat consistent course through the mass of material at hand, and his encouragement of the further stage of revision for publication.

CAVEN PRESBYTERIAN MANSE   J.C.M.
BOLTON, ONTARIO, CANADA
The Summer of 1956.

CONTENTS

We say with Augustine that the
sacramental symbols are visible words.

PETER MARTYR

The whole (doctrine of Eucharist)
was crowned by Peter Martyr,
who left nothing more to be done.

JOHN CALVIN

PORTRAIT OF AN ECUMENICAL REFORMER

Tuscia te pepulit, Germania et Anglia fovit,
  Martyr, quem extinctum, nunc tegit Helvetia
Dicere quae si vera volent, te et nomine dicent,
  Hic fidus Christi (credite) Μάρτυρ erat.
Utque istae taceant, satis hoc tua scripta loquuntur:
  Plus satis hoc Italis exprobat exilium.

(Beza: *Icones*)

THE Reformer whose history we shall briefly sketch 'belongs to all Protestant Europe'.[1] He sprang from the Reformation in Italy—Calvin called him part of 'the miracle of Italy' and Beza compared him to the phoenix, born of the ashes of Savonarola. But his chief work was performed on behalf of three great and pivotal cities in those critical times: Strassburg, Oxford and Zürich. His learning and his power in disputation and writing soon earned him a name respected by Reformer and Romanist alike. His relationship to the key figures of the Reformation, especially Bucer, Bullinger, Calvin and Cranmer, and his influence upon the Reformed teaching and order in the various spheres of his labour, are matters examined but little, although most worthy of detailed study. Here we shall simply attempt to sketch a portrait of the man, his life and teaching. Such a biographical introduction is necessary because his story is little known among us[2] and because a knowledge of the contemporary background, and of the progress of his life and thought is essential to our presentation of his theology.

I. VERMIGLI THE FLORENTINE: 1500-1526

Stefano and Maria Vermigli of Florence had vowed to consecrate their expected child to Peter Martyr of Verona, killed

[1] Schmidt, *Vie de Pierre Martyr Vermigli*, Strassburg, 1835, Intro. (Hereafter, Schmidt, I.)

[2] Nothing has appeared in English for over one hundred years. Cf. Appendix A(2), which also gives the sources for this introductory Portrait.

I

in the Arian struggle in 1252,[3] to whom a neighbouring chapel
had been built. A son was born to them on 8 September 1500,
and accordingly named *Pietro Martire Vermigli*.[4]

Peter Martyr was born into a household of wealth and social
standing, so that a thorough education was planned for him at
once. His mother taught him Latin herself, chiefly the comedies
of Terence. His formal studies began under Marcello Virgilio,
among distinguished fellow-students, such as Piero Vettori.
The boy Vermigli was soon noted for a quick understanding
and an amazing memory, which combined with his love of
study to foster that appetite for every kind of literature so
evident in his later writings.

The question of a career was settled against his parents'
wishes. Stefano had been deeply influenced by Savonarola,[5]
and suspected all monastic life of corruption and superstition.
But his son considered that such a life offered time for the study
he craved along with a relative freedom from temptation in
self-dedication to God. Moreover, at that time the Augustinian
order was noted for its severity of discipline and thorough
study of the Scriptures. Therefore at the age of sixteen, Vermigli entered the monastery of St. Augustine at *Fiesole*, near
Florence. His only sister, Gemina Felicita, followed his example and entered the nunnery of *S. Pietro Martire*.

The three years at Fiesole were pleasant, particularly on
account of the rich and extensive library gifted by the Medici,
which included books from Egypt and Asia. Elocution was
stressed, and the diligent study of Scripture involved the com-
mitting to memory of large portions of the text. Vermigli's
progress here caused his superiors to send him for further study
to a convent near Padua, where he might attend the Univer-

[3] So the *Dictionnaire de Théologie Catholique* (ed. Vacant, Paris, 1950, Tome
Quinzième, Art. Vermigli). But Simler had stated *Petro Martyri Mediolanensi*, and
Young (*The Life and Times of Aanio Paleario*, London, 1860, Vol. 1, Chapter X;
Peter Martyr Vermiglio) etc., following him, 'Peter Martyr of Milan', date
unknown.
[4] Not to be confused with *Pietro Martire Angliera* (1455-1525), noted chiefly for
his *Opus Epistolarum*, a record of all manner of events of those days, when he lived
in Spain.
[5] Geronimo Savonarola (1452-1498) came to Florence in 1489, to the convent
of St. Marc. In this city he preached fearlessly, condemning corruption in the
State and in the Church, and was finally burned at the stake for his views. Cf.
McCrie, *History of . . . Reformation in Italy*, London, 1833, pp. 27-36; Appendix
I contains specimens of his preaching.

sity. Here he lived eight years, at the monastery of *S. Giovanni di Verdaro*, under the learned abbot Albert, almost wholly occupied in the study of philosophy and the humanities, and attending the lectures of Branda, Genua and Gonfalonieri. Branda dubbed him 'our Florentine', and welcomed him to the public discussions which were the custom in those times. The chief study everywhere was Aristotle, who attracted Vermigli by his method and relative freedom from error.[6] Determining to read Aristotle in the original, despite the lack of Greek teachers, he and his close friend Cusano laboured through many nights until they mastered the language. Along with the philosophical and linguistic discipline, Vermigli studied scholastic theology under three professors, two Dominicans and an Eremite.

It was now Vermigli's twenty-sixth year, and the cloistered life of monk and scholar gave place to a career of public life which was to advance him in reputation and power, even to episcopal privileges, until his conversion to Reformed principles made him an exile, the most famous Reformer to come forth from Italy.

II.   HERESY IN HIGH PLACES: 1526-1542

In 1526 Vermigli was elevated to the office of preacher. In those days the Dominican monks alone held the honour of preaching each Sunday, other orders preaching only during Advent and Lent. But the Augustinian order enjoyed special privilege from the Pope, and its preachers, chosen for their talents and eloquence, were honoured above all. Within the year, Vermigli received the degree D.D. from the University of Padua.

[6] In his Commentaries on Aristotle's Ethics (*In Arist. Ethic. ad Nicomachum, Tiguri*, 1582), based on the lectures he gave at Strassburg during the years 1553-1556, Peter Martyr constantly examines Aristotle in the light of Scripture. He asks whether a Christian can study philosophy (p. 6) and replies that a philosophy *intra limites* is compatible with revelatory theology. Thus Aristotle's treatment of human *felicitas* is limited—and, he makes clear, positively qualified—by the doctrine of the forgiveness of sins, of which Aristotle was ignorant (p. 181). Justification through Christ is stressed as the central Christian reality which marks off its subject-matter from all philosophy: we place our felicity *in reconciliatione cum Deo per Christum* (p. 266). Theology is responsive to the Word of God only: *Discrimen hic mihi notetur inter Philosophiam moralem atque nostram Theologiam: illa facit analysim ad arbitrium sapientum ac bonorum virorum, nostra vero ad leges et sermones Dei* (p. 194).

This office involved preaching at Brescia, Rome, Bologna, Venice, Mantua, Bergamo, Pisa and Montserrat. Meanwhile he taught the Scriptures in the convents of his order, and lectured in philosophy at Padua, Ravenna, Bologna and Vercelli, in the last named also teaching Greek and interpreting Homer, at Cusano's request.

Vermigli's preaching had followed his scholastic teaching, chiefly Thomas and Arimenese, although he had already some grounding in Patristics. But the new office forced him back behind the Fathers to the Scriptures themselves. For this purpose he determined to learn Hebrew. An appointment as vicar of the prior of his convent at *Bologna* gave opportunity to approach a Jewish physician for instruction. But he proved of little help, and once again Vermigli was left to the discipline of private study. Thus he mastered the new tongue, and indeed his knowledge of Hebrew earned him in later years the name of a leading Old Testament scholar, and the position of Professor in that field.

The abbacy of *Spoleto* was bestowed upon the young scholar and preacher—an unenviable position, for not only were the convents and monasteries under his charge noted for their luxury and vice, but the town itself was split by faction and feud. Vermigli proved to be something new in abbots in that town, exerting every effort of admonition, example and discipline to reform the establishment. The results were startling, and soon the reformation spread to the townspeople, for Vermigli was able to reconcile the opposing factions and to restore order and peace. Through these activities his reputation was enhanced among the people of Italy, while enmity grew in the hierarchy of the Church.

Light at Naples

After three years Vermigli was made prior of a famous and wealthy benefice, *S. Pietro ad Ara* at Naples. This proved to be the decisive stage in his spiritual and theological awakening. Already becoming critical of the deformation of the Church through the rites and ceremonies of Rome,[7] he now read authors

[7] Italy provided the bridge over the Dark Ages and with her the revival of learning began. Moreover, even within her Church the spirit of reform was much

who gave impetus and direction to this criticism. At that time in Italy certain works of the early Reformers were being circulated in translation, under pseudonyms. Vermigli read commentaries on the Gospels and on the Psalms by Arezzo Felino (Bucer); two tracts by Abydenus Corallus (Zwingli) on true and false religion, and on providence; a well-known work, *principi della theologia, di Ipposilo de terra negra* (Melanchthon); and some writings of Erasmus.[8]

Others in Naples were searching the Scriptures too, notably Vermigli's friend Cusano, and the poet Marc'Antonio Flaminio. But most important, 'Naples was the favoured place where the glad tidings of the Gospel were first heard in Italy at the period of the Reformation', the chief instrument in this proclamation being Juan Valdes.[9] Valdes gathered about him a select group of the leading people in Church and State in Naples—then a kingdom ruled by Charles V through a viceroy —and set before them the rediscovered Gospel. In this group were accounted as three chief disciples, Vermigli, Ochino and Flaminio.[10]

Valdes stressed justification by faith and the work of the Holy Spirit, and expounded I Corinthians to the private gatherings. Vermigli had meanwhile become confident that Rome had

greater than subsequent history would suggest—but the Inquisition came in between. In particular we should mention the *Oratory of Divine Love* and its kindred associations. This society included men such as Contarini, Sadoleto and also Reginald Pole who left England to seek its fellowship of piety and study. After the accession of Paul III in 1534 the attitude of self-criticism entered the very Court of Rome, when the new Cardinals, all members of the *Oratory*, drafted their *Consilium delectorum Cardinalium . . . de emendanda ecclesia*, 1538 (text in Kidd, *Documents of the Continental Reformation*, No. 126), a 'scathing indictment of the condition of the Roman Church' in T. M. Lindsay's words (see *History of the Reformation*, II, vi.3).

[8] Cf. Simler, Young (p. 403), Schmidt (I, p. 12), Schlosser, *Leben des Peter Martyr Vermili* (Heidelberg, 1809, pp. 379f).

[9] Young, p. 201. Valdes left Spain about 1529, by which time the Inquisition suspected him of heresy because of his *Aviso sobre los interpretes de la sagrada Escritura*, based largely on Tauler's *Christian Institutions*. He became secretary to Toledo, Neapolitan viceroy. Cf. Young's excellent summary of the Valdes brothers, pp. 201-238; McCrie, *op. cit.*, pp. 134ff.

[10] Bernardino Ochino, Capuchin monk and famous preacher of Italy, became Capuchin-general, suspect for his teachings, and finally fled Italy with Vermigli. He later went to England with Vermigli, then to the Italian Church at Zürich. Unfortunately the end of his life brought the tragedy of heterodoxy (after Vermigli's death), and he became a wandering exile, finally dying of the plague in 1566. Young has a detailed survey of his life and work, *op. cit.*, Chapter IX; cf. McCrie, *op. cit.*, and R. H. Bainton's biographical study in *The Travail of Religious Liberty* (Lutterworth, 1953), Chapter VI, 'The Heretic as Exile'.

deformed the Gospel chiefly on the doctrines of grace and atonement, and began the exposition of 1 Corinthians at S. Pietro ad Ara. This would be about 1535-1536. Valdes died in 1536, by which time all Italy, especially the Neapolitan district, was stirring with seeds of reformation. The inevitable opposition was growing: in Naples this came chiefly from the Theatin monks, who began to suggest that Vermigli's teaching was heretical. They were assisted in their plans to oust him by Rebibba, vicar of Naples, later Cardinal of Pisa.

Vermigli's lectures were attended by many distinguished persons, including several bishops. When he treated of 1 Corinthians 3. 11-13, he suggested that the Fathers did not apply the 'fire' to purgatory, but referred the whole sentence to the doctrine of justification through Christ. This so angered the opposing faction that Toledo forbade him to preach. Vermigli refused and appealed to the Pope. His friends at Rome, notably Contarini and Pole, had the prohibition removed, and he resumed his activities.

Il Visitatore

Before he had completed his three years at Naples, Vermigli became severely ill of a fever then raging, of which Cusano died. In 1539 his superiors made him Visitor General of his order, an office which involved visitation throughout Italy, with great powers of discipline. His zeal in this office[11] extended not only to correcting such abuses as sprang from the monastic luxury and immorality, but even to attacking the stronghold of abuse in the hierarchy itself. With the sanction of Cardinal Gonzaga, protector of the order, he banished the rector-general and several companions, their punishment being perpetual imprisonment on the island of Diomede. For this rigour Vermigli's honour was considerably enhanced, and soon he was raised to further dignity.

Crisis at Lucca

In 1541 Vermigli was named prior of S. Frediano at Lucca—a most significant office, since it conferred *episcopal authority* over one-half the city. Vermigli's task here was no easy one, for

[11] Cf. Schlosser, *op. cit.*, p. 383—'Martyrs Eifer für Recht und Wahrheit'.

Lucca held towards Florence a deep hatred, as the city which had deprived it of freedom.[12] But 'our Florentine' gained the friendship of all, and soon laid plans for a twofold reformation, of discipline and learning. He stressed the education of the young in the public schools, and for the college procured such lecturers that St. Fridian's was surely the brightest gathering in Romanism. Paolo Lacisio of Verona taught Latin; Count Celso Martinengo, Greek; and Emanuelo Tremellio, a converted Jew, Hebrew. All three ultimately left Italy for the cause of Reformation, Lacisio becoming Professor of Greek at Strassburg; Martinengo, pastor of the Italian Church in Geneva; and Tremellio, Professor of Hebrew at Cambridge and then Heidelberg.

Vermigli himself maintained a heavy schedule, giving each day an exposition on the Pauline Epistles in Latin, and on a Psalm each evening before supper to the whole community, besides preaching in Italian every Sunday to the public. During Advent and Lent he followed the old custom of reading the Gospels with running comments. Under such instruction there gradually emerged a Reformed congregation in Lucca, which was a living example of the power of the Gospel until the Inquisition finally succeeded in crushing out its life,[13] and a monastery from which eighteen monks followed Vermigli from Italy on behalf of the Reformation.

In 1541 Charles V and Pope Paul III met at Lucca. Cardinal Contarini, whose dealings at Ratisbon had brought charges of heresy from the hierarchy, visited the Pope at Lucca to defend himself. He stayed with his friend Vermigli in the monastery, along with Tommaso Badia, Master of the Sacred Palace. This visit is a further important influence upon Vermigli's progress, since Contarini's first-hand account of the opinions of Bucer, Melanchthon and the other Reformers helped to crystallize his thoughts.

[12] Young, p. 407, attributes Vermigli's election to this office partly to the enmity of those who thought such an adverse situation would cause him harm.

[13] Cf. Young, pp. 419 and 575, concerning the *Sommario di Storia Lucchese*: charges of *la diffusione della luterane dottrine* caused the authorities themselves to take measures to forbid correspondence with heretics (such as Vermigli?) and to burn all reformed books; and McCrie, *op. cit.*, pp. 285-289, for their contribution to the Genevan Church and State. In 1547 Florence confiscated all heretical books, 'particularly those of Ochino and Martyr' (McCrie, p. 291).

B

By this time Vermigli was under definite suspicion, which was confirmed by the clergy attached to the Papal visit. On 22 June 1542 Bishop Guidiccioni wrote to Lucca warning of the spread of heretical opinions. One month later a further letter from Rome—where the tribunal of Inquisition had been erected[14]—specifically mentions certain men who should be arrested, including the vicar 'of whom we hear for certain that he has given the communion several times to many of our citizens, teaching them to partake only in remembrance of the sufferings of Christ, and not because they believed that this wafer contained His most holy body'.[15] In August the Inquisition struck, and measures were taken to trap Vermigli himself. Secret letters to Rome, plots within St. Fridian's convents, rebellion against the discipline of the order, spies to determine his movements and literary sources, all characterize this beginning of the end. His enemies called a meeting at Genoa, inviting him to attend; but realizing the true nature of this gathering, which was but a trap for his special benefit, he yielded to the advice of his friends and chose to leave Lucca.[16] He gave part of his extensive library to Cristofor Brenta, a noble of Lucca, with orders to forward the books to Germany at the earliest opportunity; the remainder he left to the monastery. He then handed over his charge to the vicar, and left the city, accompanied by Lacisio, Theodosio Trebellio and his attendant Guilio Terenziano, the beloved 'Julius' who was with him to the end of his life.

'Flee Ye Into Another'

Vermigli and his friends went first to Pisa, where he hid for a short time. A noteworthy occurrence during this visit is his meeting in secret with certain nobles and Christian friends, to whom he dispensed the Lord's Supper after the simple manner

---

[14] Cardinal Caraffa, afterwards Pope Paul IV, was notable in this work—cf. McCrie, *op. cit.*, Chapter V.

[15] 'non gia perche credino che in quell' ostia vi sia il suo santissimo corpo', quoted by Young, p. 410. His work is the best for the Italian period of Vermigli's life.

[16] Cf. Young, p. 412, quoting Caracciolo (*Vita di Paolo IV*): 'In quella città teneva scuola Pietro Martire . . . Tremellio . . . Martinengo . . . Lacisio . . . Zanehio tutti pessimi heretici . . . Questi hebbe fra Pietro Martire Vermigli che infettò Napoli, Firenze, e tutta l'Inghilterra.'

of the Gospel record. He also gave two letters to be delivered later, one addressed to Cardinal Pole, his superior, and the other to his friends at Lucca.[17] In these he declared the errors and abuses of Romanism, and especially its monastic system, 'with which he could no longer have conversation with a safe conscience' (Simler). He also mentioned the snares laid by his enemies, and reminded his people of the sincerity of his faith, lamenting the fact that he was unable to instruct them more fully in the truth. He returned the ring which was the badge of his office.

From Pisa he went to friends at Florence, and there met Bernardino Ochino, who faced the same choice as he. They agreed, on the basis of Matthew 10. 23[18] to choose the freedom of exile. Ochino departed for Geneva, and two days later Vermigli set out. Travelling by way of Bologna, Ferrara and Verona, he was welcomed everywhere, and finally entered

[17] There is some discrepancy about the events of this period, revolving round Vermigli's *Semplice Dichiarazione* or Catechism. This was published at Basle in 1544, in Italian, and there is no reason to think that it is an earlier work, or played a material part in his Italian period. Yet Schlosser identifies the pastoral letter (*Hirtenbrief*) written from Pisa in 1542, with the Catechism: 'Dieser in Form einer Exposition des apostolischen Sumbolums abgefaszte Absagebrief der catholischer Religion ist eigentlich in Italiënischer Sprache geschnaben' (p. 392). Schmidt had also thought that the Catechism was first circulated in Italy: 'Avant de quitter à jamais l'Italie, Martyr y publia encore une profession de foi, sous la forme d'une explication du symbole apostolique' (1.16), but corrected this opinion in his subsequent work of 1858 (*Peter Martyr Vermigli, Leben und Ausgewählte Schriften,* Elberfeld—hereafter cited by the numeral *II*). Here (p. 37) he relates it to the earlier letter from Pisa thus: 'es ist Vermigli's erstes auf uns gekommenes Werk, ein Absagebrief vom Papstihum . . . Da er auf der Flucht keine Bücher bei sich hatte und Eile nöthig war, hat er nur kurz seine Ansichten dargelegt.' The New Schaff-Herzog Enc. of Rel. Kn., Art. Vermigli, makes the same error: 'He issued his first Evangelical tract, *Una semplice dichiarazione* . . . for which he was summoned before the chapter of his order in Genoa.' The actual order of his writings, therefore, would be: from Pisa, the 'Pastoral letter' to Lucca, and the 'letter of refusal of the Papacy'—Simler's summary of their contents is the basis for all accounts of these; from Strasbourg, the Epistle to the Faithful of the Church at Lucca (*Loci Communes, Londini,* 1583, p. 1071—hereafter this will be cited as *L.C.*) on 25 January 1543, and the *Semplice Dichiarazione* of 1544.

[18] 'But when they persecute you in this city, flee ye into another'—cf. Vermigli's interpretation of this text in his *De Fuga in Persecutione* (*L.C.,* p. 1073). This is in the form of an Epistle 'to a certain friend', date unknown, and written originally in Italian. In this Epistle he teaches that Christ's precept in Matthew 10.23 is perpetual; and that 'flight taken for such causes is a kind of confession'. Among the 'causes' treated, he insists on a freedom from fear of a false kind (fear *per se* is not evil). The argument is twofold: whether the fear of death in a Christian is sin; and whether Christ's precept holds today. The R.C. writer Laing (*De Vita et Moribus . . . Haereticorum,* Paris, 1581, fol. 26B) writes of Vermigli and Ochino, *optimum rati sunt se conferre Genevam omnium haereticorum miserrimam speluncam.*

Switzerland, haven of refugees from Romanism, stopping at
Zürich. Here he was welcomed by Henry Bullinger, Conrad
Pellican and Rodolph Gualter. These were to become his
closest friends, and although he would gladly have stayed there
if there had been an office vacant, this desire was not to be
fulfilled until the death of Pellican in 1556.

In the Oration delivered at that time, he said:

> To Zürich I began to take my way ... those two days when I stayed here
> with those who accompanied me, I was so delighted with the godly, learned
> and pleasant conversation which I had with Dr Bullinger, Bibliander,
> Gualter and Pellican of happy memory, and others whom I cannot now
> mention, that I accounted those blessed, who might live with such men, and
> rejoiced myself for my own present exile, by which I was brought by
> Almighty God to that consolation, and the knowledge and conversation of
> such men; nor ever afterwards, believe me, could I forget this Church, those
> two days, and that fellowship.[19]

Vermigli's next stop was Basle, where he resided for a month
until he was invited to Strassburg by Paolo Lacisio who had
preceded him. Here he met Martin Bucer, through whose influence he was appointed Professor of Theology, after Capito's
death, in December 1542.

III. THE FIRST STRASSBURG PERIOD:

December 1542–October 1547

Once settled in Strassburg, Peter Martyr's[20] first thought was
for his flock at Lucca. On 25 January 1543[21] he wrote to 'the
faithful of the Church at Lucca, saints by calling', informing
them of his call to Strassburg.

> On our arrival we were most lovingly received by Bucer into his house,
> and remained with him seventeen days. His dwelling seemed to be a home
> of hospitality, he is so accustomed to entertaining strangers who travel for
> the Gospel and the cause of Christ. He governs his house so well that in all
> these days I could not once perceive any cause of offence, but found many

[19] *Oratio quam Tiguri primam habuit cum in locum D. Conradi Pellicani successisset*—
L.C., p. 1063.
[20] After he left Italy, the name Vermigli was little used, except in the formal
titles of his published works. He is known as 'Peter Martyr' or simply 'Martyr' to
friends and enemies alike.
[21] *octavo calendas Ianuarias*—L.C., p. 1071; Schlosser (p. 400) cites its date as
1 January, and its origin as Basle, and Young cites 6 January (p. 415) but re-
produces the correct date in his quotation of the letter (p. 418).

occasions of edification. At his table there is no appearance of excess or niggardliness, but only a godly moderation: here there is no distinction of meats. Before and after meat something is recited out of the Holy Scriptures to minister matter of godly and holy communications. I may boldly affirm that I ever went from that table a wiser man . . . Bucer was continually occupied by daily sermons, governing the Church, seeing that the curates watched over souls and confirming them by holy examples; he visited also the schools of learning to see that all labour had reference to the furtherance of the Gospel, exhorting and stirring up the magistrate to Christian godliness. For this purpose he daily attended the courts of justice. Being thus fully occupied during the day, he takes the night for his private studies and prayers. I never awaked out of sleep but I found him awake . . . Behold, well-beloved brethren, in our age bishops upon the earth, or rather in the Church of Christ, who are truly holy . . .

Bucer obtained for me from the senate the Professorship of theology, and has committed to me the charge of a daily interpretation of the Holy Scriptures, with an honourable stipend by which I can maintain myself. At this present time I interpret the lesser prophets as they used to call them, being now at the end of Amos; and because the greater number in this school know something of Hebrew, I expound the Hebrew text in Latin.

The letter also expresses his trust that the Holy Spirit will continue to teach the people at Lucca. He discusses the question of flight and persecution:

You will perhaps say you should have continued, waited until the most imminent dangers had actually come upon you and suffered them with a patient mind, which in the end would have greatly furthered the building up of the Church . . . but time and necessity are revealed to those who in adversity wholly commit themselves to God's protection. I was so persuaded that the right moment for me to depart was come, that I doubt not this persuasion was inspired by God. Although by my departure I avoided some bitter troubles, yet I did not escape entirely free. At Naples I suffered great vexation, and also in your city. You yourselves know what anxiety and torment I endured the last year. These, though not to be called grievous calamities, were yet the messengers and tokens of them. It seems to me that I have not preached the Gospel without afflictions. I did not therefore refuse to provide for my safety: while I am here I am by God's grace of some use.

Moreover, he continues, think of the 'variety of superstitions' he had to condone because of his office, requiring others as well to share in things 'contrary both to my judgment and conscience'. Is not his flight itself a witness to his motive?

To say the truth, my departure—I say this as setting forth the glory of God—when duly considered, carries with it no small mortification of self, the loss of honours and promotion, wherewith in the sight of man I was largely endowed, and of many comforts with which I was surrounded, besides the laying down of an authority which gave me both power and influence over men. All these things I might have increased in many ways, if I would have departed from the truth of God and of the Gospel.

A second Italian writing which is preserved for us is the work on the Apostles' Creed already mentioned. This was published in February 1544, and reveals the mature thought and precise style which was to characterize all his works. It was a 'profession of the heavenly and divine wisdom', and exhibits those basic Reformed principles which determined Martyr's future teaching and work.[22]

The Strassburg Lectures

Peter Martyr's lectures during this period are significant in both their method and subject-matter. Simler tells us that he began with Lamentations and the Minor Prophets, and then began the Pentateuch, completing Genesis, Exodus and a good part of Leviticus before he left Strassburg for England.[23] His method of exposition was, first to set forth the literal sense of the text, for which his linguistic knowledge fitted him admirably, while comparing obscure places of Scripture with clear; then he would comment on the deeper significance and the practical application. Simler says that he observed two special points, 'an exact method and a pure and plain style'. Schlosser indicates the historical significance of his method: 'As for his lectures, it is true that they were not strictly exegetical; but if one considers who the people were that attended, one will easily see that a precise exegetical lecture, explaining only the literal meaning would have been of little or no use here. Priests, monks and laymen, who either wished only to be instructed in the new teaching and its arguments, or desired to act as instructors themselves, crowded from every side to the renowned Teacher, and wished to find here the spirit and eloquence they missed from their own. Hence also Martyr's habit of dwelling on side issues and commenting on the Fathers,

---

[22] Its teaching will be considered in Chapter III, etc.
[23] Of these lectures the following are extant: commentaries on Lamentations and Genesis, propositions from Genesis, Exodus and Leviticus (*L.C.*, p. 999), see Appendix A(1).

while he explained the Scriptures. His fame soon spread through the whole of Europe.'[24]

The Patristic influence upon his teaching involves an important question: his relationship to Martin Bucer. This first Strassburg period was undoubtedly the decisive phase for Martyr's theology, for in England he was immediately put on the defensive and from that time until his death was engaged in drawing out the implications of his doctrine in the face of a variety of opponents. Simler tells us that he declared 'with singular happiness of memory, of what opinion were the Fathers', and Strype records an interesting fact: Bartlet Green, one of Martyr's Oxford students and a martyr in Mary's reign, quoted Martyr as saying that while he was a Papist, he had not read Chrysostom on 1 Corinthians 10, but later 'he was contented to yield to those doctors, having first humbled himself in prayer, desiring God to illuminate him, and bring him to the true understanding of the Scripture.'[25] We have seen that his education at Padua had given 'an acquaintance with these writings of the fathers' (Simler), while his refutation of the doctrine of purgatory in the famous lecture at Naples was based on Patristic teaching.[26] But there is little doubt that his thorough knowledge of the Fathers as the formative source of his theology, owes a great deal to his close friendship with Bucer in these years.[27]

A contrast is offered between Martyr and Bucer during this early period of his Reformed teaching. Martyr's methodical and precise style of lecturing contrasted favourably with Bucer's often inconsistent treatment of themes and irrelevancy of data, until, Simler tells us he was soon 'considered to excel Bucer'. Such an estimate speaks volumes, for 'Bucer was so highly esteemed at Strassburg that a higher eulogium could not be

[24] *Op. cit.*, p. 410. From the published commentaries it is evident that this 'deeper meaning' of the *scopus* of Scripture was for Martyr the Christological orientation of all Scripture, including the Old Testament. This will concern us in Chapter II.

[25] *Ecclesiastical Memorials* . . . John Strype, London, 1816, Vol. II, p. 197. Strype adds that this was probably while he was in Italy or immediately afterwards.

[26] His Commentary *ad loc.* cites especially Chrysostom and Augustine, but this was based on lectures at Oxford and therefore is not conclusive about his authorities for the early period.

[27] This question is dealt with in Appendix C. Calvin had left Strassburg in 1541, and no doubt experienced a similar influence from the side of Bucer.

passed on Martyr, than to equal him to this worthy divine; but in method and logical precision he was considered his superior: he owed this probably to the close study of Aristotle so much practised in Italy.'[28]

Peter Martyr's precise method and the use of unambiguous terms brought him into conflict with Bucer. Simler states 'he judged that a darkness of speech and ambiguity of words is the cause of very many contentions. And of this his writings give a clear testimony. For he wrote many things about the justification of man, and not little about God's predestination, but indeed he wrote most of all about the Lord's Supper. In the explication of this, many learned men use a certain affected obscurity, but in his writings there is nothing read, but that which is proper, plain and manifest.' But Bucer, passionate apostle of unity, had taken a different path about this central doctrine of the Lord's Supper. His opinion was that terms could well be used which allowed of interpretation by extreme Lutheran or extreme Zwinglian. And at the Diet of Ratisbon in 1541, he and Melanchthon, stirred by the great hope then entertained of unity and peace, were tempted to allow vagueness of explanation to cover differences in basic doctrines. At the beginning of Martyr's residence in Strassburg, Bucer persuaded him to follow this custom. But Martyr quickly saw that the 'grosser kind' of view involved a carnal interpretation of the terms used in the teaching of the Lord's Supper, offending the weaker brethren by such doubtful speech, and refused to share in such manner of teaching.[29] Simler tells us that this break indicated no disagreement in doctrine— 'although the manner of their teaching was diverse, yet was there a full consent of both in all the doctrine of religion, and a perpetual conjunction of life.'

'The Story of Catherine Vermilius'

At first, Peter Martyr lived with his Italian friends in Strass-

[28] Young, p. 421; cf *Dict. de Théol. Cath.* (ed. Vacant), Art. Vermigli: *Il y a resta cinq ans, très goûté et considéré comme un émule de Bucer.*

[29] Schlosser (p. 409) describes him as 'moved to passion' on this issue, because Bucer's 'principles concerning the pious fraud, and the end which justifies the means' contradicted Christian morality. But Schlosser has a bias against Bucer (and Cranmer)—for our estimate of the relationship between Martyr and Bucer see Appendix C.

burg; but at length he was persuaded to marry, a step which converted monks were then encouraged to take as proof of their sincerity. Catherine Dammartin of Metz, 'a lover of true religion', became his wife. This would be in 1545, since she died on 15 February 1553 and Simler says the marriage lasted eight years. A most striking but deplorable tragedy attaches to the subsequent history of this woman. She died in England and was buried near the tomb of St. Frideswyde at Oxford. During the Marian persecution, Cardinal Pole, once Martyr's friend and member of the liberal Italian group, but now captain of the heresy-hunters in England, advised that her body should be exhumed because of its proximity to the remains of the Saint—since no one would accuse of heresy this lady of beloved memory. Accordingly, the body was removed from its resting-place, and cast upon the dungheap in the stables of Marshall, dean of Christchurch.[30] This was about the same time that similar charges and abuse were carried out on the remains of Bucer and Fagius at Cambridge, in 1556. After Elizabeth's accession in 1558, an ecclesiastical commission composed of Parker, Grindal and Goodrich, all personal friends of Martyr, supervised an investigation of the whole affair, which culminated in the reinterring of Catherine in a common grave with the relics of the Saint, to do away with the superstitious practice of exposing the relics for adoration, and to preserve the remains of Martyr's wife from future insult. A speech on the occasion ended with the words, *Hic requiescit Religio cum Superstitione.*

'Come over and help us'

Peter Martyr's last years at Strassburg were darkened by the shadow cast by the approaching Interim[31] from which even

[30] *Ut, quoniam juxta corpus sanctissimae Fridesuidae jacebat corpus Catharinae uxoris Petri Martyris, exhumari et jactari faciat*—quoted by Young, p. 443, from the document which relates the whole affair, *Historia vera: item Catharinae Vermiliae, D. Petri Martyris Vermilij castiss. atque piissimae coniugis, exhumatae, eiusdemq. ad honestam sepulturam restitutae.* 1562. (Cf. Ant. a Wood's *Historia et antiquit. universitatis Oxoniensis, Oxonii* 1674.)

[31] The Augsburg Interim and Confession played a large part in Martyr's relationship with Strassburg. Melanchthon in 1530 had drawn up a Confession (first an 'Apology' based on the Schwabach Articles, the Lutheran view of the decisions reached at Marburg in 1529). But at the Diet of Augsburg the Confession provoked discussion but not acceptance; the Diet ended by embodying a policy of enforced conformity in its 'Recess'. The Schmalkaldic League was therefore formed by all Protestants for protection; and the Peace of Nürnberg was

Bucer was forced to flee. Although the Interim was not ratified until May 1548, and Bucer did not leave Strassburg until March 1549, yet the coming victory of Romanism caused an intensity of opposition against Bucer and Martyr which made Archbishop Cranmer's invitation doubly acceptable.[32] At King Henry VIII's death, his son was proclaimed King Edward VI, on 31 January 1547. The young King's advisers, Somerset the Protector and Cranmer the Archbishop of Canterbury, were desirous of a thorough reformation. To accomplish this purpose it was agreed that learned and godly foreigners should be invited to come to England, particularly to teach at the great Universities. The two principal Reformers who were thus invited by Cranmer and who became a great influence upon the English Reformation, were Peter Martyr, who came to Oxford in 1547, and Martin Bucer, to Cambridge in 1549. Strype says, 'It was especially thought necessary, that the corrupt opinions about the *Eucharist* should be rectified in the Universities as well as elsewhere; and both these foreigners thought aught in this great point, though differing in their judgments in the expressions to be used about them.'[33] Therefore in November 1547 Martyr was granted leave by the Senate at Strassburg, and began his journey to England. He was accompanied by Bernardino Ochino, who had also accepted an invitation from Cranmer, and who was also to play

the result, 1532. But after Luther's death in 1546, Charles V again sought concord by drawing up the 'Interim of Augsburg', a compromise backed by the sword, 15 May 1548. Bucer's influence had till now been a real force; but the Interim was a Romanist-Lutheran impossibility. Finally after strife and pressure, a similarly ambiguous settlement was effected, the 'Peace of Augsburg', 25 September 1555. Lutheranism but not Calvinism had obtained recognition. This is the background against which Martyr's first and second Strassburg residences are to be viewed. Cf. Kidd, *op. cit.*, pp. 245-364, for documents cited.

[32] Schmidt (II, p. 72) dates Martyr's Prayer from Psalm 55 as written at this period; it suits perhaps the second Strassburg period better, when the strife with the Lutheran faction, so recently brethren, was becoming so intense that it declared as enemies Martyr's friend John a Lasco and Martyr himself, who left Strassburg on its account. The prayer reads, in part: 'We are forced (O most good and merciful God) by reason of the extreme and urgent distress of the Church, to cry out daily unto thee . . . deliver us (for thy infinite mercies' sake) from subtle words and deceitful devices, and have a great foresight that thy holy Church be not sore plagued with them, who seem sometime greatly to favour her, and were partakers in the same with us, of the most pleasant and sweet food of thy blessed Sacraments . . . Let not the league be broken which those have who are at one with thee . . . sustain and increase this our feeble and slender hope with thy most present and ready help, through Jesus Christ our Lord, Amen.' (*Preces Sacrae ex Psalmis Davidis . . . Tiguri*, 1564.)   [33] *Op. cit.* p. 196.

an important role in England.[34] Martyr was appointed
Regius Professor of Divinity at the University of Oxford, and
Ochino, a Canon of Canterbury, with dispensation of residence.

IV. A Reformer at Oxford:
November 1547–October 1553

Cranmer warmly welcomed the Italian Reformers, enter-
taining them at Lambeth for some time.[35] Peter Martyr
describes his twofold task:

> Indeed I took upon myself a weighty charge. For it was necessary to
> teach Theology in the University of Oxford, but also I was often called to
> convocations held at London about ecclesiastical matters.[36]

Strype states: 'The Italian stranger, Peter Martyr, was de-
signed to read divinity in Oxford, whither he repaired from the
archbishop's, fortified by the king's authority: but, after a little
time, very rudely treated and opposed there by a popish party.
Yet, notwithstanding these oppositions and discouragements
of Peter Martyr, the king's learned professor here at Oxford,
he steadily went on in the business committed to his trust; and
besides his public lectures, he sometimes preached at St. Mary's
and had his private lectures, and his private sermons, in Italian,
at his house: whereunto resorted many auditors.'[37] But the
outstanding event of his Oxford days was the famous Disputation held in 1549.

The Oxford Disputation of 1549

In view of the state of religion in the country at that time,
which was deteriorating through the activity of the Romanists,

---

[34] There is extant (MSS. Ashmole 826, Oxford; given in full in Young, pp. 576f)
an interesting document entitled 'Expences of the Journey of Peter Martyr and
Bernerdinus Ochino to England in 1547', by one John Abell, and containing such
diverse purchases as works of the Fathers for Martyr, two daggers, and 'a peticote,
glovys, and nyght cap for Julius'.

[35] Strype (*Memorials of Cranmer*, p. 466) suggests that Martyr stayed 'till the
winter was pretty well over', not beginning lectures before March or April.
Cranmer hoped for a 'godly synod' which could 'attempt an agreement upon the
chief heads of ecclesiastical doctrine', especially the Eucharist.

[36] Zürich Oration (*Oratio quam Tiguri . . . L.C.*, p. 1063).

[37] *Ecc. Mem.* II, p. 336. Cf. C. H. Smyth, *Cranmer and the Reformation under
Edward VI* (Cambridge, 1926), pp. 108f: 'Oxford, which had not taken kindly to
the Renaissance, was violently hostile to the Reformation . . . the whole of Peter
Martyr's work was an almost single-handed struggle against overwhelming odds.'

notably Stephen Gardiner and Richard Smith, and through the ignorance of the common people, Martyr at once began to lecture on I Corinthians, as containing matter suitable to the needs of the day. In the Dedication to Edward VI of the published lectures,[38] he gives his reason for undertaking the explication of this particular Epistle:

> But that was the chief cause of this purpose, that nowhere else are treated such varied and multiple heads, which make to the controversies of our times. Undoubtedly by the doctrine of this Epistle, if skilfully and fitly used, we could easily heal completely all the faults by which the soundness of the Church is corrupted.

During the lectures of 1548 Peter Martyr was left alone by the Romanist party, even when he attacked the doctrine of celibacy. But a crisis was precipitated by his exposition of I Corinthians 10.16-17.[39] A clamour was immediately raised, headed by Smith, who claimed that Martyr ridiculed the traditional doctrine of the Lord's Supper, and treated holy things with contempt.[40] The party posted notices in the Oxford Churches, announcing a public debate the next day, in which Martyr 'would dispute openly against the presence of the body of Christ in the Holy Supper' (Simler). Needless to say, Martyr knew nothing of such a disputation. Yet the warning of his friends, the dangerous nature of the crowd that gathered that following day, even the thrusting into his hands of a challenge from Smith as he walked to the lecture, did not deter him from his accustomed routine.

At the lecture he announced that he had come 'not to dispute, but to read' and forthwith began to speak. The adversaries maintained silence during the lecture, which, Simler tells us, was delivered with his usual calmness and clarity. But at

---

[38] The Commentaries on I Corinthians given at Oxford were published at Zürich in 1562, and a second edition in 1572, from which this quotation is taken.

[39] Simler says simply 'upon occasion of the Apostle's words, he began to treat of the Lord's Supper'. Young, p. 428, locates this at I Corinthians 11.26. But in Martyr's published Commentary, 10.16 is the critical verse, where the key word *benedictio* introduces the problem of the Romanist *consecratio* and subsequent contention that *se Christum ipsum sacrificare*. Moreover, immediately following 10.16-17 is the Treatise *An in Communione Liceat Una Tantum Specie Uti*, suggesting that at this point Martyr thought a frontal attack on Romanism was in order.

[40] Cf. Schlosser, p. 423: up to this point, Martyr's moderation had kept quiet 'even the most intolerant Richard Smith, *D.T.*, who had likewise attended his lectures'.

the close the people clamoured for disputation. Martyr stated that he was not prepared, especially since he had not seen the propositions drawn up by the challenger. He refused to enter into so weighty a matter without the King's knowledge.[41] Moreover, a valid disputation required definite questions agreed upon by both parties, the presence of Judges and Moderators, and the appointing of clerks to record the debate—these things Martyr spoke from his long experience in public disputations, which began at Padua. At this point Richard Cox, Chancellor, dismissed the crowd and ordered Martyr and Smith to come to his house and arrange a formal debate, taking Martyr's arm to guide him through the crowd.

Peter Martyr's demands in drawing up the propositions are worthy of note. He states them in the prefatory speech made at the Disputation.[42] He wishes to reverse Aristotle's order of first determining the being, then the manner and purpose of a thing, since

neither of us doubts that there is a body of Christ . . . some conjunction is there of the body and blood of Christ with the signs, on which both sides agree; but of what kind of conjunction it is stands the controversy.

Accordingly, Martyr wishes to state three manners of conjunction as the grounds of the Disputation. But in the use of terms he prefers the words *corporeally* and *carnally* to the scholastic *really* and *substantially*.

But why I derived adverbs from the nouns flesh and body, rather than from thing and substance, is in order that I might accommodate myself to Holy Scripture, which in mentioning a sacrament, does not have the names of thing and substance, but only of body, flesh and blood; and therefore have I written corporeally and carnally.

[41] Strype notes (*Ecc. Mem.* II, pp. 130f) that on 27 December 1548 an Act of Parliament forbade open disputation about the sacrament, or enquiring into such questions as 'Whether the body and blood of Christ was there really or figuratively, locally or circumscriptively . . .' and advised that Paul's words be sufficient for all, 'The bread is the communion, or partaking, or the body of Christ, and the wine, likewise, the partaking of the blood of Christ.' This was to be 'until the king, with the advice of his council and clergy of the realm, should set forth an open doctrine thereof, and what terms and words may justly be spoken thereby'.

[42] Cf. his Epistle to the Christian Reader, introducing his written account of the Disputation: there are two reasons why he now sets forth in writing this and the Treatise ('of the same matter, for its clearer declaring'): the slanders of evil men, who have everywhere claimed victory in this affair, and have publicly abused his name; and the desires of friends and superiors to which he now yields. The *Disputatio* and *Tractatio* were published as one volume at Oxford in 1549.

A further point is this, that the error of attributing too much to the sacraments is as serious as their neglect—'both of which extremes we have always to our power avoided'. To deny a carnal presence, then, is not—as the Papists say— to conclude, 'it follows of necessity, that there is nothing left in the sacrament but a signification'. For they are then Anabaptists! The truth is that Christ is present 'by a sacramental conjunction, which is a most effectual signification'.[43] Accordingly, the propositions for debate were drawn up:

1. In the sacrament of the Eucharist, there is no transubstantiation of the bread and wine into the body and blood of Christ.

2. The body and blood of Christ is not carnally and corporeally in the bread and wine; nor, as others say, under the shows of bread and wine.

3. The body and blood of Christ is sacramentally joined to the bread and the wine.

The date fixed for the Disputation was 4 May. But Smith's genius for raising a tumult did not extend to such matters, and he quickly disappeared to St. Andrews, and then to Louvain.[44]

[43] Cf. Appendix D, where an extended quotation from Martyr's written Preface to the Disputation and Tract, is given. This is an important document in the problem of the influence of Bucer upon Martyr, which is dealt with in Appendix C. Martyr's explicit use of the words 'effectual signification', as well as his frequent insistence upon the real presence of Christ to faith, in the Disputation, indicate that Bucer's fears were influenced more by the enemy's demands than by Martyr's theology.

[44] Smith is a model of inconstancy. He was Fellow of Merton College and Principal of St. Alban's, Oxford, and in 1535, Regius Professor of Divinity—succeeded by Martyr. Even at that time he was 'giddy and unstable' and of 'a profligate conscience' as Strype (*Ecc. Mem.* II, p. 71) illustrates as follows. Latimer one day was in Oxford and attended Smith's lecture, on justification by faith. The next day he revoked the lecture, asserting the contrary doctrine, and acknowledging that he had spoken out of fear 'and praying, that they would attribute it to his youth; at that time plucking off his cap, whereby every one saw his grey hairs, which caused laughter'. In 1546 he published 'A Defence of the Sacrifice of the Mass', and on 15 May 1547, made a public retraction at St. Paul's Cross, London, and later at Oxford. At Louvain he published two books against Martyr, one on justification, to which Martyr makes reference in his Treatise *De Iustificatione*, in the Commentary on Romans; and one on Celibacy and Vows, to which Martyr replied with his *De Coelibatu . . . Defensio.* To this he appended Smith's retractation, and two letters of Smith to Cranmer from Scotland, written in February 1552. A similar indication of his nature is given by two letters in MS. 119 in Corpus Christi Library, Cambridge—one (No. 41) is a letter of apology to Cranmer for his book *de coelibatu patrum*, and another (No. 43) to Archbishop Parker, petitioning to have one of his bondsmen released from his bond. A marginal note adds that notwithstanding his fair promises he fled to Paris! His end was worthy of the man—expelled from Oxford for adultery, then a tavern keeper in Wales 'where, they say he has taken a wife, with the view, I suppose, of refuting all your arguments' as Jewel wrote to Martyr (1 June 1560—*Zurich Letters*, p. 81).

On 17 May, Martyr posted on the door of St. Mary's Church a notice, stating:[45]

Doctor Smith had challenged me to a disputation, as the whole University knows; I had agreed to that; we had come to an agreement about the points which should be discussed; but he is said to have absented himself from the appointed day and from this place; telling his friends at the same time that it would mean a pleasure to many people if I kept my appointment with him; so I offer publicly, for the edification of godly minds, to dispute the same points which we desired to treat, with him or any other who will appear in his place, and I take it upon me with God's help, to defend and to prove my propositions. The royal Commissioners and Visitors have appointed the twenty-eighth day of May as the day of Disputation, and given their full permission to discourse.

This challenge was accepted by three of the Romanist party, Tresham and Chedsey, both D.D., and Morgan, M.A.[46] Tresham, a Canon of Christchurch, was the chief opponent, and gave the preliminary address for their side, stating, 'I lay upon myself a mighty burden. For I have taken upon me to encounter and dispute with one who is learned, sharp of wit, and exercised in all manner of learning, both human and divine.' Yet he seeks to uphold the truth, hitherto received by the Church, and 'diametrically opposed' to Martyr's doctrine.

Peter Martyr began his positive proof by showing that Scripture says bread remains in the Eucharist—and by citing the Fathers' Christological analogy: 'a comparison to be made between the person of Christ and this sacrament: both of which, since they comprehend two natures, must preserve them both whole, which you in transubstantiating do not do'. This analogy, and the Patristic support which Martyr brings for it, guided the whole discussion through to a decided victory for Martyr's doctrine. The whole Disputation reveals Martyr's thorough knowledge of the Fathers, and his uncanny memory in quoting their words at length, or rehearsing the circumstances of their life and works.

---

[45] I take this statement from Schlosser, p. 427.

[46] None of the three presents an attractive picture: Morgan was known in Oxford as a 'Sophist' (Schlosser, p. 429); Chedsey in 1547 followed Smith's example and recanted; Tresham, after the publication of Martyr's account of the Disputation, wrote his own version, introduced by an Epistle calling Martyr *Pseudomartyr*, 'a doting old man, subverted, impudent, and famous master of errors' who fled from Germany for the sake of lust and adultery! Strype's *Cranmer*, Appendix XLV, gives the full text.

At one point, Tresham's books not having arrived, Morgan began. His petty grammatical and philological arguments fared so badly before Martyr's superiority in knowledge and debate, that Schmidt comments, 'It was a good thing for Morgan that Tresham had meanwhile received his books and could enter the discussion.'[47] Tresham and Chedsey, however, were worthy opponents, each debating with Martyr for two days—Tresham on 28 and 30 May, Chedsey on 29 May and 1 June. Morgan assisted Tresham briefly on 30 May, and Dr Cartwright gave Martyr a brief respite on 29 May. Royal Commissioners were present, and Chancellor Cox presided, summing up the debate at the end. Paying tribute to Martyr, he states: 'But Peter, who is worthily called Peter, for his assured steadfastness; Martyr, and worthily called Martyr, for the innumerable testimonies which he gives many times for the truth, ought to have great thanks at this time, both of ourselves and of all the godly: first, because he has taken the greatest care in sustaining the burden of disputation. For if "not Hercules himself against two", what say we of Peter alone against all comers? Further, whereas he undertook to dispute, he disproved the vain sayings of vain men, who spread envious and odious things against him; namely, that he would not or dared not defend his doctrine. Finally, that he so singularly well answered the expectation of the great magistrates, and indeed of the King himself, while he not only has delivered unto the University the doctrine of Christ, out of the living fountains of the Word of God, but, so far as lies in him, has not suffered any man to disturb or stop the fountains.'

Although no final decision was reached, the Disputation had two far-reaching results. *First*, it clarified the issues of the sacramental controversy, removing the false antithesis of Romanist/Zwinglian, which Bullinger's Swiss party had not helped to overcome. Thus it prepared the way for the more positive teaching of Bucer (who had just arrived at the time of Disputation, and indeed thought that Martyr had not moved far enough from the Swiss position) and of Martyr himself. For Martyr was the first Reformed Professor to hold a key position in an English University, and his doctrine in such an important

[47] II, p. 97.

and formal debate would have repercussions in all aspects of Church and State life in those critical days. *Second*, Peter Martyr's doctrine, as defended in the Disputation and set forth the same year in print along with the Treatise, and as endorsed by Cox and Cranmer, was now the recognized doctrine of the Church, and therefore normative for the drawing up of the Second Edwardian Prayer Book of 1552 and the Forty-Two Articles of 1553.[48] This introduces us to the subject of Martyr's larger part in the English Reformation, and to that we now turn.

Progress of the English Reformation

At the close of 1549 the problem of land enclosures, along with religious unrest, led to insurrection in various parts of England. The priests incited the people against the Reformers, urging the laity to demand the re-establishment of the Mass by force. The rebellion reached Oxford, where the violent mob singled out Peter Martyr as leader of the Reformed party, and cries of 'Death to Peter Martyr' echoed through the streets. He was forced to suspend his lectures, and ultimately to retire to London for safety.[49] King Edward was greatly

[48] The problem of Martyr's (and Bucer's) positive contribution to the theology of the framers of these documents is a complex one, and lies outside the scope of this work. Some contribution to it is however attempted below. Here we may note that Cranmer's 'A Defence of the True and Catholic Doctrine of the Sacrament' appeared in 1550, and shows striking agreement with Martyr's teaching; that Cox and Cranmer continued as the closest friends of Martyr, as shown by their lifelong correspondence with him; that Cranmer, at the beginning of Mary's reign issued a proclamation that he and Martyr would defend the Prayer Book against any who cared to challenge its teaching; and that Edward VI took a personal interest in Martyr and greatly respected his doctrine. In the British Museum is a copy of the 1549 edition of the Disputation and Treatise, with marginal notes on fol. 8-13 in the handwriting of the king, giving summaries of the argument. Cf. Schmidt, II, p. 128: 'die reformirten Grunddogmen in der Fassung darin aufgenommen wurden, in der sie Martyr in seinen Vorlesungen vorgetragen hatte; auch die Abendmahlslehre wurde so festgestellt, wie sie von ihm zu Oxford vertheidigt worden war'.

[49] There are extant two writings of Peter Martyr upon this rebellion, in MS. 102 (Cat. by James) in the Library of Corpus Christi College, Cambridge. No. 29 is 'A Sermon concernynge the tyme of rebellion translated from the Latin of Peter Martyr'; and No. 31 is the *Cogitationes Petri Martyris contra seditionem*. In the sermon he says 'Now the greate rebellion(s) . . . at this present tyme are to be bewailed with tears rather than with sword.' We must follow the example of Job; we must take the Word of God for our comfort and instructor; we must confess that tumult and sedition spring from sin; we must acknowledge, in the face of 'man's law and God's law', our responsibility 'in this life and in the life to come'; and above all, let this be our pattern: 'Christ did reconcyle us unto His Father, humbling Hym-

c

concerned over this turn of events, and received Martyr at Richmond. He promised him the first vacant canonry of Christ Church, Oxford—a promise fulfilled on 20 January 1551.

On his return to Oxford, Martyr resumed his busy life despite continuing opposition.[50] This so hindered his peace when he removed to Christ Church—his windows were continually broken, his studies and sleep interrupted, though 'all avowed that Martyr was the only scholarly theologian in England'[51]—that he exchanged his lodging for the cloister belonging to the second canonry, and erected a stone study in the garden, where he obtained peace to write his commentaries on 1 Corinthians. He had removed to 'the N. side of Christ Church great gate leading to Fish Street', his wife Catherine being 'the first woman, as it was observed, that resided in any college or hall in Oxon'.[52]

About this time (1550) John White, Warden of Westminster (afterwards Bishop, in Mary's reign) attempted to publish his tract against Martyr, in verse, entitled *Diacosio-Martyrion*. Strype calls it 'In truth a very trifling piece, levelled against Peter Martyr' and indeed its bigotry so distorts the facts of this period as to render its worth negligible.[53] White sent it to Louvain for publication, but he and his associates in the work were imprisoned when it was discovered and returned to London. It was finally published in November 1553, in London, and its same dedication retained: *Ad Serenissimam Illustrissimamque Principem MARIAM regis EDWARDI VI Sororem.*

selfe to His father's will, even to the death of the crosse, and He hath commanded all them that profess to be His disciples to follow His example. But alas, how farre be all from His rule and example . . .' Bucer also wrote a discourse on the Devon Revolt; and Cranmer's sermon on the same affair is based upon notes of Peter Martyr. Cf. Strype's *Cranmer*, pp. 187f, Appendix XLI; C. Hopf, *Martin Bucer and the English Reformation* (Oxford, 1946), p. 84, and Young, p. 432, n. 2. Martyr's original is in the same library, MS. 340.4, *Sermo Petri Martyri manu propria scriptus in seditionem Devonensium.*

[50] Cf. his letter to Bucer of 20 September 1550 (Strype's *Cranmer*, Appendix LX) concerning the disputations, the leadership of Chedsey, and the daily opposition.

[51] 'Der einzige gelehrte Theologe in England'—Schlosser, p. 432.

[52] Anthony a Wood, quoted by Young, p. 434. Cf. p. 579 for the formal data about this appointment, from Gilpin's Book, MS., in the Chapter-House of Christ Church.

[53] *Ecc. Mem.* II, p. 439. Its introductory epistle to Martyr not only derides his sacramental doctrine, but accuses him of wilfully causing Smith to leave the country, in order to avoid disputing with him when challenged!

During this time Martyr's work continued to mount. In a letter to Bullinger he describes his activities.

I will explain to you in few words the kind of employment in which I have been engaged. In addition to my daily expositions of St. Paul, which of themselves would almost entirely occupy the time of any one who should employ himself upon them as they deserve, a new burden has been imposed upon this University by laws lately enacted by the king's majesty. For it is decreed that public disputations upon theological subjects should be held frequently, that is, every alternate week, at which I am required to be present and to preside. Then, in the kings' college, wherein I reside, the theological disputations are held every week, which, inasmuch as all persons are freely admitted to hear them, may in like manner be called public; and over these I am appointed moderator, as over the others. I have therefore a continual struggle with my adversaries, who are indeed most obstinate; so that I am easily compelled, whether I will or not, often to lay aside other matters, and devote the whole time allowed me to the vocation to which I am bound.[54]

Young calls this 'the most useful period of Martyr's life',[55] and Schmidt says that a greater work than that of dealing with Smith and White was his contribution to the Liturgy.[56] Indeed, his influence was growing—he received the degree D.D. from the University of Oxford, and numbered among his friends Latimer, Ridley, Ponet, Hooper and Coverdale, besides Cranmer and the King.[57]

The Vestment Controversy

In the year 1550 Hooper took his famous stand against the episcopal oath and the vestments which he termed Aaronic and Antichristian. The chief answer to this question was being given by the Swiss party, Burcher, John a Lasco and others, who denied the validity of such vestments in an absolute manner. But Hooper also asked the advice of Martyr and Bucer, in

---

[54] Letter of 1 June 1550—*Original Letters* (Parker Society 1847) II, p. 481.
[55] p. 435.
[56] II, p. 120.
[57] An interesting aside is given by Strype, II, p. 337: 'Parkhurst, a Fellow of Merton, and an earnest Professor of the Gospel (afterwards Bishop of Norwich), was one of Martyr's great friends and acquaintance, and whom Parkhurst loved as his father. He, being removed from the University to the rich rectory of Cleve, in Gloucestershire, often invited him to come to his house to refresh himself: but Martyr could never find time to do it. There was a certain liquor made of rough pears, called *perry*, used much in the counties of Gloucester and Worcester, which the reverend man loved to drink when he was hot or feverish: this his friend Parkhurst used to supply him.'

October of that year. Martyr replied in detail in a letter to
Hooper of 4 November.[58]

Martyr tells Hooper that he has examined his letter (keeping
it but 'one night' since he had to forward it by the same
messenger to Bucer at Cambridge) and his first reaction is one of
elation at Hooper's zeal for the purity and simplicity of religion.

> For what should be desired by godly men more than that all things may
> gradually be removed which have little or nothing that can be referred to
> sound edification? and which are judged by godly minds rather to redound
> and to be superfluous?

The custom enjoyed at Strassburg, where all such garments
were abolished, is still, to Martyr's mind, the pure imitation
of the Apostolic Church.

> You therefore see that in the chief and principal point I do not disagree
> from you, but earnestly desire that what you attempt may have place.
> This desire of mine is kindled, partly that in ceremonies we might come as
> near as possible to Holy Scripture, and pursue the imitation of the better
> times of the Church; and partly that I perceive the Papal followers attempt
> by these relics to restore a show of the mass at least; and cling to these things
> more than the nature of things indifferent requires.

Yet even these circumstances do not cause Martyr to agree
with Hooper that this is a matter of something in itself destructive (*exitiosus*). This is rather a matter of 'things indifferent'
(*adiaphora*), which are therefore free for use or rejection. The
proper method is surely first to establish true religion in England, then the people themselves will desire to rid themselves of
such superfluous affairs. But do not let this become a hindrance
to your preaching through contention!

Martyr now answers Hooper's two objections, concerning the

<hr/>

[58] *L.C.*, pp. 1085-1088. Bucer's part in the affair is excellently described in
Chapter 4 of Hopf's work, in which he also gives, published for the first time,
Peter Martyr's letter to Bucer of 25 October 1550 (pp. 162-164). A further source,
which I have not seen published, is a work written by Peter Martyr and preserved
in the University Library, Cambridge (Tracts Mm 4.14, fol.12-14). His thesis in
this brief tract is: *Rerum indifferentium natura est per se vel usurpari vel omitti sine
impietate possint. Apparatus vestium sacerdotalium res est ex natura sua indifferens seu
ἀδιάφορος. Ergo Apparatus vestium sacerdotalium per se ex natura sua impius non est neque
exitiosus usurpartibus*: Such things as are agreeable to the Mosaic-Aaronic priesthood *possunt in ecclesias nostras revocari seu retineri*. Martyr's letter to Hooper of
4 November 1550 also figured in the Elizabethan stage of the controversy, e.g. in
the 1566 Pamphlet, 'VVhether it be mortall sinne to transgresse ciuil lawes . . .'
which gives the judgment of Melanchthon (in his Epitome of moral philosophy)
and the correspondence of Bullinger, Gualter, Bucer and Martyr 'concernyng the
apparrel of Ministers, and other indifferent thinges'. (London, 1566.)

Aaronic priesthood, and the Antichristian nature of these vestments owing to their Romanist origin. To the first he answers that although the sacraments of the O.T. priesthood are abrogated, this does not apply absolutely. Yet such things as are indifferent—not necessary to salvation—may not be restored as if they were necessary. Accordingly, with regard to the use of vestments,

this indeed I wish had been laid aside: but when it came about contrary to my mind, I thought it right to suffer the same until better times should be granted.

What may the Church use of that which comes from Romanism? Martyr warns that we must not subject the Church to a false bondage, denying a right use to everything from that quarter. For:

admit that these things were invented by the Pope, yet I cannot be persuaded that the wickedness of the papacy is such that whatever it touches it completely defiles and pollutes, by which it cannot be allowed to a holy use by good and pious men.

Moreover, Hooper's charge against human invention cannot be applied absolutely. But the great plea of the letter is this:

How can we deprive the Church of this liberty, that it may not signify something by its actions and rites, this being done without placing any worship of God in them, modestly and in few things, so that the people of Christ be not burdened with ceremonies, and better things not hindered?

And so he concludes:

This in general is enough to know by faith, that things indifferent cannot defile those who live with a pure and sincere mind and conscience . . . Nor am I lately persuaded in my mind of this opinion which I have now declared, but judged even from the first that I applied my mind to the Gospel, that these diversities of garments should not be used: but yet thought that their use, if other things prescribed to us by the Word of God remain sound, are neither wicked nor pernicious in themselves or by their own nature.

To this view of Martyr and Bucer, Hooper ultimately bowed, acknowledging 'the liberty of the sons of God in all external things . . . only the abuse, which can be pernicious to all, of those who use them superstitiously or otherwise evilly do I blame, together with Dr Bucer, Dr Martyr, and all godly and learned men . . .'[59]

[59] Letter of 15 February 1551 to Cranmer, from the Fleet prison—quoted by Hopf, *op. cit.*, p. 132.

The Second Book of Common Prayer

The Reformation under Edward VI had been furthered by the Injunctions, Homilies and Visitation,[60] and then by the first Book of Prayer, of 1549. Cranmer had charge of this work, the conservatism of which allowed even an interpretation of transubstantiation in the office of the Lord's Supper.[61] The advanced Reformers, especially Martyr and Ochino who arrived in England in 1547, and Bucer, whose dealings with England began long before his arrival in 1549,[62] taught a decisively Reformed doctrine. During the period of revision of the Book, therefore, Cranmer asked for the opinion of the foreign divines then resident in England. The problem of their influence is a complex one, on which strongly divergent opinions are held; here we shall attempt to show Peter Martyr's part in the history.

Strype[63] describes the events of that period as follows. Towards the end of 1550 Cranmer and certain bishops were reviewing the Book of Common Prayer to remove divers things 'that favoured too much of Superstition'. Cranmer asked Bucer and Martyr to submit their views upon the matter; Martyr knew the Book through John Cheke's Latin translation. 'Accordingly Bucer wrote his Censure, and Martyr his Annotations . . . A Copy of which Censure Bucer had communicated to Martyr.' Bucer's Censure had given the general opinion that nothing was enjoined in the Book not agreeable to the

[60] Cf. Strype, II, Chapter 7. 'The king by this time had made a good step in the reformation of religion. For besides the injunctions and the royal visitation and an English Communion Book, and the communion to be received in both kinds, the Holy Bible in the vulgar tongue, the Homilies, and the excellent Paraphrases of that great scholar Erasmus, were all now, by the king's command, brought in for the common use of his subjects' (p. 104).

[61] Francis Dryander wrote to Bullinger in 1549, 'some puerilities have been still suffered to remain, lest the people should be offended by too great an innovation'; and a short time later, 'You will also find something to blame in the Lord's Supper; for the book speaks very obscurely . . . it was a long and earnest dispute among (the bishops) whether transubstantiation should be established or rejected'. (Original Letters, Parker Society, I, pp. 350f, of 25 March and 5 June.) Cf. Procter-Frere, A New History of the Book of Common Prayer (Macmillan, 1941): 'the book could not be used except by applying to it a knowlege of the method of performing the Latin Service' (p. 66, n.2); cf. 67n for Gardiner's Romanist interpretation of the Book.

[62] At Ratisbon in particular, where he met Gardiner. He was in England only from April 1549 until his death on 1 March 1551. Cf. especially Hopf, op. cit., Chapter 1.

[63] Mem. of Cran., pp. 210f, 251f.

Word of God, and then had noted certain definite instances where he thought revision was required.[64] Martyr had sent his Annotations to Cranmer before he saw Bucer's Censure. The latter indicated other matter requiring correction, which he had missed because Cheke's Latin version 'was so brief and defective'.[65] Therefore Martyr wrote certain Articles and sent them to Cranmer as well. Neither Annotations nor Articles, however, are extant, our only source for his observations being his letter to Bucer of 10 January 1551.[66] This we shall quote at length as contributing to the understanding of this most important subject.

(*Censura libri Communium Precum*)

S.D.—Nothing more welcome or more pleasing could befall me at this time, than to see your censure of the holy book. Wherefore I give undying thanks that you deigned to send it to me. I myself have been asked already to comment whatever seems good to me on this matter. And since, owing to my not knowing the language, the version of Dr Cheke had been given me to read, so that I could draw conclusions from that, I have noted the things that seem worthy of correction. But because a good many things are lacking in the version submitted to me, therefore I have omitted much, concerning which I said nothing in my Annotations. But, then, when I had discovered from your writing that these things were in such manner contained in the book, I was grieved; since I had already, two or three days before, submitted my Censure to the Most Reverend man that had pressed me for it. But now I have offered this remedy: what I have learned from your writing to have been omitted in mine, I have put together in summary: and since the very same things that you have criticized seem also to me unworthy of being continued, these I have reduced into brief articles; and I have informed the Most Reverend, who already knows what you have

---

[64] Cf. Hopf, *op. cit.* pp. 65-81 for details of these. (Script. Anglic. 456-503.)

[65] Cf. Strype's 'Life of Sir John Cheke' (Oxford, 1821), p. 54: 'In this matter our Cheke was concerned: he translated into Latin the substance of the said Communion Book for P. Martyr (not understanding English), now being at Lambeth with the Archbishop: and from this translation Martyr made his censures by way of annotation. And moreover, Cheke had conference with that learned man concerning the amendments to be made, and concerning a meeting of the Bishops that were to consult and deliberate about it.'

[66] The original in MS. is in the Corpus Christi Library, Cambridge (MS. 119, No. 39), and a copy made for Strype in 1692 is in the University Library, Cambridge, Baumgartner Papers (Strype Correspondence) Add. 3 (c); Strype (*Mem. of Cran.*, Appendix LXI) gives the full Latin text; cf. G. C. Gorham, 'Gleanings of a few scattered ears during the period of the Reformation in England' (London, 1857), n. LXIII. Schmidt's source (II, p. 124) is 'Rog. Ashami epistolae, S. 147'. Peter Martyr's letter had survived in Archbishop Parker's papers, and the title *Censura libri communium precum* is in the latter's handwriting.

written to the Bishop of Ely, that in all these heads which I will offer him, noted in articles, I agree with you, that they might be changed.

However, in the first Annotations, almost everything which offended you had been noted by me. Indeed I was sending an example to you now, but do not have it so transcribed that you could read it. Yet I wondered why in the matter of the Communion of the sick, you omitted that which is stated, if it happens on the same Lord's Day as the Lord's Supper is held, then the Minister should take with him part of the elements, and should thus administer Communion in the house of the sick. In this affair it offended me, that what pertains chiefly to the Lord's Supper is not repeated there; and this when—as I think you also feel—the words of the Supper pertain rather to men than either to bread or to wine. I have advised, as seemed good to me, that all things which are required as necessary to the Lord's Supper should be said and done before the sick, and those who communicate with him as well. And indeed it is a wonder that those words are a burden to say in presence of the sick, to whom they are of the greatest utility, when they would repeat the same uselessly when the wine in the cup happens to run short during communion in the Church, since the men who are present and take the sacraments, have already heard them. These are what I thought of some moment, and why you omitted them I do not well understand. But in all things that you have recommended to be reformed, I have written of your opinion. And I thank God who has afforded occasion that the Bishops might be advised by us about all these things. It has now been decided in this Colloquy of theirs, as the Most Reverend informs me, that many things shall be changed. But what in fact they are which they have determined to have reformed, he himself neither explained to me, nor did I presume to ask him. But what Dr Cheke has told me gratified me not a little; he says, that if they themselves will not effect the changes which are to be made, the King himself will do it; and when he has come to parliament, he will interpose his Royal authority.

.   .   .   .

Yours in Christ,
PETER MARTYR

Here we see the theological unanimity of Martyr and Bucer at this time, as well as one practice that was revised on Martyr's advice alone, the reserving of consecrated elements after public administration of the sacrament, to be given the sick in private Communion. It should be noted that Martyr's view was that the sick ought to receive Communion,[67] his objection being to the false doctrine of consecration involved in the practice of

[67] In his Treatise *An in communione liceat una tantum specie uti*, 21—it is only Papist superstition that has created problems such as whether the wine should be that already used in the Mass.

reservation. It is difficult to attribute other revised portions of
the Prayer Book to Martyr specifically; however, such changes
as the prohibition of vestments, the substitution of 'Table' for
'Altar', the omission of the Agnus Dei (which was popularly
held to imply Christ's corporeal presence in the elements), are
in line with his understanding of the emphases required for
proper reformation.[68] Although the retention only of the more
active sentences in the words at the delivery of the elements
('Take and eat . . . Drink this . . .') agrees with his emphasis
upon *action* in the sacrament, the sentences omitted (and restored in 1562) also have place in his own teaching. But one
addition in the Communion Office traditionally[69] ascribed to
his hand is the second Exhortation, to be used when the people
are 'negligent to come to the holy Communion'.

Such details are but signs of the true matter at issue. The
purpose of the revision of the Prayer Book was to remove all
traces of the doctrines of transubstantiation and propitiatory
sacrifice from the central Communion Office—to cross the
Rubicon.[70] Thus the two questions to be asked were, What
form should the Prayer of Consecration take? and, What
efficacy should be attributed to the sacraments? To the first a
clear answer was given, inasmuch as the 1549 invocation for
consecration *by Thy Word and Holy Spirit* was omitted, and
indeed was not included in any subsequent revision. The
tradition of the Western Church, as rationalized by the Scholastics, was that the words of our Lord's institution form the
actual consecration, and this has been the determinative concept
ever since 1552.[71] This is an unfortunate confusion, for even

[68] For details of the changes, see Procter-Frere, pp. 81ff; E. Daniel, *The Prayer
Book* (London, 1913), pp. 41ff; etc.

[69] As early as 1579, when Marten's E.T. of the *Loci Comm.* included an expanded text of the Exhortation. F. C. Massingberd ('A Letter to the Rev. Wm.
Goode', London, 1850) notes simply, 'the address . . . is attributed to his pen',
while Blunt, *Annotated B.C.P.* (1876), p. 177, has 'This Exhortation was inserted in
1552, as Cosin thinks at the instance of Bucer.'

[70] Norman Sykes, *The English Religious Tradition* (S.C.M., 1953), comments on
the Second P.B.: 'Cranmer had crossed the Rubicon, by the removal of the am-
biguities of the first Prayer Book which had allowed a Catholic interpretation'
(p. 21).

[71] Cf. Blunt, p. 187; Atchley, *On the Epiclesis of the Eucharistic Liturgy and in the
Consecration of the Font* (Alcuin Club XXXI, Oxford, 1935): 'Consequently our
present Prayer Book (i.e. that of 1661) remains committed to the theory of the
medieval Scholastics, namely, that our Lord's words of administration are the
form of consecration; and the rubric for a second consecration in the case where

now 'the English Liturgy still lags behind its Scottish and American daughters'.[72] Whether Peter Martyr agreed with such drastic revision in the matter of consecration is a moot point. As we shall see,[73] he attributed to the words of consecration two things: a distinct role in the office of the Holy Spirit, who uses the elements as His instruments, and a sacramental mutation qualifying the elements themselves. It was Bucer, in his Censure, who objected specifically to such invocation of the Holy Spirit, and it is usually assumed that Martyr agreed on this point because of his general concurrence in the *Censura*, and because he states 'the words of the Supper pertain rather to men than either to bread or to wine'.[74] But two things must be said on this point. First, Martyr is talking about 'what pertains chiefly to the Lord's Supper' when Communion is given privately to the sick, and therefore is thinking of Consecration only as one term among others, albeit the most important. Second, his statement does not exclude the possibility that the words pertain *also* to the elements, for indeed he

'the consecrated Bread or Wine be all spent before all have communicated' emphasized this, by directing only the narrative of the Institution to be used for the blessing of the Bread or the Wine, without any prayer. It is thus far from being in accord with the belief of the Primitive Church' (p. 197).

[72] Procter-Frere, p. 474. The Scottish Prayer Book of 1637 re-stated the earlier invocation as follows: 'vouchsafe so to bless and sanctify with thy word and Holy Spirit these thy gifts and creatures of bread and wine, that they may be unto us the body and blood of thy most dearly beloved Son . . .'; yet too suffers from 'an unaccountable lapse' in its rubric for additional consecration, which is by the words of Institution alone (cf. G. Donaldson, *The Making of the Scottish Prayer Book of 1637* (Edinburgh Univ. Press, 1954), pp. 67ff, 76f, 198, 204). Donaldson comments, 'This phraseology gives no countenance to any doctrine at variance with either the Scots Confession of 1560 or the Westminster *formulae*' (68). The Westminster 'Directory' had ordered prayer, after the words of institution, including 'blessing of the bread and wine' that God would 'vouchsafe his gracious presence, and the effectual working of his Spirit in us; and so to sanctify these elements both of bread and wine, and to bless his own ordinance, that we may receive by faith the body and blood of Jesus Christ, crucified for us, and so to feed upon him, that he may be one with us, and we one with him; that he may live in us, and we in him, and to him who hath loved us, and given himself for us'. Then it states, 'The elements being now sanctified by the word and prayer . . .' (*Standards*, Edinburgh 1869.) Cf. the Book of Common Order of the Church of Scotland, in which the minister's formal words of consecration ('I take these elements') after the words of institution, lead directly into the Eucharistic Prayer, whose epiclesis invokes 'Thy Holy Spirit to sanctify both us and these Thine own gifts', and oblation follows. This in turn introduces the fraction and distribution as an act distinct from the prayer of consecration.

[73] Chapter IV, section 'The invisible word made visible' and Chapter VII, section 'The words of consecration and their effects'.

[74] The sentence is from his own *Censura*; Atchley (p. 192) quotes it as representing the theory that dictated the change in 1552.

posits a definite sacramental mutation in the elements deriving from and analogous to the mutation in the communicants themselves. Therefore it would appear unthinkable that Martyr would have simply accepted such omission of invocation of the Holy Spirit unless we assume that, under Bucer's urging, he agreed to acquiesce in what was obviously a reaction against the superstition which then abounded concerning consecration.

The other question, of the efficacy of the sacraments, received no such definitive treatment, and indeed has been a problem within the Anglican Communion ever since. On 14 June 1552, two months after the Book had passed through the Parliament, Martyr wrote to Bullinger, in part as follows:[75]

That matter which was desired by all good men, and which the King's Majesty had not a little at heart, could not be accomplished; wherefore as yet things remain to a great extent as they were before, except that the Book or Order of Ecclesiastical Rites and the Administration of the Sacraments is reformed, for all things are removed from it which could nourish superstition. But the chief reason why other things which were purposed were not effected, was that the subject of the sacraments stood in the way; not truly as regards transubstantiation, or the real presence (so to speak) either in the bread or in the wine, since, thanks be to God, concerning these things there seems to be now no controversy as it regards those who profess the Gospel; but whether grace is conferred by virtue of the sacraments is a doubtful point to many. And there have been some who altogether held the affirmative, and were desirous that this doctrine should be established by public authority. But when others clearly saw how many superstitions such a determination would bring with it, they made a primary point to endeavour in all ways to show, that nothing more is to be granted to the sacraments than to the external word of God, for by both these kinds of word is signified and shown to us the salvation obtained for us through Christ, which as many are made partakers of as believe these words and signs, not indeed by the virtue of the words or of the sacraments, but by the efficacy of faith. Moreover it was added, that it was impossible that the sacraments should be worthily received, unless those who receive them have beforehand that which is signified by them, for unless faith is present, they are always received unworthily, but if they who come to the sacraments are endued with faith, they have already received through faith the grace which is proclaimed to us in the sacraments, and then the reception and use of the sacraments is the seal and obsignation of the promise already apprehended. And as the external words of God avail to the quickening and exciting our faith which

[75] 'An Unpublished Letter of Peter Martyr, Reg. Div. Prof. Oxford, to Henry Bullinger; written from Oxford just after the completion of the Second Prayer Book of Edward VI; edited, with remarks, by Wm. Goode, London, 1850.'

is often torpid, and as if lying asleep in us, this same thing also the sacraments can effect by the power of the Holy Spirit, and their use is of no little benefit to confirm our minds otherwise weak, concerning the promises and the grace of God. But in the case of children, when they are baptized, since on account of their age they cannot have that assent to the divine promises which is faith, in them the sacrament effects this, that pardon of original sin, reconciliation with God, and the grace of the Holy Spirit, bestowed on them through Christ, is sealed in them, and that those belonging already to the Church are also visibly implanted in it. Although of those that are baptized, whether children or adults, it is not to be denied that much advantage and profit comes to them from the invocation of the Father, the Son and the Holy Spirit, which takes place over them. For God always hears the faithful prayers of His Church. We were anxious that these things should be determined and established by authority concerning the sacraments, that their use might at length be restored to a state of purity and simplicity. But it was opposed; and many are of the opinion, and those otherwise not unlearned nor evil, that grace is conferred, as they say, by virtue of the sacraments. Nor will they grant that little children are justified or regenerated before baptism. But when we come to their reasons, there are none which do not most readily admit of solution. Nevertheless no little displeasure is excited against us on this account, namely, that we altogether dissent from Augustine. And if our doctrine was approved by public authority, then, say they, Augustine would manifestly be condemned. Why need I add more? . . .

Thus the question 'whether grace is conferred by virtue of the sacraments is a doubtful point to many' and, according to Goode, accounts for the delay in publishing the Forty-Two Articles, which 'were at last published by Royal authority in the following May'.[76] In this nineteenth-century controversy about baptismal regeneration, William Goode, a follower of G. C. Gorham, published the above letter and claimed that the dispute following the publication of the Second Prayer Book proves it was not considered to have settled this question about the effect of the sacraments. Against this view F. D. Massingberd[77] admitted Martyr's influence and doctrine, but claimed 'that the opinions of Cranmer, Ridley and Bucer, concerning Holy Baptism, were opposed' to Martyr's doctrine as contained in the letter to Bullinger. This curious thesis is based on the error of judging Martyr's doctrine to be 'Zwing-

[76] Goode also points out the similarity between Martyr's doctrine and the phraseology of Articles 26 and 27. For details of this doctrine see our Chapter V.
[77] 'A Letter to the Rev. Wm. Goode . . .' (London, 1850).

lian', and involves the deduction that 'those who hold the other opinion' in the letter are Bucer and Cranmer!

What of Cranmer's own attitude towards our Reformer? Strype gives the following estimate: 'As for the learned Italian, Peter Martyr, who is worthy to be mentioned with Melanchthon and Calvin, there was not only an acquaintance between him and our Archbishop, but a great and cordial intimacy and friendship. For of him he made particular use in the steps he took in our Reformation. And whenever he might be spared from his public readings in Oxford, the Archbishop used to send for him, to confer with him about the weightiest matters. This Calvin took notice of, and signified to him by letter, how much he rejoiced that he made use of the counsels of that excellent man. And when the reformation of the ecclesiastical laws was in effect wholly devolved upon Cranmer, he appointed him and Gualter Haddon, and Dr Rowland Tayler his Chaplain, and no more, to manage that business. Which shows what an opinion he had of Martyr's abilities, and how he served himself of him in matters of the greatest moment. And in that bold and brave challenge he made in the beginning of Queen Mary's reign, to justify, against any man whatsoever, every part of King Edward's reformation; he nominated and made choice of Martyr therein to be one of his assistants in that Disputation, if any would undertake it with him.'[78]

To say the least, Anglican writers appear to have departed from the positive evaluation of Strype, and relegate Martyr to the position of a Puritan pioneer and therefore an unfortunate accident in the history of the Reformation in England.[79] The basic error in this view is the radical distinction drawn between 'Genevan Presbyterianism and Anglican Catholicity',[80] the

[78] *Mem. of Cran.*, p. 413. The reference in Calvin is as follows (*Epistolae et Responsa*, 1597, Ep. 127, p. 252), *Quanquam autem non dubito, quin haec tibi subinde veniat ultro in mentem, et ab optimo et integerrimo viro D. Petro Martyre, cuius te consilio uti plurimum gaudeo, suggerantur: tot tamen ac tam arduae difficultates quibuscum luctaris mihi visae sunt sufficere, ne supervacua foret mea exhortatio.*

[79] E.g. H. M. Luccock (*Studies in the History of the P.B.*, London, 1882) deals with Martyr under the Chapter on 'The Puritan Innovations', and decries his 'zwinglianism'. The opposite thesis is sustained by N. Dimock, *The History of the B C.P.* (Longmans, Green, 1910), in which 'an attempt is made to correct what appears to be certain prevalent misconceptions concerning our Book of Common Prayer'.

[80] Blunt, p. xxx—'It was unfortunate for the peace of the Church of England, that those who were in authority at this period were disposed to yield too much

assumption being that the 'foreign influence' period in the
history of English doctrinal and liturgical reform is an inter-
lude which the Laudian party successfully overcame in the
next century.[81] One aspect of this treatment of the history is
the claim that the Continental or 'foreign' divines forced themselves upon England as they sought refuge, and largely in-
stigated the movement for liturgical revision.[82] Both theses
must be sharply modified in the light of history. As to the first,
not only were Martyr and Bucer expressly invited to England
by Cranmer, in his desire for a 'godly synod'—Martyr, indeed
was asked back during the reign of Elizabeth—but those who
came as refugees were able to say that 'The Archbishop of
Canterbury, the special patron of foreigners, has been the chief
support and promoter of our church, to the great astonishment
of some.'[83] Moreover, Bucer's influence antedated his residence
in England, through correspondence and through the use of
Hermann's Consultation in the preparation of the 1549 Prayer
Book,[84] while Bullinger's *Decades* had played a material part in
preparing for the Edwardian Reformation.

As to the question of the origin of the movement for revision,
Procter-Frere points out: 'No sooner had the First Prayer Book
appeared, backed by the first attempt to enforce Uniformity by
Act of Parliament, than it became a bone of contention . . . it
is one of the grim sarcasms of history that the first Act of
Uniformity should have divided the Church of England into
the two parties, which have ever since contended within her

to the influence of foreigners whose principles were totally alien from those on
which the English Reformation was based.'

[81] Cf. J. H. Overton, *The Church in England* (London, 1897), Vol. II, pp. 33ff.

[82] E.g. E. Daniel: 'Unfortunately the young king gave too ready an ear to their
suggestions, and determined on having the new Prayer Book revised' (p. 40);
cf. C. Dunlop, *Anglican Public Worship* (S.C.M., 1953): 'Troubles on the Continent
caused a number of foreign theologians to seek refuge on our hospitable shore . . .
they gained a following in this country and established a more revolutionary
party in ecclesiastical circles' (p. 67). But Dimock declares, 'The idea that the
revising hand was a foreign hand, and the revision an un-English work, must be
altogether abandoned . . . our English Reformers, in preparing the second book,
were entering into a perfecting work, which was in view in their original design'
(p. 22).

[83] Micronius to Bullinger, 28 August 1550 (*Orig. Lett.*, II, p. 568).

[84] Bucer and Melanchthon had produced the 'simple and religious consultation of us Herman by the grace of God archebishop of Colone' in 1543, and
this and its answer, *Antididagma*, were before Cranmer—see Procter-Frere, pp.
28f.

on ceremonial and doctrinal matters.'[85] This indicates that the true problem is not a historical but a theological one. The influence of the Continental Reformers upon Cranmer and the Churchmen whose friendship with Peter Martyr was so close is undeniable, but to call it undesirable or 'foreign' is to miss the point that this influence was deliberately sought and cultivated by the first and second generations of English Reformers— Cranmer and Jewel for instance. No doubt the influence of the 'Swiss Party' contributed to the early Puritan point of view. But here too we must remember that after 1549 at the latest (the year of the *Consensus Tigurinus*) Bullinger's theology was wholly acceptable to Calvin, whatever be our estimate of Zwingli, and therefore once again we have the fact of a doctrine practically identical with that of Martyr and Bucer.[86] On the other side, perhaps, is the question of the significance of the famous Black Rubric, which was probably the work of John Knox.[87] This rubric, added on the eve of the publication of the Second Prayer Book, was in explanation of the kneeling to receive the Communion, and stated 'that it is not meant thereby that any adoration is done, or ought to be done, either unto the sacramental bread or wine there bodily received, or to any real and essential presence there being of Christ's material flesh and blood'. Yet even here we do not have a 'Swiss' view of the sacrament, since the term 'real and essential presence' was the traditional way of expressing the doctrine of transubstantiation.[88] Moreover, the opposition to the practice of kneeling indicates rather a horror of the sign of adoration of the elements than a low doctrine of the sacraments.[89]

[85] *Op. cit.*, pp. 66ff; but Blunt, p. xxx, states, 'It had been accepted with satisfaction by most of the Clergy and Laity', and adds, with what historical evidence he does not say, that 'A lasco, Peter Martyr, and Martin Bucer appear to have been continually corresponding about the Prayer Book, and plotting for its alteration.'

[86] Cf. the very helpful lecture by C. C. Richardson, 'Zwingli and Cranmer on the Eucharist' (Seabury-Western, Evanston, 1949).

[87] Cf. Donaldson, '(John Knox) was the "runagate Scot" to whose influence is credibly attributed the insertion, in Edward's second book, of the "Black Rubric" . . .', p. 4. Procter-Frere, p. 83, point out that the 'extreme party among the reformers' had opposed the custom, and probably Knox's 'profane recklessness' in substituting sitting for kneeling and in preaching against it, was the immediate cause. Blunt, p. 199, has no mention of Knox, simply stating, 'It was probably framed by Cranmer.'

[88] Cf. the discussion of the phrase, in relation to the 1662 reaction to the rubric, in Dimock, pp. 44ff.

[89] E.g. the Scots Confession of 1560, which reflects Knox's own doctrine, has

To the Council's request that he reconsider this question of kneeling, Cranmer made a significant reply,[90] stating in part: 'And where I understand further by your Lordships' letters that some be offended with kneeling at the time of the receiving of the sacrament, and would that I (calling to me the Bishop of London, and some other learned men as Mr Peter Martyr or such like), should with them expend, and weigh the said prescription, whether it be fit to remain as a commandment, or to be left out of the book. I shall accomplish the King's Majesty his commandment herein:—albeit I trust that we with just balance weighed this at the making of the book, and not only we, but a great many Bishops and others of the best learned within this realm appointed for that purpose.'

Cranmer's own theological position is still a subject for debate. One of the best modern treatments is that by Dom Gregory Dix,[91] who concludes that Cranmer was a thoroughgoing Zwinglian (in the traditional sense of the word), whose liturgical revision was entirely consistent with the doctrine in which he had believed ever since Ridley converted him from the error of transubstantiation. Without entering this discussion[92] about the true nature of Zwingli's own doctrine, we must consider the significance of Peter Martyr's influence upon Cranmer. Our historical summary has shown the extent of this influence, dating from Martyr's first sojourn at Lambeth in the spring of 1549 on his arrival, ending with his final visit there in the dark days of 1553, before Cranmer's martyrdom and his own flight

in its article on the sacraments (XXI) all the elements of the high Calvinistic doctrine that we shall be examining as belonging also to that of Peter Martyr: the repudiation of a doctrine of the elements as 'bot naked and baire signes'; the sacraments as seals as well as signs; the definition of faith as union with Christ; the operation of the Holy Ghost in a *sursum corda*; 'that in the Supper richtlie used, Christ Jesus is so joined with us, that hee becummis very nourishment and fude of our saules.'

[90] On 7 October 1552—text in Blunt, p. xxxi. It is difficult to understand the basis for the conclusion of Procter-Frere (p. 85): 'Thus against the Archbishop's will and without the consent of the Church, English religion reached its low water mark and the ill-starred book of 1552 began its brief career.' Yet all later revision was based on this, and not on the 1549 Book!

[91] *The Shape of the Liturgy*, 1946, pp. 640-674. 'What had largely assisted the general misunderstanding of 1549 was its retention of the traditional Shape of the Liturgy. Cranmer realized that this was a mistake if he wanted the new belief to be adopted; and in 1552 he made radical changes in this in order to bring out the doctrinal implications of 1549' (649).

[92] Between Dix and G. B. Timms. C. C. Richardson, *op. cit.*, claims to give a more proper orientation than either.

from England. Without compromising his doctrine by a simple identification with that of Bucer, we may state that the theology of these two men exerted a more personal and profound influence upon Cranmer than any other from 1549 on. Hence Cranmer's statements, often negative and one-sided, must be interpreted in the light of Martyr's more positive doctrine.[93] Cranmer's theology can be termed 'Zwinglian' only if we modify this term in two ways: by admitting that Zwingli himself, and especially his successor Bullinger, meant by 'faith' something more than a mental state,[94] and therefore Cranmer's doctrine had positive content beyond that of the Swiss party; and further, Cranmer was influenced in a more positive direction yet by Peter Martyr, although he does not explicitly pursue the distinctive direction of Martyr's sacramental doctrine.[95]

We submit therefore, that Peter Martyr's doctrine, which we shall delineate in the properly theological portion of this work, is the doctrine which Cranmer accepted as at least standing in agreement with the Prayer Book and the Articles of Edward's reign; which John Jewel and his friends considered their own theological position during Elizabeth's time; and which, although not receiving definite expression by any group in the subsequent history of the Church of England—since Puritanism, for example, cannot be called validly the true inheritor of this theology of Martyr and Calvin—yet was one whose influence is evident throughout the history of the Church in England, for example in the debates of Cheke, Whitgift and Cartwright, or Gorham.[96] And this is the full-orbed theology of baptism and

[93] As against, e.g. the interpretation of Dix and Richardson, whose main mistake consists in ignoring this influence from the side of Bucer and Martyr. But cf. Richardson, pp. 35 (n.) and 37f.

[94] As Dix, for instance, holds: 'The real eucharistic action for Cranmer . . . is something purely mental and psychological' (p. 671), and this is identical with Zwingli's 'vivid mental remembering of the passion' (632).

[95] Particularly in his failure to 'relate this theme of incorporation into Christ logically with his Eucharistic doctrine', as Richardson well states (p. 37). What a profound error, therefore, is that held by A. D. Innes (*Cranmer and the English Reformation*, Clark, 1900): Cranmer 'did not hold the view known as sacramentarian, which treated those rites as purely symbolical and commemorative. But the influence of such men as Peter Martyr was increasing. An ex-friar, who had passed on to the Lutheran stage, Martyr progressed towards a more definite Calvinism' (p. 131).

[96] In 1551 Feckenham was brought from the Tower before Sir John Cheke, for disputation 'upon the great master-controversy of transubstantiation' (Strype's

D

the eucharist which sounded its distinctive note above the abortive strife of Wittenberg and Zürich, and which must therefore command attention in our contemporary search for ecumenical truth.

The Ecclesiastical Laws

Martyr's part in the framing of Cranmer's *Reformatio Legum Ecclesiasticarum* forms a brief but significant episode. Of this Martyr wrote to Bullinger:[97]

I came to London some time since, on account of the holding of the assembly commonly called a parliament. For the King's majesty has ordained, that, as the gospel is received in his kingdom, and the bishop of Rome is driven out, the church of England shall no longer be ruled by pontifical decrees, and decretals, Sixtine, Clementine, and other popish ordinances of the same kind . . . the king has appointed two and thirty persons to frame ecclesiastical laws for this realm, namely, eight bishops, eight divines, eight civil lawyers, and eight common lawyers; the majority of whom are equally distinguished by profound erudition and solid piety; and we also, I mean Hooper, a Lasco, and myself, are enrolled among them. May God therefore grant that such laws may be enacted by us, as by their godliness and holy justice may banish the Tridentine canons from the churches of Christ!

This work ultimately devolved upon Haddon, Taylor and Martyr. Strype comments, 'These commissioners at last finished their great work; and the king lived not long enough to get it enacted; and so it fell, and that great labour frustrated.'[98]

The Articles of Religion

A final question in this problem of Martyr's influence in England concerns the *xlii* Articles of 1553, the basis of the *xxxix* Articles. In this matter also we must remember the rule— 'What the Church intends, and not what Cranmer intended, is the construction to be put upon it.'[99] Thus we are informed

Cheke, pp. 70-86, gives details of the disputations); the struggle between Whitgift and Cartwright is significant of the fact that it was *not* taken for granted that to quote Peter Martyr was a sign of Puritanism—cf. Dimock, viii; G. W. Bromiley's *Baptism and the Anglican Reformers* (Lutterworth, 1953) has given us a much needed analysis of the historical theology within Anglicanism, in relation to the first sacrament at least. [97] Lambeth, 8 March 1552—*Orig. Lett.* II, p. 503.
[98] *Ecc. Mem.* III, p. 89; cf. Burnet's *History of the Ref. of the Church of Engl.*, London, 1681, Part III, p. 208: 'Some of them were also revised by Peter Martyr: the 7th Chapter in the Title *de Prescriptionibus* is all written by Peter Martyr.'
[99] Richardson, p. 1.

that the reason Laud induced Charles to preface to the Articles the *Declaration* still in use was that 'the Puritans had been wont to read into the Articles the supposed mind of their compilers, and so to give them a kind of Calvinistic twist. This was not to be done.'[100] In the face of this warning, therefore, we shall simply note the points of coincidence between the teaching of Peter Martyr and that of those Articles that deal with the sacraments.[101]

In the sacramental theology of Peter Martyr, which we shall be examining in detail, we discover certain basic teaching: sacraments are not only tokens of divine grace or badges of human faith, but also effective signs and seals of God's nourishing and health-giving grace; a sacrament is not valid if made an object to be looked upon, for without use there is no sacrament; transubstantiation and the doctrine of efficacy *ex opere operato* are denied by Scripture and the received definition of a sacrament; the Supper in two kinds is to be given to the laity; the wicked may be said to eat the sacraments of Christ's body and blood but not Christ Himself. These are the doctrines which obviously form the 'literal and grammatical sense' of Articles XXV-XXXI. Even more explicit had been the *xlii* Articles of 1553.[102] And between then and 1562 the debate over the doctrine of ubiquity had reached its climax in the writings of Martyr and Brentius.[103] Those Marian exiles who had sat under Martyr at Strassburg and Zürich were especially zealous against the Lutheran error.[104] It is therefore most

[100] Overton, p. 65.

[101] Daniel (*op. cit.*, p. 605) has observed in Article XVII 'a close resemblance to the definition of Predestination in Peter Martyr's Commentary on the Epistle to the Romans (probably written during his stay in England, 1548-1553)'. In fact this was published in 1558, so that a definite influence cannot be ascribed. The definition begins, 'predestination is the most wise purpose of God, by which from the beginning He has constantly decreed to call all those whom He had loved in Christ, to the adoption of His children to justification by faith, and at last to glory through good works . . .'

[102] E.g. Article XXV began with a favourite theme of Martyr's, that the Dominical sacraments are 'most few in number, most easy to be kept, most excellent in signification' and had explicitly rejected the *ex opere operato* doctrine. Burnet, II, Appendix I. 55 gives the text of 1553 and 1562.

[103] See below, Chapter VIII.

[104] Cf. Jewel's correspondence with Bullinger (*Zur. Lett.*, pp. 123, 139), shortly after Martyr's death (5 March 1563): 'I do not wonder that your Hercules of Tübingen (Brentius), the forger of monstrosities, is now triumphing at his ease; I wonder whether he is able to confine himself within the ample limits of his Ubiquitarian kingdom. Should he make any attack upon our departed friend, and

interesting that Article XXIX should reject the Lutheran doctrine of *manducatio impiorum,* and that Article XXVIII should have contained in its original form a strong repudiation of ubiquity.[105] It was no doubt Elizabeth's political discernment in wishing not to alienate the German Protestants unduly,[106] which caused the substitution of Guest's third paragraph in Article XXVIII, and the temporary suppression of the whole of Article XXIX (until 1571).

The cumulative evidence we have indicated in this summary treatment of Martyr's place in the English Reformation appears to support the thesis that his influence was not only greater, but also of a more positive and 'Catholic' nature, than is recognized by many Anglican writers. No better conclusion could be given than Jewel's famous utterance to Peter Martyr in a letter of 7 February 1562: 'As to matters of doctrine, we have pared everything away to the very quick, and do not differ from your doctrine by a nail's breadth.'[107]

Volte-Face

The high hopes of the activity of reformation we have been considering were suddenly crushed by the death of the young 'Josiah' and the accession of 'Bloody Mary'. On 16 July 1553 the sixteen-year-old King died. At this time Peter Martyr was recovering from an illness, and had recently suffered the loss of his wife. A letter of his faithful Julius (Terentianus) to John Ab Ulmis gives the details of the succeeding events.[108]

'The papists, who had been always longing for this most

his writings come to my knowledge, unless some of you should be beforehand with me, I shall think it my duty to reply'; and on 1 March 1565: 'Among other things, the Ubiquitarian question is pressed upon me, which, for the sake of our old Tübingen friend, I have purposely treated of very copiously . . . in our own language, as being intended for our own people.'

[105] This stated that because of Christ's ascension and the truth of human nature, which *uno et definito loco esse,* the faithful should believe and confess no *realem et corporealem (ut loquuntur) praesentiam in Eucharistia.*

[106] Rather than her Romanist sympathies as Daniel holds (p. 649). Is this not the factor that Richardson (p. 1) misses when he states simply that the third paragraph 'represents a decisive rejection of Cranmer's opinions in the 42 *Articles*'?

[107] *ne unguem quidem latum absumas a doctrina vestra—Zur. Lett.* I, p. 100, and Appendix 59. Cf. Jewel to Bullinger, 22 May (p. 33): 'Religion is again placed on the same footing on which it stood in King Edward's time; to which event I doubt not but that your own letters and those of your republic have powerfully contributed.'

[108] *Orig. Lett.* I, pp. 365-374; from Strassburg, 20 November 1553.

wished for day, dig out as it were from their graves their vestments, chalices, and portasses, and begin mass with all speed . . . Master Peter Martyr is forbidden to leave his house; and Sidall, a truly excellent man, is ordered to guard against his running away; and thus master Peter has had his own house made a prison of these six weeks.' Meanwhile Julius went to London to assist Martyr by petitioning the Queen for his freedom to quit England, on the grounds that he had been called into England by invitation, as correspondence in the royal archives would show, and had committed no offence against law or crown.[109] 'We agree therefore among ourselves, that Whittingham should return to Oxford and remain with master Peter; for he was now almost entirely by himself, since every one, except only Sidall and master Haddon, had withdrawn from his society.' Finally Martyr himself was allowed to come to London to plead his case, which was granted him after audience; Gardiner strongly supported it.

His residence while in London was at Lambeth with Cranmer. A significant happening at this time was the public posting on 5 September, of the Archbishop's declaration, to dispel the current rumours that he was to re-establish the Mass, and even say it at the King's funeral.[110] It begins by acknowledging 'the cunning and deception of Satan', whose Latin Mass, which suffered a beginning of reform under Henry VIII but complete annulment under Edward VI, the Enemy now roars and rages to return. In this regard, many 'from malice or stupidity disparage the erudition of Dr Peter Martyr'. Therefore Cranmer declares, 'I with Peter Martyr and four or five others of my choosing', will in public and formal debate, 'prove to all that not only the common prayers Ecclesiastical, the Holy Administration, with the rest of the rites and ceremonies, but also the whole doctrine and religious order established by our supreme King and Lord, Edward the Sixth, are more pure and more agreeable to the Word of God

[109] In 1552 Martyr had been recalled to Strassburg, but Edward and Cranmer refused to let him go—cf. Strype's *Ecc. Mem.* III, p. 188.

[110] *Purgatio Reverendissimi in Christo Patris ac Domini D. Thomae Archiepiscopi Cantuariensis, adversus infames sed vanos rumores a quibusdam sparsos, de missa restituta Cantuariae.* Burnet, *op. cit.*, II, Appendix II. 8 gives the text; cf. pp. 248f. According to Procter-Frere (p. 92) this was 'a bold though exaggerated offer'; but Smyth (p. 122) calls it 'magnificent'.

'than what has been in England for the past thousand years.'

Terentianus comments: 'Master Peter commends this act, and says that had it not been done, he had intended to propose it to him. They prepare themselves for the disputations.' But the priests, formerly clamouring for debate, now 'began to change their note', choosing to 'abide by the received doctrine' and citing Cranmer on a new charge of treason, on 13 September. 'Master Peter then dined with the archbishop, who after dinner came into his chamber, and informed him that he himself must of necessity abide a trial; and that it was certain that he should never see him again.' The sad farewell was taken, and Martyr's distress at leaving Cranmer was heightened by the circumstances of danger and secrecy in which he was forced to quit the country. He crossed to Antwerp and on 30 October reached Strassburg, where Jean Sturm, Sleidan the historian, Zanchi, Hubert and others welcomed him home.

Thus ended Martyr's service to the cause of reformation in England—with cries of 'Arch-Heretic'[111] and with escape by night. Gardiner became Chancellor and Tresham Vice-chancellor, of Oxford University, and Smith was returned to his former post of Regius Professor of Divinity, to which Martyr had succeeded him for a time. With these appointments, he who had been 'the chief instrument of Cranmer's reform'[112] now cried, 'This tinkling has overthrown all my doctrine.'

V. THE SECOND STRASSBURG PERIOD:
November 1553–July 1556

Writing to Calvin from Strassburg on 3 November 1553 Peter Martyr indicates the position in which he found himself at Strassburg after six years' absence.

By what means, most worthy Sir, God snatched me from the lion's mouth even I myself have not yet ascertained, much less can I signify unto you. But, like Peter when brought out of prison by the angel, I thought that these things which were done had been seen in a dream; even now I can scarcely think it true that I have escaped. But yet I am safe and well here in Strassburg . . . I doubt not we shall have many famous martyrs, if Winchester (Gardiner) who is now in high favour, begins to show his

1   [111]*Erzketzer*—Schlosser, *op. cit.*, p. 439.   [112] *Ibid.*, p. 414.

cruelty . . . I am uncertain whether I shall remain at Strassburg. Perhaps the controversy about the Eucharist will be a hindrance. However I do not strive much about it . . .[113]

On the same day he wrote another letter to Bullinger, and said in part:

Hence it is that I am now here, but I do not yet know whether I shall again be received in this church and school; for, as I suspect, the sacramentary controversy will occasion some difficulties; however, I am not very anxious about it.[114]

Peter Martyr would like to have been with Calvin at Geneva or with Bullinger at Zürich, for in their theological climate he felt himself at home.[115] But the Senate of Strassburg was most anxious to have him return to his former position there, as Professor of Theology. He realized, however, that the extreme Lutheran faction now strong and influential in Strassburg, would cause trouble about his sacramental teaching. This happened very soon. On 15 December he wrote to Bullinger again:

My own affairs are in this condition. Our friend Sturmius, and the principal professors, with the greater portion of the clergy, have made strenuous exertions for my remaining here; and they had the governors of the school sufficiently favourable to this arrangement. But two or three of the ministers, who possess some influence, object to it on account of my opinions respecting the sacrament, and have raised such an opposition that the matter cannot yet be concluded. Since therefore I am loth to be with persons unwilling to receive me, I implore you by our friendship and affection in Christ, to look about for some situation or other, in which I may be able to exercise my calling with honour and advantage.[116]

Led by Marbach, the Lutherans objected to the Senate's desire to have Martyr re-appointed, on the grounds 'that in the doctrine of the Lord's Supper he had departed from the opinion of the Augsburg Confession, and so it was feared that he might make trouble in the Church' (Simler). They demanded that he sign the concordat between Luther and Bucer, to testify his good faith.[117]

[113] L.C., p. 1091.   [114] Orig. Lett. II, p. 505.
[115] Calvin had by this time influenced Bullinger, and the Consensus Tigurinus of 1549 was the result.   [116] Orig. Lett. II, p. 509.
[117] Marbach and his followers demanded that Martyr acknowledge an eating of the body of Christ in the Supper by the wicked, to guarantee which they brought two documents as test cases. One was the Augsburg Confession, which could be interpreted either (with Calvin and Martyr following Melanchthon) in its 1540

Martyr's reply was framed as a formal statement[118] to the governors of the College, in which he declared his acknowledgment of the Augsburg Confession, when 'rightly and profitably understood'. He further promised to give his opinions 'with all modesty, and without bitter attack'. And finally, regarding the concord between Luther and Bucer, he refused to subscribe because he could not grant that those destitute of faith eat the body of Christ in the receiving of the sacrament. Bucer himself, here in Strassburg, and also in England, taught the opposite! And to give his signature to that concord would be to offend the Church in Switzerland, England, and the brethren in Italy and France. He concluded by affirming his love for the churches of Saxony, and his desire for unity and peace.

This declaration was given on 27 December; on 22 January 1554 he wrote to Bullinger:

> Your congratulation on my being restored to my former office in this place, which business however was only concluded today, is in accordance with your friendly and benevolent disposition. May the Lord grant that I may some time reap the desired fruit of my labour![119]

The Senate appointed him to his former office in the College of St. Thomas, therefore, where he began lecturing on the Book of Judges. An additional task, and one noteworthy for this study, was that of lecturing on Aristotle on alternate weeks, along with Girolamo Zanchi, one of the monks converted by Martyr at Lucca. The formal study of Aristotle had been begun by Bucer, until Jean Sturm relieved him of the duty in 1536. Martyr now lectured on the Nicomachean Ethics,[120] and Zanchi on the *De Natura*.

form as signifying Christ's presence in the Supper, or (with Marbach following Luther) in its 1530 form as signifying His presence in the bread itself. The second is apparently the Concord of Wittenberg of 29 May 1536, a mediating formula of marked inconsistency, but specifically stating in Article 3 that *etiam indignos manducare, ita sentiunt porrigi vere corpus et sanguinem Domini etiam indignis, et indignos sumere ubi servantur verba et institutio Christi* (Kidd, p. 318). But Schlosser (p. 443) following Simler, identifies the concordat in question with the *confessio tetrapolitana* of 11 July 1530 (Kidd, p. 475). This earlier document, a mediating formula of Bucer, could have been so used at this time; but (1) Luther did not actually sign it (Kidd, pp. 468ff), and (2) Martyr himself in a letter to Calvin of this period (*Cal. Epist.* 197, p. 370) indicates the authority of the Wittenberg council over the Strassburg ministers. Cf. A. Barclay, 'The Protestant Doctrine of the Lord's Supper' (Glasgow, 1927), Chapters 7 and 8 for this period.

[118] See Appendix D.   [119] *Orig. Lett.*, p. 511.

[120] The commentaries are published, but only as far as the beginning of Book III. See Appendix A(1).

Many exiled Englishmen found refuge at Strassburg, the most noteworthy being John Jewel, later Bishop of Salisbury and author of the *Apologia* of the Church of England. He had been a reader at Oxford when Peter Martyr arrived in 1548, and became one of his closest friends and followers, being expelled at Mary's accession 'as a follower of Peter Martyr and a Lutheran'. He fled to Frankfort in 1554, and Martyr called him to Strassburg, to his own household. Jewel transcribed Martyr's Commentary on Judges 'and read the Fathers with him, especially St. Augustine'.[121] A group of such exiles gathered at Martyr's home for regular study and prayer. One happy result of this fellowship was Martyr's decision to write the *Defensio adversus Gardinerum*. Archbishop Cranmer had been preparing such a major work, a detailed refutation of the doctrines of transubstantiation and propitiatory Mass which Gardiner, now Bishop of Winchester, and the chief champion of the Papal cause, had set forth in a work which was noted for its 'extraordinary number of passages from the fathers'.[122] Cranmer's death posed a problem; but Martyr, because of his own thorough knowledge of the Fathers, was the proper man for the task. The English exiles asked him to accept the challenge, and offered to have it printed at their expense. Martyr accepted, and the work—an eight-hundred page book on the Eucharist—was published in 1559. Of this work Martyr wrote to Calvin:[123]

my Book is under the press, in which I have discovered and confuted all the fallacies and tricks of Stephen Gardiner, one time Bishop of Winchester, concerning the matter of the Eucharist. This I trust, happens at a good time: for it will be specially profitable at this time that the English Papists may understand that his book is not invincible, as they have hitherto boasted.

Letters to Poland and Lucca

In the year 1556 Peter Martyr wrote two lengthy Epistles, one 'To the Lords of Poland, professors of the Gospel, and to the Ministers of the Churches', and the other 'To the Brethren

---

[121] 'Illustrations of English Religion', ed. Morley, p. 174.
[122] Schlosser, p. 456. Cf. Appendix B. Gardiner issued two works, one under the pseudonym Antonius Constantius, which he later declared his own, in 1544. Cranmer's rebuttal was partly finished before his death, but perished.
[123] *L.C.*, p. 1121, 1 December 1558.

of the City of Lucca'.[124] All his activities of these last years of
his life further indicate his role as ecumenical Reformer, and
both letters reveal his strength of character and theological
wisdom. We shall briefly sketch the content of these before
continuing the story of the events at Strassburg.

The problem in Poland would doubtless be specially familiar
to Peter Martyr because of his friendship with the Polish
Reformer, John a Lasco. He had also been approached on
certain questions by Francis Lysman, and his letter was in part
a reply to this. The situation in Poland, which had recently
'embraced the Gospel',[125] was one of deep theological strife
concerning the doctrine of Christ and therefore also of justification. *Osiander* was the chief figure in the controversy, with
his doctrine of 'essential human righteousness', and a Christology approaching the Eutychean confusion of the Two
Natures, against which *Stancaro*, the other protagonist in the
debate, advanced a doctrine almost Nestorian in its separation
of the natures to a point endangering their unity.[126] Such a
problem of theology, common but by no means superficial,
was understood in all its implications by Martyr, whose own
strife over the Supper was rooted in the Christological
doctrine, and had constantly revolved around these two poles.

Accordingly, in his letter Peter Martyr, after expressing his
joy at their faith, immediately opens the question of Christology; warning them against false teachers, who follow human
invention and not the 'heavenly wisdom' of the Word of God.

For they say that they profess the true God . . . (but) join to this some
opinion of Arius or Servetus or some other fanatic. And they boast that they
worship and embrace Christ the true Son of God and our redeemer: but
straightway they either confound the two natures or else deny him to be

[124] *Dominis Polonis Evangelium Profitentibus et ecclesiarum ministris*, 14 February
1556 (*L.C.*, p. 1109); *Epistola D. Petri Martyris ad Fratres Lucenses, Italice edita anno
MDLVI* . . . (*L.C.*, p. 1100).
[125] In correspondence with Calvin at this time, Martyr informs him of the letter
to Poland (Letter of 16 February 1556, *L.C.*, p. 1114), describing it as showing the
scriptural doctrine of the sacrament; in another letter (of 8 April, *L.C.*, p. 1119) he
tells Calvin of a report that the Polish affairs had a hopeful ending in the Parliament, and this is clarified in a letter sent the next week (16 April, *L.C.*, p. 1124)
when he states, 'The servant of Alasco was recently here, and declared that in
Poland the Parliament is dissolved, and the affairs of Religion held over until
September.'
[126] Cf. Schmidt's account of this whole controversy, II, Book 4, Chapter 6:
'Martyrs Wirksamkeit für die Reformation in Polen—Osiander und Stancaro.'

joined to a human creature; they boldly and ignorantly say that His body is diffused everywhere, and is multiplied and closed within every piece of Eucharistic bread, and included in them; or they madly imagine that the substance of his flesh was not taken of the matter of the blessed Virgin Mary but rather brought out of heaven or else conceived and formed of the substance of the Holy Spirit . . . I do not therefore write these things unto you, my dear brethren, as though I suspect you to be infected with these evils, but so that I may very plainly show that the immortal God our Father, and Christ the Son of God and most true God and man, must be apprehended and received with that faith which shall be drawn from the very fountains of holy scripture, and not from the puddle of human dreams.

Another section on the true meaning of the sacraments warns us of the twofold error of making too much or too little of the sacrament.[127] The elements are instruments of the Holy Spirit, sacramentally therefore the body and blood of Christ, which the faithful receive by the mouth of faith, as they are raised up to Christ Himself by the action of the Holy Spirit.

I am most assured that the Church of Christ shall never have a quiet and peaceable consent of doctrine, or a sure peace between brethren, and a sincere purity from superstition, unless the sacrament of the Eucharist be delivered after this or like manner . . . in the rite of administering the sacraments, that manner is most to be embraced which shall be most plain, and most remote from the Papistical trifles and ceremonies, and which shall come nearest to the purity which Christ used with His apostles. Christian minds ought not to be occupied much in outward rites and ceremonies, but to be fed with the Word, to be instructed by the Sacraments, to be kindled unto prayers, to be confirmed in good works and excellent examples of life.

A further necessity in the reforming of the Church is *discipline*, while a great instrument of reform is the establishing of schools of divinity, where pastors are taught—their chief study being the 'reading and re-reading of the Books of the Holy Bible', avoiding vain and contentious questions.

The second part of the letter gives Martyr's answers to Lysman's four questions, chiefly concerning Christology. The question about Osiander's 'essential justice' (*iustitia essentialis*) needs little answer—it is plainly contrary to Scripture, which knows only justification by faith, and 'there is no need to light a candle in the sunshine of so clear a truth.'

Martyr closes the letter with an interesting comment on the

[127] The details of this section will be discussed thoroughly in Part III.

affair of Servetus, which was bothering the minds of the Polish Christians:

> And regarding Servetus the Spaniard, I have nothing else to say but that he was the devil's own son, whose evil and detestable doctrine must be banished everywhere. Nor is the Magistrate that put him to death to be accused, since there could be found in him no signs of amendment, and his blasphemies were altogether intolerable.

The second letter we are considering, to his brethren and former flock at Lucca, is much different in nature. The little church had come upon evil days, and the heavy hand of persecution had fallen. Many who had criticized Martyr's flight now had found recantation a way of escape. His letter is not bitter, however, but full of grief at their circumstances, and preaches the comfort of Christ.

> I had at the beginning laid among you some foundations of Christian truth, according to the will of the heavenly Father; weakly at that time as I confess before God, yet so that—not by my power but by the favour of Jesus Christ—the endeavour brought no small profit as well to me as to you ... But now when it has seemed good unto God to prove his household by tribulation and to try the constancy of your faith, alas! what lamentable proofs, what unhappy events are heard of there! For the valiant courage of a Christian heart, a wavering imbecility, a faint faith, trembling heart and most shameful denial of the truth ... how shall I keep from weeping?

.   .   .   .   .

> You knew the fury of antichrist, and the danger which threatened you when you refused to fly and profit by what some call the resource of the weak, but which I consider a wise precaution in certain circumstances ... Alas! how cruelly have these bright hopes been crushed ... Do not think, my dearest brethren, that we here are careful only of our own salvation; no wound can be given you, but the stroke pierces us too ... For Christ did so join together all members of His body, which is His Church, that they should communicate in feelings with each other.

The ground of their comfort, he continues, must be sought in Christ Himself, and their unity with Him:

> But if it behooved Christ to suffer, that He might enter into His glory, no doubt but we also must suffer if we will be there with Him.

He includes a form of prayer for them that are fallen, based on the confession of the prodigal son (Luke 15.18) and stressing the mercy of the Father in Jesus Christ; and he speaks of the true repentance as against the false and hypocritical.

After this indication of the contents of these letters, we shall return to the events of the last two years leading up to Martyr's removal to Zürich.

The 'Supper-Strife'

About a year after coming to Strassburg, Martyr was asked by the Elders of the Italian Church in Geneva to become their minister. Calvin strongly supported this call, which Martyr himself found most pleasing, as he tells Calvin in reply:

it would delight me very much if at last I could for once do service to my own countrymen from Italy. For I am not made of brass, nor is my flesh of iron.[128]

But he feels obligated to remain at Strassburg, especially since there are men like Martinengo available, whom the Church later called as minister.

In the same letter to Calvin, Peter Martyr refers to Marbach, who in the Lord's Supper maintains 'such a presence as wicked and unworthy eaters feed upon, showing clearly that he attributes not the receiving unto faith'. This was the growing issue of consubstantiation, which threatened the unity of the Strassburg churches, and the position of Martyr in particular. In his Oration given at Zürich when he removed there in 1556, he gives a summary of this strife.[129]

To the Senate, professors, and friends of old I am sure my return was most welcome, but not to all the ministers. I speak of those who are daily prepared impudently to declare—but not to prove—that cakes and pieces of bread are the very body of Christ.

The controversy became so hot that the Senate asked Martyr to hold the peace, with which he complied willingly, although 'the Saxons and our men wrote sharply against each other'. These ministers preached publicly against Martyr and his friends, whom they termed *Sacramentarii*, but refused debate. Finally they bribed a youth (*subornatus est puer*) to read a paper denouncing them:

a very bitter invective against the Sacramentarians. With great grief and sorrow godly men heard it. For what else was this than to sound a trumpet?

At this point correspondence reached Martyr from Zürich,

[128] Letter of 8 March 1555—*L.C.*, pp. 1094-1096.   [129] *L.C.*, p. 1066.

inviting him to succeed the late Conrad Pellican as Professor of Hebrew. In his reply to Bullinger on 7 May 1556 he informs him that he has told the Senate of his desire to depart:[130]

Not that I am unmindful or ungrateful for benefits received, for I know my deep obligation to this noble commonwealth; nor would I suffer myself to be separated from it if I could agree with their ministers about the sacrament. But since there is no hope of this, I have openly expressed how desirous I am to go whither I am called by most loving brethren: I seized this opportunity to complain to the magistrate of our doctrine of the Eucharist being in a public assembly both immeasurably and shamefully spoken against by the ministers of the city, and I added that I both wonder and regret that they will not treat this subject openly in the schools, though in the churches they utter both outrageous and bitter speeches against it. Briefly, I have now twice pleaded my cause before them, and also with some who were appointed to talk with me apart; and I thought that in four days they would have been able to despatch the matter. But this day the Senate answered that there was some reasonable cause for my desire to depart, but that I must not act hastily in so important an affair, and therefore they requested that I would wait patiently for at least a month for a decided answer. They promise that at the end of that time they will either offer me such conditions as I can conscientiously accept and remain among them, or they will leave me at liberty to follow my wish of going to you. This request of our magistrates, to whom I am much beholden, and who share your opinions, I could not honestly refuse, especially as they added that there are certain reasons why they could not suddenly give me a decided answer, and so against my will I yielded that period of delay which they required. But I pray you be of good cheer; as much as lieth in me I will not fail to strive that your calling me shall not be in vain. A month will soon slip away.

After the month of delay the Senate offered him the conditions, that he should avoid certain points of doctrine and restrain his zeal on others. But Martyr insisted on 'liberty of teaching, disputing and writing' (Simler). This meant severance of his ties with Strassburg—the city where he had first settled as an exiled Reformer, and where the memory of friends such as Bucer and Jacob Sturm still lingered. He had always intended to serve this city further, and while in England thought of it as his home. Thus at Bucer's death he wrote to Conrad Hubert of Strassburg:

[130] Young, p. 454. The charge of C. H. Smyth (*op. cit.*, p. 124) that Martyr could have accepted Calvin's earlier invitation, and when Bullinger's came 'quickly made it impossible for the Senate to permit him to remain' does not do justice to the facts exhibited in his correspondence and speeches of this period.

O wretched me! as long as Bucer was in England, or while we lived together in Germany, I never felt myself to be in exile. But now I plainly seem to myself to be alone and desolate . . . Oh how continually had he on his lips the church of Strassburg! what anxieties he underwent for her! . . . What discourses, what conversations took place respecting all of you, our worthy brethren in Christ! When we were talking together, we seemed to be conversing in the midst of you all at Strassburg: we were thinking of our return, but he has outstripped me, and betaken himself not to our Argentine[131] church, but to the golden one of heaven.[132]

Of these two men, then, one died in England, his life shortened by its climate, and the 'return' of the other proved to be saddened and cut short by strife and enmity. On 13 July 1556 Peter Martyr, accompanied by John Jewel, left Strassburg for Zürich.

As his final testimony to the whole debate about the Eucharist, Martyr presented to the Senate before his departure a lengthy *Confessio seu Sententia*.[133] In this he gives a clear and comprehensive account of his sacramental teaching. This begins with a statement of Christology, and the truth of Christ's humanity, then defines participation in the Supper as the growth of our union with Christ, and so concludes:

Wherefore to this union that we have with the Lord, that is, with His body, blood and bones, there is no need of a physical contact, nor of conjunction of places, continuous or contiguous—but the Spirit and faith are operative, by which we are most closely coupled to the whole Christ our Spouse and Saviour.

VI. Zürich:

July 1556–November 1562

Henry Bullinger received Martyr into his house, fourteen years since that original flight from Italy to Zürich. He lectured on the Psalms, the Minor Prophets, Samuel and Kings. At this time also he was again married, to a member of the Italian Church at Geneva, Caterina Merenda. This union proved most happy, and was blessed with several children, although none survived.[134]

[131] 'Silver'; the Latin name for Strassburg.
[132] *Orig. Lett.* II, p. 491.
[133] *L.C.*, p. 1068.
[134] Cf. the plaintive sentence in a letter of 20 March 1560, to Sampson, 'A son was born to me the 2nd of March and died the 10th day of March.'

Once again a call was extended to Martyr from the Italian Church at Geneva, this time on the occasion of Martinengo's death in 1557. Calvin wrote to the Council of Zürich urging the release of 'our venerable brother Peter Martyr'.[135] The need for such an one as Martyr among his own people was pressing at this time, because of the dangerous growth of heterodox opinion in regard to the doctrine of the Trinity. This is a complex problem, involving men such as Stancaro, whom we noted above in regard to the Polish Church, Lelius Socinus, whose works were later used by his nephew as the basis of Socinianism, and Bernardino Ochino. Ochino had become pastor of the Locarnese congregation in Zürich on 13 June 1555. His friendship with Stancaro, in whose company he had quitted Italy, had doubtless familiarized him with such teaching—or 'speculation'[136]—and now in his Zürich congregation he found Socinus, a member often under suspicion, but whose personal charm and speech could bring Calvin himself to acknowledge his innocence.[137] Ochino therefore came under strong suspicion of heresy, but Peter Martyr's mediation prevented the Zürich clergy from taking action. After Martyr's death, however, Ochino—then seventy-six years of age—was involved in a serious charge of teaching polygamy and antitrinitarianism, and was banished from the city.

It was against such a background that Calvin urged Martyr's acceptance of the Genevan call. However, the Senate and ministers of Zürich refused to give him leave, and there the matter ended. This was perhaps for the better, since Martyr's personal influence was as needful to the Italians in Zürich as in Geneva. But Martyr played his part in the Genevan problem too. In a letter to Calvin of 11 July 1558, he states:[138]

I heard of some trouble in the Italian church, which grieved me so much that my mind could scarce be quiet day or night. After the report reached

[135] Young, p. 582, gives the complete letter.
[136] Cf. McCrie, op. cit., pp. 177-187, 420-436 for an excellent account of this problem, especially as it concerned Zürich during these years. On p. 180 he says, 'The genius of the Italians led them to indulge in subtle and curious speculations, and this disposition was fostered by the study of the eclectic and sceptical philosophy, to which many of them had of late years been addicted' and cites Melanchthon's frequent mention of their 'platonic and sceptical theories', and Calvin's remark about the same—*In Italis, propter rarum acumen, magis eminet.*
[137] McCrie, p. 426.
[138] *L.C.*, pp. 1120f; Young, pp. 470f, following Marten's E.T. has *June.*

us, Georgius the physician[139] came here. He immediately began to talk to me, and I perceived that he thought I would lean to his opinion. But he was much deceived, for no man can detest this error more than I do. I conferred two or three times with this man, and saw things were as you write; namely, that these men believe but one person in the Divine nature, that of the Father only, and affirm that the Father and the Son do not form one essence . . . I referred the matter to Bullinger; he disliked it much, and desired me to break off the controversy as soon as possible, which indeed I was of myself minded to do, for opinions like these are not easily rooted out. Therefore having said to this man whatever I thought profitable, I begged him to reconcile himself with your church, otherwise he could have no place among us. Behold, at a seasonable moment I received letters, which to my great joy informed me that the Italian church had come to an agreement, and that a form of doctrine had been drawn up to which they had all subscribed . . .[140]

His greatest influence during these years, however, was not felt by his own countrymen, but by Englishmen. Elizabeth ushered in a new era in 1558, and the exiles hurried home, including Martyr's beloved John Jewel. But in their struggles for reform, their revered teacher and friend in Zürich was constantly relied upon for advice and encouragement.

The Affairs of England

Writing to Bullinger in May 1559, Jewel states:[141] 'Our universities are so depressed and ruined, that at Oxford there are scarcely two individuals who think with us', while Soto and Garsya 'have so torn up by the roots all that Peter Martyr had so prosperously planted, that they have reduced the vineyard of the Lord into a wilderness. You would scarcely believe so much desolation could have been effected in so short a time.' But the tone of subsequent letters is increasingly hopeful, as new bishops are appointed from the group which followed

[139] George Blandrata, a noted antitrinitarian—cf. McCrie, pp. 183, 414. Cf. Young, p. 582 for extract from the Genevan archives concerning the Confession of Faith drawn up at Calvin's advice in May 1558 to settle this controversy, of which Alciati and Blandrata were chief instigators.

[140] Young, pp. 469f, thinks that this situation is the cause of the rumour which Jewel reports in a letter to Martyr of 6 November 1560 (*Zur. Lett.*, p. 91): 'unfavourable to yourself, painful to us all' and confirmed even by Grindal and the Archbishop of Canterbury; but the arrival of brethren from Geneva who related 'that all is with you as we desire', settled the question. This would more likely be the heretical tendencies of Ochino and Socinus, which Martyr succeeded in overcoming in 1558 (cf. McCrie, pp. 430f; Young, p. 392), but which continued in varying degree until the sad events after Martyr's death.

[141] *Zur. Lett.*, p. 33.

E

Martyr, and reforming activity resumed with vigour. At this time it was rumoured that Martyr himself was returning. Jewel wrote on 2 November, 'I heard from the Archbishop of Canterbury that you are invited hither, and that your old lecture-ship is kept open for you'; and three days later, reports that 'nothing is at this time more talked about, than that Peter Martyr is invited, and daily expected to arrive in England'.[142] This latter report was in connection with the Queen's attitude to Martyr, a subject worthy of note at this point.

Elizabeth's early years had involved a significant period under the tuition of Hooper, and the Bishop of Aquila described her as 'saturated ever since she was born in a bitter hatred to our faith', owing to the teaching of the 'Italian heretic friars' Martyr and Ochino.[143] Thus it is not surprising to find Jewel writing to Martyr as early as March 1559, 'The queen regards you most highly; she made so much of your letter, that she read it over with the greatest eagerness a second and third time'; and the following month, 'The queen both speaks and thinks most honourably of you: she lately told lord Russel that she was desirous of inviting you to England, a measure which is urged both by himself and others, as far as they are able.'[144] The letter referred to is one written by Peter Martyr to the Queen, on 22 December 1558.[145] In this letter Martyr addresses Elizabeth as one who has not only received a kingdom, but a task and a trust to restore the true Church and to maintain genuine religion. The priests seek not the true restoration, but carry the ark of the Gospel 'on the carts of unprofitable cere-monies, and foul labours of hired servants'—a reference to 2 Samuel 6.7. Therefore he exhorts her:

> If Bishops and Ministers of Churches will not do their duty, if in handling doctrine and administering of sacraments they forsake the just rules of Holy Scripture—who but a godly Prince shall recall them into the right way?

Along with this influence over the Queen, Martyr enjoyed a popularity as a leading theological writer. Jewel writes, 'Your

[142] *Zur Lett.*, pp. 45, 54.
[143] Quoted by Lindsay, *op. cit.*, p. 368.
[144] *Zur. Lett.*, pp. 11 and 20 (of 20 March and 28 April).
[145] *Serenissimae Elizabethae, Dei Gratia Reginae Angliae, Franciae et Hyberniae, a Deo Patre, per Iesum Christum Servatorem nostrum, Gratiam et aeternam foelicitatem. L.C.*, pp. 1121-1124.

book on Vows, like all your other works, is caught up with the greatest avidity. We are all now looking for you to publish your further commentaries on the book of Judges, and on the two books of Samuel; for all our friends are now aware that you have those books in hand, and are intending to publish them.'[146] This was especially true of his *Defensio adversus Gardinerum* already mentioned, which appeared at this time, dedicated to Queen Elizabeth. Jewel writes of its expected arrival in England: 'When your present arrives, it will, I doubt not, be most acceptable to the queen; and since you wish it, although it is in itself most excellent, yet should I have an opportunity, I will set forth its value in my own words ... Your other books have long since been brought over by the booksellers, and are purchased with the greatest eagerness; for every one is most anxious to see by what hunting spears the beast has been pierced.' He later tells Martyr of Elizabeth's reception of the book: 'the queen of her own accord eagerly perused both your letter and the book itself, and wonderfully commended both your learning and character in general ... your book was made so much of by all good men, that I know not whether any thing of the kind was ever so valued before ... The queen however made diligent enquiries of the messenger, as to what you were doing, where you lived, in what state of health and what circumstances you were, and whether your age would allow you to undertake a journey. She was altogether desirous that you should by all means be invited to England, that as you formerly *tilled*, as it were, the university by your lectures, so you might again *water* it by the same, now it is in so disordered and wretched a condition. But since then, the deliberations about Saxony and the embassy from Smalcald have put an end to those counsels.'[147]

The question of inviting Martyr to England was postponed while the proposal to join the Smalcald League was considered. This, the Queen was advised, 'can by no means be brought

---

[146] *Zur. Lett.*, p. 46 (of 2 November 1559). Cf. p. 112, Cox to Martyr (5 August 1562): 'I have lately been employed in your book on Judges, which you most kindly sent to me; and I am waiting for the commentaries which you promised on the books of Kings, that I may often hold intercourse with my friend Peter, as long as I am able to range at large among his writings.'

[147] *Zur. Lett.*, pp. 21f and 53f (of 28 April and 5 November 1559).

about, if Martyr should return to us'.[148] But finally, in 1561, the formal invitation was extended by 'a most famous nobleman in England', to whom Martyr replied:[149]

But now as touching my return to England, although I am unable to answer as I could earnestly desire, do you, most noble prince, with your usual kindness take in good part what I write in reply. First of all, I would not have you think that I have anything more at heart, than the solid and firm well-being of England in the Lord. But at this present time, such is the situation in which I am placed, that I am engaged to the state and church of Zürich, and am therefore not my own master. I have therefore enquired the opinion and inclination as well of the magistrates as of my fellow ministers upon this matter; and indeed I found in them a singular zeal and most ready mind to satisfy your desire . . . But on the other hand they no less prudently than lovingly take into consideration my constitution, state, and age; and are somewhat apprehensive lest, burdened as I am and in some measure broken with age, I should be unable to bear the fatigue of the journey, which is rather long, variable, and not without difficulty. They see moreover that no small danger is to be apprehended in different places on the road; and they consider too, that I am called forth to much more severe labours than I undergo in this place. Wherefore they think it very likely that I shall be unable to serve either them or you; and are therefore of opinion that it is much better for me to remain here, where, by teaching, writing, and publishing my commentaries, I may be of use both to them and you and others, according to my ability.

Peter Martyr's influence at this stage of the English Reformation is illustrated by his part, through correspondence, in the problem of the use of the crucifix, raised largely through the Queen's own preference for this image. Once again we see, as in the case with Hooper, a more deep and decisive element introduced into the debate by Martyr.

Thomas Sampson was a constant correspondent with Bullinger and Martyr[150]; and having once already sought Martyr's advice on certain definite and detailed questions pertaining to the English Reformation,[151] he approached him in a letter of

[148] *Zur Lett.*, p. 21, Jewel to Martyr (of 28 April); the advice was given by Peter Paul Vergerio, Bishop of Capo d'Istria.

[149] *Illustrissimo Principi* (—) *in Angliam*, 22 July 1561; *L.C.*, pp. 1134f. This is thought to be the Duke of Norfolk (cf. *Zur. Lett.*, p. 20, n. 2; Young, p. 471, etc.); but in the E.T. of the *L.C.* (by Marten, London, 1583), a letter is included along with the translation of this one, addressed explicitly 'To the Right honourable the Earl of Bedford', dat. 1561 (p. 164B of final section). The contents of the two are very similar, and both mention the desire of the Queen which the Duke and the Earl must have cited.

[150] Cf. *Orig. Lett.* I, pp. 172-183.

[151] *Zur. Lett.*, p. 1 (of 17 December 1558)—questions about the title 'after

6 January 1560[152] with a more serious and urgent problem, 'whether the image of the crucifix, placed on the table of the Lord with lighted candles, is to be regarded as a thing indifferent?' If not, and if they are enjoined by the Queen upon her ministers, must not one retire from the ministry? 'Certain of our friends, indeed, appear in some measure inclined to regard these things as matters of indifference: for my own part, I am altogether of opinion, that should this be enjoined, we ought rather to suffer deprivation.' Sampson submits the question to the opinion of Martyr, Bullinger and Ochino, and suggests that any of them, perhaps Ochino in preference, since his authority 'has very great weight with the queen', might write a letter to Elizabeth on this subject.

The controversy was not an individual matter with Sampson, as Hooper's had been. Jewel wrote to Martyr the following month[153] and stated: 'This controversy about the crucifix is now at its height. You would scarcely believe to what a degree of insanity some persons, who once had some shew of common sense, have been carried upon so foolish a subject. There is not one of them, however, with whom you are acquainted, excepting Cox. A disputation upon this subject will take place tomorrow. The moderators will be persons selected by the council. The disputants on the one side are the archbishop of Canterbury and Cox; and on the other, Grindal the bishop of London and myself.' By April, Bishop Sandys could write to Martyr:[154] 'God, in whose hand are the hearts of kings, gave us tranquillity instead of a tempest, and delivered the church of England from stumbling blocks of this kind: only the popish vestments remain in our church, I mean the copes; which, however, we hope will not last very long.' But meanwhile, Martyr had given his friends definite and detailed advice about the matter. This is contained in four letters he wrote to Sampson.[155]

Christ supreme head of the Church of England'; and about the episcopal office— but no reference to the use of vestments, crucifix, etc. [152] *Ibid.*, p. 62.
[153] 4 February 1560—*Zur. Lett.*, p. 67. [154] *Ibid.*, p. 72.
[155] These letters are in *L.C.*, pp. 1125-1128—15 July and 4 November 1559; 1 February and 10 March 1560. They are addressed simply *amico cuidam in Anglia;* but there is no doubt that they are replies to Sampson, as (1) my use of their contents will show; and (2) the reference to *Jane* (Letter 1; Sampson's of 6 January 1560) also indicates. For Sampson's letters cf. *Orig. Lett.* I, pp. 181, 182; *Zur. Lett.*, pp. 1, 62, 75. Cf. Schmidt, II, p. 226.

Martyr's first letter, of 15 July 1559, addresses a man who is 'afraid on both sides'—of withdrawing from the ministry and of accepting a bishopric. Martyr agrees that these are *not* things indifferent, but 'intolerable blemishes' marring the Apostolic simplicity of the Church. He suggests two things, that Sampson should continue to preach and teach sound doctrine, and that he should 'for a while abstain from the ministering of the Sacraments' until the blemishes are removed. The second letter (4 November) replies to letters of 27 August. In this Martyr admits that he is slower than Bullinger to condemn such apparel, since he thinks it better to allow them than to be deprived of preaching. But since the matter has become one of positive offence, he declares 'I willingly yield unto his opinion'. His reason is, that what was a thing indifferent (vestments) has become identified with positive evils:

> Indeed where altars and images are preserved, I myself of my own accord, affirm just as I have written in other letters, that you must not minister . . . When I was at Oxford I would never use those white vestments in the Choir, although I was a canon.

The third letter (1 February 1560) expands and clarifies this position. Martyr distinguishes the matter of vestments from that of the crucifix. The former is basically an indifferent thing, and the need of ministers overrules, in this instance, its evil use: 'I exhort you not to withdraw yourself from the function offered, since there is so great a lack of ministers there.' Wear the vestments but preach against their use! But the question of the crucifix is of a different order:

> But I would never counsel you that when you preach or minister the Lord's Supper you should have the image of the crucifix upon the table.

Finally, the letter of 20 March in reply to Sampson's of 6 January when the controversy was reaching its height, reflects the true issue, and indicates the opinion that carried the day:

> to have the sign of the crucifix upon the holy table while the Lord's Supper is administered, I do not account among things indifferent (*inter* ἀδιάφορα), nor would I advise any man to distribute the sacraments according to that rite . . . In brief, the worshipping of images must by no means be suffered. Neither Dr Bullinger nor myself account such as things indifferent: but rather we refuse them as things forbidden.

The Poissy Conference of 1561

I am called into France to act in a colloquy concerning religion. A safe-conduct is brought here in the name of the king and queen-mother, both signed and sealed. And by letters of the king of Navarre am I earnestly invited, so that it hardly seems that my journey can be deferred. Since the affair is important and full of danger, I heartily desire your lordship that you will commend the same, and myself also, most earnestly in your prayers to God.[156]

Catherine de Medici, queen-mother of France, was largely instrumental in arranging the Colloquy. Her reasons were partly political, since she sought Protestant support against the Guise faction, but partly also deriving from her erstwhile attraction to the Protestant party of the King and Queen of Navarre, Condé, Coligny and others.[157] The Cardinal of Lorraine expected the conference to crush the Reformed group; but Beza and Martyr were summoned to represent it.[158] An invitation from Antoine, King of Navarre, addressed to the Senate of Zürich and enclosing a safe-conduct for his security, brought Peter Martyr to Poissy.[159]

On his arrival, Martyr visited Antoine, the Prince of Condé, and Admiral Coligny, and later was summoned to the presence of Catherine. In this interview, and another before he left Poissy, Martyr spoke at length to the Queen in their common native tongue.[160] He stressed the duty of Princes to reform religion within their realms, and reminded her that God was with those Princes who sought His glory. To her questions about the strife which religion had brought, he replied that

[156] Letter to Bishop Parkhurst, 23 August 1561—*L.C.*, p. 1136.

[157] Young, p. 474, says that she was attracted by the psalmody of Marot, choosing a Psalm (150) as her own, according to the Court custom then in vogue.

[158] The comparison and contrast of Beza and Martyr forms the motif of Schlosser's thesis (*op. cit.*); it should not be carried as far as he does, but is useful in understanding the events of Poissy. Beza was the leader, the man of affairs and of action: 'Beza wollte nützen und glänzen, Martyr nur erbauen . . . Beza's Eifer und Martyrs Billigken und Mässigung' (pp. 6, 8).

[159] Cf. Young, p. 583, for copy of the Letter. In Corpus Christi Library, Cambridge, MS., 119.6 is 'A safe-conduct granted by Charles IX king of France to all persons coming to the assembly at Poissy, dated at St. Germain's 25 July 1561.'

[160] I use Martyr's correspondence with Bullinger, Letters of 12 and 19 September, 2, 17 and 20 October (*L.C.*, pp. 1136-1143); with Calvin 4 October—*L.C.*, p. 1141, Lavater (19 October, *L.C.*, p. 1142), and Beza (6 November from Trois—*L.C.*, p. 1143), as the sources for this section. Cf. Beza's own account (*Hist. des Eglises Reformées*) and Condé's *Memoires*.

pure religion could not be maintained without the Cross; about her asking his consent to the Augsburg Confession, he tells Bullinger:

When she mentioned the Confession made at Augusta, I answered that the holy scriptures ought to be sufficient for us, and that she should not persuade herself, that if the Augsburg Confession were received, it would be done with the consent of the Churchmen.

Beza's famous speech which opened the Colloquy on 9 September, is described by Martyr as follows:

The matter was committed to Beza, to make the opening or preface to the conference; he spoke in French the space of one hour, as they say. But towards the end when he happened to mention the Eucharist, he said that they ought to know this, that the body and blood of the Lord is as far from the bread and wine of the Lord's Supper as heaven is from earth. These words so offended and aroused the Bishops, that they began to murmur and at last to make a din, so that Beza had much trouble in ending his speech.

The Cardinal of Tournon called for an immediate end to the conference; but the Cardinal of Lorraine desired to make his reply, and this was arranged for 15 September. It had been disputed whether to allow Martyr to be present—

However, the Queen at the hour of departure summoned me and commanded me to go. The Prince of Condé gave orders for me to be brought by his secretary, and sent his own mule by which I might be brought easily and quietly.

Martyr reports on Lorraine's speech:

When he had spoken much of these things he came to the matter of the Sacrament, where he meddled not with transubstantiation or the Mass, but mentioned no other presence of the body of Christ than did Luther and Brentius. For he affirmed that the body of Christ is present not locally nor circumscriptively, but after a heavenly manner, and supersubstantially . . . Some of the Bishops of better judgment would have us agree to the consubstantiation of Luther and Brentius. We deny this to be possible: and in this we constantly persist, that the body of Christ is in heaven and not elsewhere. But we grant that in the holy Supper the faithful communicants receive the true body and blood of the Lord, yet by faith and the Spirit, and that the distance of places hinders not the conjunction itself, since it is a thing altogether spiritual.

The debate took a new turn after Beza had replied to this speech, for Lorraine demanded that the Reformers should sign the Augsburg Confession as indicating a doctrine of real presence.[161] On this issue Martyr was finally allowed to speak. On 26 September he addressed the conference in Italian. Replying to Lorraine, he first 'defended the ministry of our Church', correcting in passing the Cardinal's historical ignorance of the Councils of the Early Church![162] But his main contribution was on the issue of the Eucharist. The Cardinal had demanded that the words 'This is my body' be taken *simpliciter*; as for Martyr:

> I objected moreover that he was greatly deceived, in daring to affirm that in God's commandments in the sacred histories, in the Testaments and Sacraments, there are no tropes or figurative speech: and from the scriptures I demonstrated that tropes are to be found: whence it cannot be concluded by him, that the words of the Lord which they call Consecration, are to be taken *simpliciter*.

The Cardinal declined to reply, feigning ignorance of Italian, but a Spanish Jesuit (Laincz), deputed by the Cardinal of Ferrara, Papal legate, gave 'a most violent oration' which precipitated a tumult. The Queen was obliged to intervene, reducing the disputants to five on each side.

There followed a quieter debate, and Martyr wrote hopefully, 'so far as I can see, we have adversaries meek enough and who disagree not much from us'. But Ferrara was especially keen to see an end to the proceedings; the five Romanist delegates 'were not only suspected by the Cardinals and Bishops, but accounted as Heretics, because they seemed to consent with us about the sacrament'. The Conference was suspended fifteen days, and finally dissolved on 19 October. No conclusions were reached; but the Gospel was being preached throughout France, and the French Confession was being urged in place of the Augsburg. An edict of 17 January 1562 gave legal re-

[161] Letter of 2 October to Bullinger is the most important in the series. Schlosser, p. 469, notes that Bullinger meanwhile wrote to Martyr advising against accepting the Augsburg Confession under any circumstances (e.g. persecution of the French Church) whereas Martyr did not like Bullinger to think more of that Confession than of the persecution.

[162] The question of the Reformed ministry was the second chief question debated along with that of the Eucharist, although four questions had been propounded, the authority of the Church, the power of Councils, the Authority of Scripture, and the real and substantial presence in the Supper (Letter of 12 September). In this regard it is interesting to note that Beza was much confused by the problem of the laying on of hands, since he believed it to be necessary to valid ordination. Martyr had warned him to avoid this question, and himself strongly denied its necessity (cf. Schlosser, pp. 469ff).

cognition to the French Reformed Church, prohibiting meetings for public worship and surrender of Church buildings, but allowing meetings outside walled towns and anywhere in private houses. The Massacre of Vassy and subsequent events brought grief and disillusionment to Martyr and his friends.[163]

The last stages of the Conference, however, had produced a document drawn up by the Reformers on 9 October, although rejected by the Romanists. But this, along with Martyr's personal statement presented to the Colloquy, is a further document significant not only for Peter Martyr's own theology, but also for that of the Reformation in general. Accordingly, both documents are reproduced in Appendix D. The Poissy Colloquy was the last great service which our Reformer was privileged to render in behalf of the Reformation, and once again his ecumenical activity is evidenced in a profound manner.

The return trip involved an incident which Schlosser terms the one blot on Peter Martyr's career.[164] It ought rather to serve as a reminder that the Reformers' ecclesiology was ordered by their doctrine and was not so systematic as their various followers would like to think! Bishop Caracciolo of Trois, a Neapolitan who had sat under Martyr at *S. Pietro* in Naples, at Poissy had been forcibly struck with the debatable nature of his office, which ignored the people's voice. He took Martyr back with him to Trois, and there put his problem before him. Martyr advised him to call a meeting of the clergy of Trois. This resulted in an acceptance of Caracciolo as Bishop over the Protestant churches, with one dissenting vote. His case remained unique, and problematic to Rome. He was deprived of his bishopric, but had already taken congregation *and* income with him! Ultimately the Queen settled a pension upon him, the only Bishop which the French Reformed Church knows.[165]

---

[163] Cf. Martyr's letters to Beza and Calvin, 25 November 1561—*L.C.*, p. 1143f.

[164] *Op. cit.*, pp. 459, 477ff. Schlosser charges Martyr with preferring 'friendship to the duty of accepting only blameless clergy to the Church'. He perhaps thinks Martyr was influenced by Caracciolo's status—son of the Prince of Melfi. But if McCrie is correct in identifying him with the Neapolitan (*op. cit.*, p. 148), Martyr would have known the Bishop's long sympathy for the Reformed cause, as well as his personal character and life. There is confusion about the details of this incident, but it is best to treat it briefly, as does Schmidt, II, pp. 272f.

[165] As Schlosser remarks, *loc. cit.* Martyr's account of the affair is found in his letter to Beza from Trois, 6 November 1561—*L.C.*, p. 1143. For Calvin's attitude

Strife and Rest

Martyr returned to Zürich full of years and weariness. But he returned to a position still active in the struggles of the period. He had been involved in debate concerning predestination.[166] He was still reckoned a major figure in the realm of teaching, and was again asked to accept a chair at the University of Heidelberg.[167] But the most significant work of these closing years, apart from his service to England and completion of the work against Gardiner, was the strife with Brentius.

The 'Supper-strife' at Strassburg, headed by Marbach and centring around the *Farrago* published in 1555, which had openly advanced the doctrine of ubiquity in support of consubstantiation in the Eucharist, now passed into a new phase under the leadership of Brentius (Johann Brenz).[168] Since

to Bishops, which is in full agreement with this action of Martyr, see Choisy, 'Calvin et l'Union des Eglises', *Bulletin de la Soc. de l'Hist. du Prot. Francais*, 1935, 87; Pannier, 'Calvin et l'Episcopat', *Revue d'Histoire et de Philosophie Religieuse de l'univ. de Strasbourg*, 1926. This attitude towards episcopacy is part of the Reformation movement as a whole, which in its original Reformers held a doctrine of the *jure humano* authority of bishops. The congruent doctrine of the parity of bishops and priests derives from scholasticism, and was of profound influence within the Church of Rome until the Council of Trent. In the Church of England the *jure divino* doctrine is supposed to be first set forth by Bancroft in 1588. But in 1604 Laud was reproved at Oxford for maintaining that there could be no true Church without bishops, 'which was thought to cast a bone of contention between the Church of England and the Reformed on the Continent' (quoted by Fisher, *History of the Reformation*, Scribner's, 1883, p. 335). There is also evidence of a group letter (Calvin, Bullinger and others) sent to Edward VI but intercepted by Gardiner and Bonner, which offered to have bishops in the Continental churches, and so to foster a greater organic unity among the Reformed—see C. S. Carter, *The English Church and the Reformation*, Longmans, 1925, p. 154, n. 3; Strype's *Mem. Cran.* II, p. 15 (p. 296).

[166] Martyr's teaching is given in the Treatise *De Praedestinatione* which follows the Commentary on Romans 9. The debate was a twofold one, first with the ageing Bibliander in his own College, then on behalf of Zanchi at Strassburg. Cf. my article on 'The Reformed Doctrine of Predestination' in *The Scottish Journal of Theology*, September 1955.

[167] Schmidt records two calls to Heidelberg, both refused by Martyr. The first was as he was preparing to leave Strassburg for Zürich (1556). II, pp. 184, 242.

[168] *Farrago confusanearum et inter se dissidentium opinionum de coena domini ex Sacramentariorum libris congesta*, Magdeb., 1552; *Recta fides de coena Domini*, Ebend, 1553; *Farrago sententiarum* . . . Frank. 1555. Calvin's *Secunda Defensio* of January 1556 replied to this; Martyr's *Confessio* . . . *de coena domini* of 1556 (to the Strassburg Senate) forms his reply. In 1560 Brentius published *De personali unione duarum naturarum in Christo et ascensu Christi in coelum, accessione eius ad patrem*; Schmidt remarks (II, p. 237): 'Brenz veröffentlichte seine, durchaus scholastische Schrift über die persönliche Einheit der beiden Naturen in Christo und dessen Erhöhung in den Himmel'.

Brentius had been an able fellow-worker with the Reformers,[169] Martyr sought to refute his doctrine in a friendly and reasonable spirit, and his *Dialogus* of 1561 was such a book. Of it Martyr wrote to Parkhurst:[170]

> I send you the Dialogue which I wrote against the ubiquity of Brentius. For a few months ago he set forth a little book in which he tried to defend with all his power this monstrous opinion. Whereupon I was here required by the brethren that I should answer him: which I have done as well as I could. But you, most reverend Prelate, along with other learned men, shall judge how thoroughly I have performed it.

But Brentius in reply launched a violent attack, *De divina majestate Christi et de vera praesentia corporis et sanguinis eius in coena*, 1562. This troubled Martyr greatly in his last days. During his final illness, Bullinger had repeated the text, 'We have a house not made with hands, eternal in the heavens', to which the dying man said, 'I know, but not the heaven of Brentius which is nowhere.'[171] Yet another incident shows his true feeling. Bullinger had remarked, 'Our true fatherland is in heaven', and Martyr replied, 'But not the fatherland of Brentius. But no—he sits there as much. I forgive him; I am angry with him no more. Had God spared me life, I had refuted him; but only for the weak-willed.'[172]

About this time a happier reaction was called forth by the publication of Jewel's Apology. In his last letter to Jewel, Martyr expresses his pride and satisfaction in the work, and then continues:[173]

> But as touching myself, if you desire to know more particularly how I do, understand that I am of a cheerful mind in Christ, and that I am occupied in the same labours in which I was engaged when you were here; but in body I am not so strong and lusty as I was heretofore. For the burden of old age daily becomes more heavy . . . Wherein though the body properly and by itself be afflicted, yet by reason of that connection which the Greeks call *sympathy*, the mind also cannot choose but be affected.

Two months later, about 5 November, Peter Martyr became

---

[169] Cf. Kidd, *op. cit.*, pp. 164, 254. Brentius played a leading part in the Swabian Syngramma of 1525, and had enjoyed the friendship of Calvin.

[170] 23 August 1561—*L.C.*, p. 1136.

[171] Cf. Gualther's verse in *Carmina Doctorum aliquot virorum in obitum D. Petri Martyris Vermilii conscripta* (intro. to *L.C.*): . . . *Nunc igitur coelum inveni sedesque beatas, Moxque suam inveniet Brentius Utopiam.*

[172] Quoted by Schlosser, p. 479.

[173] 24 August 1562—*L.C.*, p. 1147; *Zur. Lett.*, p. 339.

suddenly ill of a fever then prevalent. Trying to shake this off and resume his lectures, he suffered a relapse, and his friends soon realized that death was near. The study of medicine having long been a favourite pursuit of his, he conversed at length with the physicians that attended him. Towards the end, before taking leave of the friends gathered at his bedside, he declared, 'I believe that life and salvation have been given by God the Father to the human race through Christ alone; He is the only Saviour'. Supporting this confession with Scriptural passages, he concluded, 'This is my faith, in this will I die'.

On 12 November 1562 his strength was very low; he took fond leave of Ochino, and the pastors and elders of the Italian Church. At last he commended his soul unto God, and Bullinger, though greatly overcome, summoned courage to pay the last offices of humanity. With his own hands he closed his eyes, and dressed him in his funeral garb.[174]

. . . .

So died a Reformer of ecumenical stature, well worthy of the high honour in which he was held by his contemporaries—well worthy also of respect and imitation by those who have reaped the fruit of his labours in Italy, Germany, England, Switzerland and France. The times were great: great things, the ultimate things, were at stake: and God raised up men great in mind and in life to fulfil His purposes and to re-form His Church. Peter Martyr Vermigli was such a man.

Against such a background of life and action, we shall turn to an examination of Peter Martyr's theology. Together they may serve to bring us near to one of the greatest of the Reformers. Thus Bishop Jewel wrote to Josiah Simler after receiving the latter's biography of Martyr, along with a silver medal bearing his effigy:[175] 'In the figure indeed, although there is in many respects an admirable resemblance (to the original), yet there was a something, I know not what, in which I was unable to perceive the skill of the artist. And what wonder is it, that there should be some defect in producing the likeness

174 Young, p. 490.
175 23 March 1563—*Zur. Lett.*, p. 126.

of one, the like of whom, whenever I look around me, I can scarce believe ever to have existed? Your little book, however, I perused with the greatest eagerness and delight. For I seemed to myself to behold the same old man with whom I had formerly lived upon such affectionate terms; and to behold him too, I know not why, more nearly and thoroughly, than when we were living together.'

PART I

REVELATION AND SACRAMENT

CHAPTER I

BY WORD AND SPIRIT

Truly this Body is not destitute of its weapons: but they are spiritual, not carnal, namely the Word and the Spirit, through whom it overcomes human wisdom, casts it to the ground, and leads captive our mind and thought to the obedience of Christ. *(Catechismus* 39)[1]

PETER MARTYR's teaching on the sacraments is not only the fullest expression of his theology, but also its key doctrine. This is because he accepts the Person of Christ as the *archetype* of all theological thinking, and this material principle is most clearly operative in his distinctive contribution to the sixteenth-century sacramental controversies. The context of that contribution was the intensive Biblical studies, a part of which is preserved for us in the few Commentaries published. In these we see the source of his theology, revelation by Word and Spirit,[2] and the dynamic solution which this Biblical revelation gave him for the sacramental problem posed by scholasticism.

The Word of Life

This is the stronghold of our faith, that by the Word of God all things consist. (*in Gen.* 1.5)

No man was created by God, the Father of our Lord Jesus Christ, but through the Word of God; and therefore we must not look for man, now fallen and overthrown, to be restored by any other means than the same Word. (*Encomium Verbi Dei*)

The act of creation is the Trinitarian God in action, as the Fathers taught: Father, Word and Spirit;[3] man is created by

---

[1] Appendix A gives the complete works of Peter Martyr. Since there is no standard text for any of his works, I give the sections used in the *Loci Communes* wherever possible, although this work is reliable only for the Treatises given in full, and not for its excerpts from the Commentaries.

[2] *The Loci Communes Petri Martyri* (Massonius, first ed. 1579, Zürich) is therefore wrong to begin with the scholastic problem of natural knowledge of God as if this ever interested Peter Martyr outside its context in Scripture.

[3] *in Gen.* 1.2: *Patres putarent hic esse Spiritus sancti habitam rationem, ut tres personae ad rerum creationem concurrerent, pater, verbum et spiritus.*

the Word of God in order to image His 'holiness, righteousness and truth'.[4] But now, 'the intercourse and most sweet familiarity which man had with God at the beginning is broken off by sin'.[5] What, then, is the proper 'end of man', his 'felicity'?[6] Martyr answers: human felicity is not related to *virtue*, but to *the forgiveness of sins*.

> In this our righteousness consists, that our sins should not be imputed unto us, but the righteousness of Christ will be imputed to believers. (*in Rom.* 8.25)

> the image of God is the new man, who understands divine truth, and seeks His righteousness. (*in* 1 *Cor.* 11.17)

A 'twofold knowledge of God' there may be, but one is a barren and cold knowledge, a 'groping in the dark', since even where, as in philosophy, the existence of God may be posited, His nature and property are so described that 'one may well conclude that there is no God'.[7]

> We hold a twofold knowledge of God: but the one perception is common and by nature, which is thus slight and infirm, valid only to render men inexcusable . . . The other is had through faith, and depends on the Word of God and divine revelation. And this, which alone brings rebirth through Christ, is thus effectual, to transmute souls and make us partakers of the divine nature. (*in* 1 *Cor.* 1.21)

> God . . . continually holds open before our eyes the book of created things: He always calls and illuminates us: but we always turn away our mind from His doctrine. (*in Rom.* 1.19)

> the knowledge of Thee may be grafted and imprinted in men's minds by the form, order and most beautiful comeliness of the things that are created . . . hereunto are added Thy written laws . . . But as we are lewd and wicked wretches, so have we never made an end of abusing both these most faithful schoolmasters . . . (*Prayers*, Psalm 19(2))

In this context a basic principle of Peter Martyr's theology is operative, the distinction *per se* and *per accidens*.

> Things should be named by that which they obtain by their own disposition and nature, and not by what is annexed to them, as they say, by

---

[4] *in Iud.* 6.22; cf. *in Gen.* 1.26f, *in Rom.* 5.19: man's destiny is to be the *vicarius* of God on earth.

[5] *Enc. Verbi Dei.*

[6] *in Arist. Ethic.*, *passim*. The true *princeps facultas* or ἀρχιτεκτονικῇ is found in Scripture alone, whose wisdom is the sole path to the chief end of man. Cf. *in* 1 *Cor.*, *Praef.*: theology, not civil science is the true architectonic: 'since this science of ours treats of nothing else but Christ, it is so much the more to be judged the head of all others, as Christ is the most excellent above all other things.'

[7] *in Rom.* 1.19; cf. 8.25.

accident or chance. The Gospel has by its own institution and by God's counsel, the property to save. But when it harms, this happens externally, that is by the unfaithfulness of the receivers, otherwise Christ could not be called Saviour, since He was set for the fall and offence of many. (*in Rom.* 1.16)

Revelation is *single*, it is entirely good news, the self-revelation of the loving God. Its effect in rendering man inexcusable is not properly an effect, if we regard the Aristotelian distinction of ends, for this is accidental to the Gospel as final cause.

The Gospel is a glad tidings: by this Christ comes to us and makes us glad . . . Christ comes not to do harm, but brings His gifts and never comes empty. (*Serm. in Ioan.* XX)

There is no need to imagine that God has towards us two faces or two heads. He is always the same God, and bears one manner of countenance, although not perceived in the same way by all. For the faithful behold Him one way, and the unfaithful another. (*in* 1 *Sam.* 5.7)

This distinction is decisive in understanding the Law. For it is spiritual, and increases sin only accidentally, through human sin—'the Gospel also might be called the instrument of death'.[8] And in the doctrine of predestination Peter Martyr sounds the same note:

under the name of predestination, we will comprehend the saints only . . . the Scriptures nowhere that I know call men that shall be damned, predestinate. (*De Praedestinatione* 10.14)

The fountainhead of predestination is love, so that the order is 'love, election, predestination'; it is part of the 'Spirit of grace' —the efficient cause of life only, of union with Christ:

'Whom He has loved in Christ'. This we add because whatever God gives or decrees to give, He gives and will give through Christ . . . He is the prince and head of all the predestinate, indeed none is predestinate except to this end alone, to be made a member of Christ. (*De Praed.* 12)

Thus revelation is single, and the cause of sin is rather deficient than efficient.

in one way He may be called the author of those things afterwards evilly performed: yet not the true cause, for the proper cause is inward, that is namely their evil will. (*in* 1 *Sam.* 16.22, *An Deus Sit Causa . . . Peccati*)

The relevance of this teaching for the doctrine of the sacraments will be obvious. Is there a damning or destructive eating

[8] *in Rom.* 8.2; cf. *in Arist. Eth.* I.8 (p. 269): the law brings death not *per se* since *suopte ingenio* it is life and righteousness, and p. 289, *per se . . . temere seu per accidens.*

(*damnosa et perniciosa manducatio*) of the Body of Christ, as both
Romanist and Lutheran maintained? Martyr answers:

> Whatever the Lord instituted, He did that we should be saved . . .The
> eating of the body of Christ, which indeed Scripture hands down, is always
> a saving manducation. (*Defensio adv. Gardin.* p. 340)

There may be a twofold effect resulting from a twofold manner
of eating, but this remains firm—

> only one effect results from eating the flesh of Christ . . .The flesh of Christ
> is always vivifying. (*Def.* 342)

> It is a device of your own, to say that there is a certain body of Christ
> which the wicked eat, yet have not salvation, nor are partakers of the Spirit
> of Christ. (*Disputatio*, II, final speech)

In this whole teaching, however, we have still to examine the
fundamental assumption of Peter Martyr with regard to revelation. We have mentioned that for him, the Person of Christ
is the archetype of theological doctrine, and in the next two
Chapters we shall examine this material form in detail. But
first we must set forth his profound view of revelation as the
divine *accommodation* to the human creaturely-sinful need in
terms of earthly images or signs, and the resultant nature of
revelation as *analogical*.

The Divine Condescension

> Since God in His own nature is not perceived by sense, He yet con-
> descends to human capacity, and by sensible words shows Himself to be
> known by men, in corporeal forms and in Sacraments. (*Proposit. ex Exod.* 3,
> nec. 4)

For Peter Martyr, the *imago Dei* is not a static human deposit
but a dynamic Divine activity: God 'images Himself'. The
very fact that there *is* human knowledge of God is a wonderful
testimony of the Divine love.

> God so humbled Himself as to enter into a covenant with man: that comes
> from His own mere mercy and goodness. (*in Iud.* 2.23)

Knowledge of God means condescension, accommodation,
humility on God's part;[9] and exaltation, a being lifted up by

---

[9] This doctrine of *accomodatio* is familiar in Calvin. Since writing this, there
has appeared a stimulating book by R. S. Wallace, *Calvin's Doctrine of the Word and
Sacrament* (Oliver & Boyd, 1953), which begins, in a similar way, with the fact that
'God, in revealing Himself, adapts Himself to the capacity of man' (p. 2). Wallace
helps us to see the identity of doctrine between Calvin and Martyr. Cf. our
Appendix C.

the Holy Spirit on ours. Thus revelation by Word and Spirit
rests firmly upon the Incarnation, Death and Resurrection of
Jesus Christ and upon the office of the Holy Spirit as he joins
men to Christ according to this same pattern. We shall approach
this teaching by first examining the treatise *De Visionibus*,[10] an
analysis of knowledge of God.

Knowledge of God is not offered to the senses, since the
things understood by them 'have no affinity with God, but
are most distant from Him'. The qualities or accidents of
human cognition cannot be carried over to the knowledge of
God, 'since God, who is most simple, is not subject to these'.

The effects which Philosophers use to know God by their understanding
are not equal to His dignity, power and faculties. Wherefore they only
declared certain things common and light. But we give to Him attributes
or properties, that is, good, just, fair, wise and so on; because we have nothing more excellent, nor names more noble, which can be better applied or
agree with Him. Nor yet are these things so in Him as we speak: for, since
He is most simple, He is far otherwise good, just and wise than men either
are or are called.

There is a fundamental agnosticism in human knowledge of
God: man cannot attribute properties unto God properly, but
by a certain figure, which Martyr usually terms *anthropopatheia*.

This cannot agree at all with God, who is *purus actus*, nor suffers any
variations or changes. And so they are said of Him through ἀνθρωποπάθιαν,
not properly. (*in* 1 *Sam.* 1.19)

So is it said that God contracted His soul and was in a way sorry for the
miseries of His people. This kind of speech is not proper to God, but
improper. For God is not sorry, nor touched with affections. Wherefore
it is a speech after the condition of men. (*in Iud.* 10.15)

Thus God 'is said to' operate in the heavens, He 'is said to'
descend to signify His presence on earth.[11] In the Treatise,
Martyr explains this attribution of properties:

But the Holy Scriptures, if they sometimes attribute members to God,
doubtless this is the only reason, to help our infirmity: although we cannot
comprehend the essence of God in itself, yet by this is provided that by
certain symbols and shadows we may somewhat understand. Wherefore
members are by a most profitable metaphor attributed to God, that diligently remembering His properties, we may piously and faithfully exercise
our minds.

[10] *in Iud.*, following 6.22.   [11] *in Lament.* 1.13; *in Gen.* 11.5.

And again:

> Here we should regard the goodness of God, by which He so humbled Himself to our infirmity, that since we cannot understand His nature, He would under the name of members or parts open or rather shadow unto us certain of His properties. (*in Iud.* 8.24)

The Anthropomorphites, therefore, could not be condemned if they had retained this *impropriety* as a characteristic of their teaching, in relation to God's condescension to human infirmity.

> But they contended that the nature of God was so in very deed: wherefore they are condemned rightly and worthily.

These two ideas form the context of Peter Martyr's doctrine of the sacraments: that the invisible God images Himself according to creaturely forms; and that His relation to these forms is not one of identity but of a certain *ratio* or *proportion*.[12] In speaking of the Ark as 'a sacrament of the presence of divine help', Martyr states that because the Papists bind the sign and thing signified, 'they follow a ratio alien from piety'[13]—faith involves the sacramental-analogical relationship by its very nature. Revelation leads to faith, not sight, to analogy, not identity: it poses the problem of the meaning of earthly signs.

> By this is the excellent power of God known, when He shows forth incredible acts by abject and vile instruments ... So Christ healed the blind man with clay, and God in the signs of water and outward elements of bread and wine stirs up the faith of His people, and seals the promises of heavenly things. (*Enc. Verbi Dei*)

Peter Martyr therefore warns us that no creature can have life in itself as a fountain or principle, but only as an organ or instrument of the Divine power: otherwise we mix heaven and earth.[14] The problem of mediation is the problem of human need and the loving accommodation of God to fulfil that need.

> For since we are weak, nor easily believe the promises of God, it was needful that His goodwill towards us should be signified not only by words, but also sealed by things that could be offered to our senses. (*in Rom.* 4.11)

So God put His words in the Scriptures and in the action of the

---

[12] Cf. *in* 1 *Sam.* 29.6, a distinction between names of God *substantiala* (signifying Jehovah as *summum Ens*) and *proprietatum*. Of the latter he states, 'Other names refer to some property of God . . . yet these are not accidents in God: but only in proportion as we grasp them by our thinking. For since God is infinite, and we cannot grasp the whole, yet from the effects and notes we comprehend in some part.' Cf. *in* 15.11. *Deus Quomodo Poenitere Dicatur,* Fol. 85B ff.
[13] *in* 2 *Sam.* 15.24.   [14] *Def.* 334.

mysteries. Scripture and sacrament are the foci of the problem of mediation, although both are forms of the Word of God.

Mediation is related to human creatureliness as well as to human sinfulness; for the body is part of God's good creation, and revelation acknowledges this fact.

And I allow what is commonly spoken, 'Sacraments are visible words', they stir men up through the sight and other senses. Chrysostom rightly says, If we were spirit, we should not need those organs, but we are composed of spirit and body, the senses of the body excite the soul. (*De Poenitentia* 12)

Flesh is the workshop of spirit, as Cyprian rightly says. (*Caro est officina spiritus*) (*De Votis*, 1483)

Basically, it is human capacity to which God accommodates Himself in revelation, although Peter Martyr qualifies this thought decisively in relation to the Incarnation. Man is bodily, he is creature:

The body from our first creation was not given men to be an hindrance to our knowledge of God, nor yet to shut up our souls in a kind of dark and blind prison . . . (*in Iud.* 6.22)

A human figure is attributed to God by the Prophets . . . But they spoke thus so as to submit to human capacity. (*in Lament.* 2.1)

We must not take offence (Augustine) says, that God has so instructed us in knowledge of Himself through a glass as it were, and in dark sayings: since our nature so required it. For we are framed in such a way that we are led to the knowledge of causes by their effects, and are trained to certain truths by similitudes. (*in 1 Cor.* 13.12)

This is the first orientation of similitude or analogy, to bodily infirmity,[15] as the method of Scripture abundantly testifies:

the Scriptures do not use exquisite and subtle arguments: and rarely do they bring those most perfect demonstrations, since in respect of God, vision must be accommodated to the doctrinal capacity of the weak. For this reason a good part of its doctrine is composed of parables, narratives and similes. (*in Arist. Eth.* pp. 49f)

Thus too, the articles of our faith acknowledge our inability 'to comprehend Him fully', but we are given 'sometimes some

---

[15] The body is 'a most excellent workmanship of God'—if the heathen belief is true that the union of soul and body is evil, 'then let every man who is wise lay violent hands on himself, in order to obtain that commodity!' (*in 1 Cor.* 15.12) Body is not the prison but 'the most fit instrument' of the soul (*in Rom.* 8.11): thus instrumentality is posited in the very bodily-soul unity. Cf. *in II Reg.* 2.21, 3.27 and *De Resurrectione* in Chapter 4: the soul is the *forma* of the body.

little taste and feeling of Him, sometimes another'.[16] In this
connection we may note Peter Martyr's teaching on the resurrection knowledge of God. His stress on the value of the
body and its place in the Kingdom of Christ present and future
means that our eyes 'shall not attain to the essence of God'—

> In the life everlasting the blessed shall know the essence of God, not
> indeed by the senses but by the soul or mind . . . not that the blessed shall
> know in complete perfection the nature and substance of God: for finite
> things cannot fully receive what is infinite, nor is the creature able to com-
> prehend fully and perfectly his Creator. (De Visionibus)

It is also in relation to human sinfulness that such accommodation is to be understood; and this is the decisive relation, as
the result of the incarnational movement of humility in Death
indicates. Our felicity cannot be to have knowledge of God
'engraved on our minds' by the Spirit apart from 'outward
writings and the aid of books' because of the brokenness of
communion with God through sin.[17]

> But it was our sin that removed us from the sight of God; from this came
> to us the darkness, blindness and ignorance in heavenly things. (in Iud. 6.22)

Christ, the Redeemer, and man's union with Him, is thus the
central meaning of mediation. Speaking of Christ, Martyr
states:

> He ought chiefly to be called figurator, who while we live here takes heed
> of our infirmity through His kindness, in figures. (Def. 14)
> there are enough of God's images extant: for Christ is His lively image—let
> us behold Him and His acts, and in Him we shall know God abundantly.
> (in Iud. 8.24)

This thought is summed up best in the Preface to the Tractatio:

> And therefore the Holy Spirit, to remedy our weakness, having granted
> us light and understanding that should excel our own nature, has also
> humbled Himself to these metaphors, namely of abiding, dwelling, eating
> and drinking: so that this divine and heavenly union that we have with
> Christ may in some way be known to us.

He continues by indicating the two extremes in interpreting
these metaphors, of attributing to them too much or too little,
simple identity or simple difference. But the spiritual interpretation demands a mean between these, 'according to the
analogy and convenience of the holy Scripture', which is—'the

---

[16] Catech. 1.   [17] Enc. Verbi Dei.

hypostatic or essential unity of Christ'. Here are three factors in Peter Martyr's doctrine of sacrament: the problem of revelation or mediation, namely the relation between sign and signification; the solution of this problem according to the relationship of analogy, that is, that the sign is not simply identical with or different from, the thing signified, but related analogically to it; and the distinctive Divine analogy of the Person of Christ as the given archetype for Christian theology.

Disparates and Analogy

Those things which are so discrete or disparate, if an analogy or signification occur, may now be so conjoined that they will be valid to make a proposition. (*Tract.* 39)

The introduction of analogy as the relation between the revelatory terms means that both univocal and equivocal terms are denied in our knowledge of God, for analogy is the mean between these. In his Commentary on Aristotle's Nicomachean Ethics, Peter Martyr deals explicitly with the meaning of analogy.[18] His teaching may be summarized as follows. First he distinguishes homonyms or univocals (ὁμώνυμα, *univoca*), things having in common both name and definition; synonyms or equivocals (συνώνυμα, *aequivoca*), things having in common name but not definition; and 'between these two a medium, commonly called analogue in the schools'. In this last, the same *ratio* agrees with both, and the name is communicated from one to the other. What is proper to the one is through the definition or signification applied to the other term.[19]

A further distinction is made within analogy itself.[20] After rejecting homonymy or univocity as the mode of relation of disparates, he distinguishes a mode according to which the

---

[18] *in Arist. Eth.* I.6 (pp. 135ff, 150f) and II.6 (321 ff). Unfortunately, Martyr's work extends only to III.2, and so does not reach the *locus classicus* of analogy, the treatment of the concept of Justice in Book V, esp. ll. 1130ff. Nevertheless, these passages from his Commentary (although given only coincidental to the Aristotelian text, and not in systematic form like the teaching of Aquinas on the same subject), should prove a most valuable source for the understanding of the sacramental-analogical nature of revelation, not only in his own thought, but also in that of Calvin and perhaps of the Reformation as a whole.

[19] Pp. 135f.

[20] Pp. 150f. The context is Aristotle's question whether a common definition implies a common idea, or *an magis secundum proportionem? Quemadmodum in corpore visus, ita in animo mens, et aliud in alio.*

definition can be common other than 'absolutely or perfectly,
as it ought to be in Synonyms'. Thus pure equivocation is also
rejected, and the way cleared for the presentation of analogy
proper. 'There are these three forms of analogy': first, when
things of the same name participate also in the same ratio, not
simpliciter and by nature, but because they proceed from one
common principle (example: things *medica*, including both sur-
gical instruments and books); second, things making for the
same end share the same name and ratio, such as things *sana*
making for *sanitas*, although as various as exercise and blood-
letting.

> The third form is Analogy, which is clear enough from the example
> adduced in the text concerning the mind and the eye, where it is first
> determined about analogy or proportion that it stands, as the eye to the
> body, so the mind to the soul. Next is to be seen whether the one is the
> good of that in which it exists, and the good in this way, whether through
> itself or the other, as we say, What the eye is to the body, the mind is to the
> soul: but the eye is the good of the body: and therefore the mind is such a
> good of the soul. In this way are these shown to agree not only in name,
> but in ratio, yet only by analogy.

A third passage[21] relates this teaching to the Greek distinction between the arithmetical mean, the *medium rei*, which
is invariable and unchangeable, 'equally distant from both
extremes' (simple proportion), and the geometrical mean, the
medium quo ad nos. The latter compares two ratios or proportions,
for instance in the proposition 'as six is to three, so eight is to
four', the 'ratio or proportion' is two ($A:B::C:D$). The
medium geometricum is defined as 'the likeness of ratio or proportion'.[22] Therefore, for Peter Martyr the mode of relating
two disparate or disjunctive terms is neither simple univocity nor
pure equivocity, nor yet analogy of a determinate (arithmetical)
relationship, but analogy as *likeness of proportion*. He accepts the
Aristotelian concept of analogy which follows the Greek classic
definition of the *medium geometricum*.

---

[21] Pp. 323f. *Proportio autem nil aliud est quam collatio inter se magnitudinum AUT
numerorum* (324). This is the Ciceronic term *conlatio rationis*; cf. *in 2 Sam.* 4.11,
Jerome: *aliquem bifariam posse appellari iustum: vel simpliciter, vel ex collatione.*

[22] Cf. W. D. Ross, *Aristotle*, pp. 210ff, regarding the critical section of Book V.
In a significant footnote he states, 'Originally the Greeks seem to have recognized
three means (μεσότητες), the arithmetical, the geometrical, and the harmonic,
and only one ἀναλογία, the geometrical. Later, they applied ἀναλογία to all three
cases.'

Before considering the implications of this concept, and our reason for dealing with it at length here, we ought to note the striking similarity of Martyr's thought on this point with that of Thomas Aquinas. Aquinas rejects both univocal predication 'of God and other things', and the 'purely equivocal', distinguishing this latter from the analogical means of predication.[23] Within the analogical, moreover, he distinguishes things in relation to some other thing, and things in relation to one of themselves, the latter being the only form of analogy proper to God and other things. The proper predication within analogy is of one term to the other (*analogia quae est unius ad alterum*). The final distinction is between *proportion*, which requires a determinate relationship between the terms, and *proportionality*, which is 'a likeness of proportion' presupposing 'an analogy of similitude'. G. B. Phelan has stated, 'Since Cajetan's *De Nominum Analogia* it is customary to deal with the doctrine of analogy in the philosophy of St. Thomas under the general headings of analogy of inequality, analogy of attribution and analogy of proportionality—which correspond exactly with the three types of analogy which St. Thomas himself distinguished in his Commentary on the Sentences of Peter Lombard.'[24] Therefore 'analogy' means a relationship of proportionality, in which both 'likeness of proportion' and 'difference of proportion' are operative.[25]

What is the significance of this coincidence of the doctrine of analogy in these two theologians? Historically the significance

---

[23] *Et hoc modo aliqua dicuntur de Deo et creaturis analogice, et non aequivoce pure, neque univoce . . . Et iste modus communitatis medius est inter puram aequivocationem et simplicem univocationem.* (*Summa Theol.*, Marietti, 1952, Ia. 13.5.) Cf. Ia. 4.3, 13.4-6; *S.C.G.* I. 14-34; I *Sent.* Prol., a.2, ad 2; d. 19, q.5, a.2, ad 1.

[24] 'Saint Thomas and Analogy, The Aquinas Lectures, 1941', Milwaukee, p. 26. Moreover, 'proper proportionality' is to be distinguished not only from attribution (in which only the prime analogue 'formally possesses the characteristic signified by the analogated *ratio*', p. 37) but also from *improper* proportionality or symbolic analogy. Phelan characterizes Meister Eckhart as attributive, and Maimonides as symbolic, analogical thinking (p. 42). Karl Barth gives an excellent treatment of analogy in *Kirchliche Dogmatik*, II.1, 1946, pp. 254-275; cf. pp. 87-92 on *analogia entis*. He accepts 'as a thorough summary of all former research' Quenstedt's presentation (p. 267). Cf. Barth's *Fides quaerens intellectum*, 1931 on the *fidei ratio*, especially I.4, 'Der Weg der Theologie'.

[25] With two differences between Aristotle and Aquinas: the former is dealing with essences, the latter with modes of those essences; and more important, for the former, the resemblance preponderates over the difference, for the latter, the difference over the likeness.

lies in the fact that Peter Martyr, like John Calvin, agreed with
Aquinas that analogical proportion obtains in the mystery of
the relationship between God and man. That is to say, in God
and man an attribute such as goodness is to be understood
neither as simply univocal (identical in God and man), nor as
purely equivocal (absolutely different),[26] but as involving the
likeness and difference of proportion implied in analogical
relationship. Theologically the significance lies in the fundamental disagreement between Martyr and Aquinas as to the
material principle operative in the relation of analogy. That
is, Aquinas relates the concept of analogy to the theory
of the degrees of reality—the analogy of being is decisive.[27]
Now Martyr is well aware of the place of *analogia entis* in the
order of the categories. These, he states, do not share a common nature *ex aequo*, for

being is spoken of them not on even terms but by a certain ratio, whence an
analogy is said to be ascribed to them: for substance is first of all, in it the
other categories belong and upon it they lean. (*in Arist. Eth.* p. 138)

But Martyr does not remain in this sphere of deliberation.
Since revelation is essentially 'by Word and Spirit', he allows
the concept of analogy to become dynamic, interpreting analogical proportion in terms of the Incarnation of the Word.[28] For

[26] E. Bevan's helpful discussion (*Symbolism and Belief*, MacMillan, '38, Lecture
13: Pragmatism and Analogy) describes these two alternatives as 'a pit of anthro-
pomorphism on one side of the road (and) a pit of agnosticism on the other'
(p. 311). For a most exhaustive treatment of the doctrine of analogy, cf. James F.
Anderson, *The Bond of Being*, An Essay on Analogy and Existence (Herder, St.
Louis, 1949).
[27] Cf. R. L. Patterson, *The Conception of God in the Philosophy of Aquinas* (London,
1933), esp. Chapter 7. This is the traditional interpretation of St. Thomas, for
whom the creative bestowal of being involves the analogical participation of the
creature in the being of God Himself (e.g. *S.C.G.* I.28-34, III.16-25). Thus
Father Phelan states, 'An analogy of proper proportionality is founded on the
ontological (transcendental) relation in which each being stands to every other
being in virtue of the very act of existence whereby all that is exists. Beings are
analogical in *be-ing*. That is to say every being exercises the act of existence (*is*)
in proportion to its essence' (p. 39). But Father Balthasar makes a different point
(Hans u.v. Balthasar, *Karl Barth—Darstellung und Deutung seiner Theologie*, 1951,
p. 273): that Aquinas himself, following Patristic theology, views the *analogia
entis* as included within the *analogia fidei*, whereas subsequent Thomism drew the
false relation and distinction between the two. Even if we grant this thesis—which
is possible only by interpreting the act of creation in terms of a distinction within
grace which Aquinas does not appear to apply here (cf. *S.T.* IaIIae, 109.3, *resp.*)—
the question still remains: to what extent is modern Romanism willing to follow
Balthasar and his friends in reforming its doctrine in such terms?
[28] Cf. T. H. L. Parker, *The Doctrine of the Knowledge of God* (Oliver and Boyd,

Martyr, the theological analogy of proportionality does not rest on a doctrine of ontological continuity between God and man, but on the *unio hypostatica* of God and man in the Person of Jesus Christ, which Martyr terms 'the analogy and convenience of the holy Scripture'.[29]

The Romanist doctrine of *analogia entis* is the starting-point for God's accommodation, the possibility of the Incarnation of Deity, 'receptive and ready to be used by Him'.[30] And although its adherents may at times approach an understanding of the archetypal nature of the Person of Christ,[31] yet fundamentally they walk by sight, by their creaturely continuity of being with God, and not by faith, by the gracious Event in which God has bound Himself to man, and bound us to Him in *this* Man. These are the lines along which the battle was fought in the Reformation, as we shall see from Martyr's struggles in the eucharistic controversies. Here his weapon against the Romanists is this very concept of analogy so ably worked out by Aquinas—but the decisive factor is the acceptance of the Person of Christ as the archetypal analogue given from God's side. From grace to faith, and only then to being, this was his method: the Person of Christ, the office of the Holy Spirit, and our union with Christ.

The Holy Spirit and the 'Sursum Corda'

It is against such a background that Peter Martyr's analogical solution to the problem of the sacramental relationship

---

1952), p. 109: 'All knowledge of God is analogical and sacramental, not direct. This is what revelation means. But it is axiomatic with the Reformers that the analogy must be chosen by God Himself to be the medium of His revelation. In this sense Jesus Christ, the Scriptures, preaching and the sacraments are analogies.' This should be carried further in terms of the archetypal nature of Jesus Christ and the ectypal nature of the others; but this latter point is not so explicit in Calvin—cf. Wallace, *op. cit.*, p. 167: the hypostatic union 'at least serves to regulate his thinking on this mystery of sacramental union'.

[29] In the Preface to *Tractatio*, quoted above. See Appendix D (1). This means that the formal analogy $(A:B::C:D)$ in which a proportional relation obtains (a likeness along with a diversity of proportion in the two sides of the relationship) must be thought strictly in terms of that personal-historical Analogue in whom God has accommodated Himself to our capacity—the Incarnate Lord, crucified and risen.

[30] P. E. Przywara, *Polarity* (London, 1935), pp. 72f.

[31] E.g. Przywara states, 'The "two unfused as one" of classical Christology is pre-eminently the form of these solutions in general', i.e. Grace and Free Will, etc.—p. 85.

is to be approached. Briefly, he states that the sign and the thing signified are related according to the 'likeness of proportion' indicated by Aristotle's analysis.

> We acknowledge that disparates cannot be predicated of themselves by mutual identity, as the Scholastics say, when both are taken properly . . . But if the predicate is understood analogically, through signification, it can rightly be predicated of the other. (*Def.* 667)

> It is necessary that some analogy, that is proportion or convenience, should be retained between the sign and the thing signified. For if signs had no similitude with those things that are signified, then they should not be their signs. And yet along with this conformity there is still to be kept a diversity between what is signified and the things which signify. (*in Rom.* 4.11)

The implications are obvious: neither a simple identity nor a simple difference, nor yet a relation of proportion, but a relation of likeness *and* diversity of proportion.

This relation of analogy is essentially the *sacramental* relation. On the key verse, Romans 12.6, for instance, Martyr considers Origen's rejection of the translation 'according to the *ratio* of faith' because Origen 'counts analogy to be a competent measure', and comments, 'analogy can most properly be rendered *ratio*'.[32] Again he states:

> Nor is there a conjunction between the symbol and the thing signified, unless sacramental . . . nor may you remove the ratio or analogy between the sign and the thing signified. (*in* 1 *Cor.* 11.24)

> we have always taught thus, that the whole and complete Sacrament consists of sign and thing signified. For there can be no relation without two terminates. But the Sacrament is a certain relation between such, namely the outward symbol which we observe by eye and sense, and the things signified, which are eternal, heavenly and invisible. (*Def.* 534)

Yet the decisive thing has still to be said: the office of the Holy Spirit in this sacramental-analogical operation. In a very clear passage, Martyr points out that there is not sufficient natural analogy for us to comprehend the thing itself; for this there is required a constituting authority, the Word of God, and an effectual signification, the Holy Spirit's work: 'for assuredly by the Spirit of God, not by human reason' we derive the signification of such signs.[33] This is obviously true of Scripture:

[32] *Comm. ad loc.*   [33] *Def.* 2.

Those who come to hear the Gospel, and lack faith, receive nothing but words: and the Gospel is to them no Gospel . . . both the words of God and the sacraments, if received only as outward things, pertain to the letter, which quickens not but kills. (*in Rom.* 1.16, 2.28)

the letter kills, but the spirit vivifies, since everything kills which is offered us without the Spirit of Christ . . . Even the Gospel, if read when not supplied with the Spirit of Christ, is the letter and kills. For these outward things only teach, damn, accuse, reveal sins. (*in Lament., Praef.*)

In reading Scripture, our minds must be 'lifted up from things temporal to things eternal and heavenly'.[34] But also in the sacrament, no earthly security is offered, the relation between sign and signification remains the same. The revelation by Word and Spirit is never superseded, so that here too what is required is the movement of faith, which is always the 'lifting up of the heart' unto Christ in the heavens. The power in the sacrament is the power of the Holy Spirit—Peter Martyr's constant theme is the presence and power of the Spirit of Christ. The formal analogy becomes a positive error unless the Holy Spirit 'fills' its terms with the proportion between God and man given to faith in the Person of Jesus Christ. Now therefore we must examine Martyr's treatment of the historical record of this revelation: the presence of Christ in the Old and New Testaments.

[34] *in* 1 *Sam.* 2.10; cf. *Def.* 2: the words of the Bible are analogical signs and require the work of the Holy Spirit to be understood.

CHAPTER II

CHRIST AND THE OLD TESTAMENT 'SIGNS'

'Every Speech of God'

For the Son of God is named by the Evangelist the Word or λόγος, which we must believe was not done by him rashly, but that it might be understood that God spoke by Him, when Scripture testifies that He spoke. Wherefore as often as we read that the Word of the Lord came to this man or that, I judge that this is always to be attributed unto the Son of God.

(in Iud. 6.22)

PETER MARTYR's doctrine of the unity of Scripture is but the logic of his Christology applied to the Biblical witness. God's self-revelation is by Word and Spirit: and the Word is not merely instrumental, but is Himself the substance of revelation.[1] Whether Old Testament or New, the matter (res) is one and the same. The unity of Scripture is the unity of Christ. There are, however, two distinctions which must be noted: between Law and Gospel, and between substance and accidents of the two testaments.

Martyr's works are full of this thought of the oneness of revelation:

whatever things are said to have been spoken by God in the Old Testament, the same were made open by Christ. (in Iud. 2.1)

those things which happened then were done by the Son of God . . . whatever is uttered unto men concerning divine things is uttered by the Son of God, who has indeed given Himself to mankind, a faithful interpreter of God His Father. (De Iustificatione, 80)

the Son of God, the word and voice of God by whom He speaks. (in Gen. 3.8)

Moreover, the Son subsumes under Himself all forms of revelation, including that by angels: sometimes angels appear in

---

[1] Cf. in 1 Cor. 10.3 regarding the substance or subject of revelation: Christ is the res in all sacraments, since O.T. sacraments had the same two things, symbola and res per ea significata. But only those who approach religiose are led from the one to the other. 'Whence we acknowledge that all speech (sermo) which we read that God shared with men, is to be referred to the Son of God, who is Christ: just as the Father neither speaks nor represents His will, save through the Word.'

His name and in His power, but sometimes also Christ Himself appears as an angel:

> When in the Old Testament, as often happens, the name of angel is joined with the name of God, then is meant the second Person of the Trinity, the Son. (*Prop. ex Exod.* 3, *prob.* 1)

> Doubtless Christ was that angel that defended the Jews and fought on their side. (*in Iud.* 4.15)

Fundamentally, the authority of the Old Testament is equal with that of the New, since it too is the revelation of the Son of God.

> Christ has given to His Church the Old Testament, whose authority—let Manichees, Marcionites and other such pestilent heretics chafe at it all they want—is most stable and sure, inasmuch as by it the ancient Christians also discerned the New Testament. (*in* 1 *Cor., Praef.*)

This 'discerning the New Testament' is the key to the O.T. significance. Ultimately, the parts of Scripture are not Old and New, but Law and Gospel, distinct not historically but theologically:

> it is not lawful to divide the holy books from one another . . . whatever is contained in the holy Scriptures should be referred to two chief points, I mean law and gospel. For everywhere, either God's commandments to live well are set forth unto us, or else when we are found to depart from them through weakness or malice of some sort, the gospel is revealed, in which through Christ we are pardoned our trespasses, and promised the power and strength of the Holy Spirit, to restore us again to the image of Christ that we had lost. These two things may be seen in all the books of Moses, in the histories, in the prophets, and books of wisdom, and throughout the whole testament, old and new. (*in Iud., Praef.*)

> At the same time are given the law and Christ, for the one shows forth the other. (*in Gen.* 2.16)

> the law and the Gospel are not separated by volumes of books. For in the Old Testament are contained the promises of the Gospel, and in the Gospel the law is not only comprehended, but also most perfectly expounded by Christ. (*De Iustif.* 33)

The New Testament does not signify grace as against law, although following Pentecost 'a more ample Spirit and more plentiful grace' were given[2]—rather 'it is not the law that is abrogated, but the domination and power which follow it'.[3] The Incarnation meant a new power and freedom; this is that

---

[2] *in Gen.* 21.23.   [3] *in Rom.* 3.20.

towards which all the Divine promises point, namely the Birth of Christ,[4] and it is the sum of Scripture:

> Assuredly the highest benefit of God towards mankind is Christ: wherefore all other things must be reduced wholly to this point. (*in* 1 *Sam.* 2.10)

The O.T. Saints as Members of Christ

> as He is said to live in us, since we are His members, so also He lived and dwelt in the old fathers: wherefore they were no less His members than are we. And how the Head suffers and is renewed in His members, is most clearly declared to Paul—'Saul, Saul, why persecutest thou Me?' (*in Rom.* 10.4)

The unity of the Word of revelation implies a corresponding unity in the meaning of justification and faith. For the content of faith is always the same: *union with Christ*. Faith is 'the power by which we apprehend Christ',[5] and for Peter Martyr this apprehension involves the *whole* Christ, Divine and Human, and the *whole* man, body and soul. The apprehension of faith is based upon Christ's union with men, which He has accomplished in a twofold way.[6] By His Incarnation, Christ effected a 'general union' with all mankind, weak and 'material' but real and of ultimate significance for revelation. By 'the Spirit and grace' however, He effects a second union (*coniunctio spiritu et per gratiam*) of a very close nature:

> we are so joined with Christ that we are called flesh of His flesh, and bone of His bones; because through the Incarnation we are made of the same nature and kind as He; and afterwards, His grace and Spirit coming to us, we are made partakers of His spiritual conditions and properties. (*in* 1 *Cor.* 12.12)

The Church is the sphere of this ingrafting into Christ on the basis of His union with humanity by Incarnation and by His Spirit. But does not this presuppose the Incarnation as historical actuality, and so deny the O.T. saints membership in this same Christ which we have for our Head? To this Peter Martyr answers in strong terms: Christ is not only the prime Actor in the O.T., as we noted above, but He is this *on account of* His coming Incarnation, and in relation to it. Therefore

---

[4] *in Gen.* 22.13.
[5] *in* 1 *Cor.* 13.3; cf. *De Iustif.* 71—faith is defined in terms of its Object, Christ the Redeemer and Lord.
[6] Letters to Calvin and Beza (*L.C.*, pp. 1094, 1108); cf. Chapter V below.

before and after the Incarnation the substance of revelation—
and so of our union with Christ—is one and the same.

> The whole Church and right faith confess that the Word was the true
> God that appeared under the flesh of man. If He did this, as doubtless He
> did without counterfeit, why may He not be said to have done the same in
> the Old Testament under various forms and many figures? Without doubt
> that was much greater which He gave us in the latter time. But He that
> gave us the greater thing can surely also give us the lesser. (*De Vision.*)

The O.T. forms are thus related to the Incarnation according to the inner pattern of revelation—the future Incarnation
is their possibility. The sacrifices, for instance, are not mere
symbols:

> In the kids and goats offered, Christ could be expressed because of the
> form of perfect man which He assumed. (*Prop. ex Levit.* 1, *prob.* 5)

And what of the appearance in human form in the O.T.?
We must first acknowledge the unique nature of the Incarnation
itself:

> The similitude of angels appearing in human form must not be compared
> with the Incarnation of the Lord. (*in* 1 *Cor.* 15.47, *An Christ. ex Coel.* . . . .)

When Christ Himself appeared 'in visible species' it was because
Abraham, for instance, required confirmation 'by some effective indication of the divine presence'.[7] And such visible forms
are different in kind from the Incarnation:

> But before, when He appeared to Abraham and to the Fathers, although
> He had true flesh, yet because it was not joined to Him in one and the same
> substance, He could not be called flesh, nor was flesh God. But afterwards,
> when He took upon Him both flesh and soul, so that there was but one sub-
> stance or person, then man saw God and God, man. (*in Iud.* 13.25, *De
> Vis. Angel.*)

With this qualification in mind, Peter Martyr now declares the
basic oneness of the presence of Christ:

> Since Christ was to come and was to be offered for us on the Cross, He
> was in this way comprehended by the Fathers, by faith, and was food for
> their souls unto life eternal. For those things which are furthest away from
> us, this same faith makes present, so that they take hold of the same Christ
> which we at this time enjoy. (*in* 1 *Sam.* 1.4)

although He had not yet in actual fact taken flesh upon Him, yet was He
given spiritually for meat to the Fathers who believed in the promise.

(*Tract.* 9)

[7] *in Gen.* 12.7.

Grace and faith are the same in every age—this is the determinative category for Peter Martyr.[8] It is the gracious condescension of the Divine Person in revelation and redemption which is the content of faith: how can this differ from one age to the next?

> The death of Christ, the shedding of His blood, and the assumption of the flesh were always present, unalterable, pleasing and welcome, as God (*qua Deus*). Wherefore in the Apocalypse it is said 'a lamb slain from the foundation of the world', and to the Hebrews, 'Christ the same yesterday and today and forever'. And of Abraham it is declared in the Gospel, that he saw the day of Christ and rejoiced. Whence that connection is not firm, that 'The flesh and blood of Christ had not yet been assumed through the economy or dispensation of time, and therefore they could not be spiritual food and drink to the ancients.' For, since the salvation of the Fathers, just as ours, depended on the death and blood of Christ, it was necessary for them, as for us, to grasp these by faith: else salvation they did not have. Although the death, flesh and blood of Christ were not yet extant in nature, nevertheless the Fathers could have their force and efficacy to serve them . . . They had present the divine person, that is the Son of God, whom they grasped by faith, and indeed grasped in this promise, or as I may say, in respect of the human nature which He would assume. (*in* 1 *Cor.* 10.4)

Martyr's Christology, it will be noted, is dynamic: Christ is present as spiritual nourishment, He is grasped in a union which is a communion. The Incarnation is the great pattern and source of this union and communion, but since it means a sacramental relationship to man, it can equally well sustain such a relationship proleptic to its historical actuality. Thus Christ's union with the O.T. saints is identical in kind with that after the Incarnation: He is the substance of their faith, His human nature the mediating term in revelation, the communication of His qualities their sanctification. Their 'second righteousness' following conversion reforms them according to *the image of Christ*,[9] and therefore in the life of the O.T. saints too 'we see an express image of the Cross and Resurrection of Christ'.[10]

[8] Faith is God's instrument 'to apply Christ unto ourselves' so that we are 'grafted into Christ' (*De Iustif.* 71)—but 'that faith, in which justification consists, is the same in both testaments' (*in Rom.* 11.27).

[9] Cf. esp. *De Iustif.*, *passim*—'Because we are justified we do just things'; cf. *in* 1 *Sam.* 26.23, the *iustitia duplex, imputata et factorum*.

[10] *in* 2 *Sam.* 20.1; cf. 22. 10-26: the qualities of His saints give a valid knowledge of God, so that Martyr can even say, *Summa est, talis est Deus quales homines fuerint*.

It is this dual fact of Christ's union with His members and their reflection of His image, which is the basis of Peter Martyr's interpretation of the Old Testament.

Typology, Allegory and Analogy

Peter Martyr consistently holds that a valid knowledge of Christ is to be gained from the study of the lives and deeds of the O.T. saints. The 'argument and scope' of any passage includes two things, the historical events and the pointing to Christ, since 'in all these things Christ is celebrated'.[11]

> So far ought we thus to deal with the historical exposition, that we may understand in every act, what is set forth in the sacred books for our consideration. Two things are first to be pondered, the persons by whom the deeds are done, then the deed itself . . . what part (*persona*) they bore, what functions were theirs . . . so that we should have here two men before our eyes, Abraham and Melchizedec. (*in Gen.* 14.18)

Abraham is a lesson in piety and trust, Melchizedec in the true priesthood, the sacrifice of thanksgiving. But also each is *Christi typus*, 'between whom and Christ many symbols are evident'. This latter is most clearly that which profits believers (*utilitas sanctorum*), indeed it is 'the matter and thing itself' of the passage.[12]

In the Epistle Dedicatory of his Commentary on Judges, a clear passage sets forth this method.

> Further, this is chiefly to be marked, that Jesus Christ the Son of God is not excluded from this sacred history. For since He is the end of the law and sum of the Scriptures, since this book pertains to the law and is a part of the Scriptures, it shows and clearly preaches Christ to its readers . . . that faith which is natural and sound includes Christ Himself, unto whom particularly and in one sense only, does it refer. For by Him the promises of God are made effectual. Wherefore while we behold the wonderful acts of the Judges, we should have before our eyes the excellent faith which shone brightly in them, and also the common deliverer of mankind, namely the Son of God Christ Jesus, whom they beheld as their Captain and Commander. And that not unworthily, for He worked by them, and by them set the people free, in admonishing them by the voices of Angels, and oracles

---

[11] *in 2 Sam.* 22.1 : the *scopus* in all his Commentaries always involves the Person of Christ as chief Actor in the Biblical drama.

[12] *Haec de personis in hac historia dixisse contenti erimus : quod ad negotium et rem ipsam, videmus quantopere sancti in afflictionibus prosint.* The term *negotium* is Ciceronic, translating the Greek πρᾶγμα for *res*. Peter Martyr's Latinity has Cicero for its master.

of Prophets, in confirming them in dangers, and at last not inconstantly but faithfully performing these things which He had before most liberally promised. Lastly, when we hear that the Hebrews, who were members of the same Christ, were sometimes oppressed and killed by their enemies, let us in them acknowledge the death and torments of our Head. And in their victories and triumphs, let us behold His resurrection, kingdom and glory. For God has framed unto us wings of His Spirit and Word: but if through our own default we become fleshly and heavy, we shall not be carried up into heaven, but along with animals be drawn downwards.

Here we see the essential doctrines—the two elements in Biblical exposition, the 'sursum corda' by the Holy Spirit as the passage from the one to the other, and all based upon the membership in Christ of the saints in any and every age.[13]

Wherever in Scripture we read of a 'private rescue' of the saints, we are to look unto Christ, inasmuch as *the lesser is contained in the greater*, and the greater is that 'principal redemption' of the Incarnate Christ.[14] These lesser patterns of death and resurrection are not only shadows of the greater, but 'sure parts', because they have the same author. Therefore 'this is no allegory' when he states:

> Whatever they were that defended the people of God in ancient times, Christ was their Head and Captain. Wherefore whatever they did in defending His members, they did as His ministers and vicars. (*in Iud.* 1.1)

Peter Martyr is well aware of the allegorical method and its implications, especially as used by Origen, but he explicitly distinguishes his method from it. The Commentaries on Samuel are most valuable on this subject. Simler in the Preface, treating of Martyr's method, states succinctly, 'He does not idly play with allegories', and in his own Preface Martyr sets forth his purpose. There is a threefold end (*finis* or *scopus*) of these Books: the life and times of the nation Israel; the Divine law, exhibited by these living examples; and the 'most useful

---

[13] Such dynamic Christological exegesis compares favourably with the scholastic fourfold principle of interpretation, not to speak of much modern exegesis. But the fourfold principle has an inner relation to the Reformed, inasmuch as we may agree that 'allegory, anagogy and tropology are not so much different senses, as applications of the one literal sense' (Turretin, in Heppe's *Reformed Dogmatics* (E.T., 1950) p. 38). Calvin's strength as an exegete arises from the same basic principle as set forth by Martyr—e.g. the 'transition' from serpent to Satan is 'not only in the way of comparison, for there truly is a literal anagogy' (*Comm. on Gen.* 3.15). The term ἀναγωγή is not used by Calvin and Martyr in its traditional sense of 'mystical' so much as in their distinctive sense of a spiritual passage from sign to signification.   [14] *in Iud.*, Intro.

end of all, namely Christ' who alone is a trustworthy Guide through life. 'For Christ alone is the end, not only of the law, but also of all these actions.' Now as the greater contains the less, so we ought to look unto Christ when we see the lesser liberations of the Hebrews. In their oppression and affliction, the Divine wrath should come to mind, and every eye turn to Christ dying on His Cross:

> For whatever may be unto pious men and members of Christ, that without controversy is to be related to Christ Himself.

The basis of this exposition is the fact that Christ is the 'fountain and head' of all the earthly benefits. When he exhorts us to 'lift up our mind from things temporary to things eternal and heavenly', therefore, it is not an improper exposition on the basis of allegory, for 'those things which in the O.T. were written concerning things temporary pertain to things eternal.' Thus, 'The true David was Christ our Saviour', because 'There is therefore a fitting analogy (*collatio*) between this David and our true David, Christ Jesus.'[15] Martyr's argument of *quemadmodum . . ita* is based on the prior fact that Christ is the *archetypus*:

> This we should know, that David shadowed in himself a type of our Saviour Christ. And so in all this history the eyes are to be referred to the archetype. (*in* 1 *Sam.* 17.58)

Peter Martyr's method of interpretation, therefore, is neither allegorical nor 'typological' in the common usage of that word, but the analogical exposition of types on the basis of Jesus Christ as archetype, and Head of His members.

> I know there are those who object that we cannot expound fitly enough unless we turn aside to allegory. But there is no firm argument here. Rather I reply, this method of exposition which we follow in this place is not properly allegory. For in this history God wishes to describe to us Christ Jesus our Saviour, not less but much more than Solomon.[16]

His main concern is to see what conforms to Christ (*convenire*

---

[15] *in* 1 *Sam.* 2.10, 22.1, 28.1.

[16] *in* 2 *Sam.* 7.13: he continues, 'Yet are not all allegories useless' and acknowledges a proper use of them. Cf. *in Iud.* 7.25, where the battle is taken as an allegory as Isaiah 9 would suggest: 'this victory is to be referred unto that delivery from sin, which we have obtained through Christ. Nor do the trumpets portend anything else than the preaching of the Gospel, now spread abroad over the whole earth . . .' Further, on the Hebrew method of allegory, cf. *in Gen.* 26.22.

Christo) in the O.T. history. His 'typology' is really his sacramental analogy in action. Thus his terms are significant: not
only *type*, but *shadow, image, form, sign* and *sacrament*.[17] In all
cases, Christ is the signification, the mystery of revelation. He
joins Himself to these signs, uniquely to the humanity He took
at the Incarnation, but analogical to that union, He 'fills' these
derivative and lesser signs by the power of His Spirit. Signs
'stir up' and 'confirm' faith; they are instruments by which
men are led to believe, by which faith is 'illumined and in-
flamed'.[18]

Thus the significance of signs is in every age the same: they
are instruments of the Holy Spirit.

> the Hebrews dedicated and initiated (temples and vessels) not by simple
> and bare words, but by adding outward rites, signs I mean, and tokens
> that could be seen—not indeed that they thought any holiness or divine
> quality was in those things, since they were inanimate and incapable of
> holiness; but they thought thus, that since the rites were instituted by God,
> the consecrated things might become instruments of the Holy Spirit, by
> which men's faith should be stirred up. Nor were they deceived, since those
> things had the Word of God for that age, and what today is to us water,
> bread and wine, was for them varied and manifold symbols in holy things.
> (*in* 1 *Reg.* 8.66, *De Templ. Ded.*)

Once again we are in the category of Word and Spirit, and
therefore of the necessity for the *sursum corda* in their right use.
For the signification was heavenly as much as is that of the
N.T. sacraments.

> The old rites before the coming of Christ were testimonies and sure seals
> of the heavenly gifts, promises and favour of God to be given. For these
> are spiritual things, nor can they be discerned with outward eyes. (*in* 2 *Reg.*
> 2.21)

The sacrifices, for instance, Martyr calls 'visible sermons' which
taught the people of Christ's Death.[19] But too often, the Jews
were amazed at the sacrifices of beasts, neither did they, as was fitting, lift
up the eyes of their minds unto Christ. (*in Iud.* 11.40)

---

[17] *Nohe . . . fuit Christi umbra, in Gen.* 5.29; *imago, in Iud.* 16.31, 1 *Sam.* 18. 11;
typus . . . et forma, in Gen. 6.18, *Lament.* 5.2; *signum* (and *symbolum*), *in Gen.* 35.1,
etc. (cf. *in* 1 *Sam.* 2.34: when the Word was *rarum et pretiosum*, outward signs were
not necessary, *Signa enim instrumenta sunt, quibus homines ad credendum facilius in-
ducuntur*); *sacramentum, in Gen.* 7.19 (ark), 9.17 (rainbow). Cf. *species, in* 2 *Sam.* 20.1.
[18] *in* 1 *Sam.* 2.34, 4.3: *ut usa eorum sp. sanct. in nobis fides illustret et accendat.*
[19] *in Iud.* 11.40, section concerning Jephtha's vow and human sacrifice; cf. for
this lifting up of eyes and heart, *in* 1 *Sam.* 2.10, 6.15.

Yet in general, this signification 'was known in those days', and indeed some of the O.T. saints—Abraham, David, Jeremiah and Isaiah for instance—beheld the mystery of Christ with the greatest clearness.[20] For the sacrificial system was the schoolhouse of Christ.

The Schooling of the Mosaic Sacrifices

God does not delight in blood *per se:* but by this pedagogy He taught the people (*in Iud.* 11.40).

And that worship was a kind of pedagogy, for the Fathers were taught that the death which they had brought on themselves by their sins, was through the great goodness of God translated from them to the sacrifices. And Christ was clearly manifested, who took upon Himself all our sins and death, and so died, that we might be absolved. This was the education of the Mosaic sacrifices. (*in 2 Reg.* 3.27)

The sacrifices taught two things: the seriousness of sin, its guilt and death, deserved by the sinner but graciously transferred to the innocent sacrifice offered; and secondly,

that Christ should be that sacrifice that was to take away the sins of the world, unto whom our death and damnation should be transferred. (*in Iud.* 11.40)

It is unfortunate that Martyr's lecture notes on Leviticus were never published,[21] but we have his Propositions or summary of his notes. In those we see his doctrine of O.T. sacrifice.

A sacrifice is a ceremony in which something is offered to God according to His precept, to obtain the remission of sins, not only gracious but true, through the faith of Jesus Christ, there represented and exhibited. Faith is accommodated to various promises of God, but what justifies refers to Christ Himself. When in the Epistle to the Hebrews or elsewhere in the holy Scriptures it is said that the ancient ceremonies gave no remission of sins, that must be understood, by the power of the work, or without faith in Christ. Moses spoke nowhere more plainly of the death of Christ than in the laws of the sacrifices. (*Prop. ex Levit.* 1, *nec.* 1-4)

The O.T. sacrifices 'draw all their dignity from the sacrifice of Christ'.[22] For they consisted of three things, thanksgiving for benefits received, an exhortation to godly living, and 'a token and shadow of Christ'.[23] Of this last Martyr can speak in the strongest terms:

[20] *in* 1 *Sam.* 3.14, *in* 1 *Cor.* 10.2.   [21] see Appendix A (1).
[22] *in* 1 *Cor.* 11.20.   [23] *in* 1 *Cor.* 5.8.

And in every solemn act, through the death of the animal offered in sacrifice, the sacrifice of Christ was apprehended by faith, by which, believing in Him, they were justified. There were also in them a celebration of divine praises, a holy congregation, the administration of the Word of God, the communion of the faithful, and the confession of sins.
(*in* 1 *Cor.* 5.8)

The faith of the old Fathers, by which they regarded Christ and embraced Him in the signification of those sacrifices, justified and obtained remission of sins. (*in Rom.* 11.27)

This doctrine of sacrifice is analogical—it depends on the proper movement from sign to thing signified.

When the old Fathers knew that they were reconciled to God through the sacrifices, and yet understood that the beasts killed were not more excellent in nature than those for whom they were offered, they necessarily concluded that the worthiness of the sacrifices depended on something else: whereupon they fled to the promises of Messiah and acknowledged Him therein to be preferred before them. (*Prop. ex. Levit.* 1, *prob.* 4)

For what is pleasing to God in the sacrifices is 'the thing signified, namely Christ', apart from whom they are 'dead bodies without life'.[24] Thus were the sacrifices the chief O.T. signs, ministering 'spiritual sanctification' unto the Hebrews inasmuch as it was the 'selfsame matter' which they signified— the Death of Christ as the object of faith.[25]

Meanwhile was the sacrificing: but what were those sacrifices? They ought in the sacrifices to apprehend by faith the future death of Christ.
(*in* 2 *Sam.* 15.13)
When faith is removed, all outward things are empty. (*in* 1 *Cor.* 10.7)

For in those beasts killed, Christ's death was manifested to the faith of the Elders . . . the faith which embraced Christ in those rites brought salvation to the Elders, just as today the outward exercises of the sacraments or commandments profits not, but faith alone brings salvation, for it sees that under the enfolding of sensible signs, heavenly gifts are set forth unto us.
(*in Rom.* 3.21)

In the O.T. sacrificial system, therefore, Peter Martyr finds the elements of Christian worship, for the movement of grace and faith is always the same, making present in the union of faith the Christ who was to them *future* and is to us *above*— neither mode of separation prevents the 'effectual signification' by these instruments of the Holy Spirit, of the nourishment of

[24] *in* 1 *Sam.* 15.22.   [25] *in* 1 *Cor.* 10.6; cf. *in Gen.* 28.12.

His Person. Thus does sacrifice always pass over into sacrament: the O.T. saint is carried above the sacrificial signs to
the vivifying Lord who unites him to Himself.

The One Sacrament

> That the Fathers were justified we doubt not: and they could not be
> justified without faith in Christ . . . what have we in our sacraments, which
> we receive as the chief and principal thing? Is it not Christ? But the
> Apostle testifies that the old Fathers received Him in their sacraments.
> *(in Rom.* 8.15)

From the point of view of the substance or matter of the
sacraments, their *signification*, there is but one sacrament, Christ
Himself. Christ in His own Person is *the* sacrament, in its true
sense of *mystery*, and it is to Him that all sacraments correspond.
This is the theme of the next Chapter, but its significance here
is that the O.T. sacramental communication is equally a communication of the vivifying and nourishing Person of Jesus
Christ.

> Many infer . . . that the sacraments of the old Fathers were shadows
> of our sacraments, yet not one with them . . . There can be no other matter
> *(res)* of the sacraments appointed than Christ Himself. *(in* 1 *Cor.* 10.6)
>
> we grant that with regard to the outward signs, there is some difference
> between their sacraments and ours: but yet with regard to the things
> signified by the sacraments, this is found to be nothing at all. *(in Iud.* 2.23)
>
> the kind of signs might be diverse, but the things signified are not. Indeed
> there, as among ourselves, Christ Jesus is the same Mediator, outside whom
> there is no salvation. Therefore as to nature—or as I may say, substance
> and essence—the Church of the Jews is the same as ours. *(in* 1 *Cor.* 10.1)

The distinction between the substance and accidents in sacraments—far different from the common scholastic definition!—
reflects the nature of the Covenant:

> one and the same covenant between God and man, are the old and new
> testament . . . Briefly, what difference is between the testaments consists
> not in the substance of the covenant, but in the accidents. *(in* 1 *Sam.* 2.10)
>
> Wherefore the substance, matter and Spirit are in either testament one
> and the same: but there is found some difference in qualities . . . *(in Rom.*
> 11.7)
>
> Christ was in the covenant, as the Mediator between both parties.
> *(in Iud.* 2.32, *De Foedere)*

How false therefore is it to take the O.T. *signa* either as bare

symbols without present power, or as earthly and carnal signs![26]
For Christ was truly present to the Hebrews:

> Sacraments in the Old Testament not only signified but exhibited the
> grace of God. (*Prop. ex Gen.* 16-17, *nec.* 5)

> When the Prophets and Patriarchs were taught by the Spirit of God,
> they perceived and contemplated clearly and openly in the Sacraments of
> the Law both Christ and the redemption given through that gift, with eyes
> of faith.[27]

At this point we should note two questions which are raised
by the above outline, and which Martyr himself notes explicitly.[28] First, why are our sacraments of greater force if the
substance is thus the same with the O.T. sacraments? Because,
he replies, Christ is now given and the sacraments can exhibit
a past event.[29] Our sacraments are fewer in number, clearer
in symbolism, for 'more distinct is something done than expected'.[30]

The second question is the deeper one, already noted by us.
How could they have actually partaken of the same Christ
before the Incarnation? For Martyr's position is emphatic:

> Neither could the Jews of antiquity have life and the Spirit except
> through the flesh of Christ. (*Def.* 706)

This question is answered in two ways. A primary reference is
given to the *eternal* significance of the Incarnation and Death
of Christ, which God 'regards from all eternity'.[31]

> Of what more force unto salvation is Christ's death now, as already past,
> than it was in the old age, when it was looked for as coming? Doubtless
> on each side, faith is required. (*in Rom.* 3.9)

[26] E.g. *Def.* 54-58: the O.T. is not *tota typi*, and it is blasphemy to call its sacraments *vappae*. Cf. *in* 1 *Cor.* 10.6, they 'were types of our sacraments, but also had
the same matter spiritually comprehended'; *Def.* 702: since their sacraments
foreshadowed Christ, they are *spiritualis*; *in Iud.* 1.36: 'The Jews are occupied in
the holy Scriptures, which they do not understand aright, nor with such spiritual
sense as the Church knows them, but take them in an earthly and carnal manner';
and 2.23: God promised them 'the chief felicity, which pertains unto souls'.
[27] *Dialogus de Utr. Nat.*, pp. 131ff, where Martyr rejects the Lutheran distinction
in modes of predication—personal, sacramental and ceremonial-typical—and
identifies the latter two. Brentius wished rather to identify the first with the
unio hypostatica, the second with a consubstantial presence in the bread and wine,
and the third with the O.T. rites and figures.
[28] *in* 1 *Sam.* 1.4, a most valuable section comparing the sacraments.
[29] Cf. *in* 1 *Cor.* 10.2: *Illi venturum expectabant, nos venisse confitemur.*
[30] *in* 1 *Sam.* 21.3. Martyr often quotes Augustine on this point: *sacramenta
nostra pauciora esse, faciliora, significantiora et magis augusta quam veterum fuerint.*
[31] *in Rom.* 4.11.

The unity of grace and faith thus imply that

> they received by faith the flesh and blood of Christ which were to be given for our salvation, and we by faith and spirit embrace them as already given. (*Epitome* 2.6)

This is Martyr's constant stress, that faith always means union with Christ, so that what is demonstrated to us was promised of old, but just as we eat what is already given to suffering and death for us, so also they ate by faith 'what was to be crucified and dead'.[32] The *matter* of the sacraments is always the same— the meat and drink of their sacraments is one with our meat and drink.[33]

From this Martyr passes to a more positive historical correspondence with our Eucharist, in the *Manna* and in the *Peace-offering*. Manna is an obvious sacrament of the nourishment of Christ, which it shows 'in enigma' and our Eucharist shows 'in image' (*in specie*).[34]

> Manna rained down from heaven, which was not without miracle; in like manner Christ had the divine nature . . . Manna nourished and was given abundantly: Christ also is our meat and sufficient to nourish many, yea even all . . . (*in* 1 *Cor.* 10.3)
>
> The sacrament was the same, as regards substance, of Manna among the old Fathers, as of the Eucharist in the New Testament. Manna was an outward food, and could not give eternal life, but it had Christ joined with it. (*Prop. ex Exod.* 16, *nec.* 10, 14)

The peace-offerings show a more striking likeness to the Eucharist, since in them the Hebrews 'feasted and rejoiced together before the Lord'.[35]

> Because a participation of Christ was obtained in the eating of those things offered in sacrifices, therefore they were suitable for human consumption, just as are the symbols of the Lord's Supper . . . In the sacrifice of peace-offerings, the Holy Communion was exercised among the faithful; for there Christ was not only set forth to be believed, but was received.
> (*Prop. ex Levit.* 1, *nec.* 7; 2, *nec.* 5)

and that was the Holy Communion of those times, since in these victims the holy Fathers ate the body and blood of Christ, as we do today in the bread and wine of the Eucharist. For they not only fixed their eyes on the flesh set before them, but by faith beheld Christ, who was going to assume flesh, that by His death the sins of the whole world might be expiated. (*in* 1 *Sam.* 1.4)

---

[32] *Dial.* 133.   [33] *Tract.* 8.   [34] *Def.* 696.   [35] *in Iud.* 16.31.

There are other likenesses to our Eucharist, the showbread
and bread of Melchizedec, for instance, which the Early Fathers
often cite. In this respect, Martyr declares that the showbread
and bread of the sacrifices were two things: *signs* of the true
body of Christ and the coming heavenly food, to be eaten
spiritually by believers; and *types* of our Eucharist.[36] He also
sees a kind of dispensation of the O.T. communion, since no
flesh was eaten in the sacrifices before the Flood, but

after the Flood, they not only offered sacrifices but themselves ate of the
sacrifices: which seemed to be a singular benefit of God, as though now He
deigned to call them to His own table, and admit them to communion
with Himself. (*in* 1 *Sam.* 9.13)

In a significant passage of the *Defensio*, Martyr states that since
Christ may rightly be termed the *corpus* of all preceding shadows
and sacrifices, therefore the O.T. saints seeing the signs but
cleaving to the promise of His coming, spiritually feasted upon
their Saviour and so *ate His flesh*.[37]

Thus we find in Peter Martyr's teaching a doctrine of Christ's
presence in the pre-Incarnational age which preserves the
sacramental-analogical nature of revelation, and which gives
ultimate revelatory significance to the O.T. history.

In the oppression and deliverance of the godly which is read in the Old
Testament, we have the death and resurrection of Christ, not in a figure
but truly, since Christ truly suffers in His members. (*Oratio de Res. Christi*)
these things which preceded were not only types and shadows of the Lord's
death and resurrection, but in one way also had in them the very truth
itself of those things. For since those holy men suffered many grievous
things, and since in time help and deliverance came by God—inasmuch as
they were members of Christ it follows that Christ both suffered and was
delivered in them. Wherefore we say that the passion and resurrection of
Christ began even from the first times, but afterwards took place more
manifestly in Christ Himself, and yet become still more evident through
the present death of the Church, which it daily abides in labours and
sorrows, expecting the blessed resurrection of the flesh. (*in* 1 *Cor.* 15.3)

[36] *Def.* 400.
[37] *Manducatio carnis eius, quam veteres quoque habuerunt*—*Def.* 65; cf. p. 58: bread
and wine referred to the coming Redeemer, and so were *symbola Christi* to the
old Fathers.

CHAPTER III

CHRIST AND THE NEW TESTAMENT 'SIGNS'

The Divine-Human Person

We are constrained to confess (as faith itself witnesses to us) that this Christ is none other than a unique person in whom the divine and human natures are joined in an indissoluble bond . . . God and man in the person of Christ in perpetual society.[1]

THE Child of Mary was assumed by 'the merciful God, truly the word from eternity', who formed a union which was true and therefore eternal. The 'blessed God and man Jesus Christ' became in the Incarnation the New Man, for 'He was made to be such an one for our use and behalf'—

the Divine Word has cleansed our nature, by heaping divine gifts upon it. And this is not to be understood regarding that man which He assumed, but all those who in true faith are joined together with Him as His members.

Peter Martyr stresses, like Irenaeus, the 'for us'—He cleansed our nature and clothed Himself with it, 'to make us partakers of His divine nature'. Christians have obtained in Christ 'a participation of the divine nature', 'their nature is made divine'.

This Divine movement of Incarnation involved no denial of the truth of either nature. In a sermon on Philippians 2, Peter Martyr discusses the familiar problem of the Two Natures.[2] The determinative factor is always the Divine nature:

(Paul) sets forth Christ for an example unto us . . . Among men there is no fit example, it must be taken out of heaven. He that sees not the divinity of Christ sees nothing.

Thus although he speaks of Christ as setting aside (*seponere*) His majesty and glory for a while, this is not as if these are qualities which may be separated from the essence of God: 'neither nature is changed into the other'. Rather, Christ is

[1] *Catech.* 5. Quotations in the first paragraph are from sections 5 and 10–12.
[2] *Oratio de Morte Christi, L.C.*, pp. 1038ff.

like a king who hides his majesty while he courts his beloved as a commoner in order to reveal his love:

> First the power of the Word of God was manifested through His creation and providence, now is His love demonstrated.

The key thought is this *hiding* or *veiling* of the Divinity:

> He did not put off (*abdicare*) divinity, He cannot deny Himself; and He who is the cause that all things are, did not Himself cease to exist: but He hid Himself under man, one most abject.

Yet He did 'reveal in some way' (*aliquo modo exereret*) His divinity, so that the predestinate were able—aided by the signs given[3]—to grasp His divinity through His humanity. His humanity was like a veil (*velum*) which He put between—'As we see the sun when a cloud intervenes, so was He obscured.'

Therefore 'form' (μορφή or *forma*) is the term used for both, 'as well servant as God', showing that neither nature is changed into the other. For 'It is not the property of form to corrupt, but to preserve.' In His obedience, Christ remained equal with the Father in regard to His divinity, and obeyed *amicus amico*.[4] And yet we say,

> The Lord of life submitted Himself unto death, and being immortal, died.

If this is taken as compromising His humanity, then the Marcionites and transubstantiators will triumph, by saying 'He seemed to be man, but was not: it seems to be bread, but is not.'

How are the two natures related in Christ? Without confusion or separation:

> Between this Scylla and Charybdis we must navigate carefully, that is: Unity of person is retained thus, so that the properties of the natures remain distinct, not mixed or confused. (*Dial.* 13A)

Nestorius on the one hand and Eutyches on the other, these are the tempters to error in the doctrine of Christ. Peter Martyr's *Dialogue Of The Two Natures in Christ* is a Treatise on this very subject. There he works out the 'without separation and with-

---

[3] E.g. the Father's voice, the Angels, the Dove, the Sea's 'becoming firm under His feet'.

[4] Cf. *in* 1 *Sam.* 7.24: in the Incarnation, the Trinity acts as a whole in respect of the *actio*, but the Son alone in respect of the *opus*. Thus Christ is 'both efficient cause and effect'. The works of the Trinity *ad interna* are *singularia*, those *ad externa* are *indivisa*.

out confusion' (ἀχωρίστως, ἀσυγχύτως) of the Chalcedonian
Christology, the 'orthodox doctrine', in opposition to the
Lutheran doctrine of the ubiquity of the Body of Christ.

> Christ is one Person, but has two natures united in the same hypostasis
> with Himself: yet both of them complete and without violation in the
> properties . . . You indeed think that the persons are torn asunder if divinity
> is established where the humanity is absent. This is by no means true: it
> suffices that deity, as immense and infinite, supports and substantiates the
> humanity in the hypostasis, wherever it may be . . .Truly we make one
> hypostasis, and in that we unite two natures most compactly, but each of
> them in its own mode and extent. (*Dial.* 10A, 10F, 12D)

Martyr's debate with Brentius in the *Dialogus* is conducted
according to the teaching of the relationship of analogy as
outlined in Chapter 1 above. When Brentius (in the Dialogue,
Pantachus![5]) demands that the unity of Christ means that
humanity is to be found wherever deity is, Martyr objects that
he is speaking of the two natures equivocally (ὁμωνυμίας, *id est
aequivocationis*) so that they are confused in the manner of
Eutychean doctrine; he must learn to preserve the proper *ratio*
between them. For otherwise he will 'annul the sacrament of
the Incarnation'.[6] And just here, in the definition *sacramentum
incarnationis*, we reach the heart of Peter Martyr's sacramental
theology.

The 'hypostatic union' of the two natures in Christ means
that they are neither separated nor confused, but related in a
unique analogue according to which the human nature is the
ultimate *Signum* of revelation, the effectual medium of divinity.

> We do not perceive the divinity of Christ, except enveloped in flesh.
> Nor can our faith otherwise aspire to the divine nature, mercy, goodness
> and felicity, except through the humanity of Christ, which as a kind of
> intermediary (*sequestra*) is placed in the middle between us and God, since
> it is joined with the divinity . . . For the humanity of Christ is like a kind
> of channel, through which not only sanctification, but also all the life-giving
> grace can flow from God to us . . . For the Spirit and Word of God, that
> is the divine nature, is the efficient cause of our sanctification. But the
> medium through which He transfuses that sanctification to us, is the hu-
> manity of Christ. Therefore if we would speak rightly, the human nature is
> rather the instrument of the divinity, that is of the Word and Spirit. (*Def.*
> 590, 606, 609)

The flesh of Christ thus becomes the unique *locus* of revelation

---

[5] meaning 'everywhere'.   [6] *Dial.* 12C.

H

and the unique *medium* for communion with Him.[7] It is in this context that Martyr quotes Gelasius, that Jesus Christ is 'the principal mystery' (*mysterium principalis*). On the basis of this doctrine of Christ as Himself the unique Mystery or Sacrament, the archetypal Analogue, Peter Martyr develops his doctrine of the sacraments.

The Flesh of Christ in Incarnation and Eucharist

The analogical relationship of the Sacrament to the Person of Christ was first developed and used in controversy by the Early Fathers. Gelasius and Theodoret[8] are the most explicit. Gelasius reasoned thus, against Eutyches: the image and similitude of the Body and Blood of Christ is celebrated in the action of the mysteries; in this image, the substance of bread remains in its proper nature; therefore in the principal mystery the substance of the humanity of Christ must remain.[9] Theodoret stated, 'Compare the image with the archetype, and you will see the similitude.'[10] Peter Martyr comments:

> The Fathers proved there to be in Christ two perfect natures, through a simile taken from the Eucharist. Therefore we may argue thus: Just as two natures were in Christ not exchanged but distinct, so in the Eucharist are two natures, namely bread and the body of Christ, distinct but not confused by the conversion of one into the other . . . such bread remains in the Eucharist, as human nature in Christ . . . As the human is in Christ, so bread is in the Eucharist: But the human nature in Christ is whole and perfect: Therefore the nature of bread in the Eucharist is perfect. (*Def.* 386, 393, 395)

The hypostatic union does not divinize the humanity of Christ: the eucharistic bread is not converted into deity. The Fathers' analogy proved the nature of the relationship between the humanity and divinity of Christ from its image in the Eucharist; in the sixteenth century, when their Christology had

---

[7] Cf. *Def.* 60: the life-giving divinity of Christ is communicated through the humanity; so that we must eat His flesh by faith; *in* 1 *Cor.* 15.12: His divinity did not assume the humanity 'to shut up His benefits within its bounds, but through it to derive the strength of His goodness' to all; *Def.* 294, on Cyril: the Word of God is not edible, 'since we do not draw life from Him without some medium. But there is placed in between the human nature of Christ, which Cyril says is proper for eating . . . by the spiritual eating of faith.'

[8] See Appendix B.

[9] *Contra Eut.* (*Def.* 388, 585f, *Disp.* I.1, *Tract.* 31, etc.). It will be obvious why Rome is somewhat embarrassed by this teaching of *Pope* Gelasius!

[10] *Dialog.* 2 (*Def.* 389, 575-581, *Tract.* 29f).

been accepted but the Eucharist had become infected with the
Eutychean heresy, Martyr reverses the analogy and proves, on
the basis of the Chalcedonian Christology, two natures in the
Eucharist, bread and the Body of Christ. For transubstantiation
is essentially the error of Eutyches applied to the Eucharist.
The two errors are complementary:

the heretics who deny the flesh of Christ, destroy the sacrament of the
Eucharist. (*in* 1 *Cor.* 10.16)

you rob the bread of substance and despoil the body of Christ of quantity.
(*Disp.* II.2)

According to Peter Martyr, the true matter of the Eucharist
is plain and easy, so long as we keep to three things: sense,
Christ's humanity, and 'the received definition of a sacrament'.
But because of the adversaries it has become 'more intricate
than any blind labyrinth'.[11] Here again we see the implication
of the analogy, or *ratio sacramenti*. Christ instituted the sacrament so that all things should be done sacramentally: transubstantiation means adding something more than the ratio
of the sacrament requires.[12] Martyr explicitly acknowledges

[11] *Epit., Praef.*
[12] *Tract.* 21. Cf. *Def.* Obj. 15 on Berengarius; Obj. 20, 35, *etc.* and Part III
below on the ratio. This central doctrine of Peter Martyr's teaching on the sacraments is borne out in striking manner by the original development of the Romanist
doctrine of transubstantiation. The doctrine had its conscious beginning in the
ninth-century controversy between Radbertus and Ratramnus. The latter
opposed Radbertus' theory of transubstantiation, on the grounds that the Body
of Christ is received *in mysterio, in sacramento et spiritualiter* and not *in veritate, in specie
et corporaliter.* In the eleventh century Berengarius took up this doctrine of Ratramnus with such vigour that he was excommunicated by Leo IX. After imprisonment and threats, he accepted the form of recantation dictated by Cardinal
Humbert in 1059, which he later refuted. It is this text of the *Ego Berengarius*
which reveals the essence of the Romanist error: that bread and wine are 'after
consecration not only a sacrament but also the true body and blood of our Lord
Jesus Christ, and sensibly, not only in a sacrament but in truth are touched and
broken with the hands of the priests, and crushed with the teeth of the faithful'
(*post consecrationem non solum sacramentum, sed etiam verum corpus et sanguinem Domini
nostri Jesus Christi esse, et sensualiter, non solum sacramento, sed in veritate manibus sacer-
dotum tractari, frangi, et fidelium dentibus atteri*). This is the doctrine given the official
name of 'transubstantiation' by the Fourth Lateran Council decree in 1215:
Christ's 'body and blood are truly contained under the appearance of bread and
wine in the sacrament of the altar, being transubstantiated, the bread into the
body, the wine into the blood' (*corpus et sanguis in sacramento altaris sub speciebus
panis et vini veraciter continentur, transubstantiatis pane in corpus et vino in sanguinem*).
(Cf. Cosin's 'Hist. of Popish Trans.'; Hebert's 'Hist. of Uninspired Teaching',
II, p. 136; for the influence of Ratramnus on the Reformers, cf. A. Barclay,
op. cit., Chapter 19.) It is this 'not only . . . but also' which betrays the Romanist
destruction of the sacramental analogy, and acceptance of the relation of identity
in the Eucharist. But we ought to note the modern movement within Romanism

the Word of God as the constituting factor in 'the analogy of this sacrament and the power of signifying', which the symbols do not have before consecration; yet on the basis of the Incarnate Word as archetype and the Holy Spirit as effective Agent, he is prepared to apply the concept of analogy in its rightful meaning. The relation of the bread and wine in the Eucharist to the Body and Blood of Christ will therefore be *proportionaliter* to the relation between divinity and humanity in the Person of Christ. That is, there will be likeness *and difference* of proportion. This is exactly what we find him teaching. There must be in the Eucharist a like relationship—but we must also

retain a certain variety in the mode and form of union. For the divine nature and the human are joined in Christ otherwise than the sign and the thing signified in the Eucharist. For in Christ those two natures are joined in one hypostasis. (*Def.* 388)

Yet not in all respects is the similitude and ratio the same, concerning the two natures joined in the same union in Christ, and the Body of Christ signified by bread in the manner and ratio of a sacrament. But from that simile only this is received, namely that both natures ought to remain whole and sound. (*in* 1 *Cor.* 11.24)

it is not stated that out of the Body of Christ and the nature of bread, one subject (*suppositus*) is made, as of the divine nature and the human nature in Christ. (*Tract.* 42)

Martyr's analogy is clear: The Son of God joined Himself to humanity by the Incarnation in one *hypostasis*, yet without separation or confusion of either nature. In this gracious accommodation to man's need, God has constituted a certain form of relatedness with His creatures. The incarnational form is not to be repeated, as if the Son were to form further hypostases with His creatures, but it is to be reproduced proportionately to its nature. Thus in the Eucharistic relation between bread and the Body of Christ, Peter Martyr declares the *difference* of proportion to lie in the unique hypostasis of the two natures in Christ, while the *likeness* of proportion lies in the 'without confusion and without separation' of the two natures. Indeed, his analogical reasoning preserves the proportionality

(marked by de la Taille's *Mysterium Fidei*) which indicates 'a return to a deeper understanding of the sacramental and eschatological significance of the Eucharist' (T. F. Torrance, 'Eschatology and the Eucharist', *Intercommunion*, S.C.M., 1952, p. 303).

on all levels of Christ's relatedness to His creatures. The form of relation is 'exceptional and unique',[13] but operates variously according to the nature of the creatures: the analogy between the union of Christ with *us* and with the *signs*, for instance, is 'from the greater to the less by a negative' because His union with men is greater than with symbols.[14]

We may sum up this introductory analysis of Martyr's sacramental doctrine as follows. A sacrament is a particular form of relatedness of two disparate terms, namely the relation of *analogy*.

> In all sacraments there should be an analogy or proportion observed and retained between the sacrament and the matter of the sacrament, which analogy Cicero called a convenience. (*Disp.* II, first speech)

Therefore the *mysterium* in the sacramental relation is not so much what the elements *are* as what they *signify*[15]—and the signification in every sacrament is the Person of Christ, 'total Christ', the Divine-human Lord.

The Communication of the Properties

In this teaching about the sacramental analogy, Peter Martyr is well aware of the deep problem posed not only by the 'excessive speech of the Fathers' but by Scripture itself:

> But we ought to know that things by nature called disjunctives are yet by the institution of God so conjoined that both names and properties communicate with the other. For what could be more distant than the divine nature and the human? . . . Yet on account of the communication of properties Christ says that (the human) is truly in heaven at the same time. Thus in sacraments there is, by the institution of God, a like union between the symbols and the thing signified . . . But it is such a relation that what properly agrees with the things is attributed to the symbols, and what agrees with the symbols is in turn attributed to the things. (*in* 1 *Sam.* 26.19)

Martyr acknowledges a certain kind of communication of the properties (*communicatio idiomatum*) which attends the analogical relationship. He had worked this out in his Commentary on Aristotle's doctrine of analogy as follows:

[13] *Relatio eximia et singularis—Def.* 642.
[14] *Tract.* 53. For further analogical reasoning, cf. *Def.* 316 (Scripture 'consists in sign and thing signified'), *in Iud.* 9.25 (the Holy Spirit and human will in conversion), *in* 1 *Cor.* 3.3 (the Spirit and the ministers of the Church).
[15] *Def.* 31.

the same name is imparted to many, and by the same ratio agrees with them, but through one is communicated to the other. Nor do all things called equal in name participate straightway in definition, but the nature signified by definition belongs to one of them properly, but through this falls and passes to the other . . . they are analogues of various numbers among themselves, but not in reality univocal. (*in Arist. Eth.*, p. 136)

Analogy brings with it a sharing of the names, so that the relation appears to be univocity instead of analogy. When this seeming identity of the terms is referred to a real communication and therefore a real conjunction, heresy works itself out from the nominal communication to posit a real communication. For as Theodoret said, 'this is what causes the heretics to err, the conjunction of names'.[16]

You assert a communication between the properties not verbally but even of the thing itself! (*Dial.* 131)

Peter Martyr accepts this problem as a serious one—does not Scripture say that the Son of God suffered, and that the Risen Man is glorified?[17] In respect of the Divine nature, Martyr points out that this is a case of the impropriety of our theological language: the Lord of glory 'is said to be' crucified, although properly speaking, passion does not pertain to the Word. In respect of the human nature, only those properties are communicated (in reality) 'of which human nature is capable', so that immensity and ubiquity, for example, cannot be communicated in reality, only in name, by what Martyr terms the *verbalis communicatio*. For to grant a real communication of all the properties 'would dissolve the hypostatic union'.[18]

We grant that the things universally spoken of Christ are sometimes to be understood of the one nature and sometimes of the other: yet Christ Himself is but one person and substance. So we say, the immortal God was born, crucified and dead. For there is a certain communication of the properties by the wonderful connection of the two natures, which Nestorius attempted to separate. (*in Rom.* 9.5)

The details of this problem will concern us in Part III, but here we must understand Martyr's insistence upon the whole-

---

[16] *Et hoc est quod facit errare haereticos, nominum coniunctio*—quoted in *Dial.* 42B; again, *unio facit nomina communia* (35E).

[17] *Dial.* 30—cf. the whole of *Loc.* II, *De Proprietate Naturarum in Christo*; pp. 30ff deal explicitly with the *comm. idiom.*

[18] *Ibid.*, 42F; cf. Wallace, *op. cit.*, pp. 161ff, 229ff. For subsequent Reformed teaching on the *phraseologia sacramentalis* see Heppe, *op. cit.*, XXIV. 13.

ness of Christ even while maintaining that the 'attribution of properties' must be closely examined to see 'of which nature it is spoken'.[19]

> Wherever the Son of God is, it is undoubtedly He that has joined with Him the human nature; though not so that He makes it present in actual fact wherever He is, since for its own truth it is necessary that it should be bound within its own limits, and be contained in a certain place. (*in* 1 *Cor.* 15.47)

If we understand the 'whole Christ' in a 'personal' manner, we acknowledge His omnipresence. Therefore just as the Divine nature made room for the sufferings of the human 'by a kind of dispensation of grace for our salvation',[20] so also the human nature, in respect of the hypostasis, characterizes eternally the Son of God, so that He is always the Word made *flesh*, even though that risen Body is 'located' at the right hand of the Father:

> For wherever the Word is, He has always joined with Him the human nature; and if that is not always in as many places, yet He has it coexisting with Him. Therefore we may say, the Word of God, who is everywhere, is that Word that has conjoined the human nature in the same hypostasis, and as a true man should, this is finite and kept in heaven, and as Peter says, will be retained there until the last day. (*Def.* 295)

Thus Peter Martyr outlines a Christology which safeguards the truth of each nature, while maintaining the dynamic unity of the Person of Christ. And the nature of their relationship implies that 'verbal communication' or sharing of the names, which analogy involves.

> It is also to be observed that since the divine nature of Christ is present most truly to us, therefore through alternation and communication of the properties, the same can be said of His humanity. (*Def.* 637 (II.10))

This dynamic view of the Person of Christ, and the fact that the sacrament corresponds to Him, means that His Death and Resurrection are central in Christological doctrine, and possess a correspondent centrality in the doctrine of the Sacrament. This is because the Analogue is not an Object, nor even a passive Subject, but One who *acts in history*. The relationship

---

[19] *Disp.* II.1.—Chedsey had affirmed a real *comm. idiom.* Cf. Martyr's letter *Dominis Polonis* (*L.C.*, p. 1109) for the same doctrines answering Lysman's questions of Christology.
[20] *in* 1 *Sam.* 13.32.

of the Two Natures in Christ is not a problem of logic, for this relationship is revealed to us according to a historical pattern. We are not faced with the problem of the possibility of Incarnation, but with the problem of the Incarnate Word.[21] The heart of the analogy is His Death and His Resurrection, and this images itself in the analogical action of the sacrament as descent and ascent.

The Death of Christ

The end of all Scripture is Christ crucified. (*in* 1 *Cor.* 1.23)

there is but one principal and excellent truth, to which all other truths are directed, namely that Christ the Son of God suffered for us, that by Him we might receive forgiveness of sins—what wonder is it if our faith have respect to this one thing chiefly? . . . since He is the end of all Scripture, He is also the sum and principal object of our faith . . . For the dignity of faith, like other faculties of its kind, is derived from its objects. (*De Iustif.* 71)

Peter Martyr's constant theme is the Death of Christ, for it can 'never be praised or considered enough by us'.[22] Such a theme means that man's attitude to God will be primarily one of *thankfulness,* and this is precisely the keynote of Martyr's whole theology, especially his doctrine of the sacraments. His usual term for the Lord's Supper is simply *Eucharist,* that is, 'thanksgiving'.

Justly therefore may we rejoice, that by faith we are made partakers of so great a benefit, since Christ our Head took upon Himself all the rebukes and ignominies due for our sins, and utterly abolished them. (*Catech.* 15)

Christ is the *pascha* through a trope . . . By this sacrifice in times past the Israelites were released from their Egyptian bondage: but we through the death of Christ are rescued from hell, death, sin and the devil. (*in* 1 *Cor.* 5.7)

He gave unto us His righteousness, and took upon Himself our sins.
(*De Morte Christi*)

It is this tremendous act of grace, the humility of God's descent even unto death and hell, which bends all his thinking to its own pattern. And just as the Trinity is involved in Creation and Incarnation, so also in the Death of Christ.

[21] A notable summary of this basic Reformed position is given by W. W. Bryden in *The Christian's Knowledge of God* (Thorn Press, Toronto, 1940), where he recognizes the Incarnation as the 'final' and 'fundamental' form of the paradox of revelation. Cf. pp. 114ff regarding the Romanist doctrines of revelation, Church and Mass. 'The true Reformed Churchman finds that he must never transcend the incarnation-miracle from the human rational side' (p. 116).
[22] *Catech.* 13.

When we behold all these things, I beseech you let us with eyes of faith look into the most sacred breast of the Lord, and we shall see the incredible flame of charity, and inestimable fire of His love, by which the whole world might be kindled, if it were acknowledged with one word. As He made the world could He have redeemed us, but He would not, that we might understand His love . . . Yet the will of His Son sprang from the will of the Father: in so loving us He obeyed His Father. Now we may be sure that the Father loves us: 'For He so loved us that He gave His only-begotten Son.' This is to be drawn to the Father by the Son . . . In the death of the Son the Father's love shines upon us. (*De Morte Christi*)

Although Martyr acknowledges an objective need to 'balance' the world's sin and guilt, yet he does not think of the Father as delivering the Son according to a forensic scheme of atonement.

God could have been content with any other thing. But His will was rather to have this: not to feed His eyes or mind on the afflictions and punishments of Christ . . . He saw that by this means alone might His love towards us be most perfectly declared; and also to set forth an example of a most holy life for men to follow. (*in Rom.* 5.8)

The necessity in the Death of Christ lies in the Divine providence and will, which chose this particular way in the freedom of grace; the fact that the Death was pleasing unto God is grounded similarly in the 'unmeasurable charity and love' of the Father. The Son is 'a pledge of God's love', indeed is the very God Himself, who

vouchsafed to come Himself, and to suffer a most bitter death upon the Cross. (*in Rom.* 5.8)

Martyr notes the terrible shamefulness of the Cross and its intense suffering. Both are related to the Christian life, its consolation in humiliation and persecution.

The Cross of Christ makes all things acceptable, if it is grasped by faith. By it our sins are forgiven, our concupiscence broken and not imputed to us, the devil is vanquished, we are delivered from the law, from death and condemnation . . . By it hell is conquered. (*De Morte Christi*)

This severity in Christ's Death is also related to the justice of God, who deals not lightly with the quality and quantity of human sin, and to the human conscience, for man could not rest elsewhere than in this Death of the Son—he could find no comfort 'unless the severe sentence against Christ had preceded'.[23]

[23] *Catech.* 17.

In this teaching, the Life of Christ is not regarded as irrelevant, for Martyr takes seriously the humanity of Jesus as the Christian's example.[24] But His entire life was shaped by the approaching Death as the ultimate moment in the movement of humility. Indeed, Martyr never separates Incarnation, Life, Death, Resurrection, Ascension and Return as discrete events externally related to one another. The Death and Resurrection may be called 'the principal points of our religion', but this is because they *sum up* all the other events and circumstances.[25] Thus he states explicitly that the Death of Christ gives an understanding of 'all the mysteries of Christ' from Nativity to Cross and burial, just as His Resurrection sets forth the things that follow. It is therefore a false question to ask whether faith is directed to the Death or the Resurrection of Christ, although Martyr agrees with Augustine that faith 'chiefly consists' in the Resurrection by which we are justified.[26] What is most important in this regard, and what allows their nominal separation, is the 'elegant analogy and proportion' that obtains between the Death and our faith, and the Resurrection and our justification. For as is the Death to our forgiveness of sins, so is the Resurrection to our new life. We too must die, that we may 'enter upon a heavenly and fruitful life'.[27] This analogy determines Martyr's whole thought of the Christian life, and in particular, the Christian's use of the Lord's Supper.

The Resurrection of Christ

Christ who is our Head is raised from death, and we also are raised in Him. Tell me, I pray you, will you not judge him to have escaped the danger

[24] E.g. *in* 1 *Sam.* 11.13, Martyr speaks of the Gospel in the Law, judging that we should act with 'gentleness of mind', applying the law with clemency, since Christ's dealing with the adulteress is an example of our own sin and repentance. Cf. the passage *in* 1 *Reg.* fol. 16A, *An Dei Mand.*: Christ is able to be 'a familiar example' for our imitation because His humanity was not Docetic but real. Thus 'the ratio between Him and the heavenly Father is not to be understood *simpliciter*, since the soul of Christ, which was part of His humanity, was not immense, being a creature.' Thus also the *Sicut* of His injunction implies not equality but similitude.

[25] *in* 1 *Cor.* 15.3.

[26] *in* Rom. 4.25—cf. 10.9: 'The resurrection of the Lord is a sort of knitting together and bond by which the preceding and following articles about the faith of our salvation are very well conjoined'; *in* 1 *Cor.* 15.1: the Resurrection 'contains the sum of almost all our faith' and 15.13: 'Faith concerns the resurrection most of all.'

[27] *Ibid.*—cf. especially the *Oratio de Res. Christi* for this theme (*L.C.*, p. 1045).

CHRIST AND THE NEW TESTAMENT 'SIGNS'   113

of death who, falling into a swift river, holds up his whole head above those deep and dangerous waters, even though the rest of his members are still drowned in them? (*Catech.* 25)

Because of his doctrine of justification as union with Christ, Peter Martyr is concerned to show at every phase of his Christology, the analogy for Christian experience and life. Thus the Virgin Birth is

not only to be understood of (Christ) . . . but of all those that in true faith are joined together with Him as His members . . . For just as He was begotten without human seed, so are we born again unto new life by the power of God's Spirit. (*Catech.* 11, 32)

But it is focused primarily in the pattern of the Incarnate Christ as Death and Resurrection. The Christian's justification involves a reactive movement of descent and ascent. This reaches its climax and most fruitful expression in relation to the Resurrection and Ascension of Christ, for only in the Resurrection may we perceive

the form of that spiritual life, in which we must live no longer to the flesh, but to the spirit . . . In this stands the whole sum of Christian doctrine, that inwardly we should ever be renewed, and outwardly, as far as lies in us, we should please and benefit our neighbours; since Christ being raised from the dead, has so greatly endowed us with His benefits, by giving from that time the gift of His Holy Spirit unto His children . . . Wherefore our part is to bend all our diligence and care to that end, that we may honour Him in a godly manner: not with earthly ceremonies or various human inventions, but with spiritual worshipping, and what may be agreeable to that heavenly and spiritual state to which Christ is now raised . . . being raised with Christ, it is fitting that even as we behold Him in the place and degree in which He is set, so should we with uplifted eyes of our mind, fasten our hope upon Him. (*Catech.* 26)

This passage is striking in its clarity and implications—and comes from his earliest written work! The Christian is one united to Christ, to the dead and risen Lord. Like Christ, he experiences death and resurrection here and now. For him, therefore, the sovereignty of Death is broken, it lies in his past, even though he daily experiences—still under God's own Sovereignty—its threats and its attacks:

He leads them to the gates of death and back again, taking care that in His adopted children may shine the image whom He naturally begat to Himself before all eternity. For this first-begotten, our Brother Jesus Christ, first died before He should be raised by His own and His Father's power.

Therefore it is fitting that we also who are appointed to be made like His image, should first die before we rise again. (*Ad Reg. Angl. Ep; L.C.*, p. 1121.)

He is therefore one who is travelling away from death and towards resurrection and life—and therefore away from deadly human works and sacrifice, from Mass to Eucharist.

But now, therefore, set free by the grace of God, we are joined to Christ through the Spirit, to Christ I say being raised from the dead; by this union we shall now bring forth fruit unto God, and no longer unto death and damnation. (*De Iustif.* 12)

Union with Christ according to the double movement of death and resurrection—here is Martyr's doctrine of Christian life. The Christian is set free to perform good works by the power of the Spirit, for the Holy Spirit is the bond of His union with Christ. Thus Martyr's prayers, for example, are full of the plea for the Spirit's illumination, that the Christian may delight in God's commandments, and have strength to fulfil them.[28] The Holy Spirit communicates to us the properties of the new humanity of the Risen Head: membership in Christ means partaking of His new manhood—Resurrection and Ascension mean Holy Spirit and New Man.

The Ascension of Christ and the Holy Spirit

just as Christ being raised from the dead ascended into heaven, so it is fitting that we, being justified by His grace, should in our whole life think no more upon earthly things, but upon heavenly . . . Christ, departing into heaven, gratified us with that singular gift of the Spirit . . . The godly live in Christ, and Christ in them, and that by His Spirit. (*Catech.* 26, 32, 34)

The Death of Christ was the price of our redemption, yet it has no relevance for us apart from the movement of exaltation: Resurrection, Ascension, Intercession and Return.[29] But these are related strictly to the office of the Holy Spirit, who comes to us as the chief 'effect' of that movement.[30] He is the secret of our new life, and is unto us as the soul is to the body. His chief office is that of teaching, by which 'He works a wonderful

[28] *Preces.* esp. on Psalm 119. Cf. *in Rom.* 5.20: After justification 'the law does not lie idle but is like a mirror' showing Christian fruit, profit and *need*.
[29] This paragraph is based upon the *Catech.*, third Article.
[30] Cf. *in Rom.* 4.25: The Spirit was required to apply Christ's Death unto us, 'and to give us this Holy Spirit, Christ arose from death'; *Dial.* 69D: Christ's Ascension is for the purpose of being glorified, sending the Holy Spirit, and interceding for us.

transformation' (*mira transformatio*) in the minds of the elect. Our affections, even the members of our body as well as our mind, become instruments of the Spirit.

In a deep sense this teaching on the Ascension and the Holy Spirit is the crux of Peter Martyr's theology. He passionately returns to this article again and again in debate, because it so perfectly expresses the nature of faith: a being lifted up by the Spirit to sit in the heavenly places with Christ. So these two elements, the 'placing' of the Body of Christ and the office of the Holy Spirit, are the poles about which his sacramental teaching moves.

The Holy Spirit operative within us joins us truly to the Person of Christ and so guarantees that we shall 'one day come unto the state of Christ'.[31] Just as we already are 'spiritual men', according to Paul, so shall we one day have spiritual bodies. Yet these will not 'become spirit' but will be spiritual because they wholly *serve* spirit: 'without doubt the truth and property of human nature will still remain'. This emphasis upon the continuing humanity in resurrection is a constant one in Martyr's thought,[32] and is bound up with his teaching upon the body as part of God's good creation as well as his stress upon the eternal unity of the Person of Christ.

Martyr's teaching on John 6 is worthy of note in this regard. John 6 and 1 Corinthians 10 had special relevance for his doctrine of the sacraments. The Ascension means two things: the continuing humanity of Jesus Christ, and the office of the Holy Spirit. The former implication of the doctrine of the Ascension means that Christ in respect of His bodily presence is removed from the world of men.[33] A corporeal presence in this age of the Spirit means the inventing of a kind of 'third advent'.[34] Jesus Himself teaches this clearly in dealing with the Capernaites. They sought to take His flesh by force, to rest in a corporeal communication. So He introduced the subject of His Ascension, to raise their minds from such carnal

[31] This teaching is from the *Dial.*, *Loc.* IV (*De Christi Ascensione in coelum*) and V (*De Corporis Christi Loco in Coelo*).

[32] Cf. esp. *De Resurrectione.*

[33] *Corpus Christi sic coelo contineri ut non amplius in terris versetur* (*Dial.* 73A). The bodily Ascension destroys the *figmenta ubiquitatis*, for ubiquity means *frustra visibiliter ascendebat* (*Dial.* 86F).

[34] *Disp.* IV, conf. of Q2, no. 4; *Def.* 24, 31, etc.

ideas to the heavenly reality and therefore the spiritual nature of His communication. Why did Christ mention His Ascension?

Was it not to let us understand that He must not be eaten carnally? . . . Truly it should have been to no purpose to have mentioned His Ascension, unless He meant to note that He spoke of that kind of eating which the absence of something corporeal should not hinder. (*Disp.* II.1)

Christ plainly teaches that He understands a spiritual eating, when He sets before them His Ascension into heaven. For thereby He showed that He meant an eating in which we may eat by faith a thing absent in place and substance. And just as He recalled Nicodemus from an outward and corporeal generation to a spiritual, which we obtain in the soul and inward man, and raised up the woman of Samaria from the corporeal and outward water to the drink by which our souls are refreshed, I mean by the Holy Spirit: so Christ taught the Capernaites who now thought that His flesh should be eaten outwardly and carnally, I say He taught them that eating which we receive in the soul and embrace with faith. (*Disp.* IV, conf. of Q 2, no. 2)

Thus the teaching of John 6 is related directly to the very matter (*res ipsa*) of the sacrament.[35] Since Christ's words were spoken before the historical institution of the Supper, He could teach plainly and simply that spiritual manducation proper to faith. Therefore—

In the sixth Chapter of John is taught the manner of eating (*modus manducationis*).

Later the symbols were added, that we might be the more excited to the spiritual eating already taught.[36] Christ had already taught an eating of His flesh outside the sacrament (*extra Sacramentum*), by a direct reference to the office of the Holy Spirit (verse 63) springing from the mention of the Ascension (verse 62).

For when Christ said, 'I am the bread of life', He immediately added, 'Who comes to Me will not hunger, and who believes in Me will never thirst'. Most certainly He shows what He said later, 'The flesh profits nothing'—namely, this, if eaten by the mouth, as you think—'it is the Spirit that quickens', and 'the words that I speak to you are spirit and life'. They should be stones, not men, who deny that this pertains to the manner of eating.

[35] The teaching in this paragraph is based upon *Def.* 156f.
[36] Cf. *Tract.* 78: 'Nor must we in like manner judge that there is a difference between the spiritual eating of John 6 and that which the Lord instituted in the Last Supper, except that to that doctrine and promise which he had first taught, He added a seal.'

Martyr's teaching relates the flesh of Christ as a continuing humanity retained in heaven until its advent at the Parousia, to the present office of the Holy Spirit:

> Our argument is clear and open: if Christ is present with us wholly in the human and divine nature, there was no need of proposing the Holy Spirit as substitute . . . Christ, absent in body, sends to His Apostles His vicarious Spirit, and is Himself present with them in virtue, grace and heavenly vigour, spiritually. (*Def.* 25f).

The Holy Spirit is the Vicar of Christ, and by definition excludes a corporeal presence of the humanity of Christ upon earth during this age in between the Advents of Christ. For that humanity is a glorified humanity: its substantial presence upon this sinful earth must necessitate judgment and change, and cannot be replaced by a corporeal presence in the Eucharist.[37]

> The time of the humility and demission of Christ is past. (*Def.*, Obj. 144)

> This is unheard of by Theologians, that after His ascension to heaven, the Lord returns here in the humility of a servant . . . For how, I pray you, does He sit at the right hand of the Father in glory if He still comes here in humility? To sit in glory is to remain there, but not to sink back again to a humble servant. (*Def.* 167f)

The Return of Christ

The truth of our communion is in heaven; while on earth we have but the image,[38] which the Holy Spirit uses as an instrument to stir up and confirm our faith, that we might be lifted up to this heavenly place and commune with our risen Lord.[39] This movement of faith corresponds to the two Advents of Christ: *the presence of Christ in the Church agrees with their ratio.* This is a familiar idea in Peter Martyr's thought, based upon his grasp

[37] *Def.* Obj. 9; cf. Objs. 1, 58, *etc.* The corporeal presence of Christ in the Eucharist is a confusion not only of places (heaven and earth) but of times, before and after the Ascension (Obj. 36-37); cf. *Epitome* 2.1, *Sent.* 4, *etc.*; Christ is ascended as to His human nature, absent until He comes to judge: *Tract.* 20. The time of Christ's humility is over, yet they 'draw Him down again, communicated in respect of His body to our jaws and stomachs'; *etc.* Like the other Reformers, Peter Martyr did not work out this aspect of his Eschatology in detail—partly, no doubt, in reaction to the sectarian revival of chiliastic teaching. But that he is conscious of the implication of Christ's new humanity for 'the change of all things', his Commentaries show, especially on Romans 8 and 1 Corinthians 15.
[38] Martyr often quotes Ambrose' distinction of *umbra* (O.T. sacraments), *imago* (ours) and *veritas* (in heaven)—*rerum veritas est in coelis: quem si velimus intueri eo ascendamus oportet*—e.g. *Def.* 11.
[39] E.g. *Tract.* 50: 'we must not stay in the signs, but must worship in spirit and truth Christ sitting in heaven at the right hand of His Father.'

of the movement of grace as humility and exaltation and the correspondence of faith to that.[40]

> Scripture records no more than two advents of Christ. The first is a humble form to redeem us, the other glorious, when He shall come for judgment. But every day you invent infinite advents. For wherever there is a saying of Mass, or where the faithful communicate, you decree that the body of Christ is really and substantially present; yet to this you grant neither a humble nor a glorious form, but according to a kind of middle way you tie it to sacramental signs, of which neither does Scripture speak, nor do you bring any effectual reason. (*Disp.* IV, conf. of Q2, no. 5)

> We say that the holy Scriptures mention only two advents of Christ: you posit a third . . . You cannot deny that this fictitious advent is not altogether of the same ratio with the first and last. (*Def.* 24)

Along with this insistence upon the glorification of Christ and presence by the Spirit until the revelation of that glory, Peter Martyr places the analogical significance for Christian life. Our *summa foelicitas* is not grasped in the Eucharist, but in the Resurrection:

> We are saved by hope, not by reality. (*Def.* 229)

> But the signs and symbols that the Fathers used were changed by the coming of Christ, at whose second coming also, those that we now use shall likewise be removed. For when once we have the fruition of that chief felicity which we await, we shall then need no sacraments. (*in Rom.* 4.11)

While we live here, the sacrament sustains us not by removing Christ from His sphere of glory, but us from our sphere of humiliation. By the power of faith and hope[41] we *now* share this coming glory.

> Yet this felicity which Christ has and which we shall have hereafter, we meanwhile have by a kind of participation, while we live here. (*in Gen.* 27.28)

> we are said to have (salvation) already, because by faith and hope we enjoy it as if we held it at present . . . we possess these things as begun, although not brought to perfection. (*in* 1 *Reg.* 2.4, *An Dei Mand.*)

Of this participation and possession the Eucharist is both sign

---

[40] E.g., *Def.* 31: daily advents and ascensions in the Mass destroy the ratio; indeed, the demand for a corporeal presence is the demand for a second advent, so that transubstantiation consciously replaces the coming judgment and glory.

[41] E.g. *in Rom.* 4.5: 'Chrysostom calls (hope) a golden chain let down from heaven, which chain if we take hold will draw us up to heaven'; *De Iustif.* 4: faith has respect to things past, present and future so long as they are hidden; and 54: 'For justification and life are so joined together that the one is often taken for the other. And indeed, justification is nothing else than eternal life inchoate in us.'

and instrument. Its nourishment is the sustenance of our pilgrimage.

'Until He come': These words declare that continually while we live here, we need the administration of the Sacraments, which have no place after this life. (*in* I *Cor.* 11.26)

Manna was given by the way in the wilderness, and to us is Christ given in the Eucharist, while we make our way through this age, which agrees with the example of the desert. Manna ceased when they reached the promised land, and we in heaven shall have no need of sacraments. For Christ shall be before us, and we shall behold God as He is. (*in* I *Cor.* 10.3)

since we are not yet in the fatherland, nor see what is revealed face to face, but pilgrimage towards the Lord, do you wish us to be wholly freed from figures? We still have figures, which signify not indeed that Christ will come, but teach that He has come already, and adumbrate those good things which we expect to come hereafter, in the eternal fatherland and the eternal life . . . When we have God and Christ Himself in person (*coram*), when He is as He really is and we see face to face—then signs and figures will altogether depart. (*Def.* 66)

PART II
UNION WITH CHRIST

CHAPTER IV

THE MYSTICAL BODY

Whosoever therefore comes not into this fellowship can by no means partake of (remission of sins), since this is granted only to those who are by faith united to Christ, the Head of the Church. By this we may rightly conclude that it is a gift peculiar to those that are true members of the Body under Christ its Head. (*Catech.* 44)

And to define it, we say that it is a company of believers (*coetum credentium*), and of the regenerate, whom God gathers together in Christ, through the Word and Holy Spirit, and governs through the ministers by purity of doctrine, by the lawful use of the sacraments, and by discipline. (*in* 1 *Cor.* 1.2)

PETER MARTYR'S doctrine of the Church was born in the fires of persecution and struggle. On the one hand were the Romanists, claiming that the 'Gospellers' were schismatics and heretics and no true Church: on the other were the Anabaptists, claiming that the Reform movement was essentially the eschatological coming of the Kingdom, and disdaining the Biblical principle of reforming the Church. Martyr himself is a classic example of the Reformation, which was essentially action and life. One of the hierarchy of the Roman system, attaining episcopal functions, gaining the esteem of scholars and admiration of the Italian people, he became refugee and combatant in the ecclesiastical and theological struggles of five countries. Through all these troubled times, his one basis for understanding the Church was the fact that Christ, having joined Himself to the elect by Spirit and grace, had made them *bone of His bone and flesh of His flesh*—and therefore similarly and equally members one of another.

and these members are so completely joined to the Head, that they are called flesh of his flesh and bone of his bones. (The Church) is the soul of Christ.

For all we, who are believers, have one father, who is God, and one brother, the first-begotten, who is Christ: wherefore we are knit together in the closest friendship. (*in* 1 *Cor.* 1.2, 12.31)

The Church represents a twofold *communio*, one

inward and concerning God, unto whom we are joined in spirit by faith, hope and charity and all virtues, together with all believers in Christ,

and the other outward, according to which we partake of the sacraments and the 'conversation' of members of the Church.[1] This does not imply the doctrine of the Church invisible, but rather indicates as the formative principle of the doctrine of the Church, the 'heavenly root' and sustaining efficacy of faith, namely the Holy Spirit.[2]

The Holy Spirit, in working this union with Christ which creates a Body upon earth, although not tied to Church activity,[3] normally uses the ministry of the Church in His calling man to faith and uniting him to Christ. The 'problem' of the Church, therefore, is once again the problem of the relationship of Holy Spirit to *signum*, which in turn derives from the Christological analogy.

> The ministers of the Church . . . are but means and instruments which God uses . . . But if you consider them as they are joined to God and as He is effectual in them, and as the action of the Holy Spirit is coupled (*copulatur*) with the action of the ministers, so that in a sense one is made of these two, that which belongs unto one is by the figure (*tropo*) synecdoche attributed unto the other. In this way are the ministers of the Church said to work those things we have declared. And that which we have set down regarding the Ministers, must also be judged of the Sacraments . . . (*in* 1 *Cor.* 3.3)

'In a sense one is made of these two'—this is the mystery of the Church, reflecting the mystery of God and man in Christ Himself.[4] In the Church too we are confronted with a relationship basically *sacramental*, as we were in regard to knowledge of God: and more particularly here, because in the Church the significant 'marks' concern the Word in its threefold impact upon the membership of Christ's Body as doctrine, sacraments and discipline.

---

[1] *in* 1 *Cor.* 5, at end, Treatise *De Excommunicatione*.
[2] *in* 1 *Cor.* 2.5: 'our faith, whose root is not on earth but in heaven'; worldly wisdom cannot 'adventure to measure things divine *suis rationibus*'; and 1.20: 'the whole power of the persuasion of these divine matters must be placed in the power of the Word and efficacy of the Spirit'.
[3] Such as the speaking of doctrine or laying on of hands—*in* 1 *Cor.* 3.3.
[4] The doctrine of analogy has deep significance here too: the Church *is* not that Mystery nor even its direct proportion, yet is a Divine-human organism analogous to the unique Person of its Head.

'We go unto the Catholic and Apostolic Church'

Besides the inward cleansing of the Holy Spirit are required, as instrumental to it, the outward Word and sacraments.[5] Since the external calling and the outward signs are the ordinary means of grace, 'the faithful man, if possible, should be baptized', for example. The Church is not to be lightly esteemed, and for the Reformers it was a most serious step to depart from Rome. But this step they took on the basis that the true Church was to be distinguished by three notes:

the three marks of the Church which are wont to be shown by men of our side, namely doctrine, the right administration of the Sacraments, and the care of discipline.

On this basis, they declared themselves to be separating from what had become a false Church, and therefore:

we have not departed from the Church, but have rather returned to it . . . Wherefore in going from the Romanists we have not forsaken the Church, but have fled an intolerable yoke, and a conspiracy against the evangelical doctrine . . . We go unto the Catholic and Apostolic Church, because the Church from which we separate ourselves lacks both. For it is no longer Catholic, since it has transformed the universal Church into the Roman Church; and Apostolic it is not, since it differs so far from the doctrine and ordinances of the Apostles.

Peter Martyr's quarrel with Rome may be summed up in the phrase, 'the Scriptures, and not the traditions of men'. Again and again he insists that the Church cleanse itself by the light of the Word of God, for 'faith hangs only on the Word', not, as the Schoolmen say, on the Fathers and Councils as well.[6] This is the 'positive' Reformation principle in action, and unlike Luther's 'negative' principle, which sought only a cleansing of the Mass, it attacks the Mass as a product of human invention and therefore that which opposes the Divine institution of the Eucharist. Martyr does not regard the source of doctrine quantitatively—the notable example is his attack upon communion in one kind, with its history of five centuries' custom—but qualitatively:

[5] The material in this paragraph is from the Treatise *De Schismate, in* 1 *Reg.* 12, at the end—a most valuable study in the reasons for separating from Rome. Its distinct echo is to be heard in Jewel's 'Apology'.

[6] *in Iud.* 7.27: 'faith must be constant and wholly void of error—which two things are not found in the fathers and the councils'.

And it ought to be taken for a rule, that whatever is repugnant to the word of God, has no power to prescribe.[7]

That which alone can *prescribe* for the Church is the Word, and in relation to doctrine and sacraments, this means especially the Scriptures.[8]

To 'pure doctrine and right administration of the sacraments' Martyr always adds *discipline*. Now Schlosser interprets this as a third sacrament, that of penance,[9] which Martyr supposedly retained in his early years, after the manner of Luther. But already in the Catechism Martyr had made it clear that the sacraments are visible words, their signs being water, bread and wine:

> Unto which there ought to be adjoined brotherly correction, which in these times is so neglected, that no man will apply it, either to another's use, or will submit himself to it: such profit have we obtained in the school of Christ! (*Catech.* 42)

Moreover, in his later Treatise, *De Poenitentia*,[10] he allows no uncertainty about the falsity of the Romanist doctrine of penance. Finally, although he gives no developed doctrine of discipline in the manner of Calvin's Fourth Book of the *Institutes*, or the broad and corporate sense distinctive of the Scottish *Books of Discipline*, he does establish the principle that disci-

---

[7] *in Iud.* 11.12, where he treats of prescription as against custom.

[8] Cf. *Catech.* 38: Christians 'will never suffer themselves one jot to be led from that truth which the Spirit of God has revealed to us in the holy scriptures, but they will assure themselves of that worship alone which is lawful and acceptable unto God, which He has prescribed in those holy scriptures'.

[9] *Op. cit.*, p. 397: 'als äussere zeichen dieser Vergebung erkennt Martyr in dieser Schrift äussere den zwei Sacramenten, der Taufe und dem Abendmahl noch ein drittes, die Busse'. He is here dealing with the Catechism, and comments, p. 398n—'Man sehe den Anhang zu seinem Leben, wo man finden wird, dass er diess späterhin zurücknahm'. But in the Propositions from Genesis of 1543, Martyr had already stated: 'Since brotherly correction and accusation (*fraeterna correctio et accusatio*) is odious to the world and the flesh, therefore it must with greater diligence be retained in the Church . . . We allow a confession of sins, made not only unto God, but unto men' (*ex Cap.* 37, *nec.* 4, and *ex Cap.* 39, *nec.* 16). And in treating explicitly of sacraments (*ex Cap.* 8, 15, 16, 17 for instance) he does not mention such confession. Cf. *in* 1 *Cor.* 10.10: 'Paul retains *disciplina* most diligently—which is nothing else than a faculty of the Church divinely permitted, by which the will and actions of the faithful are rendered conformable to the divine law: as far as this is by doctrine, warnings, correction and at length by penalties, and if there is need, by excommunication.'

[10] This forms the closing section of the Commentary on II Samuel. In it, the basic definition is *Poenitentia est mutatio vitae* (sect. 3) resulting from faith, of which repentance is an effect (18). He deals in detail with the Romanist doctrine of penance and explicitly treats of *An poen. sit Sacramentum* (10ff).

pline must be cleansed of Romanist error and superstition and
re-established within the Reformed Church. For there is a 'rule
of the Gospel regarding brotherly correction' which is to be
diligently observed, guarding against 'the tyranny of one or a
few' by the 'consent of the Church'.[11]

The Church's Head and Government

Now then are we content with one head, namely Christ, the Holy Spirit
being the guide, and holy Scripture being like the outward testimony of His
will: the sure persuasion of this is sealed in our minds by the power of the
Holy Spirit. (*Catech.* 40)

The doctrine of the Church as the Body of Christ means that
He is its Head, and to speak of an earthly Head as well is to
create a two-headed monster![12] There is a Divinely-ordained
order of government in the Church, and the Bishop of Rome
overthrows this by taking unto himself supremacy.

But you will say, that although the inner sense and motion of the Church
are of Christ, yet may there be an outer head to rule ministers, and to keep
all in their duty. But there may not be; nor is it at all lawful, to change the
order appointed by God. For God wills that in the Church there should
be an Aristocracy, that bishops should have the care of all these things, and
should choose ministers, yet so that the suffrage of the people is not excluded.
(*An poss. in eccl.*)

Now although Martyr appears here, and in many places, to
limit the actual government to bishops, his normative principle
is to interpret this *aristocratia* as follows:

If you consider Christ, it shall be called a Monarchy, for He is our king,
who with His own blood has purchased the Church to Himself. He is now
gone into heaven, yet governs this kingdom of His, not indeed with visible
presence, but by the Spirit and by the Word of holy scripture. And there
are in the Church those that execute the office on His behalf: Bishops,
Presbyters, Doctors, and others bearing rule—in relation to these it may
properly be called an Aristocracy . . . But because in the Church there are
matters of very great weight and importance referred to the people, as
appears in the Acts of the Apostles, therefore it has a respect of *politia*.
(*De Excomm.*)

Paul indeed mentions bishops and presbyters, but does not teach that
they are diverse orders. (*Def.* 208)

[11] *Epist. Dominis Polonis* (L.C., p. 1109).
[12] Cf. *Catech.* 40, and *in* 1 *Sam.* 8, Treatise *An possint in ecclesia esse duo capita,
unum visibile, alterum invisibile.*

This brief indication of Martyr's attitude towards Church government is enough to show that his twofold attack upon Rome—upon its Pope and upon its Mass—has this theological foundation, that Christ is the Head of the Church, its order and its worship have their law only in His ordering and gracious self-communicating: the doors of the Church do not lead to an area of Christian life beyond the 'power of the Word and efficacy of the Spirit'.

The Church and the Word

The authority of the Church has no dominion over faith, as some wickedly think. The office of the Church is to preach, to admonish, to reprove, to testify, and to lay the holy scriptures before men's eyes: nor does it require to be believed further than it speaks the Word of God. (*in Rom.* 10.17)

The Church has no power over the Word, inasmuch as 'the Church was called by the Word' and has authority only from the Word—'the power of believing comes of the Holy Spirit'.[13] Thus Councils of the Church, of which Martyr makes much, must be subject to judgment, namely, that they have 'framed their doctrine to the rule of the holy scriptures'—

Such Councils . . . must be heard which cleave unto the Word of God. For whatever commodity or discommodity the Church has, ought wholly to be ascribed to the regard or contempt for the Word of God. (*De Iustif.* 44)

Not the Church, but the Word of God, is the 'engine' (*machinus*) by which the heretics were conquered. Christ Himself is the real Actor in the Church, in her beginning and her continuance, her justification and her sanctification. It is His Holy Spirit that establishes the Church in being,[14] but also bestows this afresh by the dynamic communication of Christ's properties to His members. Justification means an imputed righteousness, but sanctification means a real, 'second righteousness' as Christ grows in us.[15]

[13] *vim credendi esse ab Spiritu sancto*—*in Rom.* 3.22.
[14] E.g. *Catech.* 35: the article on the Holy Spirit is 'the root or stem' from which the article on the Church 'arises and buds forth as a most suitable branch'.
[15] *De Iustif. passim*, e.g.: 'Justification is derived to us from the death of Christ and the promises of God. Thus a beggar receives alms with a leprous, feeble and bloodstained hand: yet not because he has a hand thus feeble and leprous': cf. *in Rom.* 5.9: we are justified *first* 'before God by imputation', *second* 'because daily there is augmented in us a new righteousness which we obtain in holy living, by the increase of our strength which we have now received by the Holy Spirit'.

The doctrine of faith as union with Christ means that the Church is the Body of the Incarnate Word. It is related to the new humanity of its Head, and therefore to *the intercession of the Risen Man*.[16]

our Church is a true house of God . . . And this our Church has from Christ her spouse, who communicates all that is His unto her: for He is the most true house of God . . . He is to us the ark, the temple and house of God— yea, the mercy seat itself.[17]

Christ as the living Word, operative through His risen humanity and its counterpart in the new righteousness of the Church, is the basis and power of the Church's ministry of Word and sacrament.

the ministry of the Church renders service to God, and works with Him for our salvation . . . the grace of God is not bound by necessity either to the ministry or to the sacraments or to the outward Word. But we are speaking of the usual means (*de usitate ratione*) by which God leads men to salvation.

(*in Rom.* 5.21)

For this reason 'there is need of the continual ministry' of the Church, that men might behold the promises of God, both with words and with their seals, 'by sacraments, which are certain visible words'. This Augustinian definition of the sacrament as *verbum visibilis* is Peter Martyr's favourite, and points to the determinative orientation of the sacrament: *it is the Word made visible*. Although he stresses the centrality of preaching in the Church,[18] particularly in view of the appalling sermonic silence of the Romanism of his time, yet he constantly affirms the need for visibility in the Church's ministry of the Word. Since Martyr's analogical thinking begins with the Person of Christ, the origin of this stress upon the Word as clothed in flesh is obvious. For the visibility of the Word in the sacraments of the

---

[16] *in Rom.* 8.34, *in* 1 *Cor.* 13.13. The priesthood of Christ has two 'moments', the Cross and the heavenly intercession; in the latter the Church participates. See Chapter X for details of this teaching.

[17] *imo ipsum propitiatorium*: *in Gen.* 28.12; cf. *in* 1 *Sam.* 1.9: Christ is our *vera arca*, whom Paul calls ἱλαστῆριον, *hoc est vel propitiatorem, vel propitiatorium, quo alludit ad Mosaicum propitiatorium, quod Arcae superponebatur.*

[18] E.g. *in Rom.* 10.17: nothing more nourishes, maintains or confirms faith than the reading and repeating of the Word; 'To this end are holy assemblies gathered together, to hear God's word . . . And they that think a lively and pure faith may continue in Churches without frequent preaching exceedingly crr'; the Virgins' lamps (faith) soon go out unless ministered unto with oil (the Word), as Chrysostom says. Cf. *in Rom.* 1.9: there is a 'profitable dialogue' between God and man, the reading of His Word and praying unto Him.

Church is analogical to the visible *accommodation* of the Word in Incarnation. Not only must the Word be 'repeated again and again' because 'our mind is so weak',[19] but:

> on account of our infirmity, that spiritual and inward eating, though it be accomplished by the soul and spirit only, yet is assisted very much by the outward help of the senses: namely by the divine sermon and visible Sacraments. And therefore Christ joins to the inward eating the outward symbols and action of eating and drinking. And saints desire and long for that same action, so that through it the spiritual eating of the soul may be preserved more safely and increased more and more. (*Def.* 724)

The Invisible Word made Visible

> For He rules His Kingdom, which is the Church, by the Spirit and the Word, to which Word are to be reckoned also His Sacraments. (*Def.* 417)

> All such as have Thee (O most mighty God) for their shepherd, lead their life exceeding happily, as those who always have food abundantly enough of Thy heavenly doctrine . . . Thou canst refresh us if it please Thee, with a most exquisite and well furnished banquet of Thy sacred doctrine and blessed sacraments, and make us drink plentifully of the cup of Thy Holy Spirit and grace. (*Preces, Ps.* 23)

The keynote of the ministry of the Word is edification, according to Peter Martyr:

> Nor are they compacted together in this society, but that they should edify one another. (*Catech.* 39)

But edification means 'upbuilding' (*aedificare*)—growth or nurture. And this is precisely the effect of the Word of God, 'the principal food of souls' and the 'origin of the remission of sins'.[20] These two facets of the activity of the Word are constantly affirmed, the growth of our union with Christ, and the daily necessity of the forgiveness of sins. There are

> two means by which the remission of sins exists in the Church, according to the twofold way (*duplex ratio*) in which the Word of God is set forth to believers. (*Catech.* 45)

> a 'mystery' we distinguish into the Word of God and the Sacraments. (*in* 1 *Cor.* 4.1)

The Word and sacraments are the 'nerves of the Church';[21] to them the Holy Spirit joins His power of piercing to the inner man;[22] what is spoken of the one applies equally to the other.[23] Once again it is *analogy* which explains this best.

[19] *De Iustif.* 61; cf. *in Rom.* 4.11: the visible *signa* are given because of our weakness. [20] *Catech.* 31, 44. [21] *in* 1 *Cor.* 11.20. [22] *in Iud.* 19, *De Magist.* [23] *in* 1 *Cor.* 4.2.

But concerning the sacraments, we have often taught in what way justification is to be attributed to them. For they have the same relation to it as the preaching of the Gospel and the promise about Christ offered to us, to salvation. (*De Iustif.* 87)

As the sense of the words of God, through the power of signification joined to the Holy Scriptures, draws the thing itself to our souls, so the body and blood of the Lord are signified by the symbols, but are joined to our souls spiritually. (*in* 1 *Cor.* 11.24)

But the signification nothing differs, whether it is referred to sight or to hearing. Nor are the Sacraments other than seals of the words of God, the promises which are contained in them being added. (*Def.* 549)

And the Holy Spirit uses the sacraments to give us Christ spiritually, to be embraced by the soul and faith: just as we are said to receive salvation by the words of God; not that salvation lies hidden in those words, or stands in a real presence, but is contained by signification. And this comparison with divine words is very agreeable to the sacraments, since by Augustine's judgment they are visible words. (*Disp.* IV, *vs.* Ched.)

The Word itself is sacramental, because it is the Spirit's analogy of Christ, the Word made flesh. Therefore Martyr argues from the nature of the Word preached and the Word written,[24] and proves the analogical nature of sacraments, and also the effectual power of their signification—thus guarding against the two opposite errors of simple identity or simple difference.

the sacraments . . . are visible words of this absolution. For just as the word sounds and is heard in the voice, so in a visible and evident sign a sacrament speaks and admonishes us; as we have faith towards it, we indeed obtain what it promises and signifies. Nor do we otherwise have faith in its signification, than by the motion of the same Spirit of Christ . . . do not think that sins are forgiven by virtue of the work wrought (*operis operate virtute*), by our receiving the Sacrament: since this we obtain by faith, believing what it visibly teaches us by the institution of Christ: so that the Sacrament is counted just as is the Word of God. (*Catech.* 45)

no more is to be attributed to the sacraments regarding salvation, than to the Word of God. (*in Rom.* 4.11)

We make the words of God and the Sacraments equal. (*Def.* 618)

This analogy to the Word is most fruitful in Martyr's teaching. For example, he demands the very same preparation

---

[24] E.g. *in Rom.* 1.16; 3.4; 4.11; *Def.* 290 ('Both apply the ministry of the body, the mouth in communion, the ears in the address. And just as through the ears reconciliation with God, eternal life, and the forgiveness of sins come not *realiter*, so in our mouth the true body and the true blood of Christ are not received *proprie*'), 316, 334, 387.

before hearing the Word of God as before receiving the sacrament.[25] Or again, the apprehension of Christ through the Word is of the *whole* Christ, with no problem of corporeal presence or of the 'parts' which the scholastic doctrine of concomitancy sought to solve.[26] We eat Christ's flesh and drink His blood in the one as in the other—'as in the Word, so in the Sacrament'.[27] And to the Christian—·

> Since they were instituted by Christ, the symbols are no less sweet than the words of God. (*Def.* 326)

Yet the chief question remains: what profit has the sacrament over the Word? We have already mentioned the relation of the visibility of the Word to human infirmity; now we must relate it to the believer's union with Christ. For this union grows, it is augmented by the Holy Spirit, who actually 'transmutes' us into the bread and Body of Jesus Christ, in Paul's language.

> in receiving the Sacraments we are changed and converted into the body of Christ. (*in* 1 *Cor.* 10.17)

Although there are, Martyr teaches, two ways of receiving— that is, of being united to—the Body of Christ, 'through the sacrament and without the sacrament', yet through the sacrament,

> We have a kind of fruit of the Holy Spirit which by that private Communion we meanwhile grasp not so fully. (*Def.* 190)

The sacraments are seals which are not sufficient by themselves, but by the Holy Spirit's use of them as His instruments, serve positively to strengthen and confirm faith.[28]

> If you ask, what commodity the sacraments bring to us, since we have remission of sins, and have by faith obtained righteousness, we answer 'very much': for they offer themselves before our eyes, and so admonish us. For our faith is stirred up, not indeed by them, but by the power of the Holy Spirit, who uses this instrument of the Sacraments just as He uses the instrument of the Word preached. And faith, being stirred up, embraces more and more both righteousness and the remission of sins. For these things are not *in atomo* but have some breadth. (*in Rom.* 4.11)

---

[25] *in Iud.* 13.1—this implication of the analogy is equally applicable today! Cf. his *Adhortatio ad coenam Domini mysticam*: 'Admit that God asks you: Why can't you? What do you answer, pray? "I am defiled with sins"? Why not repent? Unto repentance a long space of time is not needful!'
[26] *in* 1 *Cor.* 15.47, *An Christ. ex Coel.*   [27] *Def.* 446.   [28] *in Iud.* 6.40.

In relation to the Word of God, therefore, the sacraments are that Word spoken over again, but this time related to a visible sign. In the sacraments Christ clothes His Word of grace in fleshly elements.

> The sacraments also are believed, but they are nothing else than visible words of God, to which is also joined the Word of God—as Augustine said, 'The Word comes to the element and it is made a sacrament.' (*in Rom.* 10.17)

As the Word over again in a visible way, the sacrament is a *seal* to the invisible Word of the forgiveness of sins:

> It may seem sufficient to take that definition which Paul uses here, namely to say that the sacraments are σφραγῖδες, that is, seals of the righteousness of faith. For they seal the promises by which, if faith is joined to them, we are justified . . . The head and sum of their signification we place in this, that they seal unto us the gifts and promises of God. (*in Rom.* 4.11)

This complex teaching about the effects of the sacraments will concern us in the next two Chapters. Here we should note what is perhaps the most important fact in the relationship of sacrament to Word: *it is the Word that sacramentalizes.* Martyr uses again and again Augustine's 'The Word comes to the element and it is made a Sacrament.' Strictly speaking, the elements do not profit, but only the Word added.[29] The *sermo* given over the element is that which finally profits, and that upon which the utility of the sacramental element depends.[30] In this latter context Martyr does give the element a 'lesser utility'—but derivative from the Word. We do well to remember that for him, the Word means the active Christ, not a 'five-word prayer'[31] with magic power, as the Romanist holds. For here, the work is 'by Word and Spirit'. It is not the 'power and efficacy of the words' (of consecration) that make a sacrament, but the presence of the Holy Spirit.[32] Indeed, Martyr declares that only one thing is absolutely necessary, 'the invisible operation of the Holy Spirit'.[33]

The Word of God is active in the sacrament as the determinative factor. Martyr distinguishes three parts to the sacrament:

> Three things are required in a sacrament: the promise, which is re-

---

[29] *Tract.* 57.　　　　　　　　[30] *Def.* 451.
[31] *Def.* 114: Is bread expelled *quinqueverbali prece*?
[32] *Def.* 785.　　　　　　　　[33] *in* 1 *Cor.* 11.24.

presented by words, the element by which the promise made is sealed,
finally the command of God by which what is to be done is prescribed.
(in Rom. 6.5)

First comes the outward element, then the word of promise is added . . .
third is the commandment of the Lord, that it should be done thus. What
concerns the element is received by the body, since it is an external thing;
but the promise is received by the soul. The Word must come, that the
element should have a signification to signify this. (De Poenit. 13)

Martyr identifies this Word of promise with the signification,
that is, the Body and Blood of Christ, so far as the Eucharist is
concerned. Even apart from the sacrament he can call the Word
of Scripture 'the body of Christ' and the 'bread by which our
minds are nourished', or can say with Origen, 'The blood of
the Lord is the Word of God.'[34] But more significantly, the
Word in the sacrament is the real *signifying power*:

Signs and outward actions of ceremonies are frail things: the Word of
God endures forever, therefore the ratio of the Sacrament must be judged
by that. So much is granted us, as God desires to give: concerning His will
we know nothing except what His words (*sermones*) reveal to us. (*An in
Comm. Lic.* 10)

The Word of the Lord stands as a kind of medium between the symbols
and the matter of the Sacrament, and also between us and the matter of the
Sacrament, since it should be joined both to the symbols and to us. Both
these conjunctions have regard to the Word of God . . . And so the words
of God make for a twofold union, namely to join the matter of the Sacrament to the elements through signification, but to our souls by the spiritual
perception of faith. (*in* 1 *Cor.* 11.24)

Moreover, we receive the body and blood of Christ no less in the Word
of God than in the sacrament . . . for whatever fruit or grace the bread has
in the sacrament, it has it by the Word . . . the words both express and
signify the nature of a sacrament more plainly than do the signs. (*Disp.*
IV, conf. of Q2, no. 3)

This latter teaching upon the ultimate significance of the
Word is a most helpful reminder of Peter Martyr's fundamental
reference of all theology to the Person of Christ; for in Part III
especially we shall see him struggling against adversaries in
terms which often require such a reminder of the primacy of
the Word. In this respect, too, we must develop the next
part of this teaching: the number of the sacraments. For in
relation to the Word, a sacrament should be, *formally*, related

<hr>

[34] *Epit., Sent.* 13; *Def.* 451.

to the eternal Word in His communication, and *materially*, related to a historical event of the Incarnate Word.

The Two Forms of the Visible Word of God

If you give the name sacrament far and wide, for all those things which signify some holy thing . . . you are compelled to posit not only seven, but infinite sacraments . . . (we must) limit the name of sacrament to those things which not only signify spiritual things, but also are practised by certain words, and about which there is extant a precept so to do. (*in* 1 *Cor.* 7.10)

Peter Martyr strongly opposed any general idea of sacrament, from which one might derive the validity of a certain number (two, three or seven) of 'special' sacraments—by beginning with the definition 'the sign of a holy thing', for example.[35] Such a method implies infinite sacraments, and the actual number of prescribed sacraments is relative to something external to the nature of a sacrament, such as a concern for the number seven, or for sevenfold 'times' of human life.

Wherefore we treat not of a sacrament or mystery in general, by which is signified, as Chrysostom says, anything unknown and unspeakable, having in it much admiration, and above our judgment. For in this sense there is an infinite number of sacraments. For we may thus term sacraments, the nativity of Christ, His resurrection, the Gospel . . . (*in Rom.* 4.9)

Peter Martyr rather approaches the sacraments according to their relation to the Word which sacramentalizes. The proper connotation of *sacramentum* is *mysterium*, as both the Hebrew and Greek originals testify.[36]

For who sees not that 'mystery' by the Greeks is the same as we call Sacrament? (*Def.* 163)

A Sacrament signifies a thing secret and hidden . . . Let the heathen come, he will see water, bread and wine—what they are he will not perceive: the man of faith understands their reference. (*De Poenit.* 10)

[35] *De Poenit.* 10.
[36] *in Rom.* 4.11: 'The word that signifies a sacrament is in Hebrew *Sod* and *Razi*. The first of these is common to all secret and hidden things, and more in use. And the other Isaiah used in the 24th Chapter when he said *Razi-li, Razi-li,* that is "A secret to me, a secret to me". Daniel also in his 2nd Chapter, dealing with the knowledge of the mystery, uses the same word. Such is the nature and condition of sacraments, that they contain hidden things, known indeed to some but not to all. And from this etymology the Greek word Μυστήριον does not much differ.' Cf. Wolleb (Heppe, p. 592): 'It is also called *mysterium*, so far as it signifies a secret and divine matter set forth by signs and types. But the word mystery is broader than sacrament: every sacrament is a mystery, but not every mystery is a sacrament.'

K

Thus sacrament is mystery; the ratio of mystery is signification; the signification is Christ Himself. For example, in treating of 1 Corinthians 2.7, *Loquimur sapientiam Dei in mysterio*, he introduces Chrysostom's distinction of three modes or ratios of 'mystery':[37] sacrament, when we attend to something signified by what is visible; paradox, as in 1 Corinthians 15.51, Romans 11.25, and Isaiah 24.16; and thirdly—

> one part is known, but another part is unknown, in which kind the wisdom of Christians is placed: since indeed we now see through a glass and in enigma: but then—in heaven, I mean—face to face . . . Also we can interpret Christ Himself as called wisdom in a mystery, since He held His divine nature concealed in part under the abject form of a servant.

This is the ultimate and normative meaning or *ratio* of 'mystery': the Word made flesh. The sacramental mystery must be analogical to that ratio, and therefore Peter Martyr's principle is, the mode of mystery is signification.[38] Chrysostom's dictum is most fitting: 'In the sacraments we see one thing, believe another; behold with our sense one thing, understand with our mind another.'

> A sacrament is a visible form, or a visible sign of invisible grace. And that is called a sign which, besides the form it offers to the senses, brings some other thing to our knowledge. (*in Rom.* 4.11)
>
> two things . . . an outward sign and a thing signified. (*De Poenit.* 12)

The *sursum corda* is therefore the key to the action of the sacrament:

> when Baptism or the Lord's Supper is administered, we should lead our mind away from water, from bread and wine, through faith unto Christ Himself, who is communicated to us. Wherefore in the Church it is not by chance that rule obtains, before we come to the mystery, of calling out *Sursum Corda*, that is as if to say 'Let your souls cling not to these things that are seen, but to those which are promised' . . . Thus on earth are both men who teach and sacraments by which they teach: but the matter itself is a real presence contained in heaven; on earth it can truly be said to be through signification, the apprehension of faith, and the power of the Spirit and grace. (*Def.* 9)

It is this reference to the Word-made-flesh as the signification or true Mystery apprehended in sacraments that determines

---

[37] *Comm. ad loc.*; cf. *in* 2.10: the Holy Spirit alone reveals the mystery to us, using the *sermones Dei* for this purpose.

[38] *Modus mysterii est significatio. Def.* 163.

their nature and number. For the *sacramentum* reminds us that God has bound Himself to us in a covenant, by specific promises, that is, by Jesus Christ; therefore sacraments cannot be general but must be *signs given by God's will and institution*:[39]

it is not in men's power to ordain sacraments: they are testimonies of the will of God, and like seals; and it is not of man to counterfeit seals . . . sacraments pertain to the ratio of faith. (*De Poenit.* 11)

God alone can will to signify and to seal His grace (our union with Christ) by earthly elements: for the ratio of faith is the givenness of the Word made flesh. Since the forgiveness of sins is the content of grace, we must

bind ourselves only to these two, namely Baptism and the Eucharist. (*De Poenit.* 12)

For only these two are related to the historical activity of the Word made flesh. The logic is simple: sacraments depend upon God's will; His will is revealed expressly in Scripture; Scripture shows that Christ instituted two Sacraments.[40] Thus the 'whole definition' of sacrament is this:

A Sacrament is a divine promise concerning the remission of sins through Christ, signified and sealed by an outward or visible symbol according to the divine institution, in order that faith should be raised up in us, and we should be more and more bound unto God. (*De Poenit.* 12)

The formal cause is the signifying and sealing; the material cause is the promise of God's remission of sins; the efficient cause is the Divine institution; the final cause is the erection of faith, by which we are united to God.[41]

Sacraments are therefore not physically related to grace, as the Romanist scheme of salvation implies, which 'turns grace into nature'.[42] Rather are they the gracious accommodation of God's Word of forgiveness given visibility according to the inner ratio of that grace, the union with Christ as *new birth* and *new life*:

between the state of nature and of spirit there is found a most excellent

---

[39] *in Rom.* 4.11.   [40] *Ibid.*
[41] Cf. *in Rom.* 4.11 as to the effects of the sacraments: they instruct us in heavenly things; they kindle faith in us, to desire God's promises; they join us together in a closer bond of love 'since we are all initiated with the same mysteries'; they separate us from sects; and they admonish us to live a holy life.
[42] *De Iustif.* 24.

analogy, since generation, life and nourishment are suitable to both. (*in* 1 *Cor.* 3.2)

This is the substance of God's Word, and Peter Martyr asks but one question about the Romanist sevenfold sacramental grace: 'What Word of God is in these things?' For penance 'represents no promise', nor has confirmation a Divine institution; anointing with oil 'has not the Word of God to warrant it'.[43] Or again, if marriage be a sacrament, where will you stop? What about the washing of feet, embracing children in arms, and 'almost every action of Christ', since these also are 'signs of holy things'?[44] Indeed, the washing of feet has the most reason to be called sacramental, since its element may have a signification more than common, and since a commandment was joined to it; yet

there are given no particular words, which should come to the element to make it a sacrament, and by which the promise of some singular gift of grace to be obtained is declared unto us. (*An in Comm. Lic.* 15)

Baptism and the Eucharist are the sacraments of the Church, for they are given to Christ's flock as signs and seals of His twofold activity in and among them: of joining them to Himself in the union of faith, and nourishing them by the communication of His own new humanity. In the Christian life there are these two elements: the absolute element of once-for-all death and burial related to the Cross of Christ, and the ongoing growth in grace related to the Risen Man. The sacraments signify and seal these two realities, that is, the Mystery of Christ Himself.

[43] *De Poenit.* 14, 15.   [44] *in* 1 *Cor.* 7.10.

CHAPTER V

THE SACRAMENT OF REGENERATION

Repentance and New Life

> There is one purgation set forth to us by faith, having repentance joined
> with it: by this are men purged and set at rest . . . So God governs us by
> His Spirit and Word, and those who apprehend them by faith, repent . . .
> repentance is the cross and gibbet of the old man. (*De Poenit.* 1)

IN the Treatise *De Poenitentia*, one of those gems of theological
analysis carefully set in his Commentaries,[1] Peter Martyr
deals with the basic problem of repentance and faith. The
'fountainhead of repentance' is God's manifesting His goodness
to us in Christ; when we apprehend this by faith, repentance
follows. Now the 'outward sign of taking upon us new life, is
Baptism'. What is the relation of repentance to baptism? Is it
the 'second plank after shipwreck', as it had become as early
as the Patristic period? Martyr is quite definite here: repentance *is* the change of life which baptism signifies and seals.
Regeneration has negative and positive aspects, but the emphasis must fall upon the positive new life on which we enter.

If we relate this teaching to that of the Treatise *De Iustificatione*,[2] we see the profound doctrine of grace and faith implied.
Faith has substance, a certain ontic content, namely union
with Christ. The Word completes Himself in a real or substantial indwelling in believers. Martyr's chief definition of
faith is simply 'ingrafting into Christ', with frequent mention
of Paul's *Ephesians* terminology. Moreover, this substance of
faith is imperfect, incomplete, held only in the tension of God's
promise: 'eternal life already begun (*inchoata*) in us'. The
inchoate nature of faith relates to the substantial union in terms
of the Person of Christ as hidden because of His Ascension and
awaited because of His Return. To this twofold content of

---

[1] It forms the closing section of the Commentaries on 1 and 2 Samuel.
[2] *in Rom.*, after Chapter II.

faith, a primary ingrafting into Christ and a pressing towards full union with Him, baptism and the Eucharist correspond. Their sacramental analogy both signifies and seals this content of faith to mind, soul and body.

Regeneration means a change 'into Christ', and since His work on our behalf is summed up in Death and Resurrection, therefore baptism, the sacrament of this regeneration,[3] may be 'amply defined' as follows:

> Baptism is a sign of regeneration into Christ, into His death, I say, and His resurrection, which succeeded in place of Circumcision, which consists in the laver of water in the Word, in which in the name of the Father and of the Son and of the Holy Spirit, remission of sins and outpouring of the Holy Spirit is offered, and by a visible sacrament we are grafted into Christ and into His Church and the right into the kingdom of heaven is sealed unto us, and we on our part profess that we will die unto sin and live hereafter in Christ. (*in Rom.* 6.5)

Peter Martyr notes two analogies in the baptismal rite. The chief analogy is the fundamental *washing* by which the cleansing power of God's grace is signified:

> Water is the most fitting symbol of this. For just as the dirt of the body is by it washed away, so through this sacrament the soul is purified.
> (*in* 1 *Cor.* 1.17)

the sign in sacraments should have an affinity and likeness with the thing signified by it. Wherefore since water washes away the filthiness of the body, makes the earth fruitful, and quenches thirst, it aptly signifies remission of sins and the Holy Spirit, by which good works are made plentiful, and grace which refreshes the anguish of mind.[4]

A second analogy is the specific form of this remission, death and resurrection, which has a more subjective reference:

> Chrysostom notes that the similitude of death in this place admonishes us that what was done in Christ by nature is done in us by analogy. For it is not necessary that we through baptism should die by natural death, but that in our manners and life we should resemble the likeness of Christ's death. (*in Rom.* 6.5)

> As Christ has drawn us by baptism into His death and burial, so has He drawn us out unto life. The dipping in water and coming forth again signifies this when we are baptized. (*Oratio de Res. Christi*)

This double analogy implies a simplicity about baptism which

---

[3] *sacramentum regenerationis* was the Patristic definition; Martyr also puts *Baptismus mysterium est Regenerationis* (*Def.* 557).
[4] *in Rom.* 6.5; cf. *An in Comm. Lic.* 11; *Def.* 66.

Romanism has corrupted. Its 'superstitions and inventions' have 'horribly corrupted' baptism:

oil, salt, spittle, wax, lights, breathings, exorcisms, consecration of the Fonts twice a year . . . In vain also do they give precept of three times dipping in the water, since once may be enough, or else a little sprinkling. (*De Templ. Ded.* 5)

Yet in these external matters baptism has not been so corrupted as has the Eucharist:

by God's mercy it has been somewhat less polluted with foul abuses. And although it is not used purely and soundly, yet there is less cause for you to complain of it. (*Catech.* 42)

The real sin against the sacrament of baptism is the doctrine of baptismal regeneration:

But the head of their superstition is this, that these men think sins are forgiven chiefly by outward baptism; but they are terribly deceived. This office is of Christ alone. (*De Templ. Ded.* 18)

On a deeper level, the analogy in baptism means that this sacrament cannot be repeated. It signifies and seals our death and resurrection, our beginning of a new life; its whole power lies in its relation to the once-for-all character of Christ's Death and Resurrection.

Since circumcision was administered only once to each man, and since every man has but one nativity, therefore it happens that Baptism should be given only once. (*in Rom.* 6.5)

Baptism is the sacrament in which 'the condition of spiritual nativity' is exhibited,[5] and its 'fruitful use' consists in its continual *remembrance*, which inspires the Christian's attempt to live a life 'worthy of such a sacrament'.[6] Here is the ethical motivation of baptism so familiar in Paul.

Baptism, therefore, is the sacrament of spiritual birth, of that event which begins a new creature. This new being requires strength, confirmation and nourishment; and these are given by the Word and the second sacrament, the Eucharist.[7] Birth

---

[5] *in* 1 *Cor.* 3.2.

[6] *in* 1 *Cor.* 1.17. Martyr also points out here that since God is *et author et institutor*, the nature of the sacrament is constant despite the lack either of a worthy minister or of a 'sincere spirit' in the candidate. 'Through evil ministers, good things can be ministered in the Church.' To repeat baptism is to mock God's name.

[7] *in* 1 *Cor*, 3.2: the *duplex ordo doctrinae* and the seal of the Eucharist are instruments *roborare et confirmare*.

and growth as union and communion: these are the realities of Christian life which the sacraments signify and seal.

Union and Communion

> Now should we see what it is to be in Christ. First, what is common to all mortals. For the Son of God is joined with all men because He took upon Him human nature . . . But this conjunction is general, weak, and as I may say, according to matter. For the nature of man is by far disjoined from that nature which Christ took upon Him. For in Christ the human nature is immortal, free from sin, and adorned with complete purity: but our nature is impure, corruptible, and miserably contaminated by sin. But if this is gifted with the Spirit of Christ, it is so restored that it is little different from the nature of Christ. Indeed such an affinity is made that Paul says in the Epistle to the Ephesians, We are flesh of His flesh and bones of His bones. This phrase of speech is seen to be drawn from the Old Testament writings. For brethren and kindred are there wont to be thus spoken of among themselves: My bone and my flesh. For, coming from the same seed of the father and the same womb of the mother, they acknowledge one matter common to themselves. (*in Rom.* 8.1)

There is no doubt that this doctrine of union with Christ is the dynamic of Peter Martyr's theology. All his thought of Word and Spirit, grace and faith, sacrament and sacrifice, maintains a unity in terms of the *living Body* of Christ. By this Body God speaks and acts His mercy; into this Body we are reborn in faith; in this Body we are nurtured; as this Body we offer those sacrifices peculiar unto the sons of God. It is this doctrine of union with Christ as the substance of faith that preserves the dynamic tension of Scripture, when Romanism would fossilize it in static categories of logic. The implications of this basic Reformed doctrine for all theology are staggering; but particularly in regard to the doctrine of sacraments is it fruitful and determinative.

Christ actually joins Himself to man by two unions: by Incarnation and by Spirit. The latter presupposes the former, and together they reveal a union as close as it is complete.

> By this it is manifest how faithful and godly men are in Christ, and that by the four kinds of causes. For Christ and we have one matter, also the same beginnings of form, for we are endowed with the same notes, properties and conditions as He had. The efficient cause, by which we are moved to work is the same Spirit whereby He was moved. Lastly, the end is the same, namely that the glory of God may be advanced. (*in Rom.* 8.1)

Being in Christ implies a communication of His very 'spiritual conditions and properties'.[8] But these are no Divine qualities; rather are they the qualities of the *new humanity* of Christ. Martyr is explicit and recurrent on this point, that the Incarnation was the preparation for communicating a new humanity to men, God's own humanity because it is the humanity of His Son. The purpose of the Incarnation was to unite God to this Man so that He could unite men to this Man. Christ is

the later Adam, who to enter upon marriage with the Church in the highest union, took flesh, blood, bones and true human nature from the Virgin's womb, that He might communicate in all these with us.

(*in* 1 *Cor.* 10.16)

In terms of the Incarnation, every man is 'in Christ'. But the second union means that Christ is 'in us', for His properties are truly put into us, properties that are not 'natural' as those of the first, general union were: freedom over sin, eternal life, even incorruptibility.[9] This Martyr calls a union *realiter*, since we are gathered 'into one mass' with Christ and 'are made most conformable to Him'.[10]

This doctrine is expanded in two letters extant in Martyr's Theological Epistles, one to Calvin and one to Beza.[11] Here he admits the same two conjunctions or unions with Christ, by 'the benefit of His incarnation', and a second by the Holy Spirit when we receive 'heavenly gifts'—those properties of the Risen Man which will be finally perfected in us at the Resurrection. But now Martyr adds a *third* kind or degree of union, which he calls the 'mean' (*medium*) between them:

Therefore between the first conjunction, which I name to be of nature, and the latter which I may rightly say is of likeness or similitude, I put this mean which may be termed a conjunction of union or of secret mystery.

I believe that there are three degrees of our communion with Christ, and perceive that the middle, secret and mystical degree is expressed in holy scripture under the metaphor of members and head, and of husband and wife.

---

[8] *in* 1 *Cor.* 12.12.
[9] *in* 1 *Cor.* 10.16; cf. 12.12.   [10] *Disp.* III, *vs.* Tresham.
[11] *Ioanni Calvino, L.C.*, pp. 1094ff (from Strassburg, 8 March 1555); *Theodoro Bezae, L.C.*, pp. 1108f. The latter has no date or place, but its reference to Zanchus as colleague suggests that it also should be placed in the second Strassburg period of 1553-1556.

This 'mean' is not, as one might suppose, an initial union in time, by which we are first joined to Christ in a legal manner, as in the traditional distinction between justification and sanctification. Rather is this middle degree that constant union of Christ with His members by the Spirit, apart from which there can be no likeness of the new humanity.

> Wherefore this our communion with the Head is the first at least in nature, though not perhaps in time, before that latter communion which is brought in by regeneration . . . While we are converted, Christ is first made ours and we His, before we become like Him in holiness and righteousness abiding in us. This is that secret communion (*arcana communio*) by which we are said to be grafted into Him. Thus do we first put Him upon us, so are we called by the Apostle flesh of His flesh and bone of His bones. And by this communion now set forth, that latter is always performed while we live here.

The Head unites Himself to His members by 'spiritual knots and joints', namely faith, the Word of God and the sacraments, all of which are instruments by which the Holy Spirit quickens the members 'by a just proportion' and makes them like the Head. Thus the 'second righteousness' of which Martyr speaks so often, is here shown to be itself mediate, and dependent upon the Holy Spirit's maintaining the life-giving instrumentality of the means of grace: the 'first righteousness' (by imputation) is never superseded in time. The end of it all is that we should 'become daily more and more *Christiformia*', that is, like Christ by alteration in quality.

Thus we have 'a heavenly and spiritual similitude' with Christ, of which the mean conjunction is 'fountain and origin'. When we consider these terms, *similitudo*, *medium* and *proportio* we recognize again the analogical thinking of our Reformer. The Christian is truly one becoming *like* Christ because he is *in* Christ—but the relationship of union is not direct but analogical. Capernaite and mystic are alike condemned because here the middle term is—the Holy Spirit. He is the bond of our union with Christ.[12]

[12] Cf. the significant comments on the Fathers in *Def.*, Part IV, esp. pp. 744ff. For instance, Hilary says *Christum esse in nobis naturaliter*. Martyr explains that union with Christ is based upon the Incarnation (substantial) and through faith (spiritual): 'we in turn apprehend His flesh through faith and eat spiritually'. Therefore, he concludes, the Incarnation and the Eucharist stand in a definite relationship, but it is not *identity*, for the one is substantial, the other spiritual.

The conclusion of the teaching of this correspondence relates this middle union to the sacraments.

> And of this inward union, both Baptism and the Lord's Supper are most sure and firm tokens. For just as soon as we believe in Christ, we are made partakers of this communion: and because in a profitable receiving of the sacraments faith is necessary, therefore by it is the same conjunction both confirmed and increased while we use the sacraments. Wherefore through faith are we lifted up from the degree of nature so that we are joined to Christ as members to their Head. Further, from the immortal and heavenly Head, whom we now possess in actual fact through faith, are derived unto us various gifts, heavenly benefits, and divine properties.

Both sacraments are related strictly to this middle union which Martyr has described: they are signs that such a union takes place, and seals to strengthen and confirm it. The decisive thing in this complex doctrine is that the union of faith, which is a 'secret communion' itself, leads to the communication of Christ's properties. We are first bound to Christ, as it were, then Christ to us. Our 'coming into Christ', we could say, is the gateway to His 'coming into us'. The reality of the union of faith is only present by the receiving of Christ's new human properties. And the sacraments are signs and seals of that first union, by which this second reality comes! Their purpose and effect, this context makes crystal clear, is wholly relative to the personal infilling of Jesus Christ. This is the position from which Martyr attacks all notion of a corporeal presence in the Eucharist: from his doctrine of union with Christ as the personal participation in His new humanity on the part of His members. Christ's new properties are really given to us: this is the reality of faith and the way we are related to His Body and His Blood.[13]

---

[13] Calvin's reply to this teaching is significant (*Ioan. Calvini . . . Epistolae et Resp., Ep.* 208, pp. 391ff). It was written from Geneva, 8 August 1555. 'What you had written me concerning the secret communion which is ours with Christ . . . even if of great moment, yet I think by a few sound words it can be defined well between us. I will refrain from speaking of that communication in which the Son of God took our flesh, to become our brother, participant in the same nature. For only that should be treated, which spreads from His heavenly virtue and breathes life into us, and makes us coalesce in one body with Him. But I say, as soon as we receive Christ by faith, as He offers Himself in the Gospel, we are truly made His members, and life flows into us from Him as from the Head. For no other way are we reconciled to God by the sacrifice of His death, except that He is ours and we are one with Him . . . we draw life from His flesh and blood, so that not unworthily are they called our nourishment . . . the flesh of Christ is not *per se* vivifying, nor does its power come to us without the unfathomable operation of the Holy Spirit. Therefore the Spirit is He who makes Christ abide in us, who sustains and nourishes us, and fulfils all offices of the Head (*omniaque capitis officia impleat*).

Union with Christ is effectively signified and sealed by both sacraments, inasmuch as substance is obtained in two ways, by birth and by nourishment:

> We take the same body through the same generation and the same food ... so we through Baptism are grafted into Christ, and through the Eucharist are nourished in the very same. (*in* 1 *Cor.* 12.13)

> Sacraments have regard to our union with Christ, Baptism indeed by way of generation, but the Eucharist by way of nourishment. (*Def.* 686)

Indeed, in one sense Martyr is willing to declare:

> Baptism fulfils that (union with Christ) more effectively than the Eucharist, since we obtain more through generation than by nourishment or food. (*in* 1 *Cor.* 12.12)

For this reason the Early Church considered baptism of greater moment than the Eucharist.[14] But in general Martyr is content to insist on 'an identical ratio in both sacraments'.[15] This is one of the strongest arguments against transubstantiation.

> Baptism is also a vivifying sacrament. But in it there is no body of Christ present *realiter*. (*Def.* 437)

> We are no less joined to Christ in Baptism than we are in the Eucharist: wherefore His presence and our reception of Him, which are spiritual, are to be affirmed in both alike. (*Epit., Sent.* 7)

I preclude meanwhile entering on crass comments about mixing together the substances, since it is enough for me, while the body of Christ remains in the heavenly glory, life flows from Him to us, just as the root transmits sap to the branches ... Now I come to the second communication, which to me is the fruit and effect of that prior one. For after Christ by the interior virtue of His Spirit subdues us to Himself and unites us into His body, He follows after the virtue of His Spirit by enriching us with His gifts ... Nor yet is it absurd that when we coalesce in His body, Christ communicates His Spirit to us, whose secret operation is our first effect ... even if in this communion, the faithful come at His calling the very first day: yet since in them the life of Christ grows (*augescit*) daily, He offers Himself for their enjoyment. This is the communication which they receive in the holy Supper ... I have but touched this deliberation, that you may see that we feel the very same on all points.' The doctrine and terminology is practically identical, and the closing words indicate the conscious agreement between Calvin and Martyr. Cf. Appendix C on their relationship. Calvin states clearly the difference between faith and the union that results from it: 'they consider eating to be the very same as believing; I say, that in believing we eat the flesh of Christ, because He is actually made ours by faith, and that this eating is the fruit and effect of faith; or, to express it more plainly, they consider the eating to be faith itself; I apprehend it to be rather a consequence of faith. The difference is small in words, but in the thing itself it is considerable' (*Inst.* 4.17.5).

14 As the N.T. does also!

15 *in utroque sacramento consimilem esse rationem*—*Disp.* III, *vs.* Tresham. Cf. *Def.* 522: the same *ratio et genus*; 201: the *modus* of both sacraments is by *similitudo* and therefore Baptism can as well be called *fides* as the Eucharist is called *corpus Christi*.

There is no reason why a sensible substance should obtain in the Eucharist rather than in Baptism. (*Def.* 686)

The difference between them is not one of the presence of 'the truth' of sacraments, and therefore no difference *in genere*, only *in specie*.[16]

Our union with Christ, which we celebrate in the Eucharist is not thus (sc. *in genere*) different from what we have in Baptism . . . in both we receive Christ, and are renewed both in spirit and body. Yet we often teach a difference in mode, namely that in Baptism we are changed into Christ through regeneration, but in the Eucharist through spiritual nourishment. (*Def.* 747)

In the light of such teaching we may now ask the vital question, what does baptism *effect*? Is it simply cognitive, or is it also effective?

The Effect of Baptism

Moreover, although they believe, yet when the promises are again offered, and that by the Lord's institution, and they through faith and the impulsion of the Holy Spirit effectively grasp them, the benefits of God cannot but be augmented in them. (*in Rom.* 6.5)

The only sure lodestar for this difficult path is Peter Martyr's teaching about the threefold union with Christ. As we remember that the sacraments are the Holy Spirit's instruments in order to bring to us the virtue of Christ's new humanity, we shall hold to the basic truth in the doctrine of the sacraments: that the 'thing signified' by them is not a passive substance, but the dynamic Mystery, Christ Himself. The sacraments are not superfluous, nor mere signs of something past: they have a real and positive effect. Regeneration means that 'we put on the properties of His nature' through the 'new conjunction' of the Spirit.[17] And baptism as the sacrament of this regeneration is often simply set forth by Martyr thus: 'In Baptism we are changed into Christ', since we are made 'participators in the divine nature'.[18]

What baptism concerns is the *Christiformia*, Christ's growth in us, which we have denoted as the reality of our union with

[16] *Def.* 547.   [17] *Def.* 751.
[18] *Def.* 745, 747.

Christ.[19] Indeed, Martyr himself says, in this context of the effect of baptism:

> It is possible to say that we are more perfectly in Christ than He is in us.
>
> (*Def.* 752)

For human nature exists in Him in perfection, without flaw, and it is this perfect new humanity which we begin to put on in baptism.[20] Faith means that we become 'partakers of the properties of the human nature of Christ'.[21] Faith is no less than 'a union according to the flesh'[22] since all the benefits of God are derived to us 'through the flesh of Christ' once broken for us,[23] and because we experience a mutation into this same Christ.[24] The elements of the sacraments, Martyr says, are consecrated and so changed into sacraments,

> to this end alone, to effect and induce (as much as instruments can) our mutation. (*Def.* 763)

> When the Fathers will confirm the change made in the Eucharist, they bring as example the change of our selves, which is made in Baptism: this change the Apostle too seems to declare very great. For he uses the names of life and death, between which there must needs be a very great change.
>
> (*in Rom.* 6.4)

In baptism, then, there is a definite change of ourselves, which Martyr apparently identifies with the change effected by justification. But not so: this he explicitly denies. For this is what the theologians of Trent thought, with their doctrine of the *praeparatioad gratiam*:

> But these men see not that we must far otherwise judge of Baptism. For Scripture teaches that Abraham was first justified by faith in uncircumcision and then received circumcision as a seal of the righteousness already received. This same consideration, according to the analogy, must be kept in baptism: for our baptism answers to the circumcision of the fathers of the Old Testament. (*De Iustif.* 8)

A seal to justification by faith: this is the essential meaning of the sacrament. A sufficient definition, Martyr states, is Paul's:

---

[19] Martyr's clearest teaching on this is given in the next Chapter, in the section on 'The Nourishment of the Body of Christ'.

[20] *Def.* 763.   [21] *Def.* 413.

[22] *coniunctio secundum carnem*: *Def.* 750, where Martyr deals with Cyril's doctrine of union with Christ according to three modes: Incarnation; the Spirit, who gives us that same flesh; and the communication of the properties, conditions and graces of His flesh.

[23] *Def.* 751.   [24] *Def.* 763.

sacraments are σφραγίδες, that is, sealings of the righteousness of faith. For they seal the promises by which, if faith is joined to them, we are justified . . . Wherefore every man may see how much they are deceived that think the sacraments are only marks and notes of piety . . . the head and sum of their signification is that they seal. (*in Rom.* 4.11)

Baptism is therefore not only the sign but the seal of justification by faith, which for Martyr means union with Christ. Baptism is related to the remission of sins, not indeed causally (*opere operato*), but significantly (as sign) and also instrumentally (as seal), according to the gracious working of the Holy Spirit.[25] The sealing office of baptism means that it is effective as well as cognitive. In a thorough examination of this decisive point, Martyr sums up his teaching:

The cause of sanctification is Christ Himself, who gave Himself for us, and for that reason gave the washing of water, that His cleansing might be attested by the Word and the symbol. Briefly this must be held: outward signs do not join us to Christ, but are given when we are already joined to Him . . . to be made a member of Christ precedes baptism, but to express this in manners of life follows . . . we were of the body of Christ before, but to testify and seal this, we are outwardly baptized . . . justification depends not on baptism, but precedes it. (*De Templ. Ded.* 18, 19)

Once again we see that faith is always related to the analogical nature of the activity of God's Word and Spirit. Martyr continues:

But perhaps you will say, To what end then is Baptism delivered to them, if they had the substance of baptism before? Is the labour spent there in vain? Not at all. First, because we obey God who commanded to us the work of baptism. Second, we seal the promise and gift which we have received. Moreover, faith is there confirmed by the Holy Spirit, through the Word and outward signs. And as we ourselves think of this visible Word or sacrament, the Spirit of God stirs up faith in our hearts, by which again we embrace the divine promises, and so justification is amplified, while faith is increased in believers. God specially assists the signs instituted by Him. For they are no profane or empty things. Wherefore the fruit of baptism is not momentary, but extends through the whole life. Thus those who are baptized neither waste their work nor act in vain. (*De Templ. Ded.* 20)

Does Martyr teach an *augmentum gratiae*? Not if we interpret this in terms of a deposit of grace related to external signs, or

[25] *in* 1 *Cor.* 4.11: σημεῖον is a general word, while σφραγίς is more definitely sacramental; e.g. 'an image is a sign, but it cannot be a seal'.

even to 'Spirit' in a less than Personal meaning. But inasmuch as 'grace' for him means the work of the Word and Spirit in uniting us to the new humanity of Jesus Christ, there is no reason why the personal growth of our union with Christ should not be thought in terms of additions or increases.

> The Church is a body quickened by the Spirit of God, which increases not otherwise than a living body is naturally formed, little by little.
>
> (*Catech.* 47)

Again and again Martyr stresses this positive effect of baptism as the decisive act which seals our union with Christ and gives access to that growth which is correspondingly increased through the Eucharist.[26]

> Moreover although they believe, yet when the promises are again offered, and that by the Lord's institution, and they through faith and the impulsion of the Holy Spirit effectively grasp them, the benefits of God cannot but be augmented in them . . . by the visible sacrament we are grafted into Christ and the Church . . . the right to eternal life is sealed to us by baptism.
>
> (*in Rom.* 6.5)

Martyr can even say that regeneration 'is brought with' baptism:

> a sacrament may be of the same value as is the Word of God. For just as this Word signifies and gives in truth to believers whatever it promises, so baptism being received by faith, both signifies and gives to believers remission of sins, which it promises by a visible speaking. (*Catech.* 45)

This question of baptism as deed as well as word concerned Martyr chiefly because of his Patristic studies.[27] Yet it is the obvious question in view of his basic stress on justification by faith, *if* this is related to the Church's sacramental life in categories of logic alone, which rationalizes every doctrine. If justification precede baptism, Martyr says, what profit then hath the sacrament?[28] Consider Cornelius, who possessed the Spirit before baptism, or Jacob—

> He was loved of God being an infant, was born of faithful parents, and truly belonged unto the covenant of God . . . What had he by the sacrament that he had not before?

---

[26] Cf. esp. *in Rom.* 4.11; 6.5; 7.17.
[27] Cf. G. W. H. Lampe, *The Seal of the Spirit* (Longmans, 1951) Part IV, 'Patristic Theories of Sealing' for an excellent summary of the doctrines which form Martyr's presupposition in his teaching on baptism.
[28] This teaching is from the *Comm. in* 1 *Cor.* 7.14.

Much every way: in three ways, to be precise. First, 'the commandment of the Lord must be fulfilled'. Second:

> the gifts already obtained . . . must be sealed with the outward sign, that we may be continually mindful of them, to take occasion by this to exercise our faith, and to be admonished of our duty.

Third, baptism is a Church act, a corporate act, with a corresponding significance for adult or infant:

> Moreover there are added the prayers of the minister, the vows of those who offer, things which profit the infant not a little: and the Church which stands by at the ministration of that Sacrament is taught concerning salvation.

God is pleased to amplify His gifts thus promised, 'by His goodness and Spirit'. So Martyr concludes, 'Do these things avail little, or are they unprofitable?'

A further point in relation to the sealing of baptism is that it is not to be neglected. Martyr does not regard it as necessary for salvation:

> Every faithful man should be baptized if possible: but when he cannot have a minister he is excused. (*De Schism.* 42)

But if one omit this sacrament through contempt, the omission is a positive 'hindrance' to salvation.[29] Indeed he declares:

> If any man condemns the sacrament of baptism, he will be excluded from the kingdom of heaven. For those who have entered into belief, must take special heed to this, that they be ingrafted into the Church by the sacrament. (*in Rom.* 7.25)

Finally:

> Although the sacrament is given but once, yet it ought never to be forgotten in our whole lifetime . . . For the property of signs is not to profit only at the time when they are present. Otherwise we should be baptized continually . . . The sealing of the promise of God which we receive in baptism never loses its force and strength. (*in Rom.* 6.5; 6.10)

Peter Martyr's complex and fruitful teaching on baptism involves the question provoked by the Anabaptist reduction of faith to a cognitive-subjective level: should infants be baptized? For Martyr states explicitly:

> Sacraments are seals of the promises of God, and confirmations of our faith. But if faith is absent, what can be either sealed or confirmed?
>
> (in 1 Sam. 15.22)

[29] *in Rom.* 7.17.

L

What, then, can be the reason for the baptizing of infants? Martyr brings two chief reasons, closely related: *circumcision* as the O.T. analogue of baptism, and *predestination*.

Circumcision and Covenant

> In circumcision and baptism it is a perpetual matter that those who belong to the covenant of God and are joined to the people of God should be marked by some outward sign; but yet the kind of sign was changeable and temporal. (*in* 1 *Cor.* 15.2)

Although Peter Martyr's theology cannot be termed simply 'federal', the doctrine of the one covenant of grace is operative throughout his doctrine of the sacraments as its Scriptural background. His doctrine of infant baptism rests upon the analogy which Scripture draws between the O.T. sacrament of circumcision and the N.T. sacrament of baptism—but this in turn rests upon the Christological unity of Scripture. The argument from circumcision as analogue is not an after-thought introduced by Reformed theology in defence of a Romanist doctrine carried on in inconsistency with justification by faith,[30] but is the unavoidable implication of its Christological view of revelation. Thus Martyr says of the Anabaptists:

> They seem to be wiser than God: for God doubtless knew that Circumcision contained a promise of Christ, and a profession of mortification and of new life. For by the prophets He continually urges the Circumcision of the heart, which was signified by that Sacrament, and yet He commanded that infants should be initiated unto Him by circumcision . . . They also are not to be listened to that say circumcision was only the sealing of promises concerning temporal things. (*in Rom.* 6.5)

The historical evidence is secondary: for example, that since Cyprian and Origen take infant baptism for granted, nor mention its institution, it must be Apostolic in origin.[31] What is determinative is the dogmatic element: Christ instituted baptism, and as the N.T. sacrament of regeneration (mortification and new life) it is by definition analogous to the O.T. sacrament of circumcision. Therefore unless our infants are

---

[30] As proponents of so-called 'believer's baptism' commonly charge.

[31] *in Rom.* 6.5; cf. on 5.19: 'Baptism was appointed by tradition from the apostles, to be given unto infants; because the apostles knew that the natural corruption of sin is in all men, which ought to be washed away by water and the Spirit.' As to the actual origin of the rite, Martyr says (*in* 2 *Reg.* 2.23) 'John Baptist introduced a new rite of Baptism and gave it to the Hebrews'.

'in a worse state' than the Hebrew children, they are to be baptized.

> Baptisms were before the law, in the law, and under the Gospel; and all, as regards their substance, had the same force.

> It is not true that the ceremonies of antiquity were but outward exercises, in which was no remission of sins. (*Prop. ex Exod.* 18, *nec.* 11. 12)

This dogmatic basis rests chiefly on Paul's relating circumcision and baptism in Romans 4 and Colossians 2, along with the foundational passage, Genesis 17.[32] Although these passages do not yield an explicit command to baptize infants, Martyr declares their clear teaching of this, just as the doctrine of ὁμοουσία was defended as Scriptural by Athanasius, who declared against the Arians that he contended not *de vocabulo* but *de reipsa*.[33]

> Unto doctrine nothing should be thought necessary save what is gathered from the holy Scriptures, either expressly or by clear and solid reason: such as concerning the baptism of infants, and concerning homousia.
>
> (*in* 1 *Sam.* 14.52, *De Leg. Ecc.*)

Commenting on Matthew 22.32, Martyr states that here Christ brings no express testimony, but only inference, in support of the resurrection from the dead; just so—

> whereas they contend with us for the baptism of children, they will have us to bring out of the Scriptures express, plain and manifest words by which it is affirmed that children should be baptized. Nor will they be content with reasons and conclusions derived from the Scriptures. (*De Resurrectione,* 25)

The reasons and conclusions are plain enough, according to Martyr: they are summed up in the name *covenant*.

> Baptism is given us in place of circumcision, as Paul clearly writes to the Colossians. Now unless you wish our little ones to have fallen into a condition below the sons of Israel, just as they were circumcised in infancy, so you will acknowledge our children to be admitted to baptism. What in that reason I pray you, is opposed out of Scripture? Do you doubt the infants of Christians to pertain to God as the sons of the Hebrews did?
>
> (*De Vot.* 1373D)

It is manifestly false to distinguish two covenants according to categories of law/grace or works/faith. We have already

---

[32] For Peter Martyr's detailed teaching on circumcision and infant baptism, see the Commentaries *in Gen.* 17.2 (fol. 68Aff), *in* 1 *Reg.* 8.66 (*De Templ. Ded.*, fol. 68Aff), *in Rom.* 4.9ff, 6.5, *in* 1 *Cor.* 1.17, 7.14.

[33] *De Vot.* 1345, *Obj.* V.

considered this in Chapter 2; and the implication of Martyr's doctrine of the presence of Christ in the O.T. is clear. Circumcision must be:

a sign, or to speak more properly, a sealing of the promise and covenant made with God through Christ . . . By this sacrament also the mortifying of the flesh and filthy lusts were marked. This rite was to the old Fathers instead of Baptism, and was accounted the sacrament of regeneration. Wherefore it appears that our infants should be baptized, since their lot is no worse than that of the Hebrews' children, yea rather it is many ways happier. (*in Rom.* 2.25)

Circumcision, as Chrysostom said, is double, inward as well as outward, of spirit as well as of flesh—and indeed there is between these a mean, proceeding from the one and agreeable to the other.[34] Perhaps the best summary of this phase of Martyr's doctrine is given in the Commentary on 1 Corinthians 7.14, which we shall give in some detail.

God first entered into covenant not only with Abraham but with his whole family, and willed that not only Abraham but all his household servants and slaves should pertain to the covenant—among whom no doubt were many little ones. Afterward followed circumcision. By this it is evident that the promise, pact or covenant was not brought in by circumcision but preceded it. This same fact must be understood about Baptism: for first the Word was preached to citizens or heads of families, and the covenant to be entered upon through Christ was proclaimed. When they had been kindled by faith, and admitted themselves to the covenant, baptism followed, not only with regard to them, but also to their little ones, who were recognized to be comprehended in that covenant. St. Paul says that he baptized the house of Stephanos. And in the Acts of the Apostles, as we said before, not only the master of the prison but also all those that belonged unto him received baptism.

This covenant, Martyr continues, was not temporal, since it was the revelation of God Himself, deliverance 'from sin, death and damnation'. Nor was the promise dependent upon the flesh, upon human generation, since it was preserved 'only by the power and efficacy of God's mercy'. God was *merciful* to the Hebrews and to their *children*: this was His covenant.

Nor are we to doubt that the same covenant is applied to our children, unless we will count God to be less pitiful and merciful unto us than He was to the Hebrews: as though by the coming of Christ His grace were diminished.

[34] *in Rom.* 2.25; 2.28.

This is the covenant to which the infants pertained, and which was sealed in their bodies by the sacrament of regeneration.

> In the Epistle to the Colossians circumcision is most plainly compared with our baptism. (*Col.* 2.11-12) . . . Wherefore our baptism is of no less account than was Circumcision, for it sealed the covenant and promise in the young children of the Hebrews, which we must judge to be done by Baptism.

What was sealed in circumcision? This seems to be the key to Martyr's use of the Pauline analogy. For his normative definition of a sacrament is seal, so that what is sealed is presupposed in the administration of the rite. In adults the answer is obvious. In children, however, it is the promise of the Divine words which is sealed, or the communication.[35] We count them grafted into the Church by 'the Word of God and promise of the covenant' and so include them in the sacrament of regeneration. The Word of promise is determinative:[36]

> the covenant and promise excludes them not, nay rather they are generally signified in these words, in which the Lord says, 'I will be thy God and the God of thy seed' (Gen. 17.7) under which promise we baptize them, and visibly incorporate them into the Church; who yet, when they come of age may reject the covenant and condemn the Gospel. (*in Rom.* 11.22)

Because children of Christian parents, being addressed by the Word of promise 'pertain unto the Church and unto Christ',[37] therefore they should be 'defended and confirmed' with the outward sign 'like a seal to gifts'.[38] Finally therefore,

> what faith brings about in adults before they are baptized, that the Spirit of Christ and the promise work in infants . . . God doubtless has the number of His children most certain, whom He predestinated from all eternity. But the promise of the covenant with the stock of Abraham is of no certain number, and expressly excludes none of his successors. And so when the children of believers are offered to the Church to be baptized, this has respect unto the promise as it is uttered. (*De Templ. Ded.* 20)

'The Spirit of Christ and the promise', 'whom He predestinated' —here is the ultimate theological reference of the entire discussion. For this cuts across the whole adult-infant problem in terms of the Author and Finisher of faith, and of His secret will.

---

[35] Cf. *De Templ. Ded.* 18: the covenant is the matter of infant baptism and it precedes; 'afterward follows the outward symbol'.

[36] *in* 1 *Cor.* 7.14: As a farmer seals his livestock and a king his letters patent, so the Church 'baptizes those whom it supposes to belong unto it, and who are not strangers from it'.   [37] *in Rom.* 6.5.   [38] *De Vot.* 1374A.

Original Sin and Predestination

Peter Martyr constantly refers the question of infant baptism to two related doctrines: original sin and election or predestination. For between these is an analogy, 'the consideration of seed'.[39] Original sin is like a seed 'poured in by generation'; Christ in turn begets to Himself members through His seed— election, grace, the Spirit, the Word of God and baptism. The last two are significant as the outward instruments of regeneration.

> But if a man ask whether the outward Word or the visible sign of baptism is wholly necessary, we answer that indeed the inward Word, by which men are moved unto Christ and reformed, is absolutely required, if we speak of them that are of mature age; but in children, neither has the inward Word place, nor is the outward Word the ordinary instrument. (*in Rom.* 5.19)

The distinction between the inward and outward Word is most important. God has a 'signifying' will, which extends through outward calling to all men; but His 'effectual' will is not coextensive with that.[40] But since both refer to the calling by the Word in accommodation to the human mind and the response of faith, Martyr declares the distinction irrelevant here. There is no 'deposit of faith' in infants: a biological analogy will not do to describe this beginning.

> I know that it has been thought by some, and those of no small esteem, that infants have faith, as though God works in them in a wondrous way and beyond the course of nature—whose opinion (to speak the truth) I do not embrace very readily.[41]

> Moreover (Lutherans) believe that infants are endued with faith, which neither you nor we believe, who think it sufficient unto their salvation that they are endued with the Spirit of Christ, who is the root and origin of faith, and who at such time as He thinks good, will stir up faith in them.[42]

---

[39] *in Rom.* 5.19. We may term these the negative and positive reasons for infant baptism.

[40] *in* I *Sam.* 2.25; cf. *in Gen.* 12.1: God's calling is *efficax et inefficax*: the latter is by outward sign, the former has salvation added, *plena persuasio intus et in animo*.

[41] *in* I *Cor.* 7.14: Is he thinking of Calvin here? In the *Institutes*, III. 16.18, Calvin used the biological analogy, although it represents there the expression of the eschatological nature of faith, which Martyr also sought. Cf. Wallace, p. 190: 'here Calvin is thinking of the seed of future repentance and faith . . . not as a present possession of the child but as held over the child transcendently and eschatologically through the potentiality of Baptism and the Spirit.'

[42] Letter *Ecclesiae Anglorum*, *L.C.*, pp. 1098f, written at the time when the Lutherans were persecuting Reformed Churchmen who fled England at Mary's accession. Thus the question was raised, should we allow Lutherans elsewhere to

But does this reduce predestination to an objective 'decree'? Not at all, it has a valid subjective reference: the infant 'has' the Holy Spirit, who will summon faith when response is possible.

> But since holy Scripture tells me not that little ones believe, or that these miracles (a wondrous working) are done in them, nor do I see this to be necessary to their salvation, I judge it sufficient to affirm that those who shall be saved, forasmuch as by election and predestination they belong unto the treasure of God, are endowed with the Spirit of God, who is the root of faith, hope, charity and all virtues, which He afterwards shows forth and declares in the children of God, when through age it may be done.
> (*in* 1 *Cor.* 7.14)

This means that the Holy Spirit is the 'matter' of the covenant-promise in infants that are predestinated: He may be said even to 'instruct' such infants, and to 'secretly work regeneration in them'.[43] Indeed, at one point Martyr says that the infant could be thought of as 'born again by the Word of God'.[44]

What is the significance of this debate about the 'seed of faith'? In an interesting passage he writes of original sin:

> But by the promise and force of the covenant it is forgiven—when God works this forgiveness we cannot learn from the testimony of Scripture. In infants it is perhaps forgiven when they are yet in the womb, or when they are born, or right after birth, nor is it likely given to all men at the same time. (*in Rom.* 11.14)

Martyr thus acknowledges that we cannot rationalize the mode of the Divine activity, which is accommodated differently to adults and infants. But what is more important is that he seeks to guarantee the nature of faith as eschatological: there is a delay before the reality of faith is revealed in the Resurrection, which was symbolized by the delay of circumcision until the eighth day.[45] For the sacrament of regeneration—whether

---

baptize us; and also, should we rebaptize those baptized by Lutherans? Martyr strongly speaks against repetition of Lutheran or Papist baptism. To the first he says, since baptism is a seal, we cannot deliver our faith to be sealed by those who detest it.

[43] *in* 1 *Cor.* 7.14 and *in Rom.* 2.25. In the latter passage Martyr rejects Augustine's view that salvation may come to infants by the faith of them that offer them, on the ground that in adults their own faith is required, and in children 'the Holy Spirit and grace' works the regeneration. But in his letter *Ecc. Ang.* he states that infant baptism seals the faith of the adults who offer them. This single reference ought to be compared with the former, and then related to his insistence that baptism is a corporate act, by which the whole Church benefits—e.g. *in Rom.* 4.12.

[44] *De Templ. Ded.* 20.

[45] *in Rom.* 4.12: 'the sins of the flesh can never be perfectly cut off from us, until we come to the holy resurrection.'

circumcision or baptism—is by definition a sacrament the reality of which is future and bound up with resurrection. The reality is not temporally identifiable with the sign. Baptism means *into* Christ, *into* His Body, the Body wherein nourishment is received and growth increased, as Christ is formed in us. Baptism is therefore in a profound sense *into a future regeneration*.[46]

Finally, therefore, it is the covenant promise and presence of the Holy Spirit which is the basis for infant baptism. Men are called simply to 'follow the signs and tokens of election', namely, the having of faith in an adult, the having of Christian parents in a child.

> And if with the action of the sacraments are joined election and predestination, that which we do is ratified; but if not, then is it void. (*in Rom.* 4.12)

Obviously there is a risk here! But is not the risk present in the case of adult baptism, even though different in degree? In either case a judgment is required, and human judgment is fallible.

> But you will say, you may be deceived, since perhaps the child will not pertain to the number of the elect. I answer that the same difficulty may also happen to those of adult age. For perhaps one may profess faith with a false heart, or may be led only by human persuasion, or may have faith but only for a time; so that in actual fact he does not pertain to the elect. Yet the minister has not a regard for these things . . . but waits upon the general promise; though many are excluded from this, yet is it none of his part to define which they are. (*in Rom.* 5.19)

> Since the reason of this election is hidden, and the first token we have is that children belong to them that are holy and are offered by them in the sacrament of regeneration, therefore we call them holy, although as has been noted, this token may deceive: just as also the confession of faith expressed in words by adults when about to be baptized, may lie and proceed from hypocrisy. (*in 1 Cor.* 7.14)

> Some demand that since we know not whether infants have the matter of the sacrament, why do we give them the sign, and seal what is uncertain to us? To whom we reply: this question is not brought against us but against the Word of God. For He expressly commanded and willed that children should be circumcised. Again, let them answer us, why they admit adults to baptism or communion, since they are uncertain of their mind? For those who are baptized or communicate can be false, and deceive the Church. They reply, it is enough to have their profession: if they lie, what

---

[46] Even though Martyr can say *parvulos iustificatos aut regeneratos ante baptismum* (Goode's 'Unpublished Letter of P.M. to Bullinger').

is that to us? they say, let them see to that. So say we of infants, that it is enough for us that they are offered to the Church, either by parents or by those in whose power they are. (*in Rom.* 4.12)

To conclude this account of Peter Martyr's doctrine of infant baptism, we may briefly indicate his reaction to two doctrines that developed, particularly in the England whose Prayer Book he had so greatly influenced.[47] To the doctrine of *baptismal regeneration* he would surely give a quick and decided 'No!', as our section on 'The Effect of Baptism' suggests. Apart from such specific statements as those which say 'Justification precedes baptism', there is the basic presupposition of his whole doctrine, faith as union with Christ by the Holy Spirit, which precludes the denial of the sacrament as sign and seal implied in the doctrine of baptismal regeneration. As to *Confirmation*, he has one passing reference which is significant:

> Nor do we dislike that confirmation, by which children, when they come to age should be made to confess their faith in the Church, and by outward profession approve what was done in Baptism when they understood nothing—yet of such an action we do not frame a sacrament.[48]

Moreover, his doctrine of the Church, despite its acceptance of the office of Bishop—at least in terms of his understanding of that office shared by his friends the English Reformers— would deal hardly with the subsequent arrogation of power over confirmation by the episcopal office.[49]

Martyr's doctrine ends on a note of 'hoping well' of the children baptized into the Church of Christ.

> Because we should not be over curious in searching out the secret providence and election of God, therefore we judge the children of the saints to be saints, so long as by reason of age they do not declare themselves to be strangers from Christ. We exclude them not from the Church, but embrace them as members, hoping well, that as they are the seed of the saints after the flesh, so also may they partake of the divine election, and have the Holy Spirit and grace of Christ; and for this reason we baptize them. (*in* 1 *Cor.* 7.14)

[47] Cf. introductory 'Portrait' IV, *The Second Prayer Book.*
[48] In *De Poenit.* 14 which deals with the question of the episcopal laying on of hands. The Romanist rite had preserved the sign while the signification had long since passed. In the Early Church the significance of having the bishop for this rite was *ad honorem sacerdotii, non ex necessitate praecepti* (*Hieron. contra Lucif.*), so that *Inutilis ergo est confirmatio, nisi primo modo servetur.*
[49] Cf. the Treatises noted in Chapter IV.

CHAPTER VI

THE SACRAMENT OF COMMUNICATION

A communion of spirit is a society of those men who participate in the same spirit. Thus have Christians society among themselves, and a union based on this, that they are partakers of the body and blood of Christ. (in 1 Cor. 10.16)

IN this Chapter we shall outline Peter Martyr's positive teaching upon the Lord's Supper, or to use his favourite name for it, the Eucharist. Part III will treat the details of this doctrine as these were called forth in controversy with Romanist, Lutheran and Anabaptist opposition. First we ought to sum up certain main bases of his theology. *First*, faith means union with Christ. Justification has substance in the realm of being as well as of knowledge. Sanctification means the increase of this union, but always deriving from the ongoing union from the side of Christ. *Second*, this growth has as its nourishment the Word of God as the 'chief food of the soul'. It is Christ Himself who grows in the believer, by the continual apprehension of His Person. *Third*, this apprehension is dependent upon the effective action of the Holy Spirit, who uses earthly elements as signs through and from which He raises up the mind and soul to grasp the Risen Man, Jesus Christ.

Now let us see how these bases make for a doctrine of the Eucharist as distinctive as it is fruitful, at once dynamic and personal, yielding neither to the temptation to make too much of the earthly elements, nor too little.

Communication and the Word

God everywhere required that we should hear His voice: which is nothing else than to deal with Him by faith. (*in Iud.* 2.23)

Revelation means the self-communication of God, that is, the union of men with Christ. This is the work of the Holy Spirit, who uses two instruments mutually related and apposite:

the Word of God and faith. Where the Holy Spirit unites us to Christ, there His instrument is the Word of God; where the Word of God is, there man has but one response, faith. This principle is fundamental to the Reformed doctrine of the sacraments.

> I would not admit that the sacraments, either ours or theirs of ancient times, give grace of themselves. For whatever grace we have, we obtain by faith, and not (as you imagine) because of the work done. Nor do we thus make sacraments more contemptible: since we determine that they, when received aright, help, confirm and increase faith, by which alone are we justified. For the Holy Spirit, as He uses the words of God and the scriptures like instruments to change and to save us; so likewise He uses the sacraments . . . And since faith is obtained by the Word, the more manifest that Word is, the more earnestly is faith stirred up, and the more does it apprehend the thing signified . . . the clarity and plainness of the sacraments must be chiefly regarded in the words. Because, if you compare the words with the elements, the words are their life. (*Disp.*, closing speech)

The sacraments by definition are not *per se* the communication of life, since that is a different *ordo*: that pertains to the Word of God and to faith—'Where the Word of God is not, there faith cannot be.'[1] The communication in the sacraments is thus not of the same order as the elements themselves—this is the definition of *sacramentum*!—but is located in the Word. In this sense, the body and blood of the Eucharist are the body and blood of the Word of God.[2] For it is not human blood which saves men, not even Christ's Blood 'as blood of a mere man' (*ut puri hominis sanguis*), but that which removes sin is the blood of the Word, and the Word is grasped only by faith.

In this context, faith is the one instrument from the human side, for communication of the union with Christ. It is therefore the only preparation for the Eucharist which man can have. This also agrees with the Scriptural definition of a sacrament, upon which Martyr lays such stress: a sacrament is a *seal* of that grace which comes by Word unto faith. There is a fixed and definite order to be observed, therefore, in the case of the Eucharist at least:

faith ought always to go before the receiving of the sacraments, if we receive them aright, and the order be not inverted. For as without faith men eat

---

[1] *ubi non est verbum dei, nec fides esse potest. Def.* 79.
[2] *Def.* 76: Peter Martyr cites Origen: *ne haereas in sanguinem carnis, sed disce potius sanguinem verbi . . . Novit qui mysteriis imbutus est, et carnem et sanguinem verbi dei.*

and drink unworthily, so without faith baptism is unworthily received: yet this must be understood regarding adults. For as regards the way with infants, we will elsewhere declare. Then, if faith precede, it is manifest that sins are forgiven; because the sacraments that follow seal and confirm us, concerning the will of God. (*in Rom.* 11.27)

Faith and the Soul of Man

Faith as the instrument by which alone Christ is communicated unto us, poses the question as to whether that implies a purely subjective and anthropocentric understanding of man's relation to God. Our study of Peter Martyr's theology to this point denies such a conclusion; yet we must analyse his terms in relation to the reception of the Eucharist, where he speaks much of the mind (*mens*) and soul or spirit (*animus*) of man.

> Wherefore the wicked, who are destitute of that instrument by which the body and blood of the Lord are received, namely faith, do not for that reason receive the things themselves which are signified, but receive only the signs of those things. But those who are prepared with faith, just as with the mouth of the body they eat and drink the signs, so by the mouth of the mind they truly receive the body and blood of Christ. (*Conf. Argent.* 1556)

This shows clearly not only the primacy of faith as the instrument of communication, but also the analogy which stands at the heart of the sacrament. This analogy, which we earlier traced in the objective relationship between sign and matter as upheld by the Holy Spirit, is now referred to the person of the Christian according to the distinction between the 'mouth of the body' and the 'mouth of the mind' (*os corporis* and *os mentis*). This latter is not 'mental' in our modern sense, but is identifiable with the spirit or soul—it is also called the *os animi*.

> The form (*figura*) is given by the hand and received with the mouth of the body, but the actuality (*res*), that is the true flesh of Christ, is offered by the words of the Lord and grasped by the mouth of the soul through faith; and we eat Him spiritually, while we believe that He was truly given for us on the Cross. (*Def.* 63)

The sacrament contains two things, not one—and not a *tertium quid* identifying the two in a new entity[3]—namely, sign and signification. The truth of the reception of the sacrament, therefore, depends upon a 'twofold eating' (*duplex manducatio*), one of the *res Sacramenti*, a 'spiritual and true' eating, the other

---

[3] As Chedsey claimed—*Disp.* II.

of the sign only.[4] We may note in this connection that for Martyr, the sign or symbol is usually *called* 'the sacrament', and therefore he can distinguish the spiritual eating from the 'sacramental' eating. In this sense the wicked eat the sacrament of the body of Christ. Indeed, he even calls the consecrated elements 'spiritual things' because of their signification, so that the elements, if eaten at all, make for a 'spiritual' eating—but this terminology, as we saw, depends upon the verbal communication of properties. Properly speaking, there is but one eating of Christ, that explained in John 6.

The problem of 'subjectivity' in this doctrine will be readily solved when we consider that faith is instrumental to the communication of Christ Himself. Faith is not mental knowledge, it is that by which the believer *receives* the communion of the Person of Christ. In the sacrament it is this Person of Christ that is the substance or matter, to which the elements are but instruments ordained by Christ Himself.

> The Sacrament of the Eucharist I confess is so instituted by Christ our Saviour that, His words being used, which promise a true communion of the faithful with Him, and adding symbols of bread and wine, which are effectual instruments of the Holy Spirit unto the faithful while the holy Supper is celebrated; faith is excited in us, by which we truly and unfeignedly apprehend in the soul both His body and blood, even as they were delivered unto death and to the Cross for us, unto the remission of sins. Which receiving, although of things absent, and done in the soul (*animo fiat*), yet it not only profits the soul itself, but redounds unto the body of them that receive, so that by a certain power of sanctification and of spiritual conjunction, it is made capable of the blessed resurrection and eternal life. Wherefore neither in the symbols, nor in the communicants themselves, do I admit a real or substantial or corporeal presence of the body of Christ.
>
> (*Conf. Argent.* 1556)

In this same context Martyr states that unless the communion with Christ is enjoyed before the eating of the Eucharist, we are aliens from Him since we lack faith. The object of the Supper is not to unite us to Christ by an earthly means, but to increase (*crescere*) in us that union which the Holy Spirit creates and sustains by instrumental means of grace. Faith is to be defined as 'the instrument of uniting us to Christ'.[5]

The deep question with which Peter Martyr confronts us

[4] Cf. esp. *in* 1 *Cor.* 10.17 for this teaching.   [5] *Epit.*, *Sent.* 9.

here is, what is the object of faith? He insists again and again that faith does not have fictitious objects, it grasps a real Christ, real in His Body and in His Blood. Faith cannot be dismissed as 'subjective' unless we deny that faith has power to apprehend a real presence of Christ.

The 'Real Presence' of the Body of Christ

The problematic nature of the Eucharist has arisen because men confused two categories or orders implied by the nature of the sacrament. They forgot that by the mouth only *quantity* can be received—the bodily reception does not extend to spiritual substance.[6] 'The mouth of the body cannot have a spiritual action.'[7] The difference between the mouth of the body and the mouth of the soul is the difference between spirit and flesh.[8] To annul this difference is to make the error of which the Capernaites were guilty. For the bodily mouth, by definition, cannot attain to anything but earthly elements, except by signification. The 'mouth of the body' is essentially 'the faculty for apprehending flesh', that is, for apprehending a creature. But the flesh of Christ is grasped by faith, which is 'in the soul, not in the body, not in the mouth'.

Therefore for this reason I say that the body of Christ cannot be eaten properly. For what is not chewed with the teeth and digested, is not said to be really eaten. But this no sane person will attribute unto the body of the Lord. (*Def.* 1, 3-4)

The key to this doctrine lies in the Christological thinking of our Reformer. Union with the Risen Man is not the problem of the 'divinized flesh' of transubstantiation, but of the new 'spiritual men' of the Church. Christ's flesh as creaturely is removed from us by distance of place,[9] but *we* are changed so that we apprehend Him as He truly is.[10] Indeed, Martyr declares, we only have the true Body of Christ by the spiritual presence which corresponds to faith.[11] For what if *non habeas corpus Christi*? Can that hinder what we seek?[12] In fact:

[6] *Disp.* II, *vs.* Ched.   [7] *Os corporis non potest habere actionem spiritualem*—*Def.* 160.
[8] *Def.* 161: *Tantum enim interest spiritualem manducationem, et corporealem, quantum inter spiritum, et corpus.*   [9] *Def.* 560.
[10] *Catech.* 31ff: the Holy Spirit 'works a wonderful transformation' in us: the analogical motion does something to us, not to its 'object'!
[11] *Def.* 387.   [12] *Def.* 464.

This communion with the Lord is not less than if it were given as the transubstantiators imagine: nay rather it is more excellent, since we obtain it through better instruments, and by more eminent faculties. (*in* 1 *Cor.* 11.24)

For the 'things themselves' of the sacrament are received according to the mode of faith. The fountainhead of this profound and complex doctrine is this: *the virtue of the risen Body descends from heaven.*[13] Time and again he emphasizes the 'force and power' of Christ's Body and Blood, their 'virtue and efficacy'.[14] This is our union with Christ, namely our union with the new humanity of the risen Lord, through the *virtus* and *vis* of His Body and Blood.

It will be obvious at this point that the spatial terminology used by Martyr, whose stress on the *sursum corda* is a basic factor in his sacramental theology, is not adequate for the reality it seeks to express.[15] For here we find that he is willing to speak of Christ's 'descending' to the Supper, inasmuch as 'with faith and the Spirit' the recipients feed and are restored[16] by the presence of Christ Himself. Our plea is, he says, 'that Christ should come from heaven by His Spirit'.[17] What Martyr wishes to avoid is that 'Christ-absent' sacramental teaching of the Swiss;[18] yet his doctrine is not rooted in polemical theorizing, but in acknowledgment of the positive communication which the sacrament effects. This is his principle:

the body of Christ may be joined to us in such a way that we are one with Him, though by substantial and corporeal presence in the Eucharist He is absent from us. (*in* 1 *Cor.* 12.12)

Martyr is claiming that the sacrament becomes problematical only when a false antithesis obscures the relationship: the

---

[13] *Dial.* 34C: 'How does (Christ) say that the bread of God lives and descends from heaven? . . . Because the virtue of the risen body descended from heaven. That which has virtue is ascribed to the flesh.' Cf. the remarkable homiletic commentary on the Reformed doctrine of the Eucharist by Robert Bruce in his *Sermons Upon the Sacrament* given in Edinburgh in 1589: 'I call the thing signified, togidder with the benefites and vertues flowing fra him, the verie substance of Christ himself quherefra this vertue dois flow . . . thou man discerne betwixt the substance and the fruits that flowis fra the substance; and thou man be partaker of the substance in the first roume. Then, in the nixt roume, thou man be partaker of the fruits that flow fra his substance' (Wodrow's edition, Edinburgh, 1843, pp. 12, 39).   [14] *Def.* 9; 287; cf. 298, *etc.*
[15] See below—critical note to Chapter VIII.   [16] *vescamur et instauremur—Def.* 5.
[17] *ut Christus de coelo veniat suo spiritu—Def.* 6. The context is Martyr's use of the Liturgy of Basil and Chrysostom, which Gardiner had asserted as involving adoration in the Eucharist.   [18] See Chapter IX.

Romanist teaches that the absence of a corporeal Body means the absence of grace. But, says Martyr, grace means union with Christ as the new humanity communicated to us by the Spirit: this demands that the Body of Christ be present in the mode of faith, spiritually, and absent in the mode of sense, corporeally.

The word that requires examination here is *faith*. For Martyr, faith is distinguished by one unique power: it overcomes distance to make present the reality that is its object. Hebrews 11.1 is his favourite text in this respect: the object of faith is 'substance': πίστις implies ὑπόστασις.[19] This is the property of faith, and without its correlative *substance*, faith is no true faith. Our 'firm union' with Christ is the work of faith, which leads His 'fruit and utility' to us so that the eyes of our mind 'effectively touch' Him.[20] It is this new way of using the word *substantia* that sets the Reformer over against the cavils of both sides of the contemporary eucharistic debate.[21] This concept is represented by his particular use of the word *virtus*, which he prefers as allowing him to contrast this with the Romanist restriction of *substantia* to a corporeal-physical reality. In illustration, he brings the simile of a King on his throne:

and the power of the King goes out to all parts of the Kingdom, though the King himself does not come to these parts. (*Def.* 804)

[19] E.g. *in* 1 *Cor.* 4.8: just as in hope we share the future perfection, so 'It is proper to faith to grasp things absent as though present'.   [20] *Dial.* 130.

[21] The change in the term 'substance' is as marked in Calvin as Martyr. Cf. F. Wendel, *Calvin, sources et évolution de sa pensée religieuse* (1950), IV.I, esp. pp. 178ff for the progress of his thought on this subject; J. Cadier, *La Doctrine Calviniste de la Sainte Cène* (Etudes Theol. et Rel., Montpellier, 1951, 1-2), Chapter 3 on the relation between 'substance' and 'person' in Calvin's 'modern' way of thinking. This thesis is more true of Calvin, for Martyr was content to retain the scholastic use of 'substance' and to debate about it within that realm, relying upon such terms as *virtus*, *vis* and *potestas* to convey his meaning. It is perhaps his failure to become explicit on the relation between substance and person as Calvin did, that led to the ambiguity of his terminology, which was misunderstood even by Bucer (particularly the words *signum* and *spiritualiter*): cf. Appendix C. This modern concept of substance offers one instance (cf. their doctrine of *impropriety* in theological language) in which the teaching of the Reformers stands firm against such attacks as that of the Logical Positivists. E.g. A. J. Ayer (*Language, Truth and Logic*, Gollancz, 1946) attributes the error of the metaphysical concept of being to the fact that 'it happens to be impossible in an ordinary European language to mention a thing without appearing to distinguish it generically from its qualities and states' (p. 42). Thus the scholastic concept (e.g. Aquinas, *S.T.* I, 29.1, following Boethius) is inseparable from the doctrine of transubstantiation, while the dynamic understanding of personal existence in the theology of Calvin, Martyr and Bucer (perhaps also truer to Boethius?) was able to transcend the logical *impasse*.

Thus, he concludes, may the 'virtue' of a thing be more extensive than its 'substance' or 'nature'. In the sacrament we communicate with this virtue—we may even say that

Bread is converted into the virtue of the body of Christ. (*Def.* 807)

The power of faith demonstrates two things in the sacrament: that Christ is in heaven, and that by His Spirit and grace and the celebration of His memory, He is present with us on earth.[22] The two concepts of ascent and descent are thus brought together in relation to the dynamic of faith.

We ascend in our minds through faith into heaven and there feed on Him. Yet sacramentally, just as in a sign and a figure, the body and blood of Christ are in the bread and wine, and in the same way as in the water of Baptism. But the body of Christ is in those who rightly receive the bread and wine of the Eucharist in much greater perfection than if He were present in them corporeally: for this way would profit them not. But when He is in them spiritually through the divine power, He gives them eternal life.

(*Def.* 785)

The progress of his thought may be summed up as follows. First he interprets faith as a union with Christ in which the flesh of Christ is not 'substantially' joined with us—that would mean we were made one hypostasis![23]—but is present to faith:

we constantly acknowledge Christ to be with the faithful by grace, Spirit and in respect of His divinity: yea indeed we do not deny His flesh to be present as a presence of faith. (*Def.* 22)

He then compares this presence by the Holy Spirit and faith[24] with the corporeal presence advanced by his adversaries, and concludes that the latter cannot 'bring any other profit' than is had by the spiritual reception.[25] He sums up the comparison in one place very compactly:

First, the distance of places prevents (the corporeal eating); next, the blessed nature of His body would not allow it; finally that kind of contact affords no sort of utility . . . But by the hand of the heart you take the very body of the Lord to yourself: and by an inward outpouring you drink His blood. (*Def.* 475)

Finally, he goes on to declare that the corporeal presence is no

---

[22] *Def.* 631.   [23] *Def.* 287.
[24] Cf. *in Rom.* 8.2: 'By this we see what is to be understood by the law of the Spirit of life, namely the Holy Spirit or else faith. For either is true: for indeed the Author of our deliverance is the Spirit of Christ; and the instrument which He uses to save us is faith.'   [25] *Epit.* 2.10.

M

presence and therefore is an absolute denial of the presence of the Body of Christ and of union with Him:

> O wretches! For you have not the body of Christ, but a piece of bread and a cup of wine: this you adore as Christ: this you eat as being the flesh and blood of the Lord. (*Def.* 79)

The positive teaching in this context is the nourishing quality of the new humanity of Christ, for this is what 'virtue' signifies. The communication must be in order to our union with Christ. This is the reality of union with Christ, and the analogy from which Martyr meets his opponents. The sacrament of communication is sign and seal of the nourishment of the Body of Christ.

The Nourishment of the Body of Christ

> I affirm that (the body and blood of Christ) are truly given and offered unto us both by words and by signs, when they are greatly and most effectually signified by them. And also in communicating, we truly receive the same things, when with a full and perfect consent of faith we embrace those things which are delivered by the signification of the words and signs. Therefore it happens that we are most closely joined together with Christ: and whom we have obtained in Baptism by the benefit of regeneration, Him we more and more still put on by the sacrament of the Supper: since nature provides that we are nourished by the same things of which we consist. And if we mean to be saved, we must take care that Christ dwell in us and we in Him until we are wholly converted into Him, and so converted that there should remain nothing of our own, of death I mean, which was born along with us, of corruption and sin. (*Tract., Praef.*)

There is nourishment of faith in the Eucharist: by the means of grace human faith is *increased*. But for Peter Martyr this increase has reference to the growth of Christ in us. In a letter to an unnamed friend,[26] Martyr treats the doctrine at great length, because his friend disagrees with him on this point, holding that although faith is increased, the union with Christ is an absolute and constant state. Martyr cites Ephesians 3.19, 1.23 and 4.11-14—

> unto the faithful it belongs daily to be fulfilled and perfected (*impleri et perfici*). But the same Apostle declares that it is Christ alone by whom we are filled and perfected, indeed it is He who is both filled and perfected in us . . . While one member of this body is augmented, Christ may be said to be increased in it, that is becomes greater and nearer to it . . . Nor is there any

---

[26] *amico cuidam, L.C.*, pp. 1105-1108; no place or date.

other increase of the members to be considered than that Christ Himself should be amplified and enlarged in each of His members: and this is done if the faithful are daily made the more partakers of Him.

Christ does not communicate, by the 'joints and fastenings' or means of grace, something other than Himself, a quasi-physical 'grace' for example, or a knowledge by which faith subjectively increases itself. What the Head communicates to His members is . . the Head! The Christian is daily more and more 'a partaker of the Head'. Since faith means union with Christ, an increase of faith means an increase in that union. The two are inseparably joined, and Christ appointed faith to this end, that 'by its increase we apprehend Christ more and more'. It is a 'mean or instrument' to this apprehension.

This instrumentality of faith is not derived from the elements or *opere operato*. But just as faith is aroused and made warm and increased (*nostra fides excitatur, incalescit et augetur*) when we hear the holy words, so when we receive the visible words or sacraments, our faith 'is made firmer and grows'. And the benefit of this increase of faith is a fuller incorporation into Christ. This 'follows upon the sealing' and is not simply identifiable with the sealing. The sealing, it appears, is a means to increase faith; the increase of faith is a means to the growth of Christ in us.

By this light and brightness added by the sealing, the mind is stirred up to believe the more, and by the more it believes, Christ is more earnestly apprehended, and He both comes and cleaves closer to him.

In closing this letter, Martyr assures the correspondent that he will not love or honour him less on account of 'this diversity of opinion, which is not great'.

The principle here set forth is elsewhere affirmed, especially in relation to the fact that the key to the action of the Eucharist is the analogy of nourishment. It is the nature of faith, Martyr states,[27] never to be perfect in this life, but always becoming more perfect and increased (*perfectius et cumulatius*). The sacrament therefore seals the grace given before.

But it is known that a human body is fed and nourished by the very substance and nature of bread, but not by its appearances or accidents. And therefore this most suitably and aptly signifies the body of Christ which

[27] *Def.* 738.

suffered for us on the Cross. For that, apprehended by faith, feeds us and nourishes us spiritually; since between the body of Christ and the nature of bread there is a common analogy in nourishing. For in the one the nourishment is physical, in the other spiritual. (*Def.* 739)

Christ, as the Head of every believer, is the source of life and the Spirit,

which flow from the divinity, as by the flesh and blood of Christ given unto death, these are derived unto us. (*Conf. Argent.* 1556)

The divinity of Christ is the source of our life and union, but not apart from the humanity—it is, in fact, this crucified and risen humanity which is the nourishment:

For His body given to the Cross, which is grasped by us by a true faith, is our bread, which feeds us unto life eternal. (*Def.* 94)

Christ gives bread twice: once on the Cross, to which He refers in John 6; and again in the Supper, when the same flesh is set forth to those eating in faith, the signs of bread and wine being added.[28]

In the holy Supper not only is faith required, by which we place our trust in the death of the Lord, but also outward symbols are added, by which the faith of the communicants is called forth, and which show what the spiritual manducation of the body of Christ confers: namely what, as appropriate to bread in food and wine in drink, is accustomed to guarantee the life of the eaters and drinkers. (*Def.* 94)

It is the historical Passion and Death which should be 'before our eyes while we communicate',[29] for indeed this is what 'eating His flesh' means, to believe that these were given for our salvation:[30]

to eat the flesh of Christ is nothing else than to apprehend by faith that He was given for us as the price of our redemption . . . we communicate now in the passion of Christ, if we embrace it by a living and effective faith. (*Def.* 545)

Inasmuch as the body and blood of the Lord are given for our salvation, when grasped by us with effectual and ardent faith they are for soul and mind salutary food and drink, by which we are repeatedly refreshed and recreated unto eternal life . . . such a familiar symbol of nourishment cannot be found more fitting than bread. For by it the body is daily refreshed and renewed. (*Dial.* 135f)

---

[28] *Def.* 95.   [29] *Disp.* IV, *vs.* Ched.
[30] *Epit., Sent.* 3: he adds that to that flesh and blood are joined the things Christ removed on the Cross.

Thus Martyr says 'any kind of faith' is not this eating,

but only that by which we apprehend our Lord, as once dead and crucified for us. (*Def.* 518)

For the spiritual presence is of the same kind as His death—and as 'the good things of the life to come' on which our hope is fixed.[31] The Creed should be publicly recited before Communion, since it contains the Death of Christ, with what preceded and followed.[32] The two elements are to be used as follows:

From the one part, the faith of the communicants grasps the body of Christ nailed on the Cross for our salvation, whence we are spiritually fed. The same faith apprehends from the other part His blood, shed for our salvation, and here we are spiritually watered and we drink. While communicating, the mind of the faithful is occupied chiefly about these mysteries of the death of Christ. (*An in Comm. Lic.* 10)

This orientation to the Death of Christ has an interesting implication.

As often as we fully believe that Christ is crucified for us, we eat His flesh, which metaphorically is called bread. (*Disp.* IV, *vs.* Ched.)

Therefore Martyr can say to abstainers from wine:

if a man cannot receive the Sacrament as instituted by Christ, let him abstain, for if he desire it and believe, no commodity or fruit shall in that respect be lacking to him; just as to him that desires Baptism, if he have no opportunity for it, it is imputed as if he had received it. (*An in Comm. Lic.* 22)

Briefly, 'to drink is to believe',[33] since in the sacrament itself it is still a spiritual eating, 'to the soul and faith'.[34] Once again we must recall the true effect of the sacrament.

But it is not joined to the thing itself, and corporeally: but is a sign or sacrament or memorial related to the thing indicated: or as an instrument with effect. Because these symbols are not only signs of the body and blood of Christ, but also instruments which the Holy Spirit uses to feed us spiritually with the body and blood of the Lord. (*Def.* 82)

And whereas you object that the receiving of the body of Christ by faith can be had without the sacrament, I grant it: for both with the symbols and without the symbols are we truly made partakers of Him, while we recall to mind Christ crucified for us, and His blood shed for us, and so believe. But when the symbols are adjoined, which the Holy Spirit uses as instruments

---

[31] *Epit., Sent.* 17. [32] *in* 1 *Cor.* 11.26. [33] *Def.* 146.
[34] *Tract.* 58—cf. *in Iud.* 13.25, His flesh and blood 'are an invisible nourishment'.

to better imprint faith in our minds, we are helped a great deal. For in regard to divine things we are slower, and therefore need outward symbols.

(*Disp.* III, final speech)

The sacrament is an instrument to arouse faith, not a cause which confers it.[35] Faith has as its object the Death of Christ and as its content union with Christ: believing means eating His flesh and drinking His blood. Sacraments are instruments by which this is 'performed more effectively' since such symbols 'move us more earnestly' than words alone.[36] But most significantly, Martyr is not advancing a doctrine that the Eucharist means the communication of ideas (about the Lord's Death), or even a 'benefit' impersonally conceived, but Christ Himself.

If you ask, what do we obtain through Communion? some would reply, the merit and fruit of the Lord's death, which is not displeasing to me. But I add, that we have also the Lord Himself, who is the Fountain of these goods. (*in* 1 *Cor.* 11.24)

The analogy of nourishment is continually emphasized by Martyr in treating of the Eucharist. Because of the analogy, transubstantiation, the withholding of the cup from the laity, and neglect of the sacrament are denied. This is the meaning or content of the sacrament.

Thus God acted in the Sacraments, which are names and visible words by which He effectively portrayed His promises. For He took care that the properties of the signs should agree as much as possible with the things designated. (*in* 1 *Cor.* 10.3)

Those who acknowledge a nutrition of our body from the Eucharist, which comes through true bread, obtain from this the ratio of the sacrament. For as the body of Christ feeds the soul, so bread feeds the body. Who therefore remove the grains and composition of the grains, and take away the substance of the bread, are in my judgment *Sacramentarii*, because they remove the ratio and analogy of the sacrament. (*Def.* 403)

Moreover, Martyr makes very clear that the analogy in the sacrament is not a merely formal progression from signs to signification, but derives from the prior revelation of the Person of Christ as spiritual nutrition, to which are added fitting signs. The nutritional reference of the signs is not the origin of 'the power of analogy and beginning of the comparison',[37] for

---

[35] *De Poenit.* 10.   [36] *Tract.* 33.

[37] *vis analogiae et initium collationis—Def.* 404. This whole section (*Obj.* 135, pp. 403-407) is particularly significant for this aspect of Martyr's analogical thinking.

this rests with 'the spiritual nutrition of the body of Christ':

for in mysteries, the things that are signified hold the better place, and should be altogether preferred to the signs and symbols. For as the ratio of nutrition makes clear, it is not the sense of the argument by which our body is restored by bread. But for this reason it is proved of necessity that bread is retained in the Eucharist, so that the power of nourishing, as it were, should be in the symbols just as it is in the body of the Lord, which is signified. (*Def.* 404)

Martyr uses this direction of the analogical movement to prove the presence of true bread and wine in the Eucharist,[38] but it is equally useful at this point to recall his fundamental basis for theological analogy, the accommodation of Christ in His own Person as the divine Analogue.

Martyr notes two analogies operative in the relation of bread to the Body of Christ.[39] One is, that for the Hebrews bread stands for 'all kinds of food'. John 6, for instance, cannot be understood apart from this trope of bread as food in general: Christ was to give His flesh to be 'like bread' (*instar panis*), like 'spiritual food for the soul'.

That bread of which John writes signifies the body of Christ or His flesh. Nor is anything else taught by that word than that metaphorically His own flesh, when eaten in faith by believers, will be like bread, that is real food by which they are quickened unto eternal life . . . Therefore Christ was eager to recall them by His doctrine from the food of the body to the nourishment of the soul. (*Def.* 53, 59)

This is the primary reference, to the nourishing quality of the Body of Christ, and it is to be consciously operative in the reception of the elements:

But as for the words 'Take ye and eat ye', I say that they must be understood thus: As you receive this bread and eat it with your body, so receive you My body by faith, and with the mind, that you may be strengthened thereby in place of meat. (*Disp.* III, *vs.* Morg.)

as with the body you eat bread, so with the mind you may feed upon My flesh. (*Tract.* 34)

The metaphor is this, that just as bread naturally nourishes and sustains us, so the flesh of Christ being eaten spiritually and by faith, sustains us in

[38] Cf. *Def.* 463: 'If you remove wine from the cup, the blood of Christ cannot be shown and signified by sacramental analogy' (*sacramentali analogia ostendi et significari*).

[39] *Def.* 151f. Cf. *Disp.* III, *vs.* Morg.: the analogy in the sacrament is not the breaking so much as the enjoyment of the meat; *Def.* 365: grapes not only nourish and strengthen, but also gladden (*exhilaremur*).

respect of both soul and body . . . that sacramental bread was the flesh of Christ, to be given unto death for our salvation . . . He expresses a metaphorical name for His flesh, because He should be to us for bread, or like bread, of whose property He would admonish us, to understand that the flesh of Christ is bread allegorically. (*Disp.* IV, *vs.* Ched.)

Because of this analogy, which leads us to the heart of Christ's work in us, Martyr calls the Eucharist 'our defence and shelter'[40] because it fortifies us against the enemy. How does Christ sustain His Church?

Since wars and temptations are imminent, He supplies armour, namely the Word of God; and with the meat of the Eucharist He confirms and strengthens them to the battle. (*in* I *Cor.* 4.1)

The second analogy is a favourite one in Patristic thought. The Fathers called bread *panis triticeus*, wheat bread:

that kind of bread which consists of many grains of wheat, and by that signifies the union we should have among ourselves and with Christ.

(*Def.* 152)

The sacrament excites faith in us, by which the Spirit is drawn to us more copiously and we are united in the mystical body more and more: thus the analogy of the 'many grains' and 'many grapes' signifies the mutual union among believers as well as with Christ.[41]

And as regards the mystical body, the similitude lies in this, that just as bread and wine consist of much gathering and pressing together, that is of many grains of corn and of many grapes, so the mystical body consists of many members, who grow up together into one. (*Disp.* II, beginning)

The resolution of this analogical movement of the sacrament lies in the doctrine of the *sursum corda*.

I judge the real and substantial body of Christ to be only in the heavens, yet the faithful truly receive, spiritually and through faith, the communication of His true body and His true blood, which were delivered to the Cross for our sake. (*Sent. in Coll. Poiss.*)

In this context Martyr explains that since faith is not directed to a fictitious object, a *phantasma*, the Body received spiritually must be identical with that Body which suffered on the Cross. How can this be? Simply because 'distance of places' nothing hinders, inasmuch as *the Lord's Supper is a heavenly matter.*[42] We

---

[40] *munitio et protectio—Def.* 731.　　[41] *Def.* 505.
[42] See Appendix D for the Poissy statement. Cf. *Dial.* 130D: 'The Lord's Supper is a thing heavenly and spiritual, not human and carnal.'

have already noted that this way of speaking must be related to Martyr's doctrine of the dynamic presence of Christ as virtue; yet in regard to the analogical content of the Eucharist this 'being lifted up' is his normal concept.

> In the celebration of the Supper the ancients used to say, *Sursum corda*, desiring the souls of men to be carried to heaven, but not to remain fixed to the outward elements. It therefore appears that they never thought of a real presence of the body of Christ to which the souls were rather to be turned downwards. (*Def.* 195)

> For there you must not think either of the bread or of the wine—your mind and sense must cleave only to the things represented unto you. Therefore it is said 'Lift up your hearts', when you lift up your mind from the signs to the invisible things offered you. (*Tract.* 44)

When the faithful receive the sacrament, their mind is lifted up to heaven itself, this is the motion of their faith.[43]

> For the faithful mount up like eagles to heaven itself, through faith; and there by mind and spirit experience the full enjoyment of the Lord, and grasp His body given for them on the Cross, with great profit. (*in* 1 *Cor.* 11.24)

The Renewal of the Body

> The elements . . . nourish unto eternal health, since they are instruments of the Holy Spirit to excite faith in our souls, through which the gifts of renewal (*dona renovationis*) are transfused to our body and flesh. (*Def.* 427)

A final aspect of Peter Martyr's sacramental doctrine must be noted here: the Patristic idea that the grace received in the Eucharist redounds also to the very body of the believer.

> Our bodies are in a certain way nourished and restored to eternal life by the body and blood of Christ. (*Epit., Sent.* 10)

This is not based upon a semi-physical idea of grace, for Martyr gives it a definite place within his doctrine of union with Christ and the communication of His new humanity to the members of His mystical Body:

> we understand our union with Christ to extend not only to spirit and soul, but also to body and flesh. Whence no wonder the old Fathers said, In the Lord's Supper not only is our soul and spirit quickened (*vegetari*) by the flesh and blood of Christ, but also our body and flesh are fed from thence, so that they are restored more fit and firm to the use of good works, by which Christ is served. (*in* 1 *Cor.* 6.15)

[43] *De Vot.* 1529B.

Beside this idea that the body is strengthened to do good works, and so to grow in the 'second righteousness' of sanctification, is placed the controlling idea that the renewal of the body effected in this life is simply the beginning of eternal life according to which our bodies become 'capable of immortality'.[44] The properties we receive belong unto the resurrection power of the new humanity, in which the whole man participates.

Martyr speaks of this concept in terms of a 'twofold bodily nourishment' received in the Eucharist.[45] The signs feed our body; the spiritual nourishment of the Body of Christ redounds to renew our bodies themselves unto eternal life, to make them capable of immortality and resurrection.

> There come to us by this sacrament two kinds of nourishment. One is natural, namely by the nature of the symbols, bread and wine, by which the human body is usually sustained. To this kind of nourishment, though it is not to be condemned, yet Irenaeus and other Fathers attribute little. The other nourishment is, that while we receive the sacrament, we embrace the body and blood of Christ by the soul and faith, and there is our mind first filled with the Spirit and with grace, next our body is renewed, that it may daily become a fit organ and instrument for the Spirit, and so made more capable of the blessed resurrection. (*Disp.* III.2)

This difficult thought is expressed by the Fathers in language that often suggests an identity between this present *capability* and the future state of the resurrected body, or present state of Christ's Body. Of the difficulties involved Martyr is well aware, and seeks to guard against confusion. Writing of Irenaeus and Justinian, who say that after receiving the Eucharist our bodies are no longer mortal, because the sacrament has become in the body a preserver unto everlasting life, he states:

> If these things are understood properly and absolutely, as they seem at first sight, as if they taught that the body and blood of Christ pass into the true nourishment of bodies and so there is in them the beginning of resurrection, the opinion would be terribly absurd . . . the body of Christ, being impassible, cannot be changed into other bodies . . . let us understand that in the Lord's Supper the faithful receive bread and wine with the mouth of the body, and with their mind and spirit receive the body and blood of Christ, even in the way He was given on the Cross for our salvation: and in that receiving of these things by faith, we are justified and regenerated, or we are confirmed in righteousness and

---

[44] *in* I *Cor.* 10.16—this is the best section on this theme.   [45] E.g. *Tract.* 43.

THE SACRAMENT OF COMMUNICATION

spiritual birth. But justification and regeneration, which are in the mind, make the body itself capable of resurrection. And in this way we may say that the outward elements we receive with our body are a preparation to resurrection—because they are instruments of the Holy Spirit, by which He stirs up faith in us, which is rightly the origin (*principium*) of resurrection.

(*De Resurr.* 63)

We may conclude that whatever effect the Eucharist has on our body is strictly related to the eschatological nature of faith: justification means the beginning of resurrection, 'the beginnings of our blessed immortality'.[46] It is for this reason that Martyr accepts the Patristic notion of the present renewal of our bodies as relating to the ontological content of faith, the 'beyond' of our union with Christ, which will not begin with resurrection but will be then unveiled. The full nourishment of the Body of Christ involves an area of life not sufficiently indicated by the terms 'by mind and soul'; for Christ renews the whole man, his body and his flesh as well.

[46] Letter *Ad amicum quendam . . . de causa Eucharistiae*, L.C., pp. 1144ff, in the latter part of which he states the case in almost identical language with the *De Resurr.*

PART III

REAL PRESENCE AND TRUE SACRIFICE

CHAPTER VII

THE EUCHARIST AND TRANSUBSTANTIATION

> . . . all arguments return to the extreme, to that absurd and idiotic thicket, Transubstantiation. For out of that rotten flesh, the refined concoct for us Adorations, Oblations, Reservations, Concomitances, Distentions of the body of Christ, Traffickings of Masses, *Individua vaga*, Accidents without subject, and infinitely more marvels and disagreeable dishes. *(Def., Praef.)*

PETER MARTYR had begun to depart from the doctrine of transubstantiation as early as his years at Lucca; when he left Italy for the cause of Reformation, his first written work, on the Creed, included a significant aside, about

> a full treatise of the sacraments, which I hope to perform shortly, if the Lord lend me life. *(Catech.* 42)

That was 1544; in 1549 he produced the Treatise, along with his notes of the famous Oxford Disputation, provoked by Richard Smith. Ten years later, writing against another Englishman, Stephen Gardiner, he enlarged the teaching and scope of the Treatise in his 'Defence of the ancient and Apostolic Doctrine concerning the most holy Sacrament of the Eucharist', his most fruitful and detailed work on any subject, and probably the greatest single work on the Eucharist of the entire Reformation.[1]

From these works we derive a twofold attack upon the doctrine of transubstantiation, which we may denote as a philosophical and a theological refutation. Martyr declares that the doctrine can be disproved on its own terms, chiefly with reference to the scholastic principle concerning accidents remaining

---

[1] The book is directed to Gardiner's *Confutatio cavillationum . . . ab impiis Capernaitis*, written against Cranmer, Martyr, etc., under the pseudonym *M. Anton. Constantius.* It has a most optimistic plan, attempting to give the teaching of the sacred writings, the ancient Fathers, and acts of the Councils, *de tota Eucharistiae causa,* as the note to the Reader on the title-page has it. The *Tractatio* is most excellent in its own right, and sections 2-5 sum up the Romanist arguments for transubstantiation. Martyr also wrote the *Epitome* or *Analysis*, in 1561, a brief summary intended to be like 'the sure sight of the lodestar' in the storm of controversy.

181

without their subject, *accidentia manere sine subiecto*. But from this position he always moves to the positive theological argument, the sacramental analogy which we have submitted as the centre of gravity of his doctrine. Both levels of argument deserve close attention at their crucial points.

A. The Philosophical Refutation

Dialectics is a noble gift of God: nor is there any other art of more value to the refutation of error. (*Def.* 377)

Substance and Accidents

Transubstantiation, as the name implies, means the substitution of one substance for another—in the case of the Eucharist, of the Body of Christ for that of the bread and the wine. Gardiner had accepted the medieval conception of *substantia* as prior to accidents and able to exist without them, and claimed that this was a clear teaching of Aristotle.[2] This was the usual Romanist argument, that the 'substance' of bread and wine was changed into that of the Body and Blood of Christ through the miraculous consecration of the priestly office. But Peter Martyr takes this to its source in Aristotle and points out that this is not what he said, but is a 'new philosophy'. What Aristotle taught was a distinction between accidents separable and inseparable from their substance or subject: *accidentia separabilia et inseparabilia*. Certain substances (of God and angels, for example) are without weight and quantity; but outside this class substance is not separable from its accidents—the human body, for example, as corporeal substance, cannot exist without *locus*. Moreover, to say that substance exists prior to its accidents (*prius esse posse absque posteriore*) refers only to the idea (*notitia*) and not to the thing itself (*res ipsa, existentia*).

Our indication of Martyr's doctrine of real presence as virtue has introduced us to his dynamic concept of substance, deriving from his acceptance of the Person of Christ as the architectonic of his theology. But he is quite willing to meet the Romanists on their own scholastic ground, since he is confident that it involves a logical impossibility—even Lombard denied that accidents can remain without a substance, without a sustaining

[2] *Def.*, *Obj.* 11, pp. 36-40; cf. *Obj.* 10 for this discussion.

subject.[3] For this is a philosophical problem, and for philosophy the senses must be presupposed as trustworthy.[4] Apart from this basic philosophical presupposition as to the nature of the substance-accident relation, you have only a 'despotism of accidents'![5]

> Moreover, by this unnecessary transubstantiation, they pervert the nature of things, since they pluck away accidents from their substance and proper subject, which is far more than to separate substance from a quantity . . . since an accident is a latter thing than substance. (*Disp.* IV, *conf.* 1.4)

Two arguments of Martyr's concerning the problem of substance may be introduced at this point. One concerns the term 'nature' and the other, 'action' or 'relation'. The Fathers often speak of a change in the *nature* of bread and wine in the sacrament. Martyr agrees with them: the nature of the elements is changed indeed. But nature in this case means 'property or condition', not 'substance'.[6] The Fathers do not claim that nature as substance is changed, but only as property or quality. This view Martyr himself strongly upheld against Tropism.[7] His principle in interpreting the Fathers is:

> Wherever the Fathers say 'the nature of bread is changed', it is to be received as nature in respect of properties, as in Cyprian; but wherever they say 'the nature is not changed', that nature is to be received in respect of substance, as in Gelasius. (*Def.* 640)

Transubstantiation overthrows the categories of being—for instance, the familiar cavil that mice may feed or worms breed on the accidents of the Host implies that these are really turned into substance![8] And a first principle of Dialectics is overthrown when they demand a presence of the Body of Christ *non quantum*.[9] This latter argument requires further investigation.

In the context of the philosophical problem of substance and

---

[3] *Def.* 251.   [4] *Def.* 249.
[5] *regnum quoddam accidentium*—*Def.* 528.   [6] *Tract.* 45, *Def.* 235.
[7] See below on 'The Words of Consecration'. It is unfortunate that Martyr did not relate his discussion of these terms to Boethius' *Persona est individua substantia rationalis naturae*, which he uses (*Dial.* 17F) only as an argument of Pantachus, to which Orothetes (who agrees with the definition) replies that we cannot descend below the *persona* to divide the Two Natures in Christ.
[8] *Def.* 257ff.
[9] *magnitudinem etsi posterior sit substantia corporate, tamen ab illa seiungi non posse, nisi prorsus corrumpatur.*—*Def.* 260.

nature, Martyr introduces the argument from the nature of a human body.

> And this is in opposition, for a human body to be a quantum, and to have distinct members in itself, and the same to be diffused over diverse and many places, and almost infinite: to be present, and not to be in a place. (*Def.* 42)

> One and the same body of Christ does not sustain at one and the same time such contrary qualities as passible and impassible. (*Disp.* II.2)

This argument serves against consubstantiation as well, and receives from that side the same reply that Gardiner gives:

> For whatever is most certainly objected by us about the true human nature in Christ, all that did he hope to confute by one little word, if he said 'God is omnipotent' and the body is not in the Eucharist except invisibly. (*Def., Praef.*)

Certain aspects of this argument will concern us below, but in general Martyr's position is this. Against the plea that the Divine omnipotence is able to effect logical absurdities, acceptable to faith, Martyr grants that God is doubtless omnipotent, indeed his doctrine of providence is one of the consistent and striking aspects of his theology—but God does not overrule things contrary by nature.[10] Yet the true question is not God's *posse* at all but His *velle*, which is revealed in the promises of Scripture.[11] The Body of Christ must be accepted as a quantum, whereas transubstantiation has it replace the substance of bread without occupying place. It is infinite, divinized flesh: the Docetic heresy is operative here.

> It is a perilous matter to delude the senses by transubstantiation; because the proof of the true resurrection of Christ then perishes . . . the Marcionite heretics would soon have said that Christ had no true human body, but only its accidents and figure, as you say of bread . . . Also the Fathers thought that they effectively proved Christ to be true man, by His human affections and properties, which Scripture shows . . . These arguments could be denied by the example of your transubstantiation, and the heretics could say, Just as this does not follow, namely, There are properties of bread and wine in the sacrament of the Eucharist, therefore the substance of bread and wine is truly there: so, it does not follow, In Christ there were properties and affections of a man, therefore He had a most true human substance. And thus shall there be opened a window to most grievous errors. (*Disp.* IV, *conf.* 1.3)

[10] E.g. *Potentia Dei ad ea non extenditur quae contradictionem implicant*—*Def.* 34; for Transub. cf. *Def.* 41ff, and for Consub. *Dial.* 6-7. etc., and our next Chapter.
[11] *in* I *Cor.* 11.24.

The second concept to which Martyr relates the argument about substance is the Eucharist as *actio*. Both Romanist and Lutheran are enmeshed in categories of the second causes of philosophy. Thus both fail to rise above the static relationships of logic to a regard for the office of the Holy Spirit. Martyr, however, points out that the 'mystery' is not what the elements are, but what they signify.[12] For although in logic the correlative of 'sign' may be 'thing signified', that is, a substance, yet in all sacraments is it not Christ Himself who is the *res*?[13] Consider the Last Supper itself:

Never do we read that when Christ was on earth He exhorted the Apostles to seek Him elsewhere than where He was present with them. I am persuaded that when the Apostles heard the Lord in the Supper say of bread, 'This is My body', they fixed their eyes not on the bread but on Christ Himself. (*Def.* 508)

But if the matter or substance of this sacrament is Christ Himself, static categories cannot hold the relationship, which must be personal and dynamic. This is exactly what Martyr insists upon: the dramatic action according to which the sacramental analogy operates as the Holy Spirit uses His instruments. The whole sacrament, he states, is action: remove that, and you have no more sacrament—whereas transubstantiation retains a sacrament in the element as such, even after communicating. Only *communion* can satisfy the Lord's institution, yet this is precisely what transubstantiation prevents, since Christ is in the element, and the sacrificers are not stirred up to communion with Him.[14] The Eucharist may be briefly defined: it is 'action or relation'.[15] If you disjoin 'This is My body' from 'Take and eat', you remove both Body and sacrament.[16]

The end of the Sacrament of the Eucharist is that it should be eaten and drunk: since, as you yourself know, outside of use there is no sacrament (*extra usum non sit sacramentum*); nor can you prove otherwise by holy Scripture. (*De Vot.* 1529G)

The whole Eucharist is founded on action: outside of that not even its name can be retained. (*in 2 Sam.* 6.5)

[12] *Def., Obj.* 8: Gardiner had said that Christ was in the Eucharist *non ut in loco, sed ut in sacramento, iuxta mysterii conditionem.* Martyr replies: He is not contained in a little box on the altar, nor under accidents of bread and wine, *sed sursum.*

[13] *in* 1 *Cor.* 10.3. At this crucial point we see how Martyr's doctrine of *sign* coincides with the Biblical concept of sign as event (in Hebrew thought and especially in the Fourth Gospel).

[14] *Tract.* 19—see Chapter X.   [15] *in* 1 *Cor.* 10.16.   [16] *in* 1 *Cor.* 11.24.

The promise of communication in the sacrament applies only 'while we eat and drink', for all the words and deeds together make the sacrament.[17]

> But we know that the sacrament then is, when we do those things that Christ did and commanded to be done: but He not only spoke those words, but also gave thanks, broke bread, ate and extended it for others to eat. And whereas there are many things here, all concur with the truth of the sacrament, nor must any of these things be omitted. (*Tract.* 11)

Once again we face the problem of analogical relation, and this in turn forms the transition from the philosophical level to the decisive theological refutation.

The Relation of Relatives

> . . . relatives consist in two things, as the Dialecticians say, *fundamentum* and *terminus* . . . such is their conjunction that one cannot be understood, be defined or exist without the other. Wherefore, since the sacrament of the Eucharist is a certain relation, it is necessary to establish the *fundamentum*, doubtless the signifying thing, that is the bread: and the *terminus*, that is the thing signified, which clearly is the body of Christ. But although these are so joined between themselves that the one carries the other, the nature of a Sacrament cannot remain firm, nor yet is it necessary that they should be one by local conjunction or by any contact. For they can be so joined although separated by the farthest spaces of places. (*Def.* 386)

The philosophical refutation involves the question about the relation between the two terms of any sacrament. *This is my body*: what kind of proposition is this? Martyr begins[18] from its historical setting and replies: either literal (a proposition of identity) or tropical (figurative). The former is out of the question, since that would mean 'The bread, which Christ took in hand, was His body.' For we are dealing here with disparates or relatives, which can be predicated of one another only by a certain figuration or signification. The bread therefore 'is a figure of His body, or signifies His body'.

Gardiner denies that this is a question of disparates. He admits *corpus* as disparate but holds that *Hoc* is pronominal, referring to that of which the disparate is predicated. Martyr comments:

> O elegant Dialectician! If the word *corpus* is, as you concede, disparate, from what I pray thee, is it disparate? . . . it remains that the word in this proposition is disparate from itself! (*Def.* 45)

[17] *Disp.* III, *vs. Morg.*; *Tract.* 51.   [18] *Def.* 44ff.

Gardiner has done what Martyr dismissed as impossible, namely, made this a proposition of identity, adducing as his examples the propositions *Vinum est vinum, mel est mel, lac est lac*.[19] But such examples are 'barren and irrelevant' since the two terms in question 'pertain to different kinds of species' and are therefore true disparates, such as *homo est equus*, and not *vinum est vinum*. The issue is that relationship between bread (to which *Hoc* refers) and *corpus*. Christ held bread in His hand, and the Apostles' 'common sense' perceived it to be bread. Therefore this is not the grammatical question of the relation between subject and predicate (Gardiner claimed that the predicate explained what the subject demonstrated) but the philosophical question of the relation between disparates. We have already shown the answer to this question to be the Aristotelian relation of analogy as the proportional mean between univocity and pure equivocity.

Martyr's argument is simply that by definition a sacrament involves us in the question of *relativa*, of which the one cannot be understood without the other.[20] To identify the terms destroys their nature, and 'removes all the ratio' from the sacrament.[21] In such identification a stalemate is reached, since the sacrament is reduced to one ambiguous term:

you admit an equivocation, because for metaphorical bread you always oppose to me the bread given by Christ in the Supper, which was true and natural, and a sign of this allegorical bread, that is of the flesh of Christ.

(*Disp.* IV, *vs.* Ched.)

The words of the Supper must be understood tropically—this is Martyr's summary of his position.[22] A figurative speech in the Supper (*Hoc est corpus meum*) is demanded by *Scripture*, by the nature of a *Sacrament*, and by the witness of the *Fathers*.[23] Thus comparing Scripture with Scripture, we must interpret Matthew and Mark by the figurative speech of Paul and Luke;[24]

---

[19] Cf. *Def.* 130: *Ego sum panis*, which by simple inversion yields *Panis est idem quod ego!*   [20] *Def.* 462.   [21] *Def.* 22.

[22] In the *Epitome*. The sections are entitled, 'That the words of the Supper are to be understood tropically' and 'That the figurative speech of Christ's words requires no real or substantial presence of His body and blood'. We must remember that Martyr's 'trope' is his particular analogical relationship of 'likeness of proportion'.

[23] *Disp.* II.1. Cf. *Tract.* 38 for detailed reasons for taking the proposition as figurative, including this: 'We have respect also to the ascension of Christ into heaven, to the true human nature which He took upon Him.'   [24] *Epit.* VII.

Ezekiel 37.11 uses the verb substantive 'is' for 'it signifies';[25] indeed there are frequent tropical speeches in Scripture: John Baptist is Elias, Christ's words are Spirit and life, the Gospel is the power of God, Circumcision is the covenant, the blood is the life, God is a consuming fire![26] Proving a figurative speech from the nature of a sacrament is self-evident, as the definition 'the sign of a sacred thing' shows. A distinction must be retained between the two terms—there must be two relatives extant, with some difference between them.[27] As to the Fathers, does not Augustine say 'sign', 'figure', 'mystery'? or Jerome, 'represent', Tertullian, 'figure', Cyprian, 'signify'?[28] Therefore:

> In many places of holy Scripture *Est* is taken for *significat* . . . by the antecedents, consequents and historical circumstances of the Lord's Supper; by the truth of the human nature which was in Christ; by the sixth chapter of John; and by the nature of sacraments, it is firmly proved that the word 'is' ought to be taken there for 'signifies'. (*De. Vot.* 1440)

> I say that you have not proved, nor can prove that all propositions which consist in the verb substantive (is) must be identical, because some can be predicated of the subject also through a certain analogy or convenience. (*Disp.* III, *vs. Tresh.*)

An interesting aspect of this argument about the Proposition of the Supper is Gardiner's introduction of the Scotist concept of *individuum vagum* to explain his particular type of predication.[29] Martyr has little patience with the doctrine. Scotus gave it to explain the Proposition, teaching that 'something singular or individual of a more general substance' is demonstrated,[30] to which *Hoc* refers. Christ could hold bread and yet be described as sharing in the substance. No, Martyr says—such a conception can be thought but not held in the hand. Two (sensible) substances cannot be so joined that one is concealed under the

---

[25] *De Resurr.* 43.

[26] *in* 1 *Cor.* 11.24, Martyr's best and most complete teaching on the Proposition.

[27] *Ibid.*: he brings out the meaning of analogy clearly here, as to likeness and the difference that must be kept.

[28] *Ibid.*

[29] *Def., Obj.* XIV, XV. Martyr calls the concept *haec Scotica dogmata*, arising in that scholastic sect *quae ab tenebris nomen habuit*! (p. 116). The term is difficult to translate, but conveys the idea of an 'indefinite entity'. Martyr understands it as representing an *ens unum in substantia* (p. 107), and this suits the context of the discussion of the Proposition quite well. Cf. Jewel's 'Apology' III. 5 (Parker Soc. ed.) regarding the Romanist debate as to Christ's presence in the Eucharist as *quantum* or as *individuum vagum*, etc.

[30] *Demonstrari aliquod singulare sive individuum generalioris substantiae—Tract.* 13.

other. To speak of an 'invisible' mode of presence is not the same as to speak of transubstantiation. To Gardiner's 'juggling' Martyr opposes a most apt argument. What of the other proposition in the Eucharist? he asks. 'This cup is the new testament in My blood': even Gardiner will admit a trope here![31] For 'cup' is a trope of its contents, which are not some vague abstraction, but true wine. The 'things indicated' in the sacrament are bread and wine.

The reference of *Hoc* to bread is proved by the common sense of the Disciples who sat at table with Christ.[32] Our senses must remain trustworthy with regard to the forms or signs of revelation: our senses must be retained whole and according to their proper object.[33] The common sense answer must be Augustine's 'What you see is bread', *Quod vidistis, panis est.* Otherwise—

how much material for error does (transubstantiation) offer to the adherents of Marcion, Valentinus, Eutyches and the other pests who affirm that Christ had not true human flesh? (*Def.* 110)

Since we have dealt with this argument in Chapter III, in relation to the signs of revelation, we may pass to a further aspect of the philosophical refutation. That is the literary-grammatical argument from the words of Scripture.[34] *Hoc* must refer to the substance of bread even after consecration because of texts like 1 Corinthians 10.16, 'The bread which we break, is it not the communion of the body of Christ?'

Scripture is very clear: Christ took, and gave. What did the Lord take? break? give? You can make no other answer than bread, if you retain the grammatical construction. (*Disp.* II.1)

our first and chief principle is the holy Scripture, which acknowledges bread to be in that place. (*Disp.* III, *vs.* Morg.)

In his commentary on the key verse, 1 Corinthians 10.16, Martyr derives two arguments. First, bread must remain because Paul states that bread is present as the consecrated element. Second, the element must have a similitude with the thing of which it is the sacrament. Here we pass to the true

[31] *Calicem esse vinum*—*Def.* 147.
[32] *Def.* 4, 48; cf. 108ff.
[33] *dum sensibus integris, et sanis, et in suo obiecto versantibus*—*Def.* 248; cf. *Obj.* 4.
[34] Cf. esp. *in* 1 *Cor.* 11.24 for arguments from logic and grammar.

sacramental-analogical realm of debate, and so to the ultimate theological refutation.[35]

B. THE THEOLOGICAL REFUTATION

> We dispute not about the Ideas of Plato, or the Atoms of Democritus, or the Intermundes of Epicurus, or the Enteleches of Aristotle—but about the Body and Blood of the Son of God, by which our redemption is paid in full to the eternal Father, in what manner these are joined with the symbols of the Eucharist. (*Def., Praef.*)

The Christological Analogy

Although the analogy of the Person of Christ has been constantly before us, we should note two aspects of it which concern the particular theological refutation of the doctrine of transubstantiation. First, Martyr has proved in terms of the scholastic concepts of substance and accidents, and of the relation between disparates, that the substance of bread must remain. But how can it remain when—as Martyr himself admits— the Body of Christ is 'added as a quality' by a sacramental conjunction? Martyr replies, these two 'substances' may coexist on the analogy of the Two Natures in Christ. His particular doctrine of analogy prevents our concluding an identity of proportion from the one to the other; but as archetypal analogue the hypostatic union is our guide.

> Here [in Augustine] you see the same comparison between the Eucharist and Christ: it follows from this that just as the two natures remained whole in Christ, so the substance of bread must not be removed from the Eucharist . . . I enforce the comparison between Christ Himself and the Eucharist; for the sacrament must correspond to Him: and therefore as in Christ neither of the two natures perished, so in the Eucharist both must remain.
>
> (*Disp.* I.1)

> [Gelasius] compares this Sacrament with Christ, in whom both natures, divine and human, remained whole just as in this Sacrament do the natures of bread and of the body of Christ. (*Tract.* 31)

By this analogy Martyr proves the possibility of two natures remaining whole together. This is, as it were, the negative

---

[35] Cadier therefore (*op. cit.*, p. 112) sees the issue in Martyr's Treatise when he says that Martyr's decisive argument is that accidents cannot remain without substance, since this rests on the scholastic notion of substance; but in all Martyr's teaching on the Eucharist this phase of the argument is simply the patient accommodation to childish problems, until he can lead us into the deeper realm of Christological analogy.

Christological analogy. The positive is the main attack upon the Romanist error.

Christ came to join us to Himself, and to this end gives His flesh as spiritual food, particularly through the sacramental analogy of Eucharistic bread and wine. But true bread and wine are exactly what transubstantiation removes from the sacrament.

> The Lord said, The bread which I will give is My flesh, indicating His flesh to be that bread by which He wishes to feed you. How can this be true if as that fellow teaches, between Christ or His flesh and bread, there exists no analogy, no likeness, no figure? (*Def.* 130)

For Gardiner has reduced the relationship to one of identity, making the accidents of *bread* the figure of the substance of *Christ*. Thus accidents become a figure of a figure![36] This *figura figurae* is the total destruction of the Christological analogy, for it perverts the true analogy, which derives from the side of Christ, the nourishing quality of His new humanity. Gardiner is a Capernaite, carnally minded, and so seeks likeness to Christ in accidents such as form or lineament or roundness. Finding none, he concludes that the accidents must simply be an arbitrary (accidental) physical contact for our grasp of Christ's Body.[37] But Martyr declares that it is the analogy itself which demands the retention of the substance of bread.

> When they remove the natures of the elements, the analogy of signification perishes. The bread signifies the body of Christ because it nourishes, strengthens and sustains, which we cannot attribute unto accidents. It is also a signification of many grains gathered into one, which represents the mystical body, and that cannot be attributed unto accidents. (*Tract.* 11)

> we hold here a collation of the substance and properties of bread with the substance and properties of the body of Christ. And indeed we call for nothing else than that this analogy should be retained in that proposition. (*Def.* 129)

Christ chose suitable symbols to signify His nourishing and strengthening qualities: but according to the transubstantiators He wholly extinguishes the suitability.[38] For only substance

---

[36] *Def.* 63: the accidents of bread are 'one figure made a figure of another figure', since accidents are a figure of the Body, and the Body is a figure of Christ's Death.

[37] Cf. *Def.* 130.   [38] *Tract.* 56.

'corresponds', accidents 'neither nourish nor sustain'.[39] This is clear from the witness of the Fathers. They asked,

> why this Sacrament consisted rather of bread and wine than of anything else? Doubtless because their substance consists of many grains of corn and clusters of grapes, and because by these especially are we nourished, strengthened and gladdened. When you exclude the substance and retain accidents alone, you enervate and overthrow these reasons. (*Def.* 365)

What is 'convenient'? is Martyr's question. The Analogue unites us to Himself and daily feeds us; He also unites us to each other. Either analogy proves the substance of bread to be the analogated term in the elements.

The analogy of the mystical body has a further reference. If the 'Body of Christ' involves the doctrine of the Church, does not transubstantiation involve a substantial presence of *this* Body too? The syllogism is plain:

> The Eucharist is the sacrament not only of the body of Christ, but also of the mystical body. Whence Paul says, We being many are one bread, one body. But bread is not transubstantiated into the mystical body of Christ. Therefore neither into the true body of Christ. For of both bodies equally is it declared the sacrament. (*Def.* 407)

Along with this argument[40] Martyr includes another implication of the Church as the Body of Christ. Are not members scattered throughout Britain, Spain and so on, yet truly united in one Body?[41]

A further analogical argument, and a decisive one, is the fact that the water of baptism is never thought of as transubstantiated into the Holy Spirit!

> In Baptism water is said to be the fountain of regeneration, and this agrees well since its substance is retained, for the accidents of water would not be analogous . . . just as the conjunction of Baptism with the grace of the Holy Spirit does not repel or extinguish the nature of water, even so the matter of this sacrament does not destroy and cast away the being of the signs. (*Tract.* 11.56)

[39] *in* 1 *Cor.* 11.24; cf. *Disp.* II, opening speech: 'a convenient substance should be kept in sacraments. And regarding the Eucharist it is what nourishes us, which is done by the substance of bread, not by accidents.'
[40] Cf. also *Tract.* 22, *in* 1 *Cor.* 12.12, and *Epit., Sent.* 14.15. In the last, Martyr adds a further implication: 'The poor and those oppressed for the name of Christ are His body.'
[41] *in* 1 *Cor.* 12.12, *Tract., Praef. etc.* A similar analogy is that of husband and wife still 'bone of bone' although separated in place.

We see moreover in the Sacrament of Baptism, that the Holy Spirit and the remission of sins are given: yet we do not say that these lie hidden in the waters—nay rather we put on Christ, yet no one says that the water is transubstantiated. (*Tract.* 10)

(Euthymius) compares the water of Baptism with regeneration, and makes a like analogy . . . The body and blood of Christ are so contained in the bread and wine as our regeneration is contained in the waters.

(*Def.* 243f)

Perhaps the most fruitful thing about this analogy is its implication for *our* union with Christ.

Again . . . we reason from the men themselves who are baptized, of whom Scripture plainly says that they put aside the old man and are born again—and yet is no transubstantiation imagined in them, although that generation is described as a motion by which a new substance is acquired . . . if we interpret that generation to be new, and the nativity to be spiritual, do we not allow the same to the Eucharist? (*Tract.* 15)

Martyr often brings the argument that the words of Consecration apply to us more than to bread, and that they are applied to bread only in relation to our mutation.

Yes, we ourselves are more joined to Christ than is bread. For Christ is joined in the way He is to bread to this end, that we should truly be united to Him. And the words by which bread is called the body of Christ belong more unto us than unto that, which by nature understands and believes nothing. (*Disp.* III, *vs.* Tresh.)

The Fathers were fond of stressing our change into Christ— Cyril even says *corporaliter*. And Martyr is willing to agree with this language since Christ is in us 'truly, wholly, solidly'.[42]

We ourselves by a faithful participation in the Lord's Supper are fed, and in a manner transelemented by a certain kind of spiritual change, into the body of Christ. (*Epit.*, *Sent.* 11)

We are transelemented into Christ. (*Def.* 104)

In this context of analogy of substance, we should note that Gardiner makes a feeble attempt to satisfy the sacramental ratio by claiming that for accidents, 'the power of signification

[42] *vere, integre et solide*—*Def.* 752f. Martyr says that divinity is in Christ and in us *per essentiam et per gratiam*, the difference being that in Christ one hypostasis is formed. Cf. Part IV of the *Def.*, *Sententiae ac dicta Sanctorum Patrum.* Cf. Bishop Cosin on this Patristic language (*History of Popish Trans.*, VI.8): 'Certainly, if any man would wrangle and take advantage there, he might thereby maintain, as well that we are transubstantiated into Christ, and Christ's flesh into the bread, as that the bread and wine are transubstantiated into his body and blood.'

by reason of analogy, and the virtue of nourishing are retained
per miraculum'.[43] On this Martyr comments:

> Therefore will there be a miracle to banish the nature of bread and wine,
> and again another, no less a miracle, to restore it? O incredible fertility—
> of miracles or of lies, shall I say? (*Def.* 252)

The Words of Consecration and their Effect

Peter Martyr does not spend much time over the fine points
of Romanist dogma, except to remark upon such folly as this:

> The Papists do not know to which words the Consecration owes itself.
> For Scotus and Innocent III say the Consecration is in the word *Benedixit*:
> others, *Iube haec preferri*, others, *Hoc est corpus meum*. (*Def., Obj.* 84)

Such cavilling characterizes the whole doctrine of transubstantiation. All that is necessary, claims Martyr, is the acknowledgment of a proper 'mutation of the symbols', a 'sacramental mutation'.[44] He is quite willing to admit a definite
change in the sacrament, in fact two changes. The first and
chief is our change into Christ. But there is a corresponding
change in the elements themselves. They become sacraments,
'which they certainly were not before'.[45]

The *change* in the eucharistic elements is analogous to two
things: first, the change in human words by which the power
of the Holy Spirit makes the Gospel a saving power; second,
the change in ourselves. This second is the decisive analogy:
when the Fathers say that the elements are transformed, converted and transelemented (*transformari, converti et transelemen-
tari*), this we take to mean sacramentally.[46] For we too may be
rightly said to be 'transmuted or transelemented' into Christ.
And this is the decisive principle operative here. In each case,
what Martyr means is a spiritual change (*spiritualis mutatio*).[47]

> Who doubts this, that the communication of faithful men is much more a
> commerce with the flesh and blood of Christ than with bread and wine?
> But if so, no one will pretend it to be a firm argument by denying from the

[43] Quoted by Martyr, *Def.* 251. Chedsey had used the same argument (*Disp.* II).
[44] *Def.* 273.
[45] *Def.* 70.
[46] *Def.* 805ff; cf. 410: Chrysostom, Ambrose, Augustine, Theodoret, Damas-
cenus and Theophylact all speak of our change into Christ in such terms.
[47] *Def.* 43; cf. *Obj.* 152, where he quotes Irenaeus (*adv. Valent.* 4.4): *Panis,
terrenus accepta vocatione ab Verbo dei, non amplius est communis panis: sed efficitur Eucharistia, quae constat ex duabus rebus, terrena, et coelesti . . . Ita corpora nostra illam sumentia
non sunt amplius corruptibilia.*

major to the minor. Thus it may rightly be concluded: Men are not, by the power of the Sacrament, transubstantiated into the body of Christ; therefore by much less are bread and wine by the power of Consecration transubstantiated into the body of Christ. For it is not consistent with the words of Consecration to be more able in bread and wine, than the Sacrament of Baptism is in those who are dipped. (*Def.* 409)

And this may be taken as his analogical principle in brief:

As we are changed into Christ, so is bread changed into the body of Christ (*ut nos mutamur in Christum, ita panis mutatur in corpus Christi*). (*Def.*, *Obj.* 139)

The mutation in the elements, then, is not only in order to our mutation, but analogical to that. As that is spiritual, so is this. For the 'mutation' effected through faith and repentance is one of quality:[48]

we do not cast our mind or body from us, but there is made a certain alteration in qualities . . . the whole man is changed in respect of qualities.

Such a sacramental mutation in the elements effectively refutes the charge that Martyr is merely 'Zwinglian' in doctrine,[49] but poses an even more important question: his relation to subsequent Reformed teaching, which departed from this 'high' view to declare that the words of institution consecrate 'not by the infusion of a new quality but by change of use'.[50]

In the Oxford Disputation Peter Martyr was called to answer Chedsey's argument from the Fathers' language about the change effected by Consecration. In a long speech he describes the sacramental change in detail.[51]

I answer that (Ambrose) meant to prove nothing else than the change of bread which we call a sacramental change, and meant not that the nature of bread should be taken away . . . I grant such a change to be of those natures, as they receive other conditions, and ascend to a new degree: for they become sacraments, and they were not so before.

---

[48] Rather than of quantity, substance or place: *De Poenit.* 8.

[49] Cf. 'Portrait' above, *passim*, also Appendix C. C. H. Smyth (*Cranmer and the Ref.*, 1926) has complicated the problem somewhat by his use of the term 'Suvermerian' (first used by the Lutherans in derision at Bucer's doctrine) to describe the doctrine held by Bucer and then by Martyr, who, on his thesis, 'tormented by the Oxford Papists, was rapidly driven into zwinglianism, dragging Bucer with him' (p. 25; cf. pp. 123ff). Smyth knows Martyr only through the *L.C.* and Oxford works of 1549, completely ignoring the teaching of the *Defensio* (which is not quoted anywhere in the *L.C.*); and attributes more influence to Martyr over Bucer than Hopf, for instance, would admit (*op. cit.*).

[50] Trelcatius; cf. Wolleb: 'changes not the substance or quality, but only the use of the element' (Heppe, XXIV.4, p. 593). [51] *Disp.* IV, Q.2.

The power of God effects to add 'a sacramental power' to the bread, its substance not being changed.

He is able to make common bread and wine a most effectual sacrament . . . such a change is it, in which bread and wine are translated from the natural order and profane degree in which they were, to a sacramental state and order, both by the work of the Holy Spirit and by the institution of the Lord.

The matter of the sacrament, which is 'most specially sought by the faithful', is not fastened to the elements, but 'by blessing is joined to them'; they receive a new 'quality and condition', namely the power of signifying the Body and Blood of Christ.[52] This is *the spiritual and heavenly change*.

For while this holy rite is being performed, there is brought to the signs through the institution and words of the Lord a sacramental reference. And that respect of signifying both the mystical body and the body of Christ Himself is grounded not in the accidents of bread and wine, but even in their natures, through the coming of the Holy Spirit who uses them as instruments.

Rather than meaning a physical-material change in the substance, the sacramental mutation depends entirely upon the substance remaining whole and true—because this sacramental change is nothing else than the *analogical reference* now made open to the faithful:

those things (which) now sustain another quality, and have obtained a greater dignity, namely a sacramental state . . . But who doubts that consecration is a sacramental affair? In this it appears that the sign, regarding its nature, remains bread, and yet by consecration it is sacramentally the body of Christ.

Concluding this argument on Ambrose, Martyr points to his use of the analogy of our rebirth, 'from the change made in us, when we are regenerated'. But he is told by Chedsey to re-read Ambrose at home by himself, and he will see that transubstantiation is meant!

---

[52] Cf. *Def.* 474: 'the body of Christ seems to be added as a quality'. In *Def.* 581 Martyr draws two analogies between the Eucharist and Christ. Christ's substance remained the same after His Ascension, as does that of bread after Consecration. But also, 'as bread is changed, since it is raised to a higher level and made a Sacrament, so also is the body of Christ changed, since it is endowed with glory and incorruptibility and power.' Cf. *in* 1 *Cor.* 15.38, concerning the nature of the resurrection body: 'The mutation will not be of the body as to substance, but as to accidents'; 'ornaments' and 'conditions' of a new order are given, for 'Unless the same body is raised up, death is not conquered'; and *Catech.* 24.

Instruments of Nourishment

If the body of Christ is really in the Eucharist, it must be grasped by us either by the soul or by the body. It is not grasped by the soul, for nothing corporeal enters it. If they say by the body, we ask, to what end? If they say, that man may be sanctified, that will be to act preposterously. For sanctification begins from the soul, not the body. And the Eucharist is a spiritual food, instituted to feed the mind, not the belly. (*Def.*, *Obj.* 43)

Sanctification begins in the mind, when we learn that Christ was given for us on the Cross.

We are said to be sanctified by His flesh since we place all our trust in His death and blood. (*Def.* 722)

Although it may redound even to the body, this is always indirect, through the soul as the channel of blessing. Transubstantiation, however, means that in the Eucharist the body *rather than* the soul is sanctified! For what is the instrument of the Holy Spirit here?

We know indeed the instruments which God uses—such are words and sacraments, to reach the soul through the body. (*Def.* 192)

That is, the place of the body as instrumentally valid in man's redemption must not be misconstrued as the place where redemption actually takes place. That would be to anticipate the Second Advent in a carnal manner, and that is precisely what the doctrine of transubstantiation does, throwing the coming in judgment into a remote and theologically irrelevant future.

For you in your falsity gather three advents to be set forth: the first of the incarnation, another of transubstantiation, the third of the last judgment.
(*Def.* 31)

Gardiner locates the mystery in the bread, a mystery of a special kind of visitation, of a 'real presence' of the flesh of Christ. But we must lift up our souls unto heaven, there to feed upon Him who is our bread. The nutrition is His work, and cannot be shared by bread, which is incapable of such spiritual power of sanctification.

The bread is said to be consecrated, which is separated from profane use to figure and represent the body of Christ, and the spiritual nutrition through Christ. Not that bread can be the body of Christ, for of such sanctity it is incapable (*eius enim sanctitatis non est capax*). (*Def.* 270)

The principle to be followed here is, 'Nourishment is no better than that which is eaten'.[53] Only Christ as spiritual food (*spiritualis nutrimentum*) has use and value for our sanctification.

> That real presence of the body of Christ offers no utility which we cannot have from a spiritual presence. For Christ in John 6 promised eternal life to those who eat His flesh, that He would abide in them and they in Him. But nothing more can be expected from a real presence. Therefore it is useless and superfluous, and by it nothing is gained. (*Def.*, *Obj.* 52)

The key here is the 'vivifying flesh of Christ' (*vivificam esse carnem Christi*), and this kind of eating, this manner of nourishment, dictates the nature of the Eucharist.

> The Lord's Supper has only added symbols to that manducation which is described in John: so that by those symbols we might be vehemently and effectively incited to exercise the inward manducation . . . By the outward sign the mind is excited to comprehend more closely the flesh of Christ through faith. That apprehension sanctifies us, and gives us eternal life. (*Def.* 212)

This teaching about the nutritional quality of the New Manhood of Christ may be linked with Peter Martyr's use of the Pauline distinction between the inner and outer man.[54] This inner man signifies 'not simply the soul but the soul already regenerated'. It is only by the *homo interior*, therefore, that sanctification is received—spiritual things require a spiritual instrument.

> For since those things are spiritual, nor can be taken without the spiritual instrument of faith, therefore we conclude that those who are void of faith can neither eat the flesh of the Lord, nor receive the benefits of the Holy Spirit. (*Def.* 315)

Here again the Holy Spirit is decisive. His urging and inspiration (*instinctus et afflatus*) is in nature prior to faith, in time simultaneous. The nourishment of the Body of Christ means the presence of His Spirit, therefore the eating is spiritual.[55] This is why John 6 'greatly refutes transubstantiation'—

> that word bread in John is to be referred not to the symbols, but to the spiritual food, about which doubtless Christ was then beginning to teach. (*Def.* 308)

---

[53] *Alimentum non est melius re quae alitur*—*Def.*, *Obj.* 88.
[54] *homo interior et exterior*—*Def.*, *Obj.* 94.
[55] 'About Baptism there is no ambiguity. In the Eucharist also, it is the Spirit by whom we are quickened'—*in* 1 *Cor.* 12.12; cf. *Tract.* 1-17: the Holy Spirit is the Vicar of Christ.

For to eat and drink the Person of Christ is nothing else than to abide in Him, and He in us—which is without controversy a spiritual matter. The true role of the sacraments, therefore, will be as follows:

> We, after upholding Grace, do not exclude the use of the mysteries: indeed for the fostering and increasing (*fovere et augere*) of faith and Grace, we seal the promises of God by them. (*Def.* 312)

The 'proper effect' of receiving the Body of Christ is, union with Him. This is the positive principle by which Peter Martyr refutes the Romanists.[56]

> From that opinion of the adversaries it follows that the wicked eat the body of Christ just as do the saints. But that is false: for the body of Christ cannot be separated (*divelli*) from His Spirit. Wherefore since the unfaithful have not the Spirit of Christ, they cannot eat His body. They have not the Spirit of Christ because they lack faith: by which instrument all spiritual things are received. (*Def.*, *Obj.* 94)

The Eucharist is an instrument of nourishment, but the quality of nourishment belongs wholly unto Christ as the living Lord and Saviour.

> But we say, not only the blood of Christ which was shed for us, but the whole Christ (*totus Christus*) who truly is holy, when apprehended by faith, is the proper cause of our sanctification. Assuredly the Eucharist may be called an instrument of sanctification. For through it the Holy Spirit excites faith in us, through which very cause of sanctification we clearly apprehend Christ and His blood shed for us. (*Def.* 458)

The Wicked and the Body of Christ

> The thing itself of the sacrament is received by no one to his destruction. (*Res ipsa sacramenti ab nemine recipitur ad exitium*) (*Def.* 331)

Ched.   Shall they not receive the body of Christ, then, who are without faith?

Mart.   They shall not receive it, for they lack the instrument by which the body of Christ is received, as I have showed before.

Ched.   And is it there, although it is not received by them?

Mart.   Yes, by a sacramental signification it is in the elements, since they signify, represent and give to us the body and blood of Christ.

(*Disp.* IV)

On account of the sacramental mutation, Peter Martyr allows that the carnal eating of the elements is an eating of the *sacrament*—he can even, because of the communication of the

[56] In *Def.* 160 Martyr calls Christ Host (*hospes*) as well as food in the Supper.

o

properties noted above, allow this to be called an eating of the 'body of Christ' in the sense that this is what the element may be sacramentally called. But here the vital distinction is involved:

> the thing itself of which (this) is a sacrament, was to all men for life, to none for ruin, whoever was its partaker . . . the thing of the sacrament, that is the body and blood of Christ, can be eaten by no one unto ruin. Wherefore who appropriates to himself death out of it, receives only the sacrament, but not the matter of the sacrament. (*Def.* 331)

Here we return to the distinction, *per se* and *per accidens*. Inasmuch as Christ Himself was manifested for one purpose only, namely, the giving of *life*, although by their own sinful rejection of Him men took judgment and death unto themselves, to this He is related *per accidens*: even so do the sacraments (like the word) operate.[57]

> the wicked eat the elements of the Eucharist to their judgment, just as the false and profane through Baptism attain to nothing save the outward washing. (*Def.* 328)

> the true cause of either our salvation or our rejection to satan is not to be attributed to the Sacraments or to the outward Word, except insofar as these are instruments by which faith is excited in us through the Holy Spirit, by which we can apprehend Christ Himself, and all His gifts and promises. (*Def.* 723)

In commentary on the critical text, 1 Corinthians 11.27, Peter Martyr distinguishes three kinds of unworthy eaters. The first two, those who are altogether atheist, or possess only an 'historical faith' (*fides historica*) draw damnation and death to themselves when they communicate. A third type, possessing true faith yet neglecting life and manners, receive a 'communion of health' since Christ remains in them, yet often are chastened and recalled to penitence.

> And in short, we cannot state anything else of all those kinds, except that, whatever a person has of sincere faith, so much will he receive from the Sacrament of the thing signified, and to his enjoyment.

To say that the wicked eat the Body of Christ injures the symbols, destroying their analogy, and 'pulls down the matter

---

[57] Cf. Chapter I; *Def.* 722: transub. is not necessary to the 'unworthy eating' since there was such in the O.T. too (1 Cor. 10); 820: all things were to the ancients *in figura*—and some took judgment to themselves in a figure!

of the sacrament'. But in one sense the wicked *are* 'guilty of
the matter' (*res*), since they condemn and deride the signification, even though they grasp only the symbols. But those
who are not joined to Christ cannot eat His Body. The argument is 'partly from the nature of the thing received'—since
the Body of Christ cannot be divorced from His Spirit so that
to eat His Body means to have His Spirit; and 'partly from the
condition of the receivers'—since the wicked one as regards
the life of the spirit, is dead: 'he lacks a soul by whose faculties
these things can be received'.

> Without doubt they have only the signs to be received, and that to their
> own condemnation; for Christ is not in them, nor do they abide in Christ.
> (*Epit.* 2.7)

Moreover, the relation between Word and sacrament has
obvious relevance here:

> Since the Word by itself cannot stir up its hearers, when they are desti-
> tute of faith and spirit, that they grasp the thing signified, by how much less
> do these symbols, which if they be compared with the Word, are by no
> means more firm? (*in* 1 *Cor.* 11.27)

That which is determinative in the sacrament is not the consecration as resulting in a certain entity, but, Martyr continues:

> to the worthy or the unworthy eating these have regard: faith towards the
> promises, a just and right estimation of this Sacrament, a rite lawfully
> observed, and a holy conversation.

Now this is not to be understood as accenting the subjective
element in the partaking to a false degree—it does not, for
example, mean a demand for such worthiness as to deter any
of the faithful from the sacrament; nor does it mean a temporary humility in outward things—so that the minister puts
aside ornaments or rich vestments . . . and dons them again
afterwards.[58] No, 'this dignity ought to be perpetual.' We are
therefore to examine (*probare*) ourselves, as regards 'conscience
and the inner soul'.[59] For the abuse of the Lord's Supper carries
with it, accidently but inevitably, a judgment. Peter Martyr
indicates that just as there is a public as well as a private abuse

---

[58] *in* 1 *Cor.* 11.27.
[59] *Ibid.*, 11.28—this does not mean the Papist auricular confession, since *Tota
in fide et poenitentia consistit. Fides dogmata respicit, et poenitentia conversationem.*

(the Mass as a whole is the public abuse) so there is a public as
well as a private punishment.

> So it happens today. The Lord's Supper in almost the whole western
> Church is corrupt. But who sees not, in how much evil and calamity the
> Christian world is enveloped? (*in* 1 *Cor.* 11.30)

Not only wars, plagues and so on, but even 'the high price of
corn' (*caritas annonae*) is a symptom of the judgment!

CHAPTER VIII

THE EUCHARIST AND UBIQUITY

The problems of Lutheran doctrine did not weigh heavily upon Peter Martyr in the earlier period of his eucharistic teaching—the Oxford Treatise, for example, approaches the problem with an easy hand and in few words as compared with its discussion of transubstantiation. It was the subsequent trial which he underwent at the hands of the Lutheran pastors at Strassburg, in his second period of teaching there, and in particular the violent attack of Johannus Brentius after Martyr had removed to Zürich, which called forth his detailed refutation of the doctrine of ubiquity, by which consubstantiation was upheld. We shall examine first this earlier teaching of the Treatise, and then the more important work, the Dialogue.

A. THE TEACHING OF THE 'TREATISE'

In this work Peter Martyr is chiefly concerned to refute the heretical doctrine of transubstantiation. But after having so done, he turns to two other opinions, commonly associated with the names of Luther and Zwingli—although he observes that Luther spoke 'not so grossly', and Zwingli 'not so slenderly'. Because of the common misunderstanding between the two men,

there was stirred up a contention more than was meet, and was a cause of great mischief. Whereas indeed the contention was rather about words than about the matter.[1]

Indeed, Martyr is willing to declare about these two doctrines:

which of the two is appointed we do not greatly care, if it be understood soundly. Now we shall but speak of them, in order to see what we shall judge in both to be avoided, and what to be received.

Removing the doctrines from the personalities, therefore, he proceeds to consider each in turn.

[1] Quotations in this section, unless otherwise shown, are from the second part of the Treatise, in the L.C., Tract. 65-75.

Although the Lutheran opinion begins by admitting both natures wholly present in the sacrament, and by admitting the figure synecdoche (the part standing for the whole), yet it is not consistent, and ends by allowing a presence of Christ 'really, as they say, corporeally and naturally', and a presence not local but 'definitively'. And so:

a true and real conjunction of the sacrament with the matter may be shown, which being granted, means that the wicked as well as the pious receive the body of Christ.

Martyr argues that the use of figures in Scripture is abundantly evident, and 'in teaching of doctrine there is no doubt but that figures and tropes are used'. The Lutherans, however, contend that such matters must be taken *simpliciter*, and therefore join the two natures together in the sacrament, the humanity of Christ equally and in the same way with his divinity. Martyr denies this conclusion—he does not divide the two natures,

yet it follows not therefore that what pertains to the one should be given to the other . . . Indeed we grant that the divinity of Christ is everywhere, but we shall not attribute the same thing to his body and humanity.

The risen humanity of Christ means that 'the nature of man's body is preserved'. Thus their favourite text, Ephesians 5.22, 'Christ fills all things', since the verb is middle voice, can mean either that Christ perfects the gifts of His members, or that His mystical Body is filled by Church members—but not that the humanity of Christ is equally extensive with his divinity.

This is the heart of Peter Martyr's opposition to the doctrine of ubiquity, that by the Resurrection and Ascension faith locates the Risen Man *above* the earthly elements.

But if any man, while the sacramental rite is exercised, well instructed in the mystery, shall turn his mind to worship Christ reigning in heaven, he acts rightly and dutifully . . .

For the life of faith means communion with the risen Lord, a spiritual presence which is expressly set forth in John 6: 'over and beside this what is required?' This kind of eating of Christ is not complemented by another kind of eating, for 'the two are all one', the sacramental eating means a *confirming by signs* of the spiritual.

The words of scripture drive us not to so gross and corporeal a presence; and faith is of the word of God, wherefore faith must not embrace it.

The Fathers, moreover, expressly teach the necessity of the *sursum corda* in contacting the glorified Christ. Peter Martyr, here and in the *Defensio*, quotes especially the words of *Chrysostom*:[2]

we must ascend into heaven when we communicate, if we would enjoy the body of Christ . . . being made eagles in this life, we should fly to' heaven itself, or rather above heaven. For where the body is, there too are the eagles. (*Ubi enim est cadaver, illic et aquilae.*) The corpse is the body of Christ on account of death. For if he had not fallen, we had not risen. But he calls us eagles to show that he who comes to this body must strive after Him on high, and have nothing common with earth, nor traffic or crawl with inferior things, but ever fly to things above, and behold the sun of righteousness, and have most sharp eyes of the mind—for this is the table of eagles, not of crows (*aquilarum enim, non graculorum haec mensa est*).

Further Patristic sources are Augustine, 'We are with Him in heaven by hope, He is with us on earth by love' for example; Cyril, Vigilius and Fulgentius concerning the distinction between the natures as to place; and Bernard.

Finally, Martyr warns that the likeness to the union of the two natures in Christ is a likeness and not an identity of proportion—the doctrine of consubstantiation is ultimately the same thing as transubstantiation, since it destroys the analogy and makes another hypostatic union, a false presence of Christ in this age and earth.

But if afterward you would appoint as great a union between bread and the body of Christ as there is between the divine nature and the human in Christ, that would by no means be conceded: because there would be made of bread and the body of Christ one *hypostasis*, that is, one subject (*suppositus*), so that they could never be severed from each other, which is most absurd.

Thus far the *Treatise*. But in 1555 Martyr wrote to Calvin:[3]

The Saxons do not rest. They have issued a most vain *Farrago* (for so they call it). They gather certain sentences out of the Fathers, and also out of Luther, Philip, Brentius, Pomeranus and such like. They add to this

---

[2] *Def.* 9-10, *Tract.* 72. The quotation is from Chrysostom's *Homily* 24 on 1 Cor. 10.

[3] 23 September 1555, *L.C.*, p. 1097. The debate had great interest for the English Reformers, as their correspondence shows (*Zur. Lett.* 1558-1579). E.g. Parkhurst to Bullinger, 1 September 1561 (p. 98): 'I wish the Ubiquitarians a better mind, if indeed they have a mind at all . . . persons over whom you and Martyr will gain an easy conquest.' Cf. our 'Portrait', final section.

Bucer, Illyricus and Joachim Westphal, that they may be shown to agree among themselves. Also they have inserted certain Epistles written some-time against us. But they touch neither you nor me by name. They shame-fully rebuke John a Lasco, not indeed that he maintains a private opinion, but simply under the name of a Sacramentarian. And, please God!, they have in this Fragment a special title, That the body of Christ is everywhere (*Quod Christi corpus sit ubique*). This they now openly defend, and this article they treat in three or four folios, and use no other reason than that the Son of God took the nature of man into one hypostasis.

This was the beginning of a new phase of the debate. The doctrine of the ubiquity of the body of Christ now became the central point. The following year brought good hope of Martyr's removal to Zürich, for the situation at Strassburg was becoming intolerable. But it was not until 1561 that Martyr drew up the full-scale rebuttal against Brentius, the Dialogue in which '*Pantachus* . . . sustains the person of Brentius, and *Orothetes*, myself'.[4]

B.   THE TEACHING OF THE 'DIALOGUE'

The general argument of the *Dialogus De Utraque In Christo Natura* is set forth as follows:

Dialogue concerning the two natures in Christ: how they go together inseparably in one person of Christ, meanwhile not giving up their proper-ties, so that the Humanity of Christ cannot be everywhere without the body; and contrary arguments clearly and kindly replied to, and the matter of the Lord's Supper illustrated from scripture and the testimonies of the Fathers.

The Dialogue is divided into six sections: On the Humanity of Christ, being God; On the Properties of the Natures in Christ; On Ubiquity; On the Ascension of Christ into Heaven; On the Place in Heaven of the Body of Christ; On the Presence of the Body of Christ. Much of the teaching echoes what we have set forth from his other works, especially the *Defensio*, and the many Patristic quotations are repeated there. But the main question is simply, whether the Body of Christ is every-where, as Pantachus holds.

----

[4] Letter to Parkhurst, 23 August 1561, *L.C.*, p. 113. Cf. Jewel to Martyr acknowledging the work, 7 February (*Zur. Lett.*, p. 100). Martyr represented Jewel (*Palaemon*) as the moderator in the dispute. The names of the disputants are most fitting: the one represents πανταχοῦ, 'everywhere', and the other, ὁροθέτες, 'a fixer of boundaries'.

Ubiquity as the Eutychean Heresy Revived

The Lutheran object is to prove a presence of Christ in the Supper which is 'real, substantial, corporeal'. To accomplish this, they accuse the Reformed theologians (whom they call 'Sacramentarians') of following the Nestorian heresy, that is, of dividing the Two Natures in Christ to such an extent as to deny the truth of the union in one hypostasis. Let us paraphrase a most revealing section of the dialogue in this connection.

Pantachus: Though you support your opinion a thousand times, I stick to the hypostatic union: the two natures in Christ are not two, but constitute one person.

Orothetes: We receive that union, as do the faithful and orthodox: we do not divide the two natures, like Nestorius, nor yet confuse them, like Eutyches. Christ is one person, having two natures conjoined within himself, yet both complete and without violation in the properties.

Pan.: Because of the conjunction, wherever the deity is, there also will the humanity be, since Christ cannot remain a person, unless the two thus united in him by birth are maintained, so that the one is never present without the other.

Oro.: That does not follow—you are guilty of false reasoning, because you admit an equivocation (ὁμωνυμίας, *quem nostri vocant aequivocationis*), taking the union thus made of the two natures in Christ as if the whole divine nature were included in the human, and the human were extended and expanded (*vel humana ampliata et dilatata*) so that each nature is stretched out coextensively . . . in this you follow Eutyches, who confused and mingled the two natures . . . You think the persons are sundered if He is constituted divine, when the humanity is not present. Not at all. It suffices the Deity, as immense and infinite, to support and substantiate (*fulcire et substantare*) the humanity in his person (*hypostasis*), wherever it may be. Although the body of Christ is in heaven, when the Son of God is present in the Church, or elsewhere, He is never without His human nature, having this joined unto himself in one person. (pp. 9F-11A)[5]

Now it is obvious that much of this controversy has more to do with words than facts. We must remember, however, that the beginning of the debate lay in the serious question as to the manner of presence of the Body of Christ in the Supper, whether the wicked also partook of Him. It was by forcing back the problem to its actual basis in Christology that the disputants tried to solve it. Peter Martyr felt that the doctrine of ubiquity meant the denial of the humanity of Christ, a divinizing of it after the manner of the Eutychean heresy. The

[5] 1581 edition, Basle.

critical point therefore becomes the function of the *properties* of each nature of the glorified Christ Jesus.

The Properties of the New Humanity

Una persona Deus et homo est, et utrunque est unus Christus Iesus, ubique per id quod Deus est, in coelo autem per id quod homo. (Augustine)

This sentence of Augustine sums up Peter Martyr's doctrine of the Two Natures in Christ. Christ is apprehended only and always as the Divine-human Person; yet His Divine ubiquity must not be transferred to His humanity. The reason for this is, quite simply, that then He becomes something other than a man.[6] Unless the truth of His humanity persists even in glorification, the reality of the Incarnation is denied. Peter Martyr begins from this principle, and accommodates his eucharistic teaching to it; Brentius appears to begin from the Lutheran doctrine of consubstantiation in the Supper, and accommodates his Christology to that.

What is the nature of the resurrection body? Peter Martyr asks. Pantachus answers, since you accept the Athanasian symbol, that there is one Christ—

just so there will be one infinite, one immense Being.

Oro.: You have the matter well. One, infinite and immense, do we admit. Yet the dispute by no means rests, whether this property of immensity is communicated to the human nature of Christ . . .

Pan.: But in that are we equal enough since if we speak not of the unity of the persons, but of the diversity of substances, we say that nothing prevents this agreeing with one nature *per se*, but the other *per accidens*, as is given in the schools of dialectics. For it is the common sentence spoken of Christ, 'Whatever is given to the Son of God by nature, comes to the Son of man through grace.' (pp. 19F-20A)

The *communicatio idiomatum* is for the Lutheran an ontologically real communication—Pantachus 'wants to transfuse the divine properties to the humanity of Christ'. Now although God is *simplex* and therefore without accidents, yet He has attributes, such as immensity or ubiquity. But to apply this to humanity is to destroy the human property of circumscription, to be in a place.[7] You cannot remove these properties from humanity

---

[6] *quidvis aliud quam homo*, p. 23G.

[7] *esse in loco, et quidem localiter*—p. 23F., cf. 3B: 'Four gifts are assigned to the body of Christ and indeed of the blessed, by the Scholastics, *Impassibilitas, Claritas, Agilitas et Subtilitas*.' But since Pantachus has added a new gift, a new name is required, 'the monstrous name of Ubiquity'. In this same passage Orothetes also mentions the historically interesting name associated with Luther's sarcasm, *Suermeros*.

and leave it unharmed (*incolumus*). Therefore the resurrected or glorified human body will be endowed with properties only according to its capacity.

> Paul meant not that the body should be transformed into a spirit, but taught that the human body should be drawn unto the property of a spirit in regard to knowledge and feeling (*quoad notitiam et affectum*), as much as could be done without violation to its nature . . . through this diversity of qualities and conditions, the subject, that is the substance of our bodies is not to be altered; for exactly the same body and the same flesh will be raised up. (*De Resurr.* 59-60)

Pantachus explicitly denies that this communication of the properties should refer only to the verbal-nominal communion which Orothetes holds. Orothetes teaches that such properties as 'immortality, light, glory and the rest, of which human nature is capable' are gifted to the glorified body, whereas others such as 'eternity, immensity and ubiquity' cannot be communicated.[8]

What of the power of God? Pantachus asks—does not the Divine power and industry make possible—nay, even easy!—the ubiquity of the Body of Christ?

> Nevertheless from the bare omnipotence of God we conclude the body of Christ to be everywhere, and in many places. We have divine writings as witnesses of this, and among them the most important is the word of the Supper: the Lord indeed said, 'This is my body'. (5B)

Apart from its *petitio principii*, the above argument is plainly, as Orothetes charges, an appeal to the Divine omnipotence as a last resort. But it is no let to the power of God if there are certain things, by nature contrary, which He 'cannot' unite:

> And some things I affirm to be, which are not at all through His defect or fault able to become, notwithstanding the divine power, unimpaired and whole. For what things are facts cannot by any power be undone.

Martyr's principle is, the power of God is not compromised when we say that it does not extend to what would imply contradiction,[9] as he had taught in the *Defensio*:

---

[8] p. 30B.

[9] *Ego vero e contra tibi affirmo, nulla vi, fieri posse ut res creata sit ubique* (7B); cf. 5D, quoting Augustine (*De Civ. Dei* 5.10): *Ista propterea fieri non possunt, quia seipsa destruunt, et (ut loquar in scholis) contradictionem implicant.* But the logical argument ought to give way finally to Martyr's insight *in* 1 *Cor.* 11.24: not the Divine *posse* but *velle* is at issue, and this is revealed in the promises of Scripture.

And we know, two contradictory things cannot be true at once: such as, that there should be a human body, and not be a human body, at the same time. (*Def.* 517)

In Objection 143 of the *Defensio*, Martyr uses the doctrine of ubiquity, as representing what the transubstantiator also must say, to show that Consecration cannot be thought of as introducing the Body of Christ into the sacrament, since it must have been there already. Then he reminds Gardiner that this argument is not his own, since with all the Fathers, he affirms that

wherever the body of Christ is, there is his divinity also: but not the opposite: wherever is the divinity, there also is the body. For the human nature was so assumed by the Word, that that lost nothing of its infinity and immense latitude.

God cannot effect contradiction; therefore each nature remains whole; therefore the humanity of the risen Lord retains the bodily property of circumscription, so that the Divine property of ubiquity must not be attributed to it, except according to the nominal communication which the Fathers allow. Thus speaking of the *agilitas* of the resurrected body, Peter Martyr writes:

And in this consists the fact that the soul shall perfectly govern the body, so that the weight and burden of the flesh shall be no hindrance to it. This property indeed belongs to local motion. Wherefore it is a wonder that the Ubiquitists admit this quality to be in the bodies of the blessed, as they write in their books, and yet affirm that heaven is everywhere, so that they will not attribute definite places unto Christ's body and to ours, when we shall be blessed, as though local motion can be allowed apart from a place.

(*De Resurr.* 58)

This concern for the continuing humanity of the glorified Jesus Christ leads inevitably to a concern for the *locus* of His Body. We have somewhat anticipated this concern in the teaching that the sacrament is a 'heavenly affair', requiring a 'lifting up of hearts' to its proper reception. Now we must examine in detail this conception.

The Heavenly Places—and Beyond

I marvel greatly that in beginning, you cannot shake off thoughts of the dimensions of Geometry, when there is dispute about the body of Christ—*Pantachus*.

Orothetes is charged with cleaving to a maxim of Aristotle's
—which he willingly embraces—that 'the whole body is in a
place', but he relies even more on Augustine's sentence, 'Remove spaces of places from bodies, and they are nowhere: and
because they are nowhere, neither do they exist.'[10] It is this
concern for *spaces of places* which Pantachus describes as mere
geometrical juggling.

Pan.: But the same applies to what you teach of the body of Christ, that
it is extended and diffused geometrically in every place, like a patch.

Oro.: Not like a patch, nor any other kind of covering . . . the human
body is constant, it cannot fill a place which it will not reach. Moreover,
how that can happen otherwise than by extension of its magnitude, is an
invention of yours alone in our time, although the Papists give occasion
to you, either by explaining or by defending their transubstantiation:
but you surpass them by a great length. (*Dial.* 3D)

Pantachus accused Orothetes of hiding the Body of Christ
'in a dark corner of heaven'. But although Orothetes insists on
the ascribing of a definite locus to the Body of Christ, he
qualifies this spatial-geometrical language in a most significant
and decisive manner.

But we do not assert a body as being outside heaven, nowhere in a
general way: since beyond the firmament which they make the eighth
circle, is a region most blessed, where is the body of Christ: and the saints
not only hold places, seats and mansions, but after the resurrection dwell
there. But yet if we indeed comprehend that region called heaven, it may
happen that the body is not at all discovered. (4C)

I affirm the body of Christ to be in some certain place of an outward
heaven (*aliquo certo loco externi coeli*), but in a most extended and enlarged
way, so that He is free to stand, sit, walk or roam about. But if you define
such a place with reference to the daily revolution of the earth, then your
absurdity needs no answer. (75D)

Peter Martyr is quite willing to admit that such spatial categories are not to be understood in terms of geometric and
astronomic science. There is need to recall the impropriety of
theological speech at this point.[11] But what is the doctrinal

---

[10] *ad Dard.*: *Nam spacia locorum tolle corporibus, nusquam erunt: et quia nusquam erunt,
nec erunt.* (*Dial.* 4B, 24B, etc.)

[11] Cf. *Def.* 4: 'What (Paul) says of the death and resurrection of Christ is most
clear; but what "to sit at the right hand of God" signifies is not altogether so plain.
It is a metaphorical kind of speech, taken from kings and princes, who place on
their right hand those whom they hold in great honour and esteem . . . yet we
must not think that the body of Christ is poured abroad so far as His divinity and
the right hand of the Father . . . nor can we understand anything else by "the
right hand of the Lord" than the force and power of the Spirit.'

truth he is seeking to teach and safeguard? In a most helpful
letter he states:[12]

> But I say that the human nature of Christ was always comprehended
> within some certain place . . . If he shall be in heaven as to his nature,
> until the latter day as the Apostle says, why seek we his flesh and blood
> upon the earth? . . . I believe that the human nature of Christ abides in
> the heavens separated from the lower world, even unto the end of the world,
> and that the same shall come again from thence to judge the world, as the
> Apostles were warned by the Angels and as we confess in the Article of faith.
> To speak briefly, this is my opinion about the place and presence of the
> body and blood of the Lord.

He continues by acknowledging the adversaries' charge that
they deal as natural philosophers (as to their definition of a
body and its application to the glorified Jesus Christ), and
should rather submit their reason to the mystery of the Divine
power.[13] But, Martyr argues, we simply follow the testimony
of Scripture, and to follow nature where it does not contradict
this is not unworthy of theology, 'for nature has God as its
author and defender'. Thus there is no need to fly to the
Divine omnipotence. He cites especially the Resurrection
narratives, and the promise of Christ's Return (Matt. 28.6,
Acts 3.21). This echoes the thought of the closing paragraphs
of the Treatise *De Resurrectione*:

> Truly the grounds of nature are not to be made over, except when they
> withstand the Word of God . . . But we will follow the teaching of holy
> Scripture, which wherever it speaks of the body of Christ, always attributes
> unto Him a place . . . But I withdraw myself to Scripture, which allows
> so great a conjunction between a place and a body comprehended in it, that
> when the place is removed, it forbids the thing placed . . . places also per-
> tain to the eternal felicity in the kingdom of God.

This Scriptural basis of the reality of Christ's humanity and
its continuation in His resurrected and glorified Body is the
power behind Martyr's refusal to compromise with his Lutheran opponents. Moreover, since Christ in the Transfiguration
gave 'A pattern of blessed bodies', and in the Resurrection
is 'the image and similitude of our resurrection',[14] therefore

---

[12] *ad amicum quendam*, from Zürich, 24 May 1562, *L.C.*, p. 1144.
[13] Gardiner had used the same argument (*Def.*, *Obj.* 7). But for Martyr, the
Christian's 'reason' is 'reason formed by the Word and Spirit of God', for 'human
reason will never be sane and right unless it is formed by the Word of God' (*in
Arist. Eth.* 267, 290).   [14] *De Resurr.* 64.

we cannot make an exception of the new humanity of Christ.

In this connection, his treatment of the problem of the rapture of Elijah and Enoch has relevance.

> Yet many in this our time count heaven as a kind of spiritual and incorporeal place of the blessed, wholly everywhere. But this is nothing else than to mingle the highest with the lowest, the lowest with the highest. Leaving this Ubiquarious and fictitious heaven, we say not that the seats of the blessed are bodiless, but are spread widely and extensively beyond the compass of the stars, and beyond the firmament itself . . . Nor are the seats of the blessed appointed to be in those visible heavens: for Christ is said to have ascended above all heavens. (*in 2 Reg.* 2.11)

To take up Elijah and Enoch into 'an Ubiquarious heaven' is to send them into 'Utopia, which is in no place'. If they retain their bodies, they must occupy a place:

> all things created are defined and distinguished by a certain place, although after their own manner. For bodies are corporeally in a place: but spirits are, as the Schoolmen say, definitively, since they have a finite substance and nature . . . To be everywhere is attributed to God alone.[15]

What is at stake here, then, is the ultimate significance of body, redemption as the new creation, and this as proceeding from, and guaranteed by, the new humanity of the risen Lord Jesus Christ. The Resurrection and Ascension are decisive, and lead to the necessity of speech that may be called spatial or geometrical, with the qualification that the ultimate reality is 'beyond' such spatial categories. Finally, then, Christ 'fills all things' by the *Holy Spirit*.[16] The 'moment' of the Ascension is deter-

---

[15] *Ibid.* The relation of this 'place' of Elijah and Enoch to the 'bosom of Abraham' wherein the O.T. saints dwelt until the Resurrection of Christ, is not made too clear, but the determinative principle is that none attained unto the highest heaven until Christ the firstfruits. We ought to compare the parallel passages, *in* 1 *Cor.* 10.11, where he warns us to beware of too close investigations in such 'questions that are infinite and unprofitable', the leading of the devil as he seeks to have us neglect 'the many clear and manifest things in the holy scriptures, concerning faith, hope and charity'; and especially *in Rom.* 8.23 ('the redemption of our body'): concerning the manner of change in all things, 'all these things are obscure and uncertain . . . (perhaps) figurative speech . . . when all things shall end, the state of creatures shall be disturbed'. The principle here is that 'there shall be *a certain analogy*' between our glorified bodies and 'the elements'. This is because they were bound for our sin, and in the blessing will still be related to our being. But immortality is not a 'constituted' element in anything, but 'the liberal and mere gift of God'. Finally, the future is simply 'the kingdom of Christ, which He now exercises in the Church, and which in the day of judgment he will show forth with great power'.

[16] He reinforces his argument with reference to the work of Bullinger (*De mansionibus coelestibus*): Christ fills all things with the abundance of the *charismata et dona* of His Spirit. (*Dial.* 60, 84)

minative for the doctrine of the presence of Christ—Pantachus, however, speaks of an invisible ascension of the humanity of Christ at the moment of the Incarnation.[17] Orothetes denies this as rendering vain the visible Ascension of Scripture (*frustra visibiliter ascendebat*)—it is this doctrine that destroys the 'figment of ubiquity'. The 'reign and glory' of Christ will come only at His appearing for judgment.

The Presence in the Supper

What is the real significance of this debate? First, Peter Martyr is willing—we may think too willing, as Zwingli was with Luther—to meet Brentius on his own ground of the peculiar problem of the presence in terms of bodily circumscription. For these spatial-geometrical terms and categories are essentially those of the ubiquitists' own making, and not central for the Reformed position. On this level of argument, Martyr argues that Christ's glorified Body is substantially 'above' the creaturely realm, which includes the elements of the sacraments. On such a basis he seeks to prove the impossibility of a consubstantial presence. Here his arguments, like those on the similar philosophical level against transubstantiation, can become as pedantic as those of his opponent.

But there is a deeper level to his thought, one that has ultimate significance for his doctrine of the presence of Christ. Just as against transubstantiation his real argument rested upon the analogical nature of the sacrament, deriving from his Christological thinking, so here against ubiquity his decisive doctrine is not that of the locus of the Body of Christ, but the prior and fundamental doctrine of union with Christ as the content of justification, and the end of that sanctification which comes by the Holy Spirit's instrumental use of consecrated elements.

Let us explain the reasons for such a view. First, Orothetes always insists that it is Pantachus who is choosing the categories for the discussion. For *ubique* is by definition an *adverb of place*. The distinction within Ubiquity of Local, Repletive and Personal[18]

---

[17] *in momento incarnationis*—91B.

[18] *Docendi gratia triplicem Ubiquitatem statuamus, Localem, Repletivam et Personalem* (58B). In 99B, Ps. teaches a 'personal ubiquity' as the presupposition of a 'definitive presence' in the Supper. This accords with Luther's own (scholastic) distinc-

is nonsense—how can there be a personal presence if it is not repletive? For Pantachus argues:

> For God who alone is everywhere, never is so locally, but only repletively. But after the Son of God had united humanity with himself, that humanity assumed by the Son of God into the unity of person, must of necessity be everywhere, by a personal ubiquity. (*Dial.* 58C)

Unless we are to make a new grammar, therefore, we cannot disjoin this adverb of place from *locality* (*cur ab eius significatione localitem abiungitis?*). And this question of locale receives its answer in the doctrine of Ascension, which means that just as according to a certain manner of presence the Body of Christ was removed from the Apostles, so is it removed from us.

> The body of Christ is so contained in heaven, that it no longer dwells upon earth. (73B)

It is at this point that Orothetes introduces his qualification of the whole level of discussion we have been considering: The Session at the right hand of God does not *explain* the Ascension.[19] It is a false reasoning on the part of Pantachus which says that the right hand of God, being immense, is everywhere, therefore Christ who sits at that right hand, is everywhere. For what does this Session signify? Two things: the power of God's creativity and governance, and the greatest and perfect blessedness. Just as the power of a king extends beyond his own body, so the power or virtue of the Body of Christ extends beyond its own circumscribed being. The circumscription is no hindrance to communion with Christ; to argue from the one to the other is to confuse the categories. There is a certain power of faith,

---

tion, Local (Circumscribed), Definitive and Repletive. The last may be attributable to the Body of Christ, but it is the Definitive mode by which He is present in the Supper. In debate with Zwingli, Luther's basis was (1) a Divine- or spirit-flesh of Christ ('Gottesfleisch, Geistesfleisch') and (2) a 'right hand of God' everywhere, not 'a golden chair beside the Father' (cf. A. Barclay, *op. cit.* for an able summary). Brentius, at one time close to Calvin in theology (Barclay, p. 64 quotes Ebrard: 'What is embryonic in Zwingli came to its fruition in Brenz . . . In Brenz we find first that teaching which Bucer shared, and which later reached its full development in Calvin and Melanchthon'), swung to Luther's position in the debate with Martyr and Bullinger (cf. *Dial., Loc.* III)—*quod est cum deitate personaliter et inseparabiliter unitum* shares divinity's ubiquity, as faith in God's omnipotence asserts against reason.

[19] *Sedere ad dexteram patris non explicat ascensionem. Dial.* 77B—the body *assumpti super omnes coelos exprimere videatur, demonstreturque humanitatem Christi non tantum sublatam super omnes coelos, verum et apud Deum omnipotentem supremem dignitatem et gradum esse assequutam.*

P

by which things distant are made present to the spirit and soul of the believer—a presence of faith.[20]

The decisive question to be asked Pantachus is, do the 'impious and destitute of all faith' receive the presence of Christ in the Supper? Pantachus answers, Why not? It is a substantial presence. But Orothetes teaches that the wicked, although they may partake of the outward sacrament, are excluded from the matter of the sacrament.

The nourishment of the body and blood of the Lord has eternal life joined with it in an invisible bond, as John 6 most clearly teaches. (100E)

Orothetes calls as his special witness Augustine, in many passages,[21] and also other of the Fathers. But his last witness is Philip Melanchthon. Orothetes states that Philip is worthy to be compared with the Fathers—and even with Luther, as could Zwingli and Oecolampadius. Melanchthon emphasizes the fact that Christ has been lifted up (sursum), and is not to be sought on earth.[22]

It is on this level of debate that Orothetes introduces the teaching that there is a twofold mouth of the faithful (Duplex est os fidelium):

The faithful are supplied with a twofold mouth. The one is physical, by which profane or common drink and food are conveyed into the stomach, to feed and nourish the body itself. They have another mouth—not indeed in a proper sense, but so-called by a particular metaphor, because the enlightening and edifying of faith belong to the rational part of the soul, and they receive by it heavenly nurture (coelestis alimonia) to the soul, and finally divine renewing of the whole man. Consequently, when they approach the sacred Meal, with the natural mouth they take up bread and wine, but with the mouth of the soul or of faith they grasp those things which are signified to them by the Lord's institution, the body and blood of the Lord, I say, as they were given on the cross for our salvation. Hence that mouth of the soul is a thing not earthly, but spiritual, so that eating is not literal but metaphorical. So that to eat the body of Christ and to drink his blood, is truly and effectually to believe Him to have been delivered for our sakes by God to the death of the Cross. (127 C-E)

[20] 93E.
[21] Peter Martyr's use of Augustine is abundant, but he especially cites two passages. One, Quid pares dentem et ventrem? Crede et manducasti (Joan. Tract. 25); the other is De Civ. Dei 21.25, concerning the necessity of abiding in Christ before there can be a partaking of His Body.
[22] He cites Melanchthon's Response to questions of Prince Frederick, 1559.

Now faith, says Orothetes, is wholly a work of God; yet He uses instruments—ordinarily, the outward Word and the sacraments—and what He effects by these is an increase in our union with Christ:

> While we live, faith is not absolute, but has continual accession; and our union with the body of Christ is not so intimate that it never requires to be made deeper. Wherefore in eating and drinking, when we celebrate the Lord's Supper, faith is heightened more and more, and grows, and is rendered so much the more a partner of its object, I mean the body and blood of Christ, and we are revived the more by that spiritual nourishment.
> (127 F-G)

'A partner of its object'—this is the effect of faith, and only in terms of this union with Christ can the problem of 'what presence of the body of Christ is in the Supper?' be approached. This is not 'an empty game of vacant signs', because Christ has joined Himself to these signs and so

> while we eat the broken bread in the sacred Meal, and do so faithfully, the body and blood of the Lord is more and more spiritually communicated to us. (128C)

Because of the 'inner office of the Holy Spirit', these elements become 'effective instruments'. The distance of place is overcome by the power of faith, and Christ *in His humanity* is joined to us 'in a vivifying union'.

> The Lord's Supper is a thing heavenly and spiritual, not human and carnal. Therefore the faithful, while they communicate, by the power of the Holy Spirit who is operative in them through the Word and symbols of this mystery, are carried upwards in mind above all heavens, where they delight in Christ himself, particularly in what pertains to his humanity, which they behold and contemplate, inasmuch as this Man was delivered to the cross for their salvation, a price most acceptable to God. Now you see on what grounds we claim the presence of the body of Christ in the sacred Meal. (130E)

This is the 'fruit and utility' of the new humanity of Christ.[23] The 'real presence' in the sacrament is not the philosophical question of the ability of Christ's Body to visit creaturely elements, but the theological question of the miracle of grace

---

[23] Cf. *Def.* 722: 'We confess that Christ is not only represented to us there but also given as the matter and in truth: and not only . . . what pertains to the divine nature and grace and Spirit, and other heavenly gifts, but also to the human nature of Christ itself.'

by which the Holy Spirit unites believers to Jesus Christ Himself. The Dialogue ends on a rather plaintive note:

Oro.:   I pray for you a better mind and saner doctrine.
Pan.:   Indeed I ignore your prayer. I seek this much, that as regards the
matter of the sacrament, you should hold with Luther, and as regards our
revered ubiquity you should be hereafter more correct in experience and
in speech.

Critical Note

What was the real issue at stake in this unhappy controversy
which so divided Lutheran and Reformed? Although we may
lament the Lutheran preoccupation with questions of causality,
we must acknowledge the truth for which they struggled. The
subsequent debate of the orthodoxy of the sixteenth and seven-
teenth centuries shows that what was involved was the fundamental problem of theology: the meaning of 'The Word was
made flesh' of John 1.14.

Patristic Christology had summarized belief on this issue in
the terms *anhypostasia* and *enhypostasia*. By *anhypostasia* was
signified that the human nature in Christ had no power of
existence independent of its concretion in the hypostatic union
of the two natures in the Person of Jesus Christ. *Enhypostasia*,
on the other hand, signifies the positive: the hypostatic union
gives a certain being of its own to the human nature.[24] The
development of Lutheran doctrine, symbolized by Quenstedt,
leads us to conclude that Luther had accented the enhypostatic
nature of the humanity of Jesus Christ to the detriment of the
anhypostatic, so that a doctrine of the reversal of the natures
was formulated: 'as the manhood is only through the Word
and in the Word, so also the Word has reality only through
and in the manhood'.[25] Against this, Reformed orthodoxy
stressed the anhypostatic nature of the humanity's subsistence:
even while in the flesh, the Word remained in His own nature
outside (*extra*) that flesh. Thus Calvin (*Inst.* 2.13.4) denies any
'inclusion' of the Word in the humanity, since His descent
mirabiliter to union does not imply a relinquishing of His

---

[24] Cf. the analysis of this debate by K. Barth, *K.D.* I.2, 1938, sect. 15.2, 'Wahrer
Gott und Wahrer Mensch', pp. 145-187.
[25] Barth, *loc. cit.*

heavenly rule or 'filling all things' as He had *ab origine*.[26] This teaching was branded by the Lutherans *extra Calvinisticum*; yet it opposed, not the *totus totus intra carnem* but the *nunquam et nusquiam extra carnem*. For Luther had threatened to lose the reality of the Word *asarkos* in the reality of the Word *ensarkos*.

Barth approaches the problem in terms of positive and negative principles deriving from the *unio hypostatica*. This would appear not mere dialectic but the truth of the dynamic nature of that union, as against the static and logical categories which both sides in the debate seem to have accepted. Thus we may agree that 'the Chalcedonian Christology needs to be filled out in accordance with its own fundamental position, in a more dynamic way, in terms of the incorporating and atoning work of the Saviour, for the only account the New Testament gives us of the Incarnation is conditioned by the perspective of the crucifixion and resurrection.'[27]

We have attempted to show that Peter Martyr's theology maintained a high degree of this dynamic (*e.g.* Chapters I and III), and that by stressing not only a nominal communication of properties but also a 'real presence' of *totus Christus*, he allows for the fact that the humanity of Christ always mediates His presence. Yet there is no doubt that much of his emphasis, like that of Calvin, was able to be turned to a false use by later Calvinists. However, the deeper question is whether the Reformers really appreciated the Lutheran position. It would seem that they failed to understand that the controversy arose from within the mystery of Christ Himself. The only historical exception to this failure appears to be Martin Bucer. Our Appendix C deals with the question of his relation to Martyr and Calvin in detail; here we may observe that Bucer insisted on relating the impropriety of theological language to this matter of the mode of Christ's presence in the sacrament. Therefore he utterly rejected all 'worldly' ways of speaking, and regarded spatial categories as but symbols of the mystery which language

[26] Cf. Heppe's Chapter 17, 'The Mediator of the Covenant of Grace or the Person of Christ': 'Christ's human nature had hypostatic subsistence only by its being taken up into the hypostasis of the Logos' (416); cf. Alsted (417) and Heidegger (428): the humanity is *per se* anhypostatic, becoming enhypostatic in the Logos.

[27] T. F. Torrance, *S.J.T.*,7/3, p. 247 ('Atonement and the Oneness of the Church').

cannot carry properly.[28] He sought especially to prevent the idea of Christ's local presence in a heavenly place from becoming a 'necessary doctrine', and felt that it was sufficient to stress the doctrine of the Ascension. It was on this ground that Bucer was able to find agreement with the Lutherans.[29]

Martyr's debate with Brentius, we may conclude, although an occasion for grief at such a rent in the heart of Reformation, must be accepted by us as a warning, to force us back behind the details of the controversy to that deeper mystery of our one Lord Jesus Christ.

[28] As we saw, Martyr admits as much in the *Dialogus*, but does not agree with Bucer that the Lutheran position is met by such a negative approach—unless we conclude that Brentius was abusing certain nascent concepts of Luther. But perhaps one more question this debate should raise is, how the Reformers would view our modern problem of the *Entmythologisierung* controversy?

[29] Cf. the fine study of 'The Problem of Intercommunion in the Reformation' by Ernst Bizer (*Intercommunion*, pp. 58ff), especially sections *iii* and *v* in regard to Bucer.

CHAPTER IX

THE EUCHARIST AND TROPISM

PETER MARTYR spent little time in dealing with the Anabaptists, except to note their presence as the delimiting factor in the Reformation—for instance, when treating of War, he states

> The Anabaptists, the furors and plagues (*furores et pestes*) of our time, say absolutely that it is not lawful to war. (*in* 1 *Sam.* 3, *De Bello*)

In regard to the sacrament, they occupy a similar position—a rationalized doctrine which was termed *tropism*, because they held that the sacramental signs were simply 'tropes' or bare signs of their signification. This may best be summed up in relation to two questions which are basic for Martyr, first as to the nature of the sacramental signs—the 'mutation' of which we have spoken already—and second, as to the purpose of the sacrament, its relation to sacrifice.

A. THE NATURE OF THE SIGNS

The Means of Grace as Effective Signs

Peter Martyr was too much involved in the Swiss Reformation to mistake the sacramental teaching of Zwingli for the tropism of the Anabaptists. Indeed, he says of his own sacramental teaching, in the Oxford Disputation, that it was simply what Bullinger had been teaching.[1] But he treats the so-called 'Zwinglian' view in a few sections of the *Treatise*, with the initial qualification that Zwingli himself does not speak 'so slenderly' of the signs as is supposed. His treatment serves a practical purpose—to refute the Romanist charge that the Reformed doctrine of the sacraments is mere tropism. In the struggle with transubstantiation, the terms employed often

---

[1] See Appendix C for the question of Martyr's relation to Bucer and to Bullinger.

approached the other extreme; but Peter Martyr makes clear his own position as follows:

adversaries say, If you remove Transubstantiation and real presence, it follows of necessity that nothing but signification is left in the sacrament. I answer that they are Anabaptists, who would have this sacrament to be nothing else than a badge and profession of our mutual society through love: they take no account of the Holy Spirit, whom we affirm to be in this sacrament. (*Disp.*, *Praef.*)

The problem is, if the true eating of the Body of Christ is a matter of the Holy Spirit, as John 6 teaches, can the sacramental signs mean anything more than a partial and temporary means by which a weak Christian calls to memory the Death of Christ? Now Peter Martyr deals with this question by teaching, as we have already indicated, a sacramental mutation which can be said to come to the elements because of the change in believers through the means of the sacrament. They are 'not dumb, but speaking signs'. To say, as they do, that the words 'remembrance' and 'show forth' imply an absence of Christ's Body, confuses the issue. For the absence refers only to such a corporeal-natural body as the transubstantiators demand. But

when received by faith it is not understood to be wholly absent, although He remains in heaven regarding His nature and substance. For He is spiritually eaten, and truly joined with us. (*Tract.* 77)

Moreover, the similes they cite 'could not agree with this mystery'. They suggest for example, an absent friend made 'present' when we think of him, or a mirror which reflects the likeness but not the actual presence. The difference is manifest:

For a friend being comprehended in thinking and conversant in mind, does not change him that thinks of him; he does not nourish his mind, nor restore his flesh so that it is capable of resurrection.

Indeed, the doctrine of the signs used is derivative from the doctrine of their effect; tropism means that the content of justification is not understood as union with Christ, so that 'growth in grace' is but a mental process, and sanctification may be defined anthropocentrically. Those who talk most of 'the Spirit' often do not leave Him room to breathe.

Peter Martyr wishes to define clearly the effect of the sacramental eating, and then the true being of the signs will be clarified.

For the presence which we confess of the Spirit of Christ has the power of the Holy Spirit joined with it, which unites us most closely unto Him.

Union with Christ as the work of the Holy Spirit is the 'third conjunction with Christ' which they miss, teaching only two, one natural, by the Incarnation, and the other by faith, when we apprehend that He was crucified for us. This third is the decisive one, however, 'into which we enter with Christ in the eating of Him spiritually'. Faith makes a thing 'thoroughly present', so that we are joined unto the whole Christ not only mentally and by memory but in a real union, in the realm of being.

Now Zwingli, he says, does not in his writing make the signs 'vain or frustrate'. But his followers often do, seldom mentioning any sacramental changing of the elements, *which is no light matter*. Such a change is implied in the O.T. idea of holy vessels, in St. Paul's terminology of 'the cup of the Lord', and in the frequent use of this doctrine in the Fathers.[2] Here Martyr teaches a threefold conjunction in the sacrament:

while we communicate, Christ is joined to us with an excellent union, as He that dwells in us and we in Him; who also in the next degree is joined with words, by signification; thirdly He is also coupled with signs, again by signification—which conjunction, however, is less than that which belongs unto words. And from the former, the conjunction with words, the signs take their sacramental signification.

The determinative factor is the efficacy of the sacrament, according to which:

The symbols are not only signs but instruments of the Holy Spirit.

(*Def.* 82)

The institution of the Lord and the power of the Holy Spirit mean that God condescends to work mightily through these consecrated elements.

But these symbols are through the words of God and His institution made signs and mysteries of our salvation. (*in* 1 *Cor.* 10.16)

We often call the signification of the symbols potent and effective. Why not? For the Sacraments are not common or familiar signs, but instruments of the Holy Spirit. (*Def.* 730)

Martyr contrasts these effective signs proper to mysteries[3] with

---

[2] This part of the argument is from *Tract.* 79-81.

[3] *Epit.* (*Verba Coenae* . . .): 'such as were accustomed to be assigned in other mysteries'. '

the signification of 'Tragic and Comic'[4] or of 'images and statues':[5]

so the bread of the Eucharist is called the body of Christ, because it signifies this—not, doubtless, by a common signification such as is used on a stage or theatre, but effectual, since the Holy Spirit uses that instrument to stir up faith in us, by which we may apprehend the promised participation of the Lord's body. (*Conf. Argent.* 1556)

We do not teach that the holy mysteries are a kind of common picture or promissory note. (*Def.* 200)

It was for this reason, Martyr says, that Christ used *Is* instead of *Signifies* in His words of institution.[6] There being no special word to indicate this *genus significationis*, Christ called the sacrament of His Body 'My body':

Why did Christ use the verb substantive *Est* rather than the verb *Significat*? ... lest we should suspect it to be a light and common signification. (*Def.* 71)

In these terms Martyr can grapple with Gardiner's charges that his teaching is merely 'figurative'. If by figure is understood 'an empty and vain sign', then Martyr agrees that no such figure is in the Eucharist.[7]

What, pray you, do you call an arid figure? Surely not the bread?
(*Def.* 56)

Therefore Martyr advises that the minister should

weigh the nature and dignity of the mysteries, lest he should think that he gives bread, wine or water as naked elements of the world ... Nor let him delay examining and searching those to whom he will distribute the Sacraments, that if he perceive them to be dogs, he may remove them from him.
(*in* 1 *Cor.* 4.2)

Tropes True and False

But the trope we adduce is plain, and received by the fathers, nor has it anything that opposes human nature or divine, nothing alien to the rule of faith, nothing that completely overturns the law of nature, or to which

---

[4] *Tract.* 44: it is our 'secret and unspeakable union' with Christ that proves the effective nature of the symbols.

[5] *in* 1 *Cor.* 10.1: 'not indeed commonly, as an image or statue represents Caesar, but we say it is a sign potent and effective'.

[6] *Ibid.*: 'lest it be thought a common conjunction of this communion with the cup'.

[7] *Def.* 810; cf. 52: the eucharistic figures are especially *nuda frigidaque* if they do not give the spiritual apprehension of Christ—which transub. cannot yield. What gross error in regard to both Martyr and Zwingli therefore to say, 'Il (Martyr) considérait, en effet, à la suite de Zwingli, les sacrements ... comme de purs symboles d'union Chrétienne' (*Dict. de Théol. Cath.*, art. Vermigli).

miracles and portents are necessary . . . The trope is metonymy, by which
the sign assumes the name of the signification. (*in* 1 *Cor.* 11.24)

The question in this problem of Peter Martyr's relationship
to tropism is not whether tropes are to be allowed, but which
are lawful. Both Romanist and Lutheran understood *tropos* in
terms of the doctrine of 'bare analogy' associated historically
with Arianism and the *Tropici*.[8] Thus they accused the Reformed theologians of using a rhetorical device to conceal a
doctrine of mere external symbolism in the sacrament. Against
this charge, Martyr brings the argument that the relationship
of analogy involves a verbal communication, as we saw in his
Christology. Augustine himself makes much of this nominal
communication:[9]

Sacraments (Augustine says) have a similitude to the things they signify,
and bear their names. Whence Baptism can be called faith, because it is
the sacrament of faith. And therefore baptized infants can be said to have
faith, because they receive the Sacrament of faith. (*in* 1 *Cor.* 11.24)

Here is to be noted a phrase of speech much used in the holy Scriptures,
by which what belongs to the matter is attributed to the instrument or
sign. And that this is often used in the sacrament, we have many times
proved by Augustine's opinion, although our adversaries are sore against
this. (*in Rom.* 5.3)

The technical name for such grammatical exchange is
metonymy, although it can be also synecdoche, taking the part
for the whole.[10] Further, in a significant passage he relates

---

[8] Wherever Arius found words used of God and creatures, he dismissed them
as homonyms or equivocal expressions, so that 'tropical exegesis' was reduced to
mere symbolism. Against this stood Athanasius, for whom *tropos* and *analogia* had
been synonymous, and who proceeded to attack the tropist position on the ground
that it used false analogical reasoning in its doctrine of the Trinity, 'transposing
them at will on the analogy of human generation' (*The Letters of St. Athanasius
Concerning the Holy Spirit*, trans. C. R. B. Shapland, Epworth, 1951, p. 187; cf. pp. 31,
158ff). Thus the *Tropici* were guilty of arguing from ectypal analogies, even though
these were taken from Scripture, and thereby they compromised the doctrine of
Christ and consequently of the Spirit. At the Reformation it was the doctrine of
Athanasius that came to the fore, since the Reformers were prepared to argue from
Christ as their archetypal analogue in relation to Scripture and Church (cf.
T. F. Torrance, 'Atonement and the Oneness of the Church', *S.J.T.*, September
1954). We have seen this movement in the case of Martyr's thought. But in
Oecolampadius there appears to be a doctrine of 'bare analogy' which justifies
the name of 'symbolism' and therefore 'memorialism'. Whether Zwingli himself
is guilty on this point is another question—in his 'middle period' he may be, and
this teaching was continued in Megander of Berne. Cf. A. Barclay, *op. cit.*, Chapter
6 for Zwingli's 'Nestorianism'.

[9] *Ep. ad Bonif.*: *Sacramenta habere similitudinem cum rebus quas significant, et nomina
earum gestare.*

[10] E.g. *Def.* 650. Calvin would agree—cf. Wendel, p. 262 and Niesel, *Calvins
Lehre vom Abendmahl*, 1930, p. 138 for his metonymy.

these to the figure *alloeosis*, which Zwingli and Oecolampadius had used.[11] Gardiner had accused him of using this figure in the key proposition 'This is My body', and Martyr replies:

> But I never said or wrote that anywhere. For in those words I always declared outright that I acknowledged Metonymy or Synecdoche. Yet not even there can alloeosis be denied, if one understand that figure thus, as I do. For the Sacrament of the Eucharist consists of two parts, wheat bread and the body of Christ. Wherefore when the name of the one is attributed to the other, and bread is called the body of Christ, there cannot be denied as manifest there a permutation or alloeosis of names and words. Nor is the use of these tropes Metonymy and Synecdoche much different, in my opinion, from Alloeosis and alternation. (*Def.* 598)

In the context of his larger teaching, this use of tropes may be seen as the legitimate result of analogical reasoning on the basis of Christology. Moreover, the immediate and practical concern for Martyr was the error of attributing too much to elements themselves, an error which the excessive speech of the Fathers partly induced.

> We must beware that we attribute not to the elements or symbols, considered apart from Christ, what is proper to Christ Himself; but when both Christ and the symbol are received together, the properties are there communicated. (*Prop. ex Exod.* 16, *nec.* 15)

> If at any time the holy Scriptures seem to attribute forgiveness of sins or salvation to outward signs, that must be understood by the figure Metonymy by which those things are given to signs which are proper to the things signified and the things signified are expressed by the name of the signs.
> (*De Templ. Ded.* 18)

The Office of the Holy Spirit

Martyr's teaching may be summed up in regard to the work of the Holy Spirit: it is because it is the Spirit who works here that (1) a *substantial* change is *not* necessary or proper; and (2) an *effective* change *is* necessary and proper. The error of Papist and Lutheran lay in failing to understand the centrality of the Holy Spirit in the Christian life, and seeking communication through some means other than His office. The error of the Anabaptist or 'Zwinglian' lay in failing to understand the Holy Spirit's use of instruments, based on the Christological analogy and decisiveness of the Incarnation. He refused to make any sign an effective one, and ultimately threw into doubt the Incarnation:

[11] At Marburg—*Gegenwechel*, which Luther called 'devil's mask' (*larva*).

they have not always applied to (signs) that efficacy which is due to them: for these are not made common signs but such as may mightily and effectually stir up the mind . . . these things are not attributed unto the elements for their own sake, but because of the institution of the Lord, the power of the Holy Spirit, and the plain sense of the words. . . . If they demand, how may I know that the Holy Spirit works here? it is easily answered, because it is already ordained that this is a spiritual eating. But how shall we eat spiritually without the Holy Spirit? Regarding the institution of the Lord, there is no doubt: and of the efficacy of the Word, the scriptures speak everywhere . . . (Romans 1.16) . . . that God will declare His power by this instrument (Gospel)—and what else is the Eucharist than the visible Gospel or Word?[12]

The Holy Spirit brings belief unto men, 'but He uses the instrument of Words, and of sacraments which are sensible words of God'. Martyr's theology may rightly be termed a theology of the Holy Spirit, for He is central in all Christian knowledge and life. It is on this basis that Martyr demands recognition of the change in the elements—their analogical power is not a thing of human making, arising in our cognition, and therefore external to the sacrament; it comes with the very givenness of sacraments and depends upon the Holy Spirit:

Wherefore this changing must not be removed from bread and wine, by which they are made effectual signs of the body and blood of Christ, that is, by which the Spirit of the Lord works mightily and not meanly in us, so that we are endued with faith and godliness.[13]

Here again the effect of the Holy Spirit is summed up as our union with Christ:

Indeed He is joined to us, but is every day more closely joined, and while we communicate is more and more united unto us . . . We, by the Communion, are incorporated into Christ . . . For although we affirm that the apprehension or holding fast the body of Christ is done by faith, yet upon this apprehending follows an effect, even a true union with Christ, not feigned or imagined.

Christ makes 'a certain entrance' into us, nourishing us—and mentally-present things do not *nourish*. Peter Martyr is explicit here—

all this that we teach is spiritual—and yet no feigned thing, for imagined sights, idols, or fictitious things do not nourish the mind, as here we are

[12] Quotations are from *Tract.* 80, 81.
[13] Cf. *Tract.* 49: 'by an effective and most vehement force of the Spirit'; 60: 'The Holy Spirit is the chief in this matter'; 64: 'For all depends on the institution of the Lord and the working of the Holy Spirit.'

certain happens . . . these signs both signify and offer, and most truly exhibit the body of Christ, although this is spiritually, to be eaten with the mind, and not with the mouth of the body.

This most important question of 'both signified and offered' will concern us in the final Chapter. Both extremes, transubstantiation and tropism, err in taking the sense of the offering or exhibiting of the Body of Christ in a quasi-physical sense. The one embraces this sense, the other rejects it. Martyr's doctrine of the Holy Spirit allows him to escape this false antithesis, and see that the unity of physical and spiritual in the sacrament is one maintained by the Holy Spirit and therefore real as He maintains a relation of analogy to eyes of faith, and not real as a relation of simple identity (as transubstantiation ultimately implies), or of simple difference (as tropism implies).

> Lastly, we have shown that great heed must be taken lest that which we speak of spiritual eating be understood as if it destroyed the truth of His presence . . . For wherever the faithful are, they apprehend that Christ had a true body given for us, and so they eat him by faith. (*Tract.* 81)

> But if we have regard to the work of faith (*opus fidei spectamus*), the true body of Christ is perceived to be the thing itself spiritually in the Supper.
> (*Def.* 267)

B.   THE PURPOSE OF THE SACRAMENT

In one passage Peter Martyr lays bare a most fruitful analysis of the two errors attendant upon the doctrine of the sacraments.

> And so one will establish the nature of Sacraments rather in the receiving of what God gives us than in the giving of what we offer unto God. For more excellent are the things God shows us than what we offer. Certainly we give ourselves as living sacrifices, as we die unto sin; we give confession and praises, and other things like that. But what we receive through faith are Christ, remission of sins, grace and eternal life. Against these we may sin in two ways . . . (*in* 1 *Cor.* 10.16)

The first of the 'two ways' is that of the Romanist, with his sacrifice of the altar, 'which is wholly repugnant to the ratio of a Sacrament'. The second is as follows:

> And the Anabaptists sin, who make the Sacraments only outward tokens (*tesserae*), in which they publicly declare their faith, and are distinguished from the rest of men, promising a holy life, and manners worthy of a Christian. Whence these too seem to place the whole weight in our oblation (*in oblatione nostri totum ponere*). But if so, there ought not to be so much giving of thanks. For we do not give thanks for that which we give, but receive.

The striking thing here is Martyr's conclusion that both extremes imply the same basic error: turning the sacrament (something received from God) into sacrifice (something given to God).[14] Ultimately, Anabaptism means the same legalism, with its work-righteousness and its characteristic rite of sacrifice, of which Romanism is guilty. The forms differ, for they stand on opposite sides of the Reformed position; yet the error is the same in each, and reaches its clearest expression in their turning the sacrament of the Eucharist into a sacrifice, giving it into the hands of men.

> And whereas this meat is called by Paul, spiritual, it is signified that sacraments are no common signs, as though none of these things which are signified were received: for then they should be but external and earthly meats, and not spiritual. Further, God mocks not, nor deceives, that he would promise anything in the sacraments which he will not perform by any means. Yet neither is there need of a metamorphosis (which they call transubstantiation) to the end that the sacrament should become spiritual food. We ought not to confound the nature of the signs with the things signified. Let us follow the mean and sound way; and let us judge honourably of the sacraments—not thinking them to be things altogether empty of spiritual good, nor so joining the signs with the things that they pass wholly into them. It is enough to appoint a profitable and most excellent signification, by which the faithful mind, through believing, may be made partaker of the things signified. (*in* 1 *Cor.* 10.3)

[14] A further proof of this significant teaching is Martyr's attitude to the baptismal vow (*in Rom.* 6.3; *De Vot.* 1433, 1353ff, 1369, 1576). Romanism had related the vow (of being joined (*nomen dare*) to Christ) to celibacy, making faith ambiguous, inasmuch as a further degree of faith could be attained in the post-baptismal vows. On this subject Martyr agrees that in baptism 'we are separated from satan and join ourselves to Christ', vowing never to fall away to the devil. But this is not to vow properly, since in baptism the chief point is the confession of one's faith: *fidem posse intelligi professionem in Baptismo.* Thus the Fathers understood by *votum* only *aut preces aut vehemens desiderium.* For the principle to be followed is this, sacraments are things promised by God, not vowed by men. Might we not conclude that in baptism as in the Eucharist, the two opposite errors resolve into a basic legalism in which man becomes the controlling person in the action?

CHAPTER X

THE EUCHARISTIC SACRIFICE

A. Sacrifice and Sacrament

Now a sacrifice is a religious act, since it pertains to the worship (*cultus*) of God, and is instituted by Him that we may offer our goods to him, even for this, that he might be endowed with honour, and (as Augustine says, *de Civ. Dei* cap. 7) we may adhere to him in a holy society. And here we may see how a Sacrifice, properly speaking, differs from a Sacrament: since this too is a religious work, also instituted by God, that through it the promise and good gifts should be sealed and exhibited—but there we offer nothing at all unto God, but He Himself proffers signs, and amplifies his gifts to us, while we receive the things offered with a sound faith. (*in Iud.* 2.5)

By way of preliminary definition of the Eucharist, we set forth Peter Martyr's distinction of sacrifice and sacrament: they are opposites, to be judged according to their movement, whether they proceed from God to man or from man to God. In this preliminary but fundamental sense, a sacrifice is 'wholly repugnant to the ratio of sacrament'.[1]

Since we have dealt at length with Martyr's analysis of this *ratio* of the sacraments, we may turn at once to his further analysis of sacrifice, then to his treatment of the Mass, and so to his teaching about the Lord's Supper as the 'eucharistic sacrifice' of the Christian Church.

Sacrifices Propitiatory and Eucharistic

And sacrifice is divided, according to its properties: so that one kind of sacrifice is called εὐχαριστικον, that is, a sacrifice of thanksgiving, and the other is called ἱλαστηριον, that is, a sacrifice of expiation or purging. (*in Rom.* 12.1)

The expiatory sacrifices of the O.T., as we have indicated in Chapter II, were

types of that special and unique sacrifice by which Christ Himself offered sacrifice to God, by which we are delivered. (*in Lament.* 2.7)

[1] *in* 1 *Cor.* 10.16.

For under this head of propitiatory sacrifice,

we have but one only; inasmuch as by the death of Christ alone is the eternal Father reconciled unto us, and by the merit of His one oblation alone the elect have their sins forgiven. (*in Jud.* 2.5)

The sacrifices of thanksgiving (*eucharistiae*) may be further distinguished into their inner and outer aspects, since they are characterized by the signs and tokens of the inner gratitude unto God.[2] The outward signs are of no value apart from the inner gratitude, which is always pleasing unto the Father:

among outward oblations, the killing of beasts, tithes and first fruits held in times past the last place. But the chief place was given unto the obedience shown to the Word of God, love towards our brethren, thanksgiving and prayers.

On this basis Peter Martyr proceeds a further step: in the O.T. sacrifices there was a true communion with Christ, that is, these things were also *sacraments*. And although the ratios of sacrifice and sacrament differ, yet 'one thing may be both a Sacrifice and a Sacrament'. For the O.T. sacrifices

were also Sacraments, by which Christ was set forth to the old fathers to be received by them in faith, and by which they communicated before God in eating and drinking together.

Thus of the two kinds of sacrifice, propitiatory are related to Christ as prior types only, so that no sacrifice of that kind may be offered after His self-offering. What of the claim for the Mass, then?

they say that they offer the Son of God unto the eternal Father. And that is expressly denied in the Epistle to the Hebrews: for it teaches that all things were finished by the single oblation of Christ, which being perfect we may not renew. They will have Christ to be offered up every day: the Word of God affirms that He was to be offered up once only. (*in Iud.* 1.36)

To this important subject we now turn, Peter Martyr's criticism of the Mass as overthrowing this determinative distinction between sacrifices propitiatory, which are completed in the Death of Christ, and sacrifices eucharistic, which still have place in the Christian Church.

[2] This teaching is from *in Iud.* 2.5. Martyr's doctrine of O.T. sacrifice relates the sacrifices of thanksgiving to the peace-offerings (e.g. *in* 1 *Sam.* 1.4, 2.28, 11.15, etc.), part of which was eaten. In this class of *sacrificium pacificum et gratiarum actionis*, therefore, we have a striking analogy in name, content and action, to our Eucharist. Cf. Chapter II above, 'The One Sacrament'. Calvin draws the same distinction within sacrifice—cf. *Inst.* 4.18.13ff.

B. The Roman Mass

O thou holy Supper of the Lord, how many ways art thou here miserably dishonoured and polluted! O mass, mass, mass, what remains sound in thee? (*Catech.* 42)

In Missa Papistica non est Coena domini. (*Def.* 195)

But I affirm that it is so perverted as in a sense to agree not at all with Christ's institution, yea to be wholly contrary to it . . . They may rather give any name unto it, than the Lord's Supper. (*in Iud.* 1.36)

Peter Martyr examines the Mass in detail, inasmuch as this is the stronghold of Romanist error. To the English Church he writes:

But perhaps you think that the controversy about the Eucharist is a kind of small dissent, which is not so, since in it there is strife about the principal points of religion. (*Epist. Eccl. Ang.*)

And to Calvin about the latter's sacramental controversies,[3]

I judge its manifestation to be so great a good, that without it God cannot be sincerely worshipped in His Church . . . unless this fountain of many evils is abolished, there shall be lacking a great part of Christian doctrine in the Church of Christ.

There is a twofold objection to the Roman Mass. First, in its external forms, it is to be deplored as a falling away from the original simplicity of the Lord's Supper. Second, because of the doctrines of transubstantiation and propitiatory sacrifice, it is to be absolutely denied as a means of grace in the Church.

The Institution of the Lord and its Corruption

in the sacrament of the Eucharist we must not depart from the institution of the Lord. (*An in Comm. Lic.* 5)

In a detailed examination of the parts of the Mass,[4] Peter Martyr explains their original meaning. Certain parts of it have excellent use, notably the *Sursum corda*—

to think upon no carnal or earthly thing, but wholly bend their mind unto heaven, where Christ is to be sought, and not on earth, as though He were inclosed in bread and wine . . .

and the Giving of Thanks—

the mystery itself of Christ's body and blood is called *eucharistia* because its whole construction depends upon the giving of thanks.

---

[3] 16 February 1556, *L.C.*, p. 1114—Calvin's 'Second Defence against Westphal' appeared the previous month.   [4] *in Iud.* 1.33; cf. *in* 1 *Cor.* 5.5.

Considering all its parts, Martyr concludes:

Although all these things led the Christian people away from that first simplicity of the Lord's Supper, many things being added as seemed good to various men, yet in one sense they could be allowed, and not rightly accused of superstition and idolatry . . . but afterwards the Roman Antichrist corrupted everything.

This corruption which followed the Patristic age has its source in the divorcing of sacrament from Word, and is clearly illustrated by the use of Latin in the Mass.

For the Sacraments in those first and purer times were commonly known to all, but are unknown today (a fact to be much lamented) to the greatest part of Christians. But the use of a strange tongue has introduced this misery, which Antichrist has added to all sacred rites and ceremonies: by this it happens that the people understand nothing, and are only amazed at certain outward gestures and ceremonies, and on them place all their confidence and salvation.[5]

The key term in this debate is 'edification': are the people edified by what is done?[6]

Nor are they joined together in this Society except to edify one another.
(Catech. 39)

Our doctrine banishes superstition, removes idolatry, teaches the pure use of the sacraments, uses the language by which the people are edified, renders to devoted men the Word of God, frees the faithful of Christ from the elements of this world. (Def. 50)

But the Mass, he continues, has introduced shameless idolatry and untold abuses—adoration of stones, pictures, bread and wine; the use of an unknown tongue; neglect of the Word; and truncation of the elements. Yet the infant Church (ecclesia incunabulis) knew none of these—where do we read in the older writings of carrying the elements about, of lights and wax, invocations and adorations? Martyr's conclusion is, it was the new doctrine of transubstantiation which introduced the abuses; the superstitions were born of that opinion and its corporeal presence.[7]

[5] in Rom. 6.2. The context is the analogical nature of baptism. Martyr continues our quotation: 'And chiefly from this too springs that mischief that infants are often baptized either at home or else in Church when none are present . . .'
[6] Cf. in 1 Cor. 14.40: 'decently' means, not bells, lights, golden vessels, but holiness, modesty, 'and especially edification'; in Iud. 8.24: 'ecclesiastical traditions may be changed or removed, if edification require.'
[7] Cf. Disp. III, vs. Morg., that transub. is 'the newer opinion'; in Rom. 1.16: 'Why do you object antiquity to us? . . . you have introduced things new'; 3.21:

But the old fathers distributed the sacrament in this Supper to the faithful with gravity and dignity, and afterwards burnt the remainder, as Hesychius testifies. They appointed clerics to eat what remained among themselves, somewhere or other. Women had the rest at home sometimes, as can be read in Tertullian and Cyprian. Sometimes the bread of the Eucharist is given to the sick, being carried even by children, as the Ecclesiastical History teaches . . . (*Def.* 51)

We have departed that Society which . . . forces upon us idolatry towards bread and wine. (*De Schism.* 46)

In the Mass, then, we see the classic example of the way in which human invention has corrupted a Divine institution until the latter has been inverted in nature and purpose.

What is today more adorned and set forth with colours than the Mass? In it is a wonderful decking with garments, alluring songs, musical instruments, waxen lights, sweet perfume, bells . . . where is even one among the miserable people who understands the causes of these signs? . . . And the thing is so deformed and so greatly degenerated, that it may be counted or perceived to be anything rather than the Lord's Supper. (*in* 1 *Cor.* 3.12)

The simple institution, making for remembrance and communion, has become a matter of onlooking and superstition.

Christ instituted the Lord's Supper, that the Lord's death should be held in remembrance there, and the communicants be partakers of its fruit, and be joined to Christ, and always joined together among themselves with greater amity, and mortify their evil lusts, and through that heavenly meat more and more practise a new life. This is the worship which God requires of His own in this sacrament. Yet men were not content, since it was a hard thing to do, or because they always willed to add their own inventions to divine matters, and invented outward ornaments, vestments, gold, silver, precious stones, wax, tapers, bells and infinite ceremonies, to set forth the sacrament by these. And they would have men stand by at their Mass, and be but onlookers and listeners, while they meanwhile mumble their prayers . . . This is the profit that comes from human inventions. (*in Rom.* 1.21)

The great sin here is that by transubstantiation there has been a complete inversion of the sacrament, into a sacrifice of expiation, attended by the ceremonial and legal externalities

'in the Gospel, newness must especially be shunned'; *An in Comm. Lic.* 3: *Deus dixit* is divinity's first principle; 18: 'They say that they have the consent of the Church, wherein they impudently take to themselves what is ours: since the Churches of Greece, and the whole East and universal antiquity, hold with us. For the foul mangling of the Eucharist is but lately arisen.' But in the Reformed Church 'we most faithfully recite the history of the Supper as delivered by the Evangelist, and what Christ did in the Supper, so do we also to the last word' (*Def.* 209).

which accompanied the Temple worship of the Old Covenant. These outward aspects of the Mass, therefore, indicate a deeper root to the matter.

The 'Miserable Bondage'

(Paul) calls that a miserable bondage, when we take the signs for the things. In this is great offence committed these days, in the Sacrament of the Eucharist. For how many shall one find, who beholds the outward signs of this Sacrament, and calls to memory the death and person of Christ, of which most certainly they are signs? or thinks within himself that the body and blood of Christ is the spiritual food of the soul by faith, just as bread and wine are the nourishment of the body? or ponders the union of the members of Christ among themselves, and with the Head? These things are not regarded, but they cling only to the sight of the signs. And men think it is enough if they have looked on, bowed their knee, and worshipped. This is to embrace the letter . . . (in Rom. 2.27)

The errors of transubstantiation have thus destroyed the analogy, the sacramental ratio itself, and turned everything upside down. Think of this, says Martyr—this food, which they surround with pomp, incense, bells and all manner of adoration, they deign to call (please God!) *Viaticum*, the rations of soldiers and pilgrims![8]

The Mass represents the denial of the Holy Spirit, and the recourse to the dead letter of legalism and bondage. When the analogy is lost, it is inevitable that the sign should become the object of faith. Moreover, because such bondage implies 'Christ in a little box' as Martyr terms it, sight has taken the place of faith, and therefore the Word of God and the response of faith are irrelevant.

For we in the sacrament venerate the body of Christ which is in heaven. But since you declare that a real and crass presence is altogether necessary, of what use can the Archetype be for that affair? (*Def.* 281)

For adoration belongs unto the Archetype only. Indeed, adoration of the sacrament does not yield the proper effect and utility of the sacrament, which is by eating and drinking to have union with Him. And since this Papist doctrine exposes the Church to idolatry, whereas God always recalls His Church from idolatry, it must be false. For think of the dangers attendant upon the priestly Consecration! The people worship

[8] *Def.* 509.

an idol, the priests must consecrate aright, the words are muttered and not understood even if audible, the material must be such as is prescribed . . . but Christ at the Last Supper spoke with words that all heard and understood, as Paul clearly relates.[9]

The two symbols of this miserable subjection to signs are the use of Latin and the withholding of the cup from the laity. These two Peter Martyr mentions often as decisively indicating how the Word of God has been set aside in this inverted rite. Indeed, Romanism proves itself sectarian in the latter regard,[10] since it comes under Cyprian's censure of the Aquarian heretics:

> Cyprian blamed them because they did it against the Word of God. Today the Papists use not indeed water instead of wine, but they tear and mutilate the sacrament, and pluck away one part from the people, nor meanwhile consider what Christ taught or did, but only what some men have decreed against the Word of God. (*De Vot.* 1556G)

The use of Latin has no justification, either from the original institution of Christ, or from the purpose of the sacrament.

> It is no part of the pastors of the Church of Christ to keep secret the words of God. (*in* 1 *Cor.* 14.4)

> And those words, which should bring great consolation unto the by-standers, when the participation of the body and blood of the Lord is promised to them, they speak so softly, yea mutter them so darkly, that even if a man know Latin he is unable to understand them . . . But in my opinion these men therefore mumble those words because they are wary lest their lies be perceived. (*An Christ. lic.*)

For instance, they say 'Take ye and eat'—and then only the priest communicates. He continues:

> Therefore faith has no place in those things, which they do in their Mass, since it has place only where God's Word offers itself to us . . . the old pagans may with much better probability excuse and plead for their

---

[9] *An in Comm. Lic.* 9: 'Christian liberty consists not in this, that we may change the institutions of Christ, but in this, that Christ has reduced many ceremonies to few, and for laborious has given easy and plain, and for obscure ceremonies has set forth those that are most clear.'

[10] Cf. the whole Treatise *An in Communione Liceat Una Tantum specie uti* (*in* 1 *Cor.* 10.17, ff. 138B-141A): the two parts of the sacrament are parts of Christ's Word, but human sin desires to mutilate that Word—recently, at any rate, since 'the Fathers greatly feared to depart from the Lord's order in this Sacrament'. 'They judge it a grievous error if they omit any sign of the cross or most minute kind of thing: which are nonetheless human inventions, mere absurdities and trifles (*hominum inventa, merae ineptae et nugae*). Why should we not rather beware lest we overlook what Christ Himself commanded in His Word?'

sacraments, than these men may defend their Masses . . . Let them therefore cease from dandling that little daughter of theirs, and say no more that
it should be taken for the institution of Christ and of His Apostles.

The Mass has become the highest mark of Romanism, and
may well be called 'a public profession of popery'. Although
ceremonies may be classed as 'things indifferent', yet must the
institution of the Lord be renewed, and occasion of superstition be removed entirely. In a trenchant passage depicting
the contemporary situation, Peter Martyr lays bare the basic
inversion which Romanism has effected:

If today, under the reign of Antichrist, some godly man should approach
a sacrificing priest and say to him, 'I pray you, make me a Mass, but so
that I may plainly understand the confession of sins and absolution; expound to me the praises of God which you have at the Introit of the Mass,
and the Hymn, the Gloria in Excelsis, that I may worthily magnify God
along with you, and give Him thanks; neither hide from me the meaning
of the prayers, that I may respond, Amen. Teach me the Epistle and
Gospel, that by it I may learn wholesome doctrine and admonition from
you; let us say together the creed of the catholic faith; and when you come
to the blessing and consecration of the mysteries, keep me not back, for
those words pertain also unto me; and in the breaking of bread and drinking of the cup, communicate with me, that we may at last give thanks unto
our God. And since neither wealth nor food is lacking to you, all this you
have freely received, freely bestow upon me.' He that asks these and like
things from the sacrificer, I ask, how will he be received by him? He shall
be excluded with taunts of Lutheranism, and the reproach of heresy shall
be flung violently at him. But let there come likewise another who says,
'Come, I must hunt today, but because on this Lord's day I will not be
without the Sacrament, take this money, and at some time in the morning,
make me a Mass, and despatch it quickly and speedily.' Believe me, there
will be no delay by the priest! Think you that this is to be a minister faithfully, in the way the Apostle commanded? I think not. (*in* 1 *Cor.* 4.2)

Facias mihi Missam—so the buying and selling of the sacrifice
goes on, while the communication of the Body and Blood of the
Lord is almost wholly neglected. The key to reformation is the
return to the institution of the Lord, which is above all else a
communion with Him and with the brethren. Because this Meal
refers to 'the Kingdom of Christ' in which is no division of class
or wealth, therefore it is by definition a shared sacrament.

The Papistical Mass cannot rightly be called a Supper. For Supper
indicates communion: but in the Mass the sacrificers alone devour everything. (*Def.* 402)

This sacrament is called the Supper, because it refers to that first institution made by the Lord at supper. By which word, moreover, is designated a communion of many. (*in* 1 *Cor.* 11.21)

In the same context Martyr reminds us that the Early Church associated the mystery with a common meal, the *convivia Christianorum* or *Agape*. Faction abused the gift and perverted the love-feast, so that today we have 'a minimum of sacred symbols', since the purpose of the Supper is sanctification. It is to be administered both simply (according to the institution of Christ), and clearly (the words heard and the elements seen). Just as every human art returns to the head and font for renewal, and just as Jesus Himself returned to the chief commandment of the Law, so we must return to the Lord's institution to remedy this evil; and the sum of the Scriptural institution is, the Lord's Supper ought to be a common meal.[11] Private masses are a human invention and a new addition.

Martyr's deepest examination of the Mass is given in a treatise entitled, 'Whether the Mass Is a Sacrifice'.[12] He begins by noting the distinction between sacrifices propitiatory and eucharistic. The first has power to satisfy God and earn the forgiveness of sins; the latter has no such quality, but presupposes the offering of the propitiatory sacrifice, since it is offered by 'those already received into favour'. On this basis Martyr considers the Mass in respect of each kind of sacrifice.

The first section seeks to prove that 'The Mass is not a propitiatory sacrifice', because of a difference in ratio:

Therefore as great a difference is there between a sacrament and a sacrifice as between giving and receiving, since in a sacrament we receive of God what He promised, but in a sacrifice we give and bring what He requires of us. Wherefore to speak properly, since the Lord's Supper is,

---

[11] *coenam communem esse debere*—in 1 *Cor.* 11.23. Cf. *Tract.* 19: only communion 'satisfies the institution of Christ'; *in* 1 *Cor.* 10.18: 'For if the table and company, as Chrysostom says, unite us and make us intimates and friends, how much more the Sacrament?' In this regard we should notice Martyr's attitude to the problem of private communion for the sick. His basic principle is, 'where many do not communicate the nature of the sacrament is not retained' (*Tract.* 51) and therefore such a rite outside 'the holy congregation and the rite appointed by the Lord' is not properly 'a just communion'. However, they should receive the sacrament 'if they repeated the holy words, and if some faithful men communicated there'. Elsewhere (*An in Comm. Lic.* 21) he states that the sick ought to receive the Communion, it being only the Papist superstition that created problems about the 'remnant' of the consecrated host, etc.

[12] *An Missa Sit Sacrificium. L.C.*, pp. 995-999.

as they will agree, a sacrament, it cannot be a sacrifice, unless we would have giving and receiving to be the same!

Christ's offering on the Cross was 'the one propitiatory sacrifice'. According to the communication of names obtaining within the sacramental relation, the Lord's Supper can be called a propitiatory sacrifice—by metonymy, as Augustine said. But we are not discussing what the Supper represents, but what it 'properly is'. And against the claim that daily sins require daily sacrifices of expiation, Martyr stresses the 'once and for all' note of the Epistle to the Hebrews. In fact, he points out, to follow Christ's example literally, as the Roman priest claims to do, one should not slay Christ but oneself! Moreover, a sacrifice must spring from an express commandment of God:

if obedience is not the root of the sacrifice, it becomes deadly unto him that offers it.

Christ's sacrifice fulfilled the O.T. priesthood, so that now we require rather

a feast prepared, of which the minister of the Church is not the offerer but the dispenser; nor has he a little altar, unless you figuratively call a table an altar. Therefore those who labour to renew the priesthood, altar and outward sacrifice, doubtless try to transform the new testament into the old.

Finally, the Patristic witness is clearly against the idea of propitiation in the Supper:

They do not speak of propitiatory but of Eucharistic, to which kind belong praises, thanksgiving, confession, alms, oblations, and especially that we give ourselves wholly unto God to be ruled and governed . . . among them 'To sacrifice' signifies nothing else than to represent a sacrifice, to commemorate, to lay before the eyes, to give thanks for it.

Now Martyr moves on to the crucial point. Since the Mass has placed the whole weight upon propitiation to the neglect of *eucharistia*, and since propitiation has been wholly translated unto the Cross and so removed from the Church—therefore the Mass completely misses the only valid sacrifice remaining to Christians, the eucharistic.

In the Papistical Mass this Eucharistic or gratulatory sacrifice has no place. (*Deinde in Missis Papisticis sacrificium hoc Eucharisticum sive gratulatorium non habet locum.*)

This is a terrible charge, but Martyr explains his reasons:

for those that stand by understand not what is said by the sacrificer, so that they cannot answer 'Amen' to the praises of God and thanksgiving; he alone communicates, the others receive nothing; of offerings of alms there are scarcely any; the Lord's death is preached least of all. So it seems they have overthrown everything by their private Masses. And whereas there are two kinds of sacrifices, propitiatory I mean, and eucharistic, and they have not the propitiatory any more than we have (for Christ wholly and perfectly offered that), further they have not the Eucharistic which we have —what remains to their Mass, except that it is mere hypocrisy, and a feigned and damnable imitation of the Lord's Supper?

Thus in terms of the twofold nature of sacrifice, Martyr declares that the Mass has completely failed to fulfil the function of the Lord's Supper in relation to the role of sacrifice in the Church.[13] What he has to say now about the positive part which the Supper plays in the Church reflects the great new element of Reformed theology. For Martyr, the Lord's Supper is the active memorial of the propitiatory sacrifice of Christ, and the true sacrifice of thanksgiving which the Church is commanded to offer on that foundation.

C. THE EUCHARISTIC SACRIFICE OF THE CHURCH

The work of faith is to give thanks. (*in* 1 *Cor.* 15.57)

Nor wouldst Thou for any other cause gather Thy chosen and good people so wonderfully together, but that a true way to worship Thee . . . might at length be universally known among all nations . . . that we might offer Thee an acceptable sacrifice of thanksgiving. (*Prayers*, Ps. 50)

We sacrifice indeed . . . the giving of thanks is the victim . . . therefore since (thank God!) the mass has been removed, which was a superstitious and detestable sacrifice, as we declared, let us apply ourselves with all our hearts to this sacrifice alone. (*Exhort. Iuven.*)

In this final and greatest aspect of Peter Martyr's doctrine of the sacraments we may distinguish three elements: the priesthood of Christ, the propitiatory sacrifice remembered or re-

[13] As mentioned already, modern Romanism reveals a marked tendency towards a more Biblical understanding of the eucharistic sacrifice—that is, a departure from the univocal doctrine of sacrifice in the life of Christ and of His Church, implied in the traditional Tridentine doctrine of the Mass. In this sense our contemporary battleline is not to be drawn up in exactly the same place as it was in the sixteenth century. Nevertheless in Martyr's polemic upon the Mass we have much more than a matter of historical interest; we have indeed an attack based upon the positive doctrine of eucharistic sacrifice which informed his doctrine of the Church.

presented, and the Eucharist or sacrifice of thanksgiving offered. The Romanist dialectic had reduced the relationship between God and man to a simple distinction between God's offering to man, and man's (propitiatory) offering to God. The qualifying assertion that man makes his offering on the basis of faith was invalidated by the expiatory nature of his sacrifice, which meant that he was in a position to make God's own offering to Him. The determining factor in the Mass was the priestly power of consecration which gave control of the Body of God's Son. It was this sacrifice which gradually became extended over the whole fabric of Romanism until the system of work-righteousness reached logical completion—heaven was in the power of earth, the earthly activity forged the pattern for heaven to follow.

Thus the whole Biblical dimension of the sacrifice offered by responsive faith had been lost. This was recovered in the sixteenth century largely through the return of the dynamic content of faith as union with Christ. The analogical or sacramental content of justification meant a complete inversion of the meaning of the life of the Church. In a clear passage[14] on the central problem of the authority and function of the ministry, Martyr sets forth the elements of the Reformed view.

They are called dispensers of the mysteries of God, but not of sacrifice, nor sacrificers—yet not as though every kind of sacrifice were removed from them. For praises and confessions by which the goodness and mercy of God is declared, are pleasing sacrifices to God: no less are prayers, confession of sins, the offering of almsgiving, and repentance by which the heart becomes contrite and humble, and finally the sacrifice of our own bodies, which we offer to God as a living and reasonable sacrifice. We do not deny that these are made in the Church through the ministers of the Church. And in the last place is the sacrifice by which unbelievers are brought to Christ, as Romans 15 plainly teaches, in which Evangelical ministration (*liturgia Evangelica*) the ministers of Christ are occupied most of all. But those who favour superstition boast that they sacrifice the Son of God, which is most absurd: because Christ offered himself, nor needed other priest. By one oblation he consummated and perfected whatever was to be done for our redemption: nor is it meet that man be held sacrificer in so great an oblation. For it always obtains that the offerer must be equal or more worthy than the thing offered: which is sacrilege to think concerning our-

---

[14] *in* 1 *Cor.* 4.1; cf *in.* 2 *Reg.* 2.23 (on *Manuum impositio, Successio* and *Vestitus*): the ministry is given not with laying on of hands but with the Apostolic succession of true doctrine, which reveals the Church's line of ancestry.

selves, as compared with Christ. Moreover who can offer the Son of God, since he is continually in the sight of the Father, where he is both our propitiation and our Advocate? But, if by sacrifice they understand the giving of thanks for his death, and because for our salvation he would give his body to the cross, and his blood to be shed, we do not deny such a sacrifice to be offered to God in the Lord's Supper, both through the ministers of the Church, and through all those standing by.

1. *The Priesthood of Christ*

Peter Martyr distinguishes two 'moments' in the priesthood of Christ: the oblation on the Cross and the heavenly intercession at the right hand of the Father.

He thought it not enough to die for us, but would also by His ministry advance our salvation. He is our bishop and priest. But the office of a bishop is both to offer sacrifice, and to pray for the people. Christ has offered Himself upon the Cross: and when He had finished that ministry, there remained another ministry, which He should exercise continually, namely to make intercession for us . . . And continually by the priesthood of Christ are our sins forgiven, and we are reconciled unto God . . . In the kingdom of Christ which he exercises most mightily at the right hand of the Father, all things are governed: and the prayers which He continually pours out for us are most welcome and acceptable to the Father . . . Christ makes intercession to the Father, because He is always at His hand . . . Therefore the Father is perpetually put in mind of the sacrifice once offered by Him, and smells the same like a sweet-smelling savour, and by that is made merciful unto us. And therefore Christ is called our mediator and advocate. (*in Rom.* 8.34)

The implications of this passage alone are of the deepest significance for the doctrine of the Eucharist. How is the Cross related to the present mercy of the Father? Through the heavenly intercession of Christ Himself, answers Martyr—Christ 'puts the Father in mind' of that sacrifice. In this same context Martyr indicates a further fruitful line of thought:

the intercession of the Son is the cause of the intercession of the Holy Spirit.

Now the Spirit's intercession, Martyr makes clear, is related to our prayers in the most significant way. On the text 'By Whom we cry, Abba, father', he points out that this prayer of Christ's ('our first-begotten Brother') becomes our own invocation by the work of the Holy Spirit. It is the Holy Spirit who stirs us up to acknowledge our inheritance, and who confirms our faith by these prayers.[15] Without the Spirit's testimony we

[15] *in Rom.* 8.15-16.

should not believe our inheritance, which is presently held, but only imperfectly, awaiting its coming revelation and the perfection of its bestowal. For the Spirit is particularly the One that confirms us with hope.[16]

The intercession of the Spirit is ultimately *our* intercession *inspired* by Him: He does not properly pray unto the Father (or to the Son, as the Arians said) since He is 'not less than the Father'.[17] And yet our prayers are decisively related to merit, which is their root, and are of 'great force', because the prayers of the Church are related through the intercession of the Spirit (through His inspiration, to speak properly) to the intercession of the Son.[18] Here we reach the heart of this doctrine of the priesthood of Christ: *the Son prays as man.*

> The Son prays and makes intercession for us, because He is less than the Father in respect of His humanity. The Spirit makes intercession, because He makes us to pray and cry . . . 'Abba, father' . . . The Son prays to God, not in that He is God, but in that He is man, and a creature . . . And that those words of Paul are to be referred to the humanity of Christ, those things spoken before sufficiently declare. Paul had written before that Christ died, rose again and was carried up to heaven to the right hand of God: all such things agree not with the divine nature of Christ. (*in Rom.* 8.34)

The new humanity of Christ is the origin of His intercession to the Father.[19] He is 'the propitiatory place itself',[20] and so:

> the priesthood is translated unto Christ; He is now our high priest.
> (*De Poenit.* 26)
> now also He executes before the Father the office of an intercessor and high priest. (*in Rom.* 4.25)

> He is now able a great deal more to relieve our necessities, by the grace and power of His Father, to whom He always has such familiar access, and to whom He continually offers prayers of particular efficacy for us that He wins us His favour and procures us His strength. (*Catech.* 25)

Perhaps the most decisive aspect of this intercession of Christ is that His prayers 'have satisfaction joined with them'.[21] This is the difference between His prayers and ours: His cannot be repulsed. To speak of 'merit' and 'satisfaction' therefore, is to speak of the heavenly intercession of the New Man, and not of the work of earthly priests. This is the first and fundamental

---

[16] *in Rom.* 8.19-20, 24.   [17] *in Rom.* 8.26-27.   [18] *in Rom.* 8.16.
[19] *in* 1 *Cor.* 11.3: Christ is *caput viri* as to His Divine nature, but God is *caput Christi* as to His human. His consubstantiality with us is not denied in the Ascension.   [20] *in Gen.* 28.12.   [21] *in Rom.* 8.34.

element in Martyr's doctrine of eucharistic sacrifice: the unique nature of the propitiation obtained by the eternal, continuing priesthood of Christ. On this basis the Church may build: but it has no hand in the foundation.

The earthly life of the Body of Christ works its work on this basis: its good works, for instance, mean that it has ceased from fleshly corruption to begin a new life of participation in Christ's Resurrection; its Christian friendship and brotherly love flow from His love, for this is 'faithful and continuing in Christ alone'; even the death of its martyrs pleases God only on the ground that 'they belong to the body of Christ and are now become His members by regeneration'.[22] In short:

our gifts are acceptable unto God, when we offer them upon the rock which is Christ. There our actions are purged by the fire of the Holy Spirit, and what is in its own nature unclean is received by God as holy. (*in Iud.* 6.21)

Christ is not acceptable unto God for the Church's sake but the Church is acceptable unto God for Christ's sake. (*in Iud.* 13.22)

Christ is not acceptable unto God for the sake of the sacrifice, but on the contrary we are acceptable unto God for the sake of Christ. (*in* 1 *Cor.* 5.7)

Whatever our sacrifice may be, it cannot be the offering of Christ to the Father, because He is continually with Him, the eternal Priest.[23] On the other hand, some positive relation to His sacrifice is to be expected on the basis of the nature of the Church as the Body of its Head. The mystery of the Church's earthly life and activity is the mystery of the life and activity of its Head, in which it shares and which it reflects in the sacramental analogy. If communion of worldly goods among the brethren is but the loving response to His communication of 'His eternal and greatest goods',[24] how much more will the Eucharist exhibit this responsive and reflective character of the Church's service!

2. *The Propitiatory Sacrifice Remembered and Represented*

If by oblation or sacrifice you understand a memorial of that sacrifice which He offered on the Cross, and the giving of thanks for that, these are not properly done by the ministers, but pertain also to all the faithful who

---

[22] *in Gen.* 12.1, *in* 1 *Sam.* 18.1, *in* 2 *Reg.* 3.27.
[23] *in* 1 *Cor.* 4.1, 11.24; cf. on this whole subject, Wm. Manson's *The Epistle to the Hebrews* (London, 1951), Chapter 5, 'The Oblation of the Body of Christ'.
[24] *in Rom.* 15.27—the goods are to be distributed 'by a just proportion'.

communicate with them. The minister leads this with words, but does not celebrate the memory alone. (*De Vot.* 1531A)

The People of God are called unto two things that pertain to sacrifice: first, the celebration of the memory of Christ's sacrifice (*recordatio sacrificii Christi*); second, the proper sacrifice of thanksgiving for that propitiation. The latter is the chief element in Martyr's positive teaching upon the Lord's Supper:

> We count the sacrifices of Christians to be a contrite heart, prayers, thanksgiving, alms, mortification of fleshly affections, and so on. Since the abrogation of carnal sacrifices, these are left to us to offer as the fruit of our faith, and testimonies of a thankful mind. But as to placating God, Christ offered Himself once upon the Cross, nor need anyone offer Him again: for by one oblation He fulfilled all. It remains for us to embrace His sacrifice by faith, and we shall have God merciful (*propitium*) to us, who of His goodness will accept through Christ the sacrifices just mentioned.
> (*in Iud.* 13.22)

Following justification, the People of God have a positive offering to make. But its nature must follow the teaching of the Epistle to the Hebrews, which affirms

> one sacrifice only, and one oblation, namely the death of Christ, by which sins are blotted out and satisfaction made for men. Wherefore justification is not to be looked for by works; and it should be enough for us that the good works we do after justification are sacrifices of thanksgiving—but let us not establish them as propitiatory, for then we should do great injury to Christ. (*De Iustif.* 16)

Moreover, these 'proper' sacrifices, summed up in the name 'eucharistic' or 'sacrifices of thanksgiving', are the effects of the deliberate act of the Church in recalling to mind the Death of Christ. This has been a constant element in Martyr's doctrine of the sacraments as visible Gospel, used in dramatic analogy by the Holy Spirit to lift up our souls unto the heavenly Saviour. But it serves as a basis for the further, positive action of the sacrament, the 'right sacrifice' (*iustus sacrificium*) which is offered in the Church *because* Christ has instituted His memorial:[25]

> the offering of prayers, thanksgiving, contrition of heart, almsgiving and continual mortification of the old man.

For this reason we must examine the nature of this 'memorial' carefully.

---

[25] *Def.* 194: 'But how can the Church be destitute of sacrifice, since it constantly worships the true and only victim, Christ, and as He instituted, commemorates Him?'

The problem of the memorial of the Cross is, whether in the sacrament in some way or another the Death of Christ is not only recalled as memory but recalled as event, repeated and so recalled to God's mind by a priestly offering. This problem concerned the Fathers too, and Martyr sums up the teaching of Ambrose as follows:

> To offer Christ, or His body, is to make a remembrance (*recordationem facere*) of His death, and to exhibit the same as example, and to repeat the commemoration of what was done before: thus we may be said rather to make a remembrance of a sacrifice, than to offer it (*magis recordationem sacrificii operari, quam offerre*). (*Def.* 13)

Martyr's sacramental teaching involves the 'real presence' of Christ in the action of the mysteries, and to this end he uses the words 'represented and exhibited' to signify Christ's presence.[26] The critical term is *repraesentare*. According to Gardiner, the 'representation' in the Eucharist meant that the matter itself was exhibited as present. Martyr replied to this by interpreting representation as reference to, not exhibition of, the matter of the sacrament: *repraesentare* means *referre*.[27] As a real presence to faith, however, the Body of Christ is truly 'exhibited', but Martyr refuses to compromise his basic analogical doctrine of the sacrament in order to interpret 'represent' as 'make present' in a false way. Obviously the problem here is partly one of terminology, since Martyr constantly teaches a real presence of a real Body; his demand that sacrament be seal as well as sign implies a doctrine of representation as something more than 'signification' and involving an actual 're-presentation' at least correspondent with the ratio of faith.

In relation to this central problem of eucharistic sacrifice, Peter Martyr stands by his doctrine of analogy as the sacramental ratio.

> That word *Repraesentare*, which Tertullian uses in the same way (Jerome) takes for this, namely to refer by some image or similitude. (*Def.* 513)

> Baptism exhibits faith and the Eucharist, the body of Christ. But these

[26] Cf. esp. the 'Propositions' from Genesis and Leviticus. A sacrament is instituted 'to signify and exhibit grace'; sacraments *non modo significabant sed exhibebant gratiam* (*ex Gen.* 16.4-5); in the O.T. sacrifices Christ was 'represented and exhibited' (*ex Lev.* 1.1, 10).

[27] *rem ipsam praesentem exhibere*—*Def., Obj.* 160. Gardiner stated, *Ex pane fieri praesentiam corporis Christi, mutata quidem substantia, cuius tamen accidentia significant corpus Christi*. Martyr replied, *Repraesentare aliquando positum esse pro referre*.

are not exhibited by the sacraments, but by the Holy Spirit, who uses them as instruments. Wherefore that term is not to be taken *simpliciter*. For sacraments are to be referred to the ratio of instrumental cause (*Sacramenta enim revocanda sunt ad rationem instrumentalis causae*). (*Def.* 548)

It is this fundamental orientation of the sacrament which must guide us in this question. The doctrine of analogy reminds us that we deal here not with a substance but with an action or relation,[28] with a living Person who is the mystery we seek to 'represent'.[29] When Martyr speaks of 'memory' he does not mean something 'bare and simple' as the 'Sophist' Gardiner would make out, but a presence of Christ 'with all His effects, gifts, fruits and merits'.[30]

The *recordatio sacrificii* must be related to the nature of the sacrament as an instrument of the Holy Spirit. In this sense the 'memorial' is not the sign of Christ's absence but the guarantee of His presence, since apart from the Spirit we do not communicate with Him. Now just here Martyr's dynamic view provides the answer to the demand for realism in the sacrament:

> In the Lord's Supper not only is the memory of Christ in regard to His death re-opened (*refricare*) but all the benefits which follow from that and which excel that, should be recalled. (*in* 1 *Cor.* 11.24)

> We grant a sacrifice to be there, since there is the commemoration of a true sacrifice, and the Sacraments, that is outward symbols which are proposed, are signs of the same true sacrifice, and refer it to the communicants by the institution of the Lord. (*Epit., Sent.* 20)

These terms *refricare* and *referre* indicate the positive, beneficial effect of the sacramental representation. Christ Himself is present, therefore the sacrament is the 'holy of holies',[31] and

---

[28] *Sacramentum tantum esse in usu, dum re ipsa sumitur* (*Def.* 491): 'nothing without use' (*Tract., Praef.*); the Holy Spirit joins Himself to the elements 'as efficient cause, as the other is the instrument, or seal of the promise'. (*Def.* 14)

[29] This is the decisive issue in the Reformers' sacramental teaching, even though much of their eschatological reference is implicit rather than explicit. Yet their greatness lay in understanding that the medieval concern for 'relating the eucharist *to the passion*' indicated a deep break with the thought of the primitive Church so that 'the eschatological conception of the primitive rite has been almost entirely lost to view' (Dix, *op. cit.*, pp. 621f). By recognizing that the true and archetypal mystery or sacrament is Christ Himself, and that the efficacy of the sacrament derives from His new humanity, the Reformers returned to the dynamic Biblical view in which the living Christ 'presents' Himself as the chief actor in the eucharistic drama, as the judge of the Church's liturgy as well as the bread of its life.

[30] *Def.* 590—the context is his exposition of Bernard's antithesis between *memoria et praesentia*.   [31] *Def.* 796.

R

He sanctifies us there—but He does not redeem us at the holy table any more than He sealed a testament in His Blood at the Last Supper, which was no substitute for the Cross that lay ahead.[32] We are not to constitute 'two sacrifices of Christ' as if the Father were not pleased by the first.[33] Martyr does not, however, deny a real offering of redemption to the believer in the sacrament as in the Word, and on this basis he states:

> And so that cry *Oblatio* is to be referred not to God but to those who with pious spirit feed in the sacrament. For to them is the remission of sins offered. (*Def.* 175)

Martyr supports his doctrine with extensive Patristic quotations, which he sums up as follows:

> By countless Fathers we prove to be there: memory, monument, example, commemoration, thanksgiving about the offering of Christ already made on the Cross in the past; after these, that the sacrament obtains the name of the thing; nor is it granted that a proper sacrifice of Christ can be made there.
>   (*Def.* 332)

The nominal communication in the sacrament is once again Martyr's explanation of the Patristic language:

> Certainly the Fathers often called it a sacrifice on account of the memory and recollection of a sacrifice (*propter memoriam et recordationem sacrificii*).
>   (*in* 1 *Sam.* 11.15)

In terms of the celebration of the memory, therefore, and the communication of names involved in the sacramental relationship, the Eucharist is called a sacrifice: but it has nothing to do with slaying Christ in its action.

> . Now if you can, bring forth one testimony out of the Gospel or the Apostles, from which you declare that the flesh of Christ is today offered in sacrifice for the living and the dead. (*De Vot.* 1531)

> We know that we celebrate the memory of His sacrifice . . . (but) in the Eucharist the immolation of Christ is not repeated. (*Def.* 7)

The Romanist identification of 'Do this' with 'Sacrifice this' (*facere* with *sacrificare*) is a frivolity, a burning of straw for wood because nothing better is available: when does one apply this interpretation? Does one sacrifice a garment when one makes it? Or a fire, when one makes it? What did Christ sacrifice in the Last Supper? What oblation, what blood? For He said, 'Take, eat, drink, do this that I have said (namely eat and

---

[32] *Def.* 66.   [33] *Def.* 81.

drink) for a remembrance and monument of My death.'[34]

The Fathers, on the basis of the communication of names in the sacrament, called the Supper 'sacrifice' and 'immolation'. But since Scripture does not use this word in any sense as applied to the Supper, Martyr refuses to do so. Moreover, he complains that such language on the part of Patristic and Scholastic writers

did not edify the people, but drove them to pagan and Jewish rites, when from a blind and foolish zeal they borrowed both altars and other rites. (*in* 1 *Reg.* 13.1)

The word 'altar' receives a good deal of consideration from Martyr, since it is a prominent term in Patristic writings.

It is also to be noticed that when the Lord's Supper is celebrated, the holy table is not properly to be called an altar, although the Fathers used that word indiscriminately; but when they did this, the people believed that holy table to be no less a symbol of Christ than the altar of the Hebrews . . . since we no longer have an altar, that kind of figure and symbol should not be found among us. (*Def.* 173)

Much more wisely did some of the Fathers instead of Altar put Table . . . from which the faithful took symbols of the Eucharist. (*in* 1 *Reg.* 13.1)

The Church is centred around a Table, from which Christ spreads out the commemoration of His Sacrifice, thanksgiving for it and its fruit.[35] The Church is *less* destitute of priests since Christ Himself is its Priest, and therefore

In the Christian Church they have no altar proper . . . We rather have tables, since we see that Christ instituted the mystery of the Eucharist not at an altar but at a table. (*Def.* 710)

'Table' is also an allegory, from which we learn of that pleasure and conviviality that Christ offers us.[36] But decisively, Martyr states:

Now Altar refers to outward sacrifice: but because this has place among us no longer, since we offer no more outward sacrifices of beasts slain, our sacrifices being nothing else than prayers, praises, thanksgivings, mortification of the flesh and almsgiving: therefore since the correlative, as the Logicians say, of an Altar is removed, neither can the thing itself remain. (*in* 1 *Reg.* 13.1)

Peter Martyr's stress on the heavenly intercession of Christ, and on the Eucharist as communion, prevents his speaking of

---

[34] *in Iud.* 13.16; cf. *in* 1 *Cor.* 11.24 concerning *facere* and *sacrificare*.
[35] *in* 1 *Cor.* 9.13.   [36] *in Rom.* 11.9.

an 'offering' or even 'representation' in the sacrament except in terms of the celebration of the memory of the Cross, and the proper sacrifice of thanksgiving.

> What is objected from the Nicene Council is but weak, that it makes no mention of an unbloody host or victim—which we deny not if you refer it to a memorial or thanksgiving. But to them it is not unbloody, since they boast that they have true or, as they say, real blood in the sacrament.
>
> (in 1 Cor. 5.7)

He limits the Patristic use of *offerre* as follows:

> We contend in the holy mysteries for a giving of thanks, a commemoration and memory of the body and blood of the Lord delivered for us, to be made and to be what the Fathers called to offer . . . But in the Church are ministers or as (Ambrose) says, priests of His *imago*, in whom or through whom Christ Himself or in image, is said to be offered, when the memorial of His death is celebrated in the congregation.[37]

Although Peter Martyr is zealous to guarantee the proper use of *sacrificia*, he does not relate his doctrine of eucharistic sacrifice to the intercession of Christ in the explicit way that Augustine and Calvin do, as a true offering of Him by prayer and memory,[38] although this is involved in his treatment of this

---

[37] *Def.* 15, 10-11. The latter context is Ambrose's distinction of *umbra, imago* and *veritas*. It is the heavenly Christ, who has the truth in Himself (*rerum veritas est in coelis: quam si velimus intueri eo ascendamus oportet*) that gives 'the ministry of His image' to the Church. Martyr concludes that the Fathers mean by offering the Body and Blood of Christ on earth nothing other than 'to celebrate the memory among us in the Church, and to give thanks to God for that true and perfect sacrifice once offered of old on the Cross'.

[38] Cf. Augustine's *De Civ. Dei* X. 6 and 20: in Christ the High Priest, the Church shares a corporate sacrifice—'This form He offered, and herein was He offered; in this is He our priest, our mediator, and our sacrifice . . . By this is He the Priest, offering and offerer. The true sacrament whereof is the Church's daily sacrifice: which, being the body of Him the Head, learns to offer itself by Him.' Martyr quotes his words on the Psalms, *Memoria et cogitatione Christum quotidie immolari* (in 1 *Cor.* 5.7). Calvin has a striking passage on Numbers 19.2f (*Harm. of the Pent.* II pp. 37ff, Cal. Trans. Soc.): 'that we may be partakers of ablution, it is necessary that each of us should offer Christ to the Father. For, although He only, and that but once, has offered Himself, still a daily offering of Him, which is effected by faith and prayers, is enjoined to us, not such as the Papists have invented, by whom in their impiety and perverseness the Lord's Supper has been mistakenly turned into a sacrifice, because they imagined that Christ must be daily slain, in order that His death might profit us. The offering, however, of faith and prayers, of which I speak, is very different, and by it alone we apply to ourselves the virtue and fruit of Christ's death . . . Thus the people offered vicariously by the hand of the priest; and in this way also at present, although we set Christ before God's face in order to propitiate Him, still it is necessary that Christ Himself should interpose, and exercise the office of a priest.' The problem of the relationship of sacramental *recordatio* or *anamnesis* to Christ's heavenly intercession thus touched upon by Augustine and Calvin, is virtually untouched by Martyr, although the elements of his doctrine are essentially of the Augustinian-Calvinist type. Probably his failure

intercession and the prayers of the Church in the passages from Romans 8 cited above. In general, his doctrine extends primarily to the giving of thanks in the sacrament, so that his use of 'eucharistic' follows its proper O.T. sense, and not explicitly a sense that in the Eucharist there is a positive relation to the Death of Christ by which we 'plead His merits'.

> The substance of our sacrifice is, a giving of thanks for the body of Christ given on the Cross. And because of this thanksgiving, faith and confession, the Fathers said that the body of Christ is offered in the Supper. (*Disp.* IV, Q. 2)

Therefore when he states,

> Although the Lord's Supper is not a sacrifice, yet it cannot be done without a sacrifice (*Prop. ex Lev.* 2, *nec.* 6)

he means by the latter two things: first, the celebration of the memory of the Sacrifice of Christ, which may be called figuratively (by the metonymy operative in the sacramental relationship) an offering of that Sacrifice; and second, the only true and proper sacrifice of the Church of Christ, the offering of the *eucharistia* or sacrifices of thanksgiving.

3. *The Eucharistic Sacrifice Offered*

> In the Eucharist we admit no other sacrifice than the sacrifices of thanksgiving (*sacrificium eucharistiae*), of prayers, and of the offering of our own lives: and these sacrifices must be offered not only by the minister, but also by the people that communicate. (*Epit., Sent.* 20)

Peter Martyr's distinction of the O.T. sacrifices according to the twofold oblation means that

> Although Christ by one oblation consummated our salvation, there are still remaining to us many and various sacrifices in the New Testament.
> (*Prop. ex Lev.* 1, *nec.* 12)

The paraphernalia of the Mass, however, betray a false understanding of the nature of these sacrifices, of what God requires of His people. The true 'ornaments and works' of the Christian Church should be:

> First, praises of God, second, confession of sins, ministration of holy

---

to extend the implication of these elements in this way is due to his reaction to Romanist terminology, causing him to limit 'sacrifice' to the strictly eucharistic (in its proper sense), just as he limited 'substance' to the presence of the Body of Christ in heaven.

doctrine, prayers, receiving the Sacraments, the exercise of ecclesiastical discipline, and offerings for the poor. (*in* 1 *Cor.* 3.16)

This concept of the Church's activity as properly sacrificial, and therefore as the offering which the Body of Christ makes to the Father through the sustaining Spirit of its Head, forms the general background for the doctrine of sacrifice in the Eucharist. Martyr often calls this whole sacrificial life of the Church 'eucharistic' since all are expressions of the gratitude of faith—and therefore the Eucharist embodies these in its fourfold oblation, as we shall see below. In one sense, the chief element of the sacrificial response of faith is the offering of self and conversion of fellowmen:

> (Paul) wishes us to make ourselves oblations unto God . . . And doubtless there is no sacrifice more noble . . . all Christians are now sacrificers, who ought to sacrifice not only themselves, but also others, which they especially effect who preach, teach, exhort and admonish their neighbours to return to Christ . . . God is so desirous of our salvation that He counts the conversion of every one of us a most acceptable sacrifice. (*in Rom.* 12.1, 15.16)

This doctrine of the 'human sacrifice' of the Church[39] is especially telling in relation to transubstantiation and the priestly office in the Church. The Romanist priest thinks that he is called chiefly 'to manufacture the Eucharist',[40] but the Epistle to the Hebrews teaches a priesthood which consists rather in offering tribute and sacrifice for sins unto God, which Christ alone did. That oblation being past, the ministry is called to preach the Gospel, since 'Sacraments without doctrine are useless and frigid',[41] and since their true sacrifice is the offering up of men, if they succeed to the Apostolic office which Paul describes.

> Doubtless is this kind of sacrifice committed unto me by the preaching of the Gospel, to offer up the Gentiles a most acceptable sacrifice unto God. My sword, says Paul (as Chrysostom writes) is the Gospel: the sacrifice killed with my right hand, the Gentiles. Let our consecrators of pieces of bread boast that they are priests because by their enchantment they transubstantiate bread and wine. This is that sacrifice, this I say is that priesthood, which the Apostles exercised, and which also the pastors of the

[39] Romans 12.1 is Martyr's favourite text in this regard; but cf. the section in 2 *Reg.* 3.27: not only the offering of self, but of others and of our children, is the true oblation, 'And these now suffice in respect of human sacrifice'.
[40] *nisi qui conficere possit Eucharistiam*—*Def.* 207.   [41] *Def.* 209.

Church should now exercise . . . here we offer a human sacrifice by the precept of God: but in that fiendish juggling of Popery the souls of simple men are most cruelly murdered . . . by our sacrifice we spread abroad the worship of God: but there under a form of piety the most horrible idolatry is retained in the Church. (*in Rom.* 15.16)

The Romanist priest thinks that he has 'no other office than to change the substance of bread', while the common people 'think that Christ is taken from them' if the doctrine of transubstantiation is denied.[42]

I would to God the Romish priests would also consider this, and not count all their honour to consist in their transubstantiating the nature of bread (which is but legerdemain and a vain device) but that they would finally understand themselves to be called by God to this, that by Word and doctrine as by good manners and examples, they should transubstantiate men into Christ and make them His lively members. (*Serm. ex Hagg.* 1)

The minister of Christ has a true sacrifice to offer, indeed a more important sacrifice than had the O.T. priest:

What more excellent and honourable thing can they have, than to be the ambassadors of Christ, and to reconcile the world unto God by their preaching? (*in* 1 *Cor.* 5.7)

At the heart of Martyr's doctrine of Christian sacrifice stands this concern for a living sacrifice, a spiritual offering which begins when 'we crucify our own flesh'.[43] The Christian carries in his own body a living monument or altar of the heart, on which is engraved 'Christ is my Peace'.[44] But the Lord's Supper is the Church ordinance in which Christian sacrifice finds its special basis and greatest expression: here all sacrifice meets in the particular Thanksgiving.

When the Lord's Supper is celebrated, inasmuch as the body and blood of Christ are by faith and the Spirit given us to be received, and the promise of that conjunction which we have with Christ sealed, so that we are members of His body, in this respect I say it is and is called a Sacrament, since in that action God gives His gifts to us. But inasmuch as by the same action we celebrate the memory of the death of Christ, give thanks for the benefits received, consecrate and offer ourselves to God, it is and may be called a proper Sacrifice, since we give most acceptable oblations unto God.

(*in Iud.* 2.5)

The Eucharist itself involves a fourfold offering:[45] almsgiving

---

[42] *Disp.*, prefatory speech.
[43] *in Rom.* 1.19.
[44] *in Iud.* 6.24.
[45] This teaching is found *in* 1 *Cor.* 5.7.

(including the offering of bread and wine), thanksgiving, the offering of self, and lastly the memorial of Christ's Death sacramentally called a sacrifice. Martyr illustrates these from the Early Church practice and doctrine.

But since Christ is said to be immolated, what do these sacrificers mean that say He is sacrificed every day in the Mass? Concerning these things, it is to be noted that in the Lord's Supper there may be four oblations. The first is of the bread and wine brought in by the people. From a certain part of this the Eucharist was celebrated; from this source the faithful communicated among themselves; and what remained was distributed to the poor.

Under this first head, Martyr cites Irenaeus and Tertullian, and also Philippians 4.18, in which Paul

shows that alms are sacrifices, when he writes that he received those things which they sent him as a sweet smelling sacrifice unto God.

The question of how bread and wine are offered to God is answered in this context of their relationship to almsgiving.[46]

Moreover we deny not that the bread in the Lord's Supper is in a sense offered unto God to be sanctified, and that it is made a sacrament by Him. The difficulty and question under debate is whether Christ Himself is offered unto God the Father by those who sacrifice.

He now turns to the three other kinds of sacrifice in the Eucharist.

In the next place is the giving of thanks (*gratiarum actio*), which in the holy Scripture is called the sacrifice of praise (*immolatio laudis*). Thirdly the communicants offer themselves unto God to be ruled and mortified ... Fourth and last, when it is spoken there of the memorial of the death of Christ, which was the true sacrifice, by a figurative speech the Eucharist or Lord's Supper takes its name from the thing it represents and is called a sacrifice, as Augustine says upon the Psalms, 'By memory and meditation Christ is offered daily'.

The Eucharist therefore involves the whole of Christian sacrifice, and serves both as a true oblation offered unto the

[46] Cf. *Def*. 75, where Gardiner states that Melchizedec offered 'the true body and blood of Christ under those species', to which Martyr points out that historically, he offered the food and drink to Abraham, not God, and theologically, we are not priests after his order, but Christ is, the High Priest in heaven; also *Def*. 73: what is the *nova oblatio* of the Church in the Supper? Martyr asks. Two things: first, bread and wine, since part is offered by the people to the holy assembly, and part to the poor; second, the people's prayers, thanksgiving, *et omnia illa quae communicando ad cultum dei facimus*. This oblation is 'new' because we are freed from the rites and places of the O.T. dispensation, and because we give thanks for what is done and therefore present, while those foreshadowed something future.

Father and as a means of grace to establish believers in their faith,[47] so that its whole purpose may be summed up as 'communion' and 'thanksgiving':

> But we teach that pious men are provoked by these symbols or visible words, to think upon the things themselves, which are represented by these symbols, and feed on them in spirit and in mind . . . the matter itself is gone: only its memory is retained in the mysteries, and for that thanks are given publicly. (*Def.* 793, 676)

The eucharistic sacrifice is thus for Martyr the essence of Christian life and action. He regards it as the summary and highest expression of the Church's being, since it embodies all that Christ commanded His Church to do in her service of God.[48]

Here, then, is the normal and normative worship of the people of God. Although Peter Martyr does not state so explicitly as Calvin[49] that the Eucharist should be celebrated 'at least every Sunday', this is his constant presupposition. Thus describing the worship of the Lord's Day in connection with almsgiving (which he relates internally to the Eucharist) he writes:

> And to inflame our minds to give alms Paul very fitly chose the day of the holy congregation, because of the Word of God, the public prayers and holy lessons used on that day, through which we are put in remembrance of the benefits which God has bestowed on us for His mercy's sake. Also we receive the sacraments, by which the memory of that most excellent benefit is renewed, I mean of the death of our Lord Jesus Christ.
>
> (*in Gen.* 2.1)

The question of the frequency of Communion is simply the question of the divinely-appointed means by which the Church responds to the love of its Lord: since we 'cannot be thankful enough' of His Sacrifice, the sacrament of the Eucharist ought to be 'most familiar to the faithful'.[50]

> And since so great a price is paid for our salvation, we must not suffer so great a benefit to lightly slip from memory. To avoid this, we are helped

---

[47] *quod dignatus esset usque ad finem illos constantes in fide servare*—*De Vot.* 1531C.

[48] *An in Comm. Lic.* 21: 'All that Christ commanded may be reduced to four words'; cf. in *Iud.* 1.33. He follows Augustine's interpretation of the 'four words' of I Timothy 2.1, which he relates to the eucharistic service: δεήσεις, supplications which precede the celebration of the sacrament; προσευχαί, prayers in the administration of the sacrament (we vow ourselves unto Christ); ἐντεύξεις, petitions by which the minister prays for all present; and εὐχαριστία, general thanksgivings.

[49] *Articles* of November 1536.

[50] *Catech.* 17, *in* I *Cor.* 10.15f; cf. *in* I *Cor.* 4.2: frequent communion is urged against Romanism, which thinks it 'lawful for them to communicate only at Easter'.

not only by doctrine and Scripture, but also by sacraments. For just as the frequent sacrifices shadowed the coming Christ among the Elders, so now the frequent use of the mysteries brings to memory His death and blood shed for us. (*in Rom.* 3.24)

In this respect also, the Patristic age may be our guide, according to Martyr, whose contemporary situation demanded the replacement of daily Masses by frequent Communions:

> First, there were not innumerable daily private Masses, as there are today. Once or twice in seven days, not every day, was the Supper held. Next, although strangers passed by, they were unwilling to abstain from holy communion, but it was proper to minister as it suited those that arrived.
>
> (*De Vot.* 1395B)

Ambrose, for instance, exhorted ministers of his day to be ready

> to distribute the holy mysteries, which, he says, used to be done once a week, unless more often because of strangers.[51]

Finally, the nature of faith itself demands such regular communication, since faith corresponds to the promises of God: regenerate men co-operate with the Holy Spirit and so must come frequently to the holy mystery to express the assent of soul and faith to the promises.[52]

Thus Peter Martyr's doctrine of eucharistic sacrifice brings us to the heart of the problem of Christian service and worship. This it answers by interpreting the movement of faith as the grateful response to God's Word of mercy in which we are lifted up in soul and mind to the Heavenly Redeemer Himself, and in which we are enabled to offer unto Him the sacrifice of thanksgiving for His benefits. *Communion* and *thanksgiving* are the two chief elements involved in the response of faith, and both find their central meaning and deepest expression in that which is both the Gospel of God made visible and the sacrifice of the Church made actual, the sacrament of the Eucharist. Just as Melchizedec, priest of the Most High God, offered to Abraham and his soldiers food for their hungry and weary bodies, so Christ our High Priest offers us nourishment for soul

---

[51] *in Iud.* 4.5—according to Jerome and Augustine, 'Christians communicated every day'; cf. *in* 1 *Cor.* 7.5.

[52] *in* 1 *Cor.* 11.25. Cf. *Def.* 325: what broke down this normal worship of the Church was the doctrine of transubstantiation, because 'Corporeal presence hinders frequency of communion', the Mass making it sufficient for people to 'see Christ being made' or 'putting on' bread (or accidents!) so that they 'never get as far as communion' (*communionem nunquam accedere*).

and body by the real presence of His own Death and Life. And this gracious movement of accommodative love summons from our side a grateful praise and thanksgiving, the eucharistic sacrifice of the Church of Christ. As He becomes our Head through grace so we become His Body through gratitude.

This study in the sacramental theology of Peter Martyr could end on no more worthy note than this of the eucharistic sacrifice as the great offering of the Church unto God. The Church is the very Body of Christ, sharing His life and activity, enjoying His real presence and offering Him its true sacrifice. The prayers of the Church, its good works, its devotional life and theological service—all derive meaning and purpose only as the Church centres about this Table, receives this Food, offers this Sacrifice.

PETER MARTYR's *Prayer Against False Worship*

Come at length, we beseech Thee O heavenly Father, and illuminate the hearts and minds of all thy Christians with the Spirit of Jesus Christ Thy Son, that forsaking idols and superstitions they may be converted unto Thee alone, who ought to be purely and sincerely served . . . Thy holy name hath been long enough dishonoured with reproaches, the pureness of Thy Gospel long enough polluted, more than enough have men abused the institution of Thy Son's Supper in most impure idolatry. Stop at last these furies of men, O Lord . . . and Thou Jesus Christ, the true and eternal God, confirm this work which Thou hast begun, and bring it to the desired end: or else, if there be no hope of recovery, if no more shall Thy truth have public and open place in Thy Church, come quickly and hasten Thy judgment, and for the glory of Thy name turn away such shameful abuse from Thy holy Supper, which Thou hast instituted in Thine incredible mercy and excellent goodness: who, with the Father and the Holy Spirit livest and reignest world without end,   Amen.

APPENDICES

BIBLIOGRAPHY

(1) The Works of Peter Martyr

1. *Principal Works*

1543—*Proposita ad disputandum publice in Schola Argentinensi, ex Gen., Exod., Levit. et Iudic.* (published 1582)

1544—*Una Semplice Dichiarazione sopra gli XII Articoli . . . Basilea,* 1544. (later pub. as *Catechismus sive Symboli expositio . . .*)

1549—*Disputatio de Euch. Sac. in celeb. Angliae schola Oxon. habita: ad haec Tractatio de Sac. Euch. habita Oxon. cum iam absolvisset interpret. XI Cap. prioris Epist. ad Corinth.—Londini* 1549. (Tiguri, 1557, 1562, 1579)

1558—*Commentaria in Epist. S. Pauli ad Romanos*, 2 tom.—*Basil.* 1558. (fol. *Tiguri* 1559; E.T. ('by H.B.') Lond. 1568)

1559—*Defensio doctrinae veteris et Apost. de ss. Euch. . . . adv. St. Gardin.—Tig.* 1559.
—*De Votis Monasticis . . . adv. Ricc. Smyth.—Basil.* 1559.
—*Aristotelis Ethicae cum illis in Sacra. Script collatae—Basil.* 1559 (*Tig.* 1582; included in *Meditationes Ethicae*, of Hyperius): Books I, II and beginning of III only.

1561—*Dialogus de Utraque in Christo natura*—1561.
—*Comm. in librum Iudicum*, fol.—*Tig.* 1561. (*Argent.* 1582; E.T. Lond. 1564)
—*Brevis Epitome (sive Analysis) disputationis de Euch. in Gardinerum.*

1562—*Comm. in priorem Epist. ad Corinthios*, fol. (*Tig.* 1572).

1564—*Comm. in Samuelis Proph. libros duos—Tig.* 1564. (*Tig.* 1595)
—*Preces Sacrae ex Psalm. Dav. desumptae—Tig.* 1564.

1566—*Comm. in duos posterios libros Regum.* fol.—1566 (*Tig.* 1581, *Heidelb.* 1599): only to 2 Kings 11; Joh. Wolfius completed the work.

1572—*Comm. in Gen.—Tig.* 1572 (*Heidelb.* 1606); only to Chapter 42; Lud. Lavater completed the work.

1629—*Comm. in Lament. Jer. Proph.—Tig.* 1629.

2. *Lesser Works*

De Vitandis Superst. . . . excusatio ad Pseudonicodemos . . . 4to. Genevae, 1549 (French trans. 1582, 'Excuse aux faux Nicodemites'): this work of Calvin's included the opinion of Melanchthon, Bucer and Martyr; the purpose was to warn against 'too great rigour' during the initial stages of Reformation.

Clariss. et Magnif. Dominis Schol. Argent., 27 December 1553.

Oratio ad Acad. Argent. . . . de studio Theologico, 1553.

Confessio seu Sent. de Coena Dom . . . Argent., 1556.

Oratio quam Tig. prima habuit . . . 1556.

Sent. de praesentia Corporis Christi in Euch. . . . in Coll. Poiss. habito, 1561; 'Brève instruction de M. Martyr de la Sainte Cène . . .', Poissy, 1561.

An Missa Sit Sacrificium.

Oratio de utilitate et dignitate sacri Ministerii: Exhortatio iuventutis ad sac. lit. studium (on Malachi 2; given at Oxford).

De Morte Christi (sermon on Philippians 2).

De Resurrectione Christi (sermon).

Sermo in Locum Ioan. XX Cap. (on John 20.19-23).

Sermo ex Hagg. I (given at Oxford).

Encomium Verbi Dei in Scripturis Traditi, et ad harum studium adhortatio.

Adhortatio ad Coenam Domini Mysticam (the second exhortation of the Book of Common Prayer, from the Sunday before the sacrament is to be celebrated).

(Collected works):

Epistolae partim Theologicae, partim familiares.

Epistolarum ὄγδοας.

Loci Communes Pet. Mart., quatuor classes, R. Massonius, Ed.— Londini, 1576, 1583 (*Tig.* 1587; *Genev.* 1623; *Heidelb.* 1603; *Amst. et Franc.* 1656; E.T. by A. Marten, Lond. 1579).

Locorum Comm., Tom. Tert., Grynaeus. Ed.—*Basil.* 1580 (I: *L.C.*; II: *Dial., Def., Disp.*; III: *Preces, Epist.* etc.).

The Editions used in this work are as follows: *Def.*: 1559; *Tract.* and *Disp.*: 1557; *Dial.* and *De Vot.*: *Basil.*, 1581; Commentaries are cited according to Chapter and verse; Treatises according to the sections of the *L.C.* of Lond. 1583, as below.

Treatises in the Commentaries: *De Iustificatione, in Rom.* 11 at end (*L.C.* III.4); *De Poenitentia, in 2 Sam.* at end (*L.C.* III.8); *De Resurrectione, in 2 Reg.* 4.37 (*L.C.* III.15); *An in Communione liceat una spec., in 1 Cor.* 10.17 (*L.C.* IV.11); *De Templorum Dedic., in 1 Reg.* 8.66 (*L.C.* IV.9).

3. Problematic Works

1. M. Young (*op. cit.*, pp. 584ff) includes in his Bibliography a reference to *Comment. in priores libros*, which should be continued in the next item, *Ethicarum Aristotelis*. He misread these as two separate works, from A. Teissier's list (*Eloges des hommes savans*, I. 217). However, his reference to *Comment. in Exodum; Comment. in Prophetas aliquot minores* introduces an important problem: were Martyr's lectures upon Genesis, Exodus, part of Leviticus, and the Minor Prophets (given at Strassburg, 1553-1556) ever published? Simler (*Oratio*) had stated that the Commentaries on Samuel and Kings were to be published, 'and perhaps' those on Genesis, Exodus, Leviticus, the Prophets, Lamentations, and the Ethics of Aristotle. Of these, only the first and last two were published. Schmidt (II, p. 294) examines the question of the others: Simler and Lavater 'undertook the editing of the Lectures on the O.T.' and found notes on Genesis 1-42, Exodus 1-34, Samuel, Kings, Lamentations and the Minor Prophets. They wrote to Conrad Hubert in England about Martyr's other works, but he had 'only a copied note-book on the third Book of Moses'. From his study of the correspondence, Schmidt concludes that Martyr's notes 'on the second and third Books of Moses, and the fragment on the Minor Prophets, appear to have remained unprinted'. A further interesting comment in this same passage is Simler's note about a reference in this correspondence to a work of Martyr's on 1 John, which seems to be an error based on a confusion of the data available to Simler. In hopes that the notes on Leviticus might be extant, I made enquiries which resulted in the following: Martyr took all his notes with him on leaving Strassburg and the Simler Collection at Zürich contains any remaining material; but enquiries about the document in question proved fruitless. It would seem that Hubert's own note-book was the only source available to Simler, who decided against publishing that or the notes on Exodus 1-34 he had in his possession. Martyr's own words on the subject are perhaps of interest: he wrote to Bullinger from Oxford on 2 October 1551, at which time he was preparing his Commentary on Romans for publication: 'As to those other commentaries of mine which you enquire after, I do not see how they can possibly be published in so short a time: for what I have written upon Genesis, Exodus, Leviticus, and the minor prophets, are brief and hasty annotations; so that there needs leisure for revising, and copying over again, what I at first wrote out for my own sole use, and for that of others. But if it please God to spare my life, and I should obtain a little leisure, I shall not

s

object to publish them; not that I consider any work of mine as of any value, but that I may not seem arrogantly to disregard the wishes of my friends.' (*Orig. Lett.* II, p. 499)

2. In the *Loc. Comm.*, Massonius included three works of Bullinger's, *De Libero Arbitrio, De Providentia et Praedestinatione*, and *An Deus Sit Causa et Author Peccati*: L.C., pp. 971, 992, 994. These were composed by Bullinger in 1553, and being found among Martyr's papers without signature or name, were carelessly taken for Martyr's work—Schmidt (I, p. 102n). For Martyr's own teaching see his *Comm. in* 1 *Cor.*, f. 26B, *De Libero Arbitrio; in Rom.* 9, *De Praedestinatione; and in* 1 *Sam.* f. 19A, *An Deus Sit Author Peccati.*

3. There is extant a little volume printed in 1555, consisting of a Sermon by Henry Bullinger, and a Treatise ascribed to him: 'A Treatise of the cohabitation of the faithful with the unfaithful . . . A Sermon of the true confessing of Christ . . . made in the convocation of the clergy at Zürich the 28th day of January, 1555 by H.B.' There has been some doubt as to whether it was Bullinger or Martyr who wrote the Treatise. Now this is actually a Treatise written by Peter Martyr and found in his Commentaries on the Book of Judges (*in Iud.* 1.36, ff. 27B—35B, *Tig.* 1582) entitled *An Christianis Liceat Cum Infidelibus Habitare*. A careful comparison reveals that it was an English translation of this section of the Commentary, which dealt with the difference between the Mass and the Lord's Supper. Since the Commentary was not published until 1561, Martyr must have written the Treatise earlier, no doubt during his residence in England, when his and Bullinger's teaching had such influence, and allowed it to be published in this form. The Treatise and Sermon were later published along with 'The chief grounds of Christian Religion, set down by way of Catechizing . . . By Ezekiel Rogers . . . London, 1642'.

4. A quaint, short work entitled *Narratio historica viciss. rerum quae in inclyto Brit. regno acciderunt A.D.* 1553 *mense Julio. Scripta a P.V.* (Antwerp, 1553) sets forth the hypothesis that King Edward VI's death was 'caused or accelerated by unfair means' and 'boldly ascribes the king's death to the agency of the duke (of Northumberland, the king's guardian) by violent means, poison, or the dagger'. The quotation is from the E.T. (London, 1865) of J. Ph. Berjeau, whose researches were thought to prove that Peter Martyr (P. Vermigli) was the author. This has since been disproved, and authorship remains uncertain (although Peter Viret was in England about that time). The copies in the Bodleian Library, Oxford, and the University Library, Cambridge, however, are still erroneously ascribed to Peter Martyr.

4. *Manuscripts*

Corpus Christi College, Cambridge: MS 102. 5-8, 29-31 (Cat. by James), Letters to Bucer *de causa et argumentis Mag. Yungi, de Statu Germaniae, consolatoria de morbis;* a sermon and cogitations concerning the Devon. revolt; *Epist. ad quendam episcopum ubi multis argumentis contra August. probat, quod post justum divortium utrisque licet altero superstite matrimonium denuo contrahere.* MS 119. 37-40, 44, Letters to Bucer *de fide Christi generale et de concordia de re sacramentaria; ut non det se in disputationem nisi adsint judices idonei; de libro precum communium; de Smitheo et libellis eius;* and *de adversa eius valetudine.* MS 340. 4-6, Sermons *in seditionem,* and *Dialogus regis et populi Italice.*

University Library (Anderson Room), Cambridge: Tracts Mm 4.14, brief Treatise on the Vestment controversy. Baumgartner Paper (Strype Corr.) Add 3 (c), copy of the *Censura Libri Comm. Prec.* (Corp. Christi 119.39). Baker MSS, vol. 31, Mm 1.42, copy of the Letter of consolation to Bucer (Corp. Christi 102.8).

Bodleian Library, Oxford: MS New College (*Nov.* cccxliii.12), two letters to Bucer of 25 October 1550, concerning the Vestment controversy; MS Queen's College (*Reg.* cclxxxiv.181), Letter to Edward VI.

(2) SECONDARY SOURCES

Simler, Josias, *Oratio de Vita et Obitu Clarissimi Viri et Praestantiss. Theologi D. Pet. Mart. Verm.* . . . 1562—printed in Gerdes, *Scrin. Antiqu.* III.ii, and in all the *Loc. Comm.*

Beza, Theo., *Icones,* Geneva, 1580; slightly longer account in *Les Vraies Pourtraits,* 1581.

Schlosser, F. C., *Leben des Theo. de Beze und des Peter Martyr,* Heidelberg, 1809.

Schmidt, C., *Vie de Pierre Martyr Vermigli,* Strassburg, 1835.
Peter Martyr Vermigli, Leben und ausgewahlte Schriften, Elberfeld, 1858. (Vol. VII of *Leben und aus.* . . . *der reformirten Kirche,* Hagenbach, Ed.)

Young, M., *The Life and Times of Aanio Paleario,* London, 1860, Chapter X, 'Peter Martyr Vermiglio'.

The above are the main biographical works; Schmidt's 1858 work is the only one of a seriously critical nature. Simler is the basis of the rest, but Young has included much material from the Italian scene, while Schmidt has examined sources of the Strassburg and Zürich periods thoroughly; Schlosser's constant comparison of Martyr with Beza often distorts the history, nor is he so careful a scholar as Schmidt. In 1860 Young wrote (*op. cit.*, p. 492), 'The life of Peter Martyr is worthy of a more extended history than the limits of a chapter can afford, and is still a desideratum in sacred literature. The materials are abundant, and would well repay a scholar's diligence if taken up as a separate work, incorporating his correspondence with the chief men of the day.' The desideratum still exists, and the materials are even more abundant. Below we shall give the chief, with works of adversaries first.

White, John, Bp. of Winchester, *Diacosio-martyrion . . . de veritate corporis et sanguinis Christi in Euch. . . . adv. P. Martyrem*, London, 1553.

Chorus alternatim canentium ('A satire in verse on the controversy between G. Haddonus and J. Osorio da Fonseca, Bishop of Silves, attached to a caricature in which Haddon, Bucer and Peter Martyr are represented as dogs drawing a car on which Osorio is seated in triumph'), 1563?

Laing, Jas., *De Vita et Moribus atque rebus gestis haereticorum nostri temporis . . .* Paris, 1581.

Schulting, Cornelius, *Bibliotheca catholica et orthodoxa, contra summam totius theologiae Calviniae in Institutionibus J. Calvini et Locis Communibus Petri Martyris, breviter comprehensae*, Col. Agrip. 1602. (This 'brief' work contains 5 vols. in 2, mainly directed against Calvin's work.)

Parker Society literature: *Original Letters*, 2 vols. Camb., 1847; *Zürich Letters*, Camb. 1842.

Strype, John, *Ecclesiastical Memorials*, vols. II, III, London, 1816; *Memorials of Cranmer*, London, 1694.

Burnet, G., *History of the Reformation of the Church of England*, London, 1681. (Part III has appendices of Letters to Martyr of Jewel, etc., and one of Martyr to Bullinger on the state of the U. of Oxford, 1 June 1550: App. 6.)

The materials in the nineteenth-century Gorham controversy include 'Gleanings' and 'Extracts' (G. C. Gorham, 1849-1850) of passages from Martyr and Bullinger, in relation to the doctrine of infant baptism in the Book of Common Prayer. Also Wm. Goode's editing of a Letter of Martyr to Bullinger of 14 June 1552 on this subject, 'An Unpublished Letter etc. London, 1850'.

Young, (*op. cit.*, p. 585) mentions 'a useful little book by the Rev. E. Bridge, vicar of Manaccan, Cornwall. *A Voice from the Tomb of P. Martyr against Popery*, 1840', which I have been unable to locate.

APPENDIX B

PETER MARTYR'S PATRISTIC SOURCES

Peter Martyr's theology is Patristic in a profound sense: exten-
sively, a work such as the *Defensio* is actually a commentary upon
the writings of the Fathers; intensively, his Patristic sources have
authority because of their relation to holy Scripture. Martyr's first
and formative principle is that theology has as its subject-matter
the Scriptural and not the Patristic text: *Deus dixit* is the sole norm
of theological activity (*in 1 Cor., Praef.*). He warns explicitly against
converting theology into patrology:

> We are called Theologians, and such we would be accounted:
> let us answer to the name and profession—unless instead of
> *theologi* we would be *patrologi*! (*Exhort. Iuv.*)

An example of this process is offered by 'Smyth the brawler of
Oxford' who armed himself with the Fathers without correcting
them by Scripture (*Def.* 68). It is the activity of such men that
draws from Martyr the detailed interpretation of the Fathers that
characterizes his polemical writings.

> Because we have certain adversaries who depend very little
> or not at all upon Scripture, but measure all their religion
> by the Fathers and Councils, so that they might rather be
> called *Patrologi* than *Theologi*, and—even more intolerable—
> collect little sentences out of the writings of the Fathers, and
> obtrude them to the people, to obscure truth more easily . . .
> (therefore) we also will allege out of the Fathers. (*De Iustif.* 36)

This gathering of *sententiolae* from the Patristic writings is characteristic of the Romanist *doctores tabularii* 'who have more skill in
indices than in books' (*De Iustif.* 24), listing every mention of words
like *sacrificium* and *praeparatio* as if these support their theories of
propitiatory Mass and preparatory grace. Against this custom
Martyr brings two principles for interpreting the Fathers. First is
the *Deus dixit* which alone makes for sound doctrine:

> First we should define doctrines soundly out of Scripture itself.
> Then afterwards may the Fathers be read with judgment.
> (*in Rom.* 4.7)

We must read them warily and with discrimination, correcting

267

them by Scripture, and not *vice versa* as the Romanist declares. To the latter's claim that Scripture is obscure and the Fathers a surer source, Martyr says:

> yet who see not meanwhile, or pretend they do not see, what Labyrinths are in the Fathers . . . when there are obscure places in the Fathers, what shall I do, where shall I fly? Other Fathers succeed, who may interpret the former—and when obscurity and difficulty occur again in them, later interpreters are further appointed, so that the thing will never end! (*Exhort. Iuv.*)

Thus Augustine uses Basil, Chrysostom, and so on; others use Augustine—and when there could be neither end nor measure 'Peter Lombard came, to make all hard places plain!' And even Lombard had infinite interpreters, chiefly Scotus and Occam. Then Thomas was expounded by Cajetan and Capreolus, Scotus by Zorobellus and Leschetus, Occam by Gabriel Biel and Gregory Ariminensis. Martyr concludes the passage—

> Let us return, I beseech you, let us return to the first fountains of the Scriptures.

Along with this principle Martyr places another, that there are 'degrees of the Fathers' (*Disp.* III, *vs.* Morg.). Thus Theophylact, for instance, lived in the time of great dissension between the Greek and Latin Churches concerning the Holy Spirit, and must be read accordingly—and this was the time when 'the doctrine of transubstantiation began to sprout'. In contrast, Martyr adds, Augustine 'lived in purer times'. This becomes a general principle of interpretation: he distinguishes 'the Fathers that were of greater antiquity and the purer age' from 'the latter writers of the Church' (*De Templ. Ded.* 21), for in the main, 'Later Fathers speak less prudently' (*Def.* 97). This requires certain qualification, inasmuch as even in Augustine's time the sacraments had too much attributed to them, but in general Augustine 'weighs these things more diligently and closely' than other Fathers (*in Iud.* 19.14). This second principle introduces the question of particular Patristic sources for his theology.

Peter Martyr's remarkable knowledge of the Fathers is evident throughout his whole life, and soon became known among his contemporaries as worthy of their notice. In Naples he had opposed the doctrine of purgatory on Scriptural authority, supported by testimonies of the Fathers; in Strassburg his lectures were noted for their regular inclusion of Patristic exegesis of the Biblical text; in England his lectures on 1 Corinthians and his Disputation at

Oxford opposed the doctrine of transubstantiation on the basis of Patristic analogical thinking. An interesting account of one document indicates Martyr's place as a Patristic scholar—Chrysostom's *Ad Caesarium Monachum*, fragments of which are preserved in Greek by Jo. Damascene, Anastasius and Nicephorus. A Latin version for the remainder was brought to England by Martyr, and presented to Cranmer, who used it in his 'Defence of the True and Catholic Doctrine of the Sacrament, etc.' of 1550 (see 1907 ed., note by H. Jenkyns on p. 52, Book II, Chapter 5). Gardiner disputed its genuineness (doubtless because of its expressions against transubstantiation) and it has remained a subject of controversy. Cranmer's copy disappeared after his death, and since Martyr 'had not stated from whence it was procured, Cardinal Perron ventured to charge him with having forged it'. But in 1680 the original MS was discovered in the library of the Dominican monastery of St. Mark at Florence, and finally published in 1685 by Le Moyne, whose defence of its genuineness induced scholars such as Bigot and Dupin to accept it. This 'discovery' would have been made much sooner, and in circumstances less striking, if Martyr's adversaries had troubled to read his *Tractatio* more carefully. For there he clearly states the location of the document under discussion: 'Chrysostom to Caesar the Monk, in the time of his second exile, against Appolinarus and others who confounded the divinity and humanity of Christ (the Epistle is kept in the Library at Florence, although it is not imprinted) . . .' (*habetur in bibliotheca Florentina haec Epistola, licet non sit impressa*)—*Tract.* 31.

When Martyr and Ochino went to England, one of the purchases which the former made in preparation for the journey is listed as 'Pd. for the works of S. Augustine, Cyprian and Epithanius for Petrus Marter at Basell . . .' (Expences of the Journey . . . by John Abell, 1547). Apart from this incidental reference, we do not know the extent of his library. But in his writings we see clearly that *Augustine* was his chief Patristic source—in the *Defensio*, for example, there are approximately sixty-four places of Augustine quoted over one hundred times, as against thirty-four places from Chrysostom, twenty from Ambrose, and so on in descending order of use. Such quantitative incidence merely reflects the profound reliance of Martyr upon Augustine's works, and in particular certain passages which are foundational for his sacramental teaching, which we have noted throughout our work—the sacrament as *verbum visibilis*, the necessity of abiding in Christ to eat His Body, etc.

The problem of Martyr's use of *Theodoret* also deserves mention. In his 'Treatise', 'Disputations' and 'Defence' Martyr makes extensive use of Gelasius and Theodoret—both of whom are rejected by his opponents as 'Nestorians'! The reaction to his quoting Theodoret in the Disputation is interesting. Tresham's first objection to Theodoret is that he 'was a Nestorian heretic, as appears plainly enough from the history of Nicephorus, and the Council of Chalcedon'. To this Martyr replies by rehearsing the events of the Synods of Ephesus and Chalcedon; the former (the Robber-synod of 449) had condemned him along with Nestorius, the friend of his youth, although he had already refuted his earlier support of the Nestorian hypothesis, and the latter accepted him as a leading theologian, since he had been reinstated by Pope Leo (cf. O. Bardenhewer, *Patrology*, E.T. by Shahan, 1908, sec. 78,' Theodoret of Cyrus'). Tresham then brings another objection: 'He is but an obscure author, and no man has him but you: wherefore he must not be cited for the defining of so great a matter.' Martyr answers, 'The book is printed, and may be bought at Rome.' Tresham then concludes most appropriately, 'I answer that it would be a long and tedious thing to go to Rome for such a book.' Besides reminding us of Martyr's singular acquaintance with Patristic documents, this passage raises the question of what this book was which Martyr had bought at Rome. Was it perhaps the lost work of Theodoret, his *Pentalogium* against Cyril and the Council of Ephesus, which has perished except for a few fragments? (cf. Migne, *Pat. Gr.* 84, 65-88). An examination of all the passages in which Martyr uses Theodoret against the doctrine of transubstantiation leads us to reply in the negative: at least, if this was what he possessed, he did not use it. His quotations are all from Theodoret's first two Dialogues against Eutycheanism or Monophysitism, entitled *Eranistes Seu Polymorphus* (Migne, *PG-L* 83). The first concerns the *immutabilis* of the divinity of Christ, and the second concerns the *inconfusus* of the divinity and humanity. Martyr uses their *analogia Christi* as a principal argument against the doctrine of transubstantiation. We must therefore conclude that we have no evidence to prove conclusively that a full 'Theodoret' was available to Peter Martyr.

A final aspect of this brief comment upon Peter Martyr's Patristic sources is the problem of his relationship with Cranmer. Strype (*Mem. of Cran.* II, Chapter XXV) relates the hypothesis that Martyr came to England as 'a Papist, or a Lutheran, as to the belief of the Presence' in the Eucharist. It was Cranmer's influence which brought Martyr to the true doctrine, which he subsequently set forth in his Treatise, and upheld in the Disputation. Our historical and theological study proves conclusively, however, that this hypothesis is untenable; the 1544 Catechism alone proves that Martyr left Italy with a consistently Reformed doctrine of the sacraments, and already stated therein his hopes concerning 'a full treatise of the sacraments, which nevertheless, I hope shortly to bring to pass, if the Lord lend me life' (*Catech.* 42). The charge of suiting doctrine to governmental desires was levelled at both Bucer and Martyr (cf. Strype, *Ecc. Mem.* II, pp. 196ff), and indeed pursued Martyr all his life, caught as he was between Lutheran and 'Zwinglian' sides of the Reformation—in 1555 he wrote to Bullinger about charges of inconsistency, 'I have ever taken the greatest possible care not to blow hot and cold out of my mouth' (*Orig. Lett.* II, p. 517). Now Strype's claim is that Cranmer's Patristic theology was the deciding factor in Martyr's theological development. His evidence, at least for Cranmer's Patristic knowledge, is significant: there is still extant in the Library of Corpus Christi College, Cambridge, Cranmer's own note-book entitled in his own hand *De Re Sacramentaria*, and comprising a remarkable collection of Patristic quotations about the Eucharist. His conclusions from this study are identical with Martyr's doctrine, as are his arguments against 'the crass Papists, or Capernaites', first of which is *Quod Accidentia maneant sine subiecto*. Martyr himself stated in his Preface to the *Tract.*, dedicated to Cranmer, 'Nor is there any book old or new in which I have not seen with these eyes notes in your own hand, whatever pertained to this whole controversy'. But the facts of the Patristic studies pursued by Bucer and Martyr at Strassburg prior to 1547, plus Martyr's authority as a Patristic scholar when he came to England suggest that he had as much to offer Cranmer as he received, and in the case of such Continental documents as those of Chrysostom and Theodoret mentioned above, much more. Thus for instance, Cranmer's extensive use of Theodoret in the 'Defence' of 1550 (Book III, Chapter II) is directly the result of Martyr's influence, if Tresham is to be trusted that only Martyr had a copy of the Dialogues. Finally we should note that it is this Patristic theology which Martyr introduced to the English Church which has been such a profound influence in its history—through the theology of the Caroline divines, for instance Especially is this true of his use of the analogical reasoning of Gelasius and Theodoret. Cf. Cosin's 'History of Popish Trans.' (1676), Chapter V for extensive use of these two Fathers (edition of 1840), pp. 104ff; cf. p. 101 (note in reference to Martyr's *Defensio*).

APPENDIX C

BUCER, CALVIN AND MARTYR

The question of Peter Martyr's relationship to his contemporaries has concerned us at certain points throughout our historical and theological study, and now merits closer attention in terms of its own. The key would seem to lie with the Strassburg Reformer, Martin Bucer. It was in Strassburg that both Calvin and Martyr dwelt on the closest terms with Bucer, during the critical period of their lives; and the theological coincidence among the three men is more than accidental. In the dilemma of the Reformation, which so quickly separated into two rival camps, symbolized by Luther and Zwingli, a new and distinctive note was sounded, first by Bucer, and most distinctively and permanently by Calvin, although equally as much by Martyr. Despite their individual differences, they consciously worked for the same ends—truly ecumenical ends, it should be noted—and these are most clearly revealed in the doctrine of the sacrament.

Bucer and Calvin

By way of introduction to this complex problem, we may take the reaction of Bucer (and Capito) to Calvin's *Confessio Fidei de Eucharistia* of 1537 (presented to the Synod of Bern: text in *Calv. Epist. et Resp.* 348). Calvin's typical stress upon the dynamic virtue flowing from Christ, the office of the Holy Spirit, the *totus Christus*, and the use of the terms *substantia* and *exhibere*—all this is accepted by Bucer's subscription as 'orthodox', complying especially in the localizing of Christ's continuing humanity, the ascending motion of faith, and the rejection of the view that reduces the symbols to *nuda et inania* and ignores the reception of *ipsum Dominum verum Deum et hominem*. Along with this early document we should place Bucer's important letter to Calvin in criticism of the *Consensus Tigurinus* of 1549 (dated 14 August 1549, Lambeth and London: text in *Corpus Reform.* XLI—*Ioan. Calv. Op.*, vol. XIII, pp. 350ff). Bucer begins with a general agreement (*Magnas vero gratias ago Domino . . .*) and then notes three points of criticism. First he would stress the true communion with Christ more than the formula does. This stress, he states, does not imperil the truth of Christ's heavenly glory and

272

human nature if we define it as 'not of this world, not of sense, not of reason': we must say together *et gloriam coelestem, et simul eius inter nos praesentiam, inhabitationem in nobis, manducationem.* He is horrified by the tendency to avoid Christ's words of consolation as to the real communion by which we are united as bone of His bone. He stands against those that preach 'Christ rather absent than present in His mysteries', labouring 'rather to explain what the minister might not effect, than what Christ confers through it, rightly administered and received by faith'. For thus the Spirit increases our communion with Christ: this should be stated explicitly, he concludes. Second, he agrees with what is said about the truth of Christ's humanity—but 'Let them not make a new article of faith concerning the certain place of heaven in which the body of Christ is contained.' He would define the mode of Christ's presence merely negatively—'not of this world'—and demand only that the doctrine of the Ascension be firmly held. Scripture does not press us to enquire further about the heavenly place. Third, as against their damning the Lutheran words by which they understand Christ to be enclosed or affixed locally in the symbols, Bucer objects that 'I have dealt again and again with so many Lutherans' and only discovered them to wish 'Christ to be truly given and received in the Supper' without determining about Christ's descent or ascent, or implying that sense or reason perceive anything apart from faith. Bucer concludes with *Mihi vos satisfecistis . . .* Now these points are the identical ones upon which Bucer criticizes Martyr, and revolve about the question whether the manner of Christ's presence in terms of His humanity is to be indicated negatively or positively. Bucer's negative delineation allowed him to accept the Lutheran terminology, and on this point we may feel that he thereby succeeded in accepting that other aspect of the truth of the mystery of Christ (of the anhypostasia) that we noted in Chapter IX above. Yet we must also point out that Calvin's absolute rejection of the Lutheran *manducatio impiorum* was based upon something deeper than a misunderstanding.

Bucer and Martyr

The key document here is the correspondence of the two men concerning Martyr's Disputation of 1549 (text in full in *Mart. Buc. Scripta Anglicana . . . Basil.* 1577, pp. 545ff). Bucer had attended the Disputations, and voiced some disapproval of Martyr's terminology at least. Martyr wrote to him on 15 June 1549, wishing to make it clear that his teaching 'dissents not at all' from Bucer's. He states:

if you consider all things well, you will easily understand, when I say, the body of Christ is made present with us by faith: and we are incorporated by that communicating, and transmuted into Him, that I deviate not much from what you yourself teach. I acknowledge that we truly receive the thing of the sacrament, that is the body and blood of Christ; but I say thus, as this is done by soul and faith, meanwhile I grant that the Holy Spirit is effectual in the sacraments, by the power of the Spirit and institution of the Lord. But I endeavour to hold this particularly against superstitions, lest the body and blood of Christ be mixed with bread and wine themselves, carnally and through a corporeal presence. But that we ourselves are truly joined to Him I do not question, nor would I have the sacramental symbols to be without honour and dignity. Only one thing remains by which you could perhaps be offended, that I claim that it does not agree (*convenire*) to the body and blood of Christ, as so greatly glorified, to be in many places. But as you see, Scripture does not signify this to be believed, the reason of a human body contradicts it, and the Fathers declare that this is granted to no creature, God excepted, nor does any greater utility come to us for that. You see that to the use of the sacrament, I grant as much as I can through the Word of God whence I am persuaded, equally with what you would grant . . .

Martyr concludes by reaffirming their agreement, and inviting criticism.

Bucer's reply is a most significant document. Bucer knew the English situation well, and was aware of the temptation to cater to the more symbolic view of the Supper held by the Swiss party in England. He too (letter of 20 June *Sc. Ang.* p. 54) acknowledges their unity of thought and life, and trusts that Martyr will accept his suggestions as to what he would have altered in the Acts, which he has read thoroughly. We may set out Martyr's Propositions, with Bucer's alterations.

1. *In sacramento Eucharistiae non est panis et vini transubstantiatio in corpus et sanguinem CHRISTI.* (Bucer: accept this *simpliciter*).

2. *Corpus et sanguis CHRISTI non est carnaliter aut corporaliter in pane et vino, nec ut alij dicunt, sub speciebus panis et vini.*
   (Bucer: replace by these or similar words: *Corpus Christi non continetur localiter in pane et vino: nec iis rebus affixum aut adiunctum est ulla huius mundi ratione*).

3. *Corpus et sanguis CHRISTI uniuntur pani et vino sacramentaliter.*
   (Bucer: add this: *Ita ut credentibus Christus hic vere exhibetur: fide tamen, nullo vel sensu vel ratione huius seculi intuendus, recipiendus, fruendus*).

Bucer explains his alterations in terms of the sad state of the German Church (the Interim had begun) and the need for maintaining the reception of Christ in the sacrament *planius pleno ore.* In the second Prop. therefore, he would not deny a real and 'substantial' presence of Christ, and in the third, he would prefer an explicit reference to the 'exhibition' of Christ. The problem of concord among the churches on this question has been to him like the stone of Sisyphus (*quasi saxum Sisyphi*) which has ground him down. Yet he will not admit 'either an impanation of Christ or a local connection of this world in the symbols'. On the other hand, he cannot agree that the elements are 'signs of a wholly absent Christ' by which we make a memorial only. Others, of course, wish the *recordatio* to lift up the soul into heaven and enjoy Christ there, or judge that Christ is there exhibited wholly (as God and man) and 'they would use those words and say that the body of Christ is exhibited corporeally because His body is exhibited, substantially because His substance, carnally because His flesh'. Further, Bucer agrees with Martyr in rejecting an eating of Christ by the wicked ('the presence of Christ is exhibited in the Sacrament simply to one's salvation'—cf. *Sc. Ang.* 623 for Bucer's denial of the *mand. imp.*, following Aug. just as Martyr does). He also reminds Martyr that he and Philip (Melanchthon) have always utterly abhorred *Ubiquitatem Christi secundum hominem.* He rejects a presence of Christ *localiter*, or by a connection *huius mundi*— these are his typical phrases delimiting the mode of presence, and he feels that these do not exclude the Lutherans. Finally he states that by faith comes 'a receiving and presence not feigned nor only verbal (*dictam*) but real and of the substance of Christ Himself'. Therefore, Bucer concludes, omit those terms from Prop. 2.

This letter indicates the teaching of Bucer to be essentially one with Martyr's, a difference in emphasis, strongly advanced by eirenical motives, making for a distinctive difference in Bucer's manner of speaking. Martyr emphasizes a 'local' presence of Christ's Body in heaven, and the *sursum corda* as the movement of faith in the Supper; Bucer will not give these a like emphasis, as his 54 English aphorisms (*Exomologesis, sive confessio . . . de s. Euch. . . .* 1560, *Sc. Ang.* pp. 538-545) clearly show. In these he refers to this 'high mystery' of communion with Christ, which is above reason and therefore only metaphorically indicated by human terminology (9-13); although he agrees with the truth of the humanity of Christ, which is now in a heavenly place, he refuses to follow Aristotle's doctrine (*De Nat.* IV) about this (25-27); he allows the non-Scriptural speech of the Fathers, but is cognizant of the errors to

which they have led, and agrees with their localizing the Body of
Christ in heaven so long as this is not made a necessary doctrine
(28-30); he reaffirms the weakness of human capacity, and need
for emphasizing a real presence; he describes the symbols as *signa
exhibitiva*—(Calvin's distinctive phrase) (45), and such exhibition is
well termed by the Fathers 'representation' (54).

Bucer was genuinely sorry for Martyr's terminology in the
Disputations—he wrote to Brentius: 'I am as sorry for master
Martyr's book as any one can be; but that disputation took place,
and the propositions were agreed upon, before I arrived in England.
At my advice he has inserted many things in the preface whereby to
express more fully his belief in the presence of Christ' (*Orig. Lett.*
II, p. 544—15 May 1550). He continues by describing a powerful
group in England who would confine Christ 'to a certain limited
place in heaven; and talk so vapidly about His exhibition and
presence in the supper (nay, some of them cannot even endure these
words), that they appear to believe that nothing else but the bread
and wine is there distributed'. A letter to Niger (quoted by Hopf,
op. cit., p. 79) extends this idea: 'he acknowledges the presence and
exhibition of Christ; but, since the Zürich people have here many
and great followers, this excellent man was drawn, I hardly know
how, to consent to use the word "Signification", although he added
"efficacious", by which he understands the exhibition of Christ,
as he himself explains it in the Preface to his Disputations, in which
by my advice he added many observations to his own, and withdrew
some; for he is most desirous of a pious concord. Those who had
hitherto listened to my explanation of this Mystery, especially those
who care for the kingdom of Christ, approved it.'

In Appendix D we give extended quotations from the Preface
which apparently owes so much to Bucer. But we submit that all
Martyr says there does not extend the doctrine of the sacraments
he had taught ever since his Catechism of 1544. For in that earliest
publication (sect. 42) he taught explicitly that the *verba visibilia*
were signs by which 'all the promises of God's mercy are effectively
represented to us' so that 'we are sure partakers of the matter
itself'. Martyr's understanding of *signum* does not follow that of the
'Zürich people' but rather that of the *semeion* of the Fourth Gospel,
related especially to the flesh of Christ as the archetypal *signum*—
so we tried to show in Part I of this work. Certainly Martyr's
teaching in the *Tract.* and *Def.* rejects the very same errors which
Bucer fights to keep out. And in the Disputation itself, Martyr's
teaching upon the sacramental mutation in the elements can hardly
be called 'Zwinglian'! Nor did the Swiss party in England accept

Martyr as ally, as their correspondence shows. Hooper wrote to Bullinger the month before the Disp. that 'Peter Martyr and Bernardine (Ochino) so stoutly defend Lutheranism, and there is now arrived a third (I mean Bucer), who will leave no stone unturned to obtain a footing'; in November he sent the Disp. to Bullinger, with no comment; but by October 1551, he could call Martyr 'a brave and godly soldier in the army of the Lord' (*Orig. Lett.* I, pp. 61, 70, 97). Burcher, it is true, made a sharp distinction between Martyr, whose Treatise he sent to Bullinger, 'being unwilling to deprive you any longer of so great a pleasure' (*Orig. Lett.* II, p. 660) and Bucer, whose death he hailed (*ibid.*, p. 678) as affording England 'the greatest possible opportunity of concord' (cf. p. 662).

What was Martyr's true relation to Bucer and to Bullinger? Martyr consciously identified his doctrine of the Eucharist with Bullinger's: 'You congratulate me upon the happy result of the disputations, which however is rather to be attributed to you than to me, since you have for so many years both taught and maintained that doctrine which I there undertook to defend' (*Orig. Lett.* II, p. 478); and about the *Cons. Tig.*: 'What you have mutually agreed upon respecting the sacrament of the eucharist is very gratifying to me . . . I go along with you altogether, and scarcely deliver any other sentiment in this place' (*ibid.*, p. 493). Martyr's First Zürich Oration (1556) mentions 'the orthodox opinion of the Eucharist, which also you men of Zürich, as the prime and in one sense the only patrons, always defended most constantly'. Nevertheless, Martyr does not seem to have been accepted at Zürich so openly (cf. Hospinian, *Historia Sacramentaria, Tig.* 1598—a brief reference in Part II suffices for Martyr), except perhaps by Bullinger himself, who did not meet Martyr until 1543, when the latter was en route to Germany, and who probably became intimate with him only from 1549 onwards. Certainly the closing years of Martyr's life show as close a relationship to Bullinger as was enjoyed to Bucer in the Strassburg period of 1543-1547. C. H. Smyth's thesis (*op. cit.*, p. 125) is quite untenable: 'the doctrine which (Martyr) held when he arrived in England was very different from that which he held when he left it in 1553. In 1547 he was a Bucerian, albeit rather by force of circumstances than by natural inclination; five years with Bullinger at Zürich, instead of with Bucer at Strassburg, would have brought him far sooner to that solution of the sacramental problem at which he finally arrived.' Smyth fails to reckon with the significance of the *Consensus Tigurinus* in the history of Zürich, with Calvin's relationship to Martyr, and especially with Martyr's doctrine as revealed in the *Defensio* of 1559 and the *Dialogus* of 1561. These latter works cannot be dismissed as Zwinglian, or as departing substantially from Bucer's position—yet both were written during his residence at Zürich!

These complex and often apparently contradictory facts mean this at least, that there was a degree of unity existing among the Reformers far beyond what their successors allow, or have since maintained. It means that between the cleavage of Lutheran and Zwinglian emerged a positive theology which was in a profound sense the true gravitational centre of the Reformation: not Wittenberg or Zürich, but the Strassburg of Bucer, from which both Calvin and Martyr went forward to a massive and powerful theology. It means that the more comprehensive and influential theology of John Calvin was representative of the Reformation as a whole as no other could be. Such implications are particularly borne out by Martyr's personal history, for he was a truly 'ecumenical' Reformer, closely associated with Bucer, Calvin, Cranmer and Bullinger among others.

To conclude this section on Martyr's relationship to Bucer, we may say that although Bucer had some cause to suspect Martyr's liking for the Zürich doctrine, yet in the context of Martyr's whole theology, and his personal and theological unity with Bucer himself (on Bucer's death he wrote to Hubert 'I seem mutilated of more than half of my self') we must conclude that the two men were essentially one in their doctrine of the sacraments. Hopf (*op. cit.*, p.18) therefore is wrong to make so much of Bucer's criticism of Martyr's terminology. The fundamental theological doctrines, and even expressions, are common to both—for instance, the teaching of *duplex os fidelium*, the unity of Word and sacrament in effectiveness, the doctrine of analogy as operative in the sacramental relationship, and the *analogia fidei* as normative (cf. A. Lang, *Der Evangelienkommentar Martin Butzers* . . . Leipzig, 1900, esp. pp. 435ff).

One basic problem operative in all this history was the concept of *substantia*. Bucer's use of this word led the Lutherans to regard him as an ally, but Martyr interprets his doctrine as identical with his own, so that substance for Bucer signifies that true Body of Christ which faith apprehends (in *Def.* 634 Martyr deals at length with Gardiner's appeal to Bucer's use of the term *substantia*). It is in Calvin's new and distinctive use of the term that we find the resolution of this problem.

Calvin and Martyr

Martyr regarded Calvin as 'the most eminent and noble expositor of holy Scripture of our times' (*De Vot.* 1424D), while Calvin termed Martyr *optimus et integerrimus vir* (to Cranmer, *Epist. et Resp.* 127), and again, speaking of the struggle to refute the doctrine of local presence in the sacrament, stated, 'The whole was crowned by Peter Martyr, who has left nothing to be desired' (*True Partaking*, etc.—*Tracts.* II, p. 535). The relations between Calvin and Martyr were always cordial, and represented a steadily increasing bond of thought and purpose which made their teaching identical. Through controversy, Calvin in regard to the doctrine of predestination and Martyr to the Eucharist, each stressed certain points quite differently from the other; but basically their theology is one. Our study of Martyr's sacramental theology has shown that the basic elements of accommodation, analogy, the office of the Holy Spirit, faith as union with Christ, and the *triplex munus* of the mystical Body of Christ, so clearly expressed in Calvin's theology, are equally present in Martyr's. Does this apply to the doctrine of sacrament as much? Yes: a comparison of Calvin's Tracts on the Eucharist and the teaching of the Institutes (IV. 14-19) reveals a similarly striking coincidence of doctrine and phraseology. This is particularly obvious in respect of the doctrine of analogy. (Cf. Barth's teaching on analogy already referred to; also the work of Niesel. Although Calvin is neither so explicit nor detailed as is Martyr on the subject of analogical reasoning, it seems just to interpret Calvin in terms of Martyr's categories.) A significant question in this respect would be whether Martyr places more stress on the analogated reality than does Calvin, at least in controversy, and what effect this had on his doctrine of the increase of our union with Christ. In this respect, too, both theologians appreciate the Patristic doctrine of the bodily renewal through the Eucharist (accepted rather in terms of Augustine's 'participation' than of the Greek 'deification') and *analogia entis* that comes through the *analogia fidei*—a doctrine very marked in Martyr's O.T. commentaries, as we saw in Chapter II. A further comparison here is Barth's doctrine of the 'soteriological inversion' operative in the sacramental action: Martyr says, 'outward things nothing profit to salvation, unless there be a mutation or change made by the Holy Spirit in our hearts, either before or during their use' (*in Rom.* 2.25).

An excellent modern study (cf. Nevin's *Mystical Presence*, Phil. 1846 for an older work) of this question is given by Jean Cadier (*op. cit.*), whose careful examination of the history of the Calvinistic teaching yields significant conclusions. In dealing with Martyr's doctrine of the *Tractatio* he says 'Sa pensée est essentiellement calviniste' and cites the principal elements of the Calvinistic

doctrine to be found there: inner witness of the Spirit, faith en-
gendered in our hearts by His testimony, incorporation into Christ,
life in Him—and comments, 'Pierre Martyr insiste peut-être plus
que Calvin sur un bienfait de la Cène, qui est d'établir un lien entre
les croyants, membres du même corps, grains formant un même
pain' (p. 112). At Poissy, continues Cadier, his private declaration
(see our Appendix D) is 'an excellent résumé of doctrine, in all
points according with the calvinistic doctrine', and his final conclusion is: 'On peut donc considérer Pierre Martyr comme pleine-
ment d'accord avec Calvin dans sa doctrine sur la Sainte Cène' (p.
115).

We may well conclude that Martyr and Calvin teach the same
doctrine of the Lord's Supper, and in relation to the central thesis
of this Appendix, we submit: that these three Reformers, Bucer,
Calvin and Martyr, represent a unified theology of ecumenical
dimensions and purpose, reflecting their historical position as
united in a task of reformation which was essentially catholic. The
distressing controversies with the Lutherans which involved both
Calvin and Martyr in bitter debate, must be judged in relation to
Bucer's acceptance of the Lutheran position as compatible with
the theology shared by all three men, and indeed to the caveat
we entered in our Critical Note to Chapter IX, that perhaps Martyr
(and Calvin) failed to appreciate the Lutheran position as one
arising from within the mystery of Christ Himself. At any rate,
what is most striking is that while Lutheran could agree with Bucer,
and 'Zwinglian' with Martyr, Bucer and Martyr were conscious of
being one in doctrine and purpose. Martyr said the week after
Bucer's death, 'I am now torn asunder from a man of the same mind
with myself, and who was truly after my own heart' (to Hubert,
Orig. Lett. II, p. 491).

The unity existing among the Reformers may be indicated by
one final reference. A MS letter of Martyr's to Bucer, from Oxford
on 11 November 1550 (Corp. Christi Lib., Cambridge, MS 119.37)
contains a few sentences upon a most significant matter. Alasco
had written to Martyr expressing a desire that a confession about
the sacrament should be drawn up, and signed by Martyr, Bucer,
Ochino and himself (cf. Strype, *Mem. of Cran.*, p. 250). Martyr
wrote to Bucer as follows: 'I do not know whether Alasco has written
to you what he signified to me so earnestly, about some kind of
confession *de re sacramentaria*, as he termed it, enquiring whether you,
Bernhardino, himself and I would consent to this . . . if you should
subscribe, I also shall easily accord.' This MS not only supports
the thesis of the basic unity of Bucer and Martyr as to doctrine of

the Eucharist (and of Ochino's share in that unity), but reminds us
that Alasco (who identified himself with Bullinger as to doctrine)
was much closer to that unity than is often appreciated. In a sense
it is not Martyr but Calvin who succeeded in drawing together these
precious strands into the golden chain of a theology historically
and doctrinally representative of the Reformation. Yet the three,
Bucer, Calvin and Martyr, must be considered as holding an
essentially identical doctrine of the Eucharist, a doctrine positive
and dynamic, in general transcending the false antithesis that so
hampered the Reformation, in their teaching the 'real presence' of
the Divine-human Person who nourishes His people by the virtue
or power of His new humanity.

APPENDIX D

DEFINITIVE STATEMENTS OF PETER MARTYR'S EUCHARISTIC TEACHING

1. From the Preface to the *Tractatio* of 1549
(Epist. Nunc. pp. 9-34 of 1557 Ed.)

'I have determined to explain certain matters in a few words, lest by keeping silent I perhaps be held unwise, an innovator, a bold, rash and ungodly man, as though I took from the Sacrament of the Eucharist its honour and dignity, or would obtrude the holy Supper to the Church without Christ . . . But for my part I attribute so much to this sacrament as to say that in its exercise, the faithful obtain the greatest benefits which can be hoped for of God in this life . . . just as the bread and wine (which feed the body) are given outwardly to the communicants, so is it truly granted unto their minds that by faith they eat the body and blood of Christ (given for our redemption): whereupon the whole man, both inward and outward, is restored to the greatest felicity. And this is the only way that Scripture allows and knows of eating the body and drinking the blood of the Lord, namely when we apprehend by a constant and firm faith that Jesus the Son of God our Saviour and Lord, gave His own body on the Cross and shed His blood for us, and that He has so embraced us who are given to Him by the Father, and so joined and incorporated us to Himself that He is our head, and we flesh of His flesh and bone of His bones, while He dwells in us and we in Him. In this stands the whole power and reason of this meat and drink, to which our faith is stirred up and kindled by the threefold Word: sometimes inwardly, while the Holy Spirit, by His secret yet mighty power, clearly incites our souls to renew these things with ourselves, that they may be embraced with lively and willing faith; to the same end are we many times moved by the help of the words of God (which pierce us either by outward sound or writing); and finally, that there should not lack any help to our infirmity, Christ added in the Supper bread and wine for signs, which are made sacraments by His words and institution, that is, organs by which the Holy Spirit excites faith in our minds, that by this we

282

may be spiritually yet truly fed and sustained by his Body and blood . . .

'And in receiving the sacrament of the Eucharist, the memory of the Lord's death and of the whole mystery of our redemption through the incarnate Word of God is re-opened (*memoria refricatur*), the acknowledgment of God's testament is renewed, and there is offered the blessed communion of Christ and remission of sins through the sacrifice of Christ offered upon the altar of the Cross . . . Lastly, because a man is not made to solitude, but is desirous of social and civil life, therefore when he is now convinced that he has the gracious divine will through Christ, and that through Him his sins are forgiven, nothing else is required to his perfect and absolute life while he lives here, except that he should live together with other men called in the Scripture neighbours, both in harmony and with the greatest justice and charity. But this sacrament most effectively and earnestly admonishes us of this. For in the mysteries we become sharers in the one Table: what else would we resolve in mind than that we are one body, members one of another under Christ our Head, one bread, so conjoined among ourselves just as almost infinite grains of wheat coalesce in that bread which we take? . . . If a profane table reconciles men to one another when they meet together, why should not the Table of Christ effect this the more? . . .

'But concerning the body of Christ, which you (adversaries) so greatly dislike me to deny as present: I will say a little for your satisfaction. If I should demand of you why there should be affirmed any such presence as you invent for yourself, you will, I believe, make me no other answer than that the body and blood of Christ may be joined to us. But since the whole work of this conjunction is heavenly and spiritual, this presence of yours which you so zealously contend for, is not at all required for this! What need is there of either physical contact or nearness of places? . . . are not the faithful in Spain, Italy, Germany and France so joined with us as to be (as Paul says) members together with us? . . . A plainer simile and more expressive may be yet used: Man and wife . . . that unity of flesh is nothing hindered if the man should sometime be at London while the wife remain at Cambridge or Oxford . . . Yet I would not have it thought, on account of these similes alleged by me, that I but lightly account or too much extenuate the union we have and daily enter into with Christ. For I know well that Scripture, to demonstrate its great compactness, is accustomed to declare that not only are we endowed with the Spirit, merit and intercession of Jesus, and act and live by His inspiration and Spirit, but also He Himself is with us, and dwells in our hearts by faith: He is our Head, He dwells in us and we in Him, we are born again in Him, His flesh is both given and received to be eaten and drunk. But I understand statements of this kind to be metaphorical, since proper speech cannot easily be had for these things—for words signify this or that as they are appointed to serve human ends. Wherefore when it comes to heavenly and divine things, natural man who understands not such great secrets, cannot as much as name them.

'Whence the Holy Spirit would take heed of our infirmity by this—having granted us a light and understanding to excel our nature, He also humbled Himself to these metaphors, namely abiding, dwelling, eating and drinking, that this divine and heavenly union which we have with Christ may in some way be known to us. And since these forms of speech consist of two things, the highest efficacy and a signification not proper but translated, they must be interpreted not rashly but with prudent and spiritual caution. This is used if we do not extenuate their sense more than is fitting, especially as applied to the Sacraments, nor attribute to them more than is suitable. The excessive speech of the Fathers and contempt of the Anabaptists (*Hyperbolae patrum et Anabaptistarum contemptio*) wonderfully obscured the Sacraments (particularly this one which we treat)—these judge it only a token of mutual charity, and cold and bare sign of the death of Christ, but those leave no divine thing not attributed to this sacrament, by which they impudently take a step into horrible idolatry.

'And no other way can that mediocrity we desire be retained, but by interpreting the phrases which we have rehearsed according to the analogy or convenience of holy Spripture. This requires that we tear not asunder the hypostatic (as they say) union of Christ on account of which the properties of the two natures (I mean the divine and the human) are communicated with each other; but yet this requires us to distinguish with sound understanding what we have communicated by alternation of the properties, so that the divinity is not made subject to human infirmities, and the humanity is not so much deified that it leave the bonds of its own nature and be destroyed. Therefore by a spiritual wisdom, such as is not elsewhere provided than in holy Scripture, we must discern what is agreeable to Christ in respect of the one nature, and in respect of the other . . .

'Why have I used the words *realiter*, *substantialiter*, *corporaliter* and *carnaliter* in the questions of these disputations, since these are foreign words, wholly alien to the phrase of holy Scripture? I thought this too, and if I had been allowed to speak my own will would have utterly abstained from them, as being strange and even barbarous and ambiguous. But partly the use received in the schools, and partly the importunity of the adversaries has forced me to these; they, to hinder me more certainly (as they thought), paraded me before the people and ruder sort of priests, as though I overthrew the foundation of the sacrament of the Eucharist—by these grosser words they zealously affirmed the presence of Christ under the species (as they say) of bread and wine, and also published as effectively as possible the charge that I most heretically denied them . . . When I deny the body of Christ to be present *localiter, substantialiter, corporaliter et carnaliter*, it must not be inferred that we eat the body of Christ *ficte, simulate seu phantastice*. For if by these words they understand the truth of the thing, I will not deny the body of Christ to be truly received by us. For what we comprehend by faith must not be held false or feigned, counterfeit or a phantom . . .

'I wished to write at greater length of this matter, since I easily think that many are offended by these words, as I understand that some, and those, men excellent in godliness and learning, would not willingly have suffered them. Perhaps they will be more friendly to me when they understand both why I used them, and in what sense I affirm or deny the body and blood of the Lord to be present in the Supper. And that I may again make this manifest in fewest words, I declare those to be truly given and offered to us, by both words and symbols, while they are potently and most effectively signified through these. And again, in communicating, we truly receive the same when with full and solid assent of faith we grasp those things which are offered by the signification of words and signs. Whence it is that we are most closely joined with Christ, and whom we have obtained in Baptism by the benefit of regeneration, Him we again put on more and more by the sacrament of food, since it is provided by nature that we are nourished by the same things of which we consist. And if we wish to be saved, we should always take care that Christ dwell in us and we in Him, until we are wholly converted into Him, and so converted that nothing of ours remains—of inborn death I mean, or corruption and of sin . . .'

2. Judgment on the Eucharist delivered to the Strassburg Senate, 1553
(*Clariss. et Magnif. Domin. Sch. Argent.*)

'To the most renowned and esteemed governors of the Strassburg Academy, my most honoured masters, grace and peace from God through our Lord Jesus Christ.

'Since doubt is raised about the matter of the sacrament (*de re sacramentaria*) and the ministers of this Church fear lest any contentions arise in that respect through me, it seems well to repeat now in writing the same thing that I affirmed in your presence a few days ago. First, I readily embrace and acknowledge the Augustan Confession, and whatever others do not differ from it, if rightly and profitably understood. Next, no disputes or contentions shall be called forth through me: but rather, if any place in Scripture is to be treated, or if any other necessity require that I declare my opinion about such a question, I promise to do it with all modesty and without any bitter attack. But what my opinion is can be understood by the books already published by me. From these I wish to detract or alter nothing either by writing or by promise, until I shall be persuaded otherwise by the teaching of Scripture or Spirit. But since I have not subscribed to the concord made between Dr Martin Bucer and Dr Luther and his fellows, it is for this reason that I cannot grant, through the Word of God and conscience, that those who are destitute of faith eat the body of Christ in receiving the sacrament (*illos qui fide sunt destituti, percipiendo sacramenta corpus Christi sumere*). Nor is it a wonder that I would not assent to this article, since Bucer himself in this School of ours, when I was present, publicly taught otherwise, when he expounded the Acts of the Apostles, and wrote far otherwise when he was in England (as I can show from certain of his articles). And indeed he judged rightly, since faith is the only instrument by which Christ's body and blood are received by us; if this is removed, the mouth of the body receives nothing unless sacraments of the body and blood of Christ, bread I mean and wine consecrated by the minister or officer of the Church. Just as a man of adult age, if he come to Baptism without faith, we would say received nothing but the sacrament, that is water, since by not believing he could not obtain the grace of regeneration: so without faith no one is admitted to the communion of the body and blood of Christ. Finally, I fear lest by subscribing to this concord proposed to me, I might seem to condemn the Church of Zürich, Basle, Berne, Geneva and England, and all the brethren scattered throughout Italy and France. But I do not think this is lawful to me through the Word of God. Accordingly, as I both honour and esteem the Churches of Saxony, so do I embrace in the Lord and greatly love these others which I have mentioned. May God, as He is the Author of peace, give us to speak and think all the same at last. And to you, my masters, most honoured for the courtesy and goodness which you show to me, I give the greatest thanks, since I can return you nothing else. And I pray the most good God, that through our Lord Jesus Christ He may be always gracious unto you—27 December 1553, in my hired lodgings at Strassburg.'

3. Statements from the Colloquy of Poissy, 1561
(A: *Sententia*; B: Private opinion, preserved
in Condé's *Memoires*, II, p. 513)

A. 'I judge the body and blood of Christ to be really and substantially only in the heavens, yet the faithful truly receive, spiritually and through faith, the communication of His true body and His true blood, which were delivered to the cross for our sake. Wherefore I absolutely reject transubstantiation and consubstantiation in the bread and wine of the Supper. Further, I affirm that the distance of places nothing hinders our conjunction with the body and blood of Christ, because the Lord's Supper is a heavenly matter, and although on earth we take bread and wine by the mouth of the body, sacraments of the body and blood of Christ, yet by faith and by the work of the Holy Spirit our souls, to which this spiritual and heavenly food pertains, are carried up into heaven and enjoy the present body and blood of Christ. And therefore I hold there to be no need of positing the body of Christ as present truly, substantially and corporeally, by a presence not local, either with us or with the symbols. I hold that the things signified by these are joined with the outward symbols not otherwise than *sacramentaliter*, since they are signified by them not profanely or lightly but effectively, by institution of the Lord. This is the sum of my faith which I follow in this dogma, and therefore I admit formulas adduced which consent with this reason, able to be referred or accommodated to the sense now explained: if any pervert or misinterpret these, I publicly disagree with him. And whereas in these speeches the substance of the body of Christ is mentioned, by that name or term I understand nothing else than the true body of Christ. For our faith is not directed to a fiction or phantom, but to the true and natural body, which the Word of God took of the blessed virgin, and gave for us on the cross. Wherefore there is no cause why we should be thought to believe that His real presence is elsewhere than in heaven . . .'

B. 'Since the promises of the New Testament are not at all vain, but full of efficacy and virtue, presenting us truly with what is promised there, and since a living faith makes us actually participate in and enjoy what is offered us in them, it is necessary to believe and confess the presence of the Body of Jesus Christ in the Holy Supper, in which the substance of His flesh and of His blood is truly promised, offered and given to us as true meat and drink for the soul, according to this most holy Word: 'Take, eat, this is My body; take, drink, this is My blood.

'The Holy Supper by a secret and ineffable operation effects in us, here on earth, this communication and participation of His Body, which dwells in heaven and not elsewhere, divinely accommodating His grandeur to our capacity, and joining places far distant: and as if visibly He unites heaven with earth by His power, to place His royal throne in the midst of the Supper (*pour poser son siège royal au milieu de la Cène*) and to give Himself more closely as the food of our soul; in the same way and still incomprehensibly, faith, by its wonderful property (*vertu admirable*) accommodates and lifts up our soul to heaven, and gives it opening and entrance to the throne of His majesty . . . in this respect the Holy Spirit is, with faith, the sole medium and eternal minister of this heavenly and spiritual participation and manducation of the body and blood of Jesus Christ, and not bread and wine, corruptible creatures which serve only as signs to teach the faithful that Jesus Christ is present at the Supper and gives Himself to them: thus do the creatures remain bare and stripped of all other substance: and the most one finds in them is the simple analogy of material signs, bread and wine, with the thing signified, which is heavenly bread: Jesus Christ the only true meat, drink, nourishment and life of our souls.'

GENERAL INDEX

Unio hypostatica, 83, 102ff, 190f, 205
Union with Christ, 88, 101, 123,
      132, 139ff, 164, 168f, 193, 223,
      282ff

Valdes, Juan, 5f
Vestment controversy, 25ff

Vision of God, 78

White, John, 24
Word of God, 128ff, 160f

Zanchi, Girolamo, 8, 44, 46, 65
Zwingli, 5, 37f, 203, 216, 221ff, 272